MARK
JOHNSTON

The Authorised Biography

MARK JOHNSTON

The Authorised Biography

Nick Townsend

highdown

A **RACING POST** COMPANY

Published in 2006 by Highdown
an imprint of Raceform Ltd
Compton, Newbury, Berkshire, RG20 6NL
Raceform Ltd is a wholly owned subsidiary of Trinity Mirror plc

ISBN 1-905156-26-X

Cover designed by Tracey Scarlett

Interiors designed by Fiona Pike

Printed in Great Britain by William Clowes Ltd, Beccles, Suffolk

DEDICATION

This book could not have been completed without the time, patience, commitment and humour of Mark Johnston or the contribution of his ever-buoyant and charming wife Deirdre, not to mention the help of Debbie Albion and Mikaelle Lebretton. I am also grateful to Mark's sister, Sharon, for her assistance, and also to the Duke of Roxburghe and Ron Huggins for their assistance. Finally, thanks to my agent, John Pawsey, for being his usual imperturbable self under pressure; to Jonathan Taylor and Julian Brown at Highdown, for their encouragement; to editor Daniel Balado; and not least to my wife Louise, for her support throughout.

CONTENTS

INTRODUCTION	9
CHAPTER 1	12
CHAPTER 2	26
CHAPTER 3	37
CHAPTER 4	51
CHAPTER 5	63
CHAPTER 6	69
CHAPTER 7	82
CHAPTER 8	90
CHAPTER 9	103
CHAPTER 10	120
CHAPTER 11	129
CHAPTER 12	141
CHAPTER 13	151
CHAPTER 14	166
CHAPTER 15	176
CHAPTER 16	194
CHAPTER 17	203
CHAPTER 18	217
CHAPTER 19	229
CHAPTER 20	242
CHAPTER 21	253
CHAPTER 22	265
CHAPTER 23	279
CHAPTER 24	288
RACING RECORD	294
INDEX	311

INTRODUCTION

*The noblest prospect which a Scotchman ever sees
is the high-road that leads him to England.*
SAMUEL JOHNSON

If you could rewind the years to 1969, you'd discover a student skulking in a betting shop, in a fog of cigarette fumes, armed with just a copy of the *Daily Mirror*, a pencil and one of those scruffy sheets of paper on which to scribble a bet, the scene set off by that evocative sound of the 'blower' which brought commentaries. No television screens and betting monitors then, just a bored board-man chalking prices. Problems with examinations would disappear as the student sidled through that door with those plastic streamers, into a Tardis-like room of like-minded individuals.

He surveyed those trainers' names. Evocative surnames. The 'Hs' alone were sufficient: Hern, Hobbs, Harwood, Houghton. And some young pretender, in his first season, named Hannon. There was a mystique about them. He could only envy those who made a living from racehorse training. Even then he harboured a belief that it was for those of a certain birth; those possessing the right family name or connections; or as a natural conclusion to a riding career after a jockey retires from the saddle. That student could not have imagined that in a few years' time he would be interviewing such characters for a living, as a sportswriter. In the years from that date, the notebook and tape recorder have been produced at the stables of probably over 100 trainers, from the opinionated to the discreet, the distracted to the engaging and welcoming.

That student, this writer, admires many. But just occasionally a man stands out, not merely because of his achievements, but because of the life that brought him there. One such horseracing figure was Barney Curley, with whom I collaborated on his autobiography. Another is the subject of this book, a character who has become synonymous with that prodigious stayer Double Trigger, for which Mark Johnston remains famed despite a more recent association with that remarkable, speedy filly Attraction.

Words such as 'relentless', '100 per cent', 'stamina' and the inevitable 'Always Trying' – his stable slogan – apply to him. And many others too. Bombastic. Arrogant. Analytical. Contrary. Argumentative. Trenchant. They all come to mind. He has over 200 horses in his yard. He also has as big a stable of hobby-horses. And he gallops them frequently. It can rarely be said about Mark Johnston that 'he preferred to maintain his own counsel'. He can be as contrary and provocative as George Galloway MP; as spirited and rebellious as Rob Roy MacGregor, who coincidentally hailed from the Trossachs, on the periphery of which Johnston spent his formative years. In short, it would be fair to suggest that a quiet night in with Mark Johnston is an oxymoron. It is impossible to enjoy idle chit-chat with a man who gnaws away at issues and won't let them be removed from him. Just like his bull terrier, Gnasher.

On the racetrack he has consistently stayed the course. More than a century of winners in each of thirteen seasons. There is a fascination with the fact that such a record has been achieved by a man who was not blessed with a distinguished training name, had not been an ace in the saddle (by all accounts, nothing could be further from the truth), and had not worked as a pupil with a doyen of the sport. Mark Johnston is self-made. He has hauled himself up by his boot-straps – or, as certain Sassenach rivals might say, by his jockstrap. I wanted to discover what motivates a man to set out so single-mindedly to create so impressive an empire. I hope this book goes some way towards revealing that.

If the genesis of this book can be traced back to 1969, the catalyst for it was a newspaper interview I conducted in a café near Harrogate station in the summer of 2005. Johnston had a dentist's appointment in the Yorkshire town. I needed, rather urgently, a trainer to talk about Royal Ascot – which that year had been moved to York because of rebuilding work at the Berkshire course – for an article to feature in the next edition of my newspaper, the *Independent on Sunday*. Speaking to a 'local' Yorkshireman, albeit one of very defined Scottish origins, sounded appropriate, particularly as he had frequently been the leading trainer at the Royal meeting over the years. We spoke for an hour, and the seed was planted.

Some of the inspiration for this book comes from Simon Barnes's admirable and, at the time, ground-breaking insight into the life of a racing stable, *Horsesweat and Tears* – one year, 1987, spent by that fine writer in John Dunlop's racing stable. Quite why it did not feature in the *Racing Post*'s top 100 books remains a mystery. So, although this is a biography, it is also intended to give an insight into one year of the career of the trainer who began with an eight-horse stable in Lincolnshire and who nearly two decades later is master of Kingsley House and much of what he surveys in Middleham, North Yorkshire.

A long distance has been travelled, not just physically but emotionally, between today and the day I met up with Mark Johnston in Harrogate. When you write about a racehorse trainer, you become almost institutionalised; you end up taking every defeat personally and relishing every victory almost as though you have saddled the horse yourself. It has also been an education. When we started this project, we could not have known what frustration and exhilaration lay ahead; nor what other events would be unfurling, with former champion jockey Kieren Fallon and others appearing in court on charges relating to alleged race-fixing. The vagaries of racehorse training could never have been more amply demonstrated than in 2006, a year in which despair and delirium so often walked hand in hand.

Nick Townsend
Oxfordshire
September 2006

CHAPTER ONE

Part of my success story is that, from the outset, I've never made any excuses for my failures. The buck stops here. But at the same time, there are times when I think, 'Anybody could do this job, it's not rocket science. It's not particularly clever to be a good racehorse trainer.'

It's the first Sunday in December 2005 and autumn's hand is already in winter's harsh grip. On the moorland above the North Yorkshire town of Middleham a raw, blustery wind chastises you as harshly as a Victorian mother scolding a recalcitrant child, bringing a ruddy glow to your features. Those heady days of summer – of Goodwood, York, Royal Ascot at York, and the lesser meetings – when Mark Johnston's yard hammered out winners like a demonic blacksmith seem an age away.

As you clamber out of Johnston's four-wheel-drive you can only envy the winter wear of the sheep that occupy the grassland surrounding the 270-acre Park Farm, his latest acquisition. It's another annexe to an operation which is less a presence in the town and beyond, more an occupying force.

This is a dormant period for Flat yards, when they find nourishment in the past season's glories to carry them through the winter and prepare to gorge themselves once more, come the spring – as all must believe they will. Johnston's is no exception. Like a kitchen which can be consistently guaranteed to produce cordon bleu fare, there is the tantalising whiff of Classic and other big-race potential emanating from the Johnston premises. For the moment, though, the stables' principal hopes, including Nakheel, Black Charmer, Atlantic Waves, Prince Of Light and In Full Cry no more than simmering pots on the back-burner. Who knows what kind of dish they will serve up. This limbo-land in Flat racing's journey through the year is an opportunity for the horses to rest and recover from their wear and tear, while the trainers themselves reflect on and re-evaluate their operations.

We tour Johnston's latest property purchase. It is located a mile from his principal yard, Kingsley House, near the centre of the town. Park Farm was originally owned by brothers Peter and Tony Walton, the former of whom is the husband of trainer Kate. The additional yard has become a necessity now that Johnston invariably has to accommodate a roster of over 200 horses – assuming that as many new charges as he hopes and expects to train next season arrive in the spring. It means he now has three bases in and near Middleham, and it reaffirms the yard's position as one of the country's largest training establishments. At this rarefied level of training equine populations are fluid, so it is difficult to ascertain who is superior numerically. Suffice to say that Johnston vies for that status with Richard Hannon, Mick Channon, Barry Hills, Sir Michael Stoute and the Maktoum family's Godolphin operation. 'Richard Hannon probably runs the most runners in a season, followed by Mick Channon, followed by me,' Johnston opines. 'But what you can say is that the six of us consistently have all got 200 horses.'

As we survey Park Farm, he elaborates on his plans for the facilities with the enthusiasm of an estate agent determined to claim his percentage. He explains the various uses to which the new yard will be put. One block, in particular, is for horses out of training, recovering from injury, and for those to be quarantined (horses coming in from other yards are isolated for a month). That is all the responsibility of one of his yard managers, Penny Skilton. Though Johnston has his preferred methods, he does not attempt to create some great mystique out of the skill of training. 'Part of my success story,' he says, 'is that, from the outset, I've never made any excuses for my failures. The buck stops here. But at the same time, there are times when I think, "Anybody could do this job, it's not rocket science. It's not particularly clever to be a good racehorse trainer."'

On this day, Johnston is clad in fleece, jacket and cords. He would not strike the casual onlooker as the patriarchal figure he has become; indeed, at such moments there is almost a diffidence about the Scot. He is an observer, a listener, casting glances at anyone in his proximity like a salmon fisherman watching his fly. Yet there is an inescapable presence about him that perhaps has – no, it *must* have – its origins in the Caledonian blood that surges through him. It is an ebullience, a self-confidence and self-belief frequently found in many of his compatriots who dominate public life throughout the UK, including within the seats of government. Even in his quieter moments, such as now, he exudes a vehement pride in all he has achieved – a demeanour that can be mistaken for arrogance.

As you swiftly discover, for all the polished civility of his television appearances, it doesn't take much to provoke the former president of the National Trainers' Federation and columnist in many newspapers and periodicals, including the *Racing Post*, *The Times* and *Horse & Hound*. When roused by contentious issues, he can be a vocal and intimidating opponent, mounting his soap-box with the animation of a particularly garrulous speaker at Hyde Park Corner. He keeps his verbal flick-knives well concealed, but he will readily produce one, and produce it at your throat. Certainly he enjoys puncturing balloons of conventional wisdom. Sometimes an adversary is unnecessary. Johnston could start a row in an empty barn, as he often, self-mockingly agrees. What's more, if he doesn't happen to be inside such a construction, he'll go out and search for one. Around here, there are plenty.

You'd need to be a confirmed townie, damned with a soul of stone, not to be captivated by the scene before you. Newmarket may boast a greater equine population, but the horses there do not work before such an idyllic backdrop as the verdant and fertile Wensleydale, the largest valley in the Yorkshire Dales. John Wesley was entranced by it when he travelled through here in 1790. Anyone enraptured by the miracle that is the racehorse in motion should make the pilgrimage here, to the acres surrounding this North Yorkshire town.

Middleham was granted its first charter in 1389, and despite its two market squares it is the smallest town in Yorkshire, you are told. Which is probably why everyone appears to refer to it as 'the village'. Here, the ghosts of equine legends gallop past, nurtured to the finest pitch by the skills of men such as Captain Neville Crump, who once trained at Warwick House Stables, the entrance to which stands across the road from Kingsley House. The captain trained his three Grand National winners here: Sheila's Cottage in 1948, Teal in 1952, and the 1960 victor Merryman II. Crump, who also trained five Scottish and two Welsh

National winners, died in 1997, aged 86, and is buried in Middleham cemetery. In common with a considerable portion of Middleham, Warwick House has been assimilated into the Johnston operation. It has been in Johnston's ownership since 1994. Like a feudal baron, much of what Johnston surveys he owns, or exerts some kind of influence over. Much of the remainder, including the gallops, he shares with his neighbours.

You can understand why these acres were a ready invitation to Johnston's training forebears. The area evokes a sense of history, with evidence of a Celt, Roman, Viking and Norman presence, and in the last half-century much of it equine. Listen, and you can almost hear the pounding hooves of Surrey, the white mount of Richard, Duke of Gloucester, later King Richard III. It is said the horse was ridden on what are now racehorse gallops more than 500 years ago. According to Shakespeare, Surrey was King Richard's charger at the Battle of Bosworth Field in August 1485, which ended the Wars of the Roses. Few are unfamiliar with Richard's cry in the heat of bloody conflict, 'A horse! A horse! My kingdom for a horse!' Middleham's upper market square has what is called the 'Swine Cross' because it bears a stone carving resembling a pig. A guide to Wensleydale, written by Stephen I. Robinson, tells us that it is thought to represent the white boar emblem of Richard III, who granted the market a second charter in 1479.

Richard apparently came to Middleham in 1461 as a boy of eleven, and it was here that he was educated and received his training to be a knight. He married Anne Neville, daughter of the Earl of Warwick, a man so powerful in the land that he was known as 'the kingmaker', and they lived at Middleham Castle. After that, this romantic tale takes a decidedly sinister twist. When King Edward IV died, Richard became protector to the new king, a boy of twelve. Richard then seized the throne and confined the young king and his brother to the Tower of London. Whether he also murdered them has never been confirmed. However, Richard's reign ended prematurely when he fell at Bosworth Field.

What can be substantiated is that racehorses have been trained in the area for some 250 years, and the Cistercian monks of nearby Jervaulx Abbey were breeding horses even before then. There was horseracing on the High Moor as early as 1739. Isaac Cape, who was a jockey in the first half of the eighteenth century, became the first specialist racehorse trainer here. Meetings were held regularly for many decades, but they ended in 1873 after disputes between trainers and local gait owners, the landowners with grazing rights on the moorland. Since then, the High Moor has been used only for training and the surrounding area has become a haven for its practitioners, who have settled here.

Middleham has suffered periods when its fortunes have waned and stables have stood empty. Kingsley House was but one yard that became desolate. The weeds grew to chest height. That was the scene when the Johnstons first arrived here late in 1988 like a family of pioneers in the Old West, following their wagon as it rolled into a new town. But today the training industry is thriving again, in and around Middleham. Horseracing has brought prosperity. And nowhere more so than within Johnston's accumulated properties.

An aircraft stands in a tractor shed, a makeshift hangar, at Park Farm. It is more than merely a symbol of affluence and success. Indeed, it is no Lear jet. It is a 30-year-old Piper Cherokee, which set Johnston back £85,000. But what that purchase does reflect is the amount of travelling he undertakes, countrywide and within Europe, to supervise the running of his charges, and to attend sales. A drive to Goodwood, for example, can be a twelve-hour round trip. The Piper Cherokee reduces it to four, even if there are taxi rides at the other end. 'It's been life-changing,' he says. 'I should have done it five years ago.'

He explains enthusiastically that new gallops are to be laid alongside the 'airstrip', which is an adjacent field. Johnston is a compulsive expansionist, as though he lives in mortal fear of having to post a 'House Full' sign, and having to turn away a horse. He should have CBE after his name, for 'Constantly Building the Empire' describes him accurately. 'I've spent my whole career building and expanding,' he says. 'When I stop doing that, I'll give up.' He has a rapacious desire to transform fallow land into gallops, derelict sheds into rows of boxes. He is the project manager who is his own architect.

Though he has clambered up to a plateau of sorts, consistently accumulating well over 100 winners a season and remaining among the leaders in the trainers' table, he is still riven with ambition. It is an ambition so naked it's surprising he's never been arrested for indecent exposure. 'Always Trying' has long been the Johnston motto, and statement of intent. It originated when a punter leant over the rail of the paddock at Hamilton one day and asked him if a particular horse would win. 'Always trying,' he retorted in an impatient tone. 'Always trying.' And it stuck, as much for its ambiguity as anything else, one suspects. Certainly it makes people think. His approach is summarised, quite simply, by the declaration, 'I constantly strive for more because I want to be regarded as number one; not just champion trainer in Britain, but in Europe. I need to be up there, top of the Premier League.' The Manchester United manager Sir Alex Ferguson, a fellow son of the city of Glasgow, and one of his owners, would empathise with such aspirations – and, no doubt, remind him what a daunting prospect it is.

The previous evening, purely by coincidence, we'd both travelled to Old Trafford to watch United play. I was there to write about the game for my newspaper; Johnston had been invited into the directors' box by Ferguson. It was a rare interruption in Johnston's work schedule, although, like a soldier, a trainer can never stand easy. He is always, to an extent, on parade. Johnston can never be accused of underselling himself. Everyone he meets through social contacts is a potential owner. Though he boasts many distinguished names among his owners – Sheikh Mohammed and the extended Maktoum family, the Duke of Roxburghe, former British Horseracing Board chief Peter Savill, and Ferguson, to name but a few – there can never be an assumption about their patronage.

For the major Flat training establishments, the closure of turf racing in November can be likened to the end of the summer season for an end-of-the-pier show. A kind of depression sets in. Perhaps more appropriately, we should refer to it as the end-of-the-peer show, as the more precocious blue-bloods of the sport who lord it in the spring and summer give way to the hardier, generally more durable stock of National Hunt racing. (Johnston is by no means a total stranger to the National Hunt game. His first runner ever was over jumps, and, as he will readily remind you, the stable has actually won Newcastle's Fighting Fifth Hurdle.) Flat racing continues, but, in truth, apologetically so, on the all-weather racecourses – despite the increasing utilisation of that surface – as the jump season swaggers

17

increasingly into the consciousness of many racing folk. Back in Johnston's office, administration manager Debbie Albion and staff are as occupied as ever on this Sunday morning – there is no rest on the Sabbath for these workers – a few prospective runners for the Wolverhampton and Southwell meetings chalked up on their wall. But these meetings are but minor trespasses on jump territory. For now, the debate about prospective victors of the Cheltenham Gold Cup and the Grand National takes precedence over discussion of next year's Classics. This year, however, a significant vacuum has been created. The much-loved three-time Gold Cup winner Best Mate collapsed and died during his seasonal pipe-opener at Exeter.

Despite the vast scale of the Johnston enterprise, it remains very much a family business. When you talk of 'the yard', you refer not just to the trainer but to his vivacious wife of two decades, Deirdre, who is his assistant, and the elder of his two sons, Charlie, fifteen, who rides work and has even made television appearances on behalf of the stable. (Yes, I agree, as a general rule we should be spared the outpourings of precocious, know-all offspring of sporting or any other kind of personality. But there are exceptions, and Johnston Junior is a bright, articulate boy who does his parents proud.) Charlie is determined to become a trainer. His younger brother, Angus, thus far shows no inclination.

And there is an enormous extended family. By mid-summer, the busiest time for the yard, Johnston will employ no fewer than 119: 85 full-time staff and 34 part-time. They include seven yard managers – the equivalent of departmental heads in a conventional business – and two full-time vets, James Tate (son of trainer Thomas Tate and nephew of Michael Dickinson, the man who trained the first five home in the 1983 Cheltenham Gold Cup) and Dr Rogerio F. De Sousa Filho, from Brazil. Their facilities include an equine pool, two endoscopes and two X-ray machines. Later in the season, Johnston will outlay £16,000 on an ultrasound scanner, for the diagnosis of pelvic and soft tissue injuries. It will probably be the only yard in the country with such an advanced piece of equipment.

Many trainers believe that a visit to the box of every horse every day is an essential part of their schedule. Johnston doesn't believe it is a necessity. It would also be logistically impossible for him. 'Every night I get a written report from my yard managers regarding any veterinary problems or changes to a horse's well-being,' he says. However, although Johnston recognises the benefits of delegation to an efficient workforce, he cannot find it within himself to purge totally the control-freak from within his psyche. God forbid that circumstances remove him from the entire process of management. That would be anathema to him. 'If things aren't going so well, I have to be out there, hands-on and involved myself,' he says. 'I have a fantastic staff, but you have to be continually striving to make them better, and to push them all.'

Johnston is not one for small talk. You sense he feels that it is *his* time being wasted. Certainly he will not countenance loose talk. He corrects false impressions and errors of facts with the venom of Freddie Flintoff smacking a loose ball over the boundary ropes. And he is obsessed with statistics. 'Not quite *as good as ever*,' he had corrected me politely but firmly the previous year after I had cheerfully suggested that his team was in its pomp. 'We're sixth in the trainers' table. I have been as high as second.' He can recall most statistics readily, particularly those of the yard's winners to runners. Those he can't are at his fingertips: his mobile phone doubles as a mini-computer and contains every detail of every horse's current progress. He'll remind you that the zenith was 2003, in which year the stable was responsible for a record number of winners, 146. They earned £2,454,440 in prize money. The following year, 124 winners produced record prize money of £3,121,282. Whatever the fate of his team in the coming year, you sense he will be bitterly disappointed if he doesn't pass, or at least approach, the targets he set with those achievements.

Those within the lower echelon of the training ranks tend to covet and cherish every individual victory. These days, Johnston is only genuinely thrilled by big-race triumphs, such as those of his formidable Cup horse Double Trigger and the remarkable dual 1,000 Guineas winner Attraction, who, in September 2005, after the 10th success of an outstanding career, had been retired to the paddocks of her owner, the Duke of Roxbroughe.

There are those who maintain that such an attitude confirms the perception that this is more a winner-churning works than a stable. That appearance could be said to be reinforced by the fact that Johnston asks his staff to 'clock in', as though this were Johnston & Johnston, Widget Manufacturers. Sceptics contend that such a trainer cannot possibly possess an intimate knowledge of all his horses. That was the author's suspicion too, but he was swiftly disabused of that notion. Johnston appears meticulous in the knowledge and preparation of all his runners. I cannot recall his being anything but *au fait* with any of his charges at any one time. And anyway, confirmation of a horse's condition and future plans is only one phone-call away.

'Size is everything', they say. That has long been Johnston's maxim when it comes to the population of a stable, although he will reluctantly concede, if reminded of it, 'We actually hit the first Classic winner (Mister Baileys in the 1994 2,000 Guineas) when we had around 70 horses.' He is disdainful of those trainers who will settle for less than half his complement, as though the number they train is some kind of optimum for the industry. From the journalistic side of the great divide, I confirm to him that many trainers consider the preferred number to be considerably less than his. 'That's what they say,' he scoffs. 'They'll tell you, "Oh, I'm comfortable with 50, 70", whatever, but that's only because they can't get any more. My view is, if you're not moving forwards, the only way is back. I remember James Given, an ex-assistant of ours (and also, originally, a vet) who went into training on his own account, being quoted as saying, after a couple of years, "Seventy is as many as I want. When you have over 100, it gets too much like a factory." Well, I took that as a direct slur against us. It's strange that James now has over 100 horses ...' Johnston shrugs, and continues mischievously, rather like a teenage hot-head who feels he has been slighted and needs to settle the issue, 'I've never challenged him on it. Perhaps I should.' When he chances upon a theme he would like to develop, the 46-year-old Glaswegian's normal throaty growl threatens to become a bark. For once, he lets that particular matter drop. For now.

He will concede that a large complement of horses was not penned on his original blueprint for success. 'When I started out I was naive and didn't realise that if you want to train Classic winners you need 150-plus horses,' he says. 'It was footballer and manager Kevin Keegan, I think, who once said that the strength of a team on the pitch is dictated by the strength of those sitting on the bench. The same applies to us, to some extent. If you select a small team and think you're going to go to war all season with them, you're wrong. You need reserves, a pressure from behind of others coming through. I wasn't the only one who made that mistake. Godolphin had a huge pool to draw on from their other trainers, and they originally thought they'd operate with a 40-strong team of elite horses drawn from those yards. They rapidly realised that couldn't be done. They had to have a big team. There's pressure every day to stay up there. Some people say to me that I've got to get away from that kind of thinking. Yet the fact is that, comparing years, the curve is upwards. Each individual horse has a better chance of winning a race with me now than ten years ago, and a better chance than with the vast majority of smaller trainers.'

The figures certainly tend to confirm that theory. The 2005 season resulted in another prodigious yield for the yard, culminating in Crosspeace winning on the last day of the turf season at Doncaster, the Listed CIU Serlby Stakes. It has left everyone in the best of spirits, anticipating a grand season to come. Crosspeace's triumph left the yard with a total of 144 winners from 883 runners, and a record of just under £1.8 million in first prize money earned. Johnston finished fourth in the trainers' league table, based on prize money. Only Michael Stoute, Aidan O'Brien – both of whom benefit from a better quality of resources overall from their patrons than other handlers – and Richard Hannon, who had run significantly more horses (1,259), boasted higher tallies. In May 2006 the yard would record its 1,700th winner when Peter Savill's Peppertree Lane won at York. It is a testament to the consistency of Johnston's achievements that the 1,000th winner, Double Honour at Hamilton, had been celebrated fewer than six years earlier, on 4 September 2000. 'Owners look at those records, of course they do,' Johnston insists. 'Generally all those trainers at the top are doing their job pretty well.'

First thing every day he scours the *Racing Post* for the Today's Trainer section which gives handlers' records over the previous fortnight, in terms of wins and places. It offers a telling insight into current trends. 'The measure is to look at the percentage of horses getting placed,' Johnston says. 'If we're hitting 50 per cent then we're really flying.

That's incredible. It usually only happens at certain parts of year. If we're running at a third everything's fine. But if it drops below 25 per cent we're in dire straits. If we don't have a winner in a week, then we're really going badly.' Like his football counterparts, Johnston is acutely conscious that future prosperity is all about today's results. 'If you're getting plenty of winners for an owner, they're never going to leave,' he asserts.

Unfortunately, you can train them just *too* well. Those owned by members of the Maktoum family which excel on the racecourse – although not necessarily every horse – tend to be transferred to Godolphin to continue their careers. Johnston experienced such a loss after Shamardal had won the previous season's Dewhurst Stakes. 'Nobody wants to lose such a grand horse, but we all know that's the name of the game,' he says. 'Sheikh Mohammed knows it hurts, and there was a very generous compensation from him, including a huge present for the staff.' And it is not only Maktoum horses that are vacuumed up by Godolphin. Sometimes, as we discuss later, his other owners are made offers they can't – and, Johnston believes, certainly shouldn't – refuse. The revolving doors here tend to be frequently in motion. Some of the best horses have already gone to Godolphin, such as Winged Cupid, runner-up to another Godolphin recruit Palace Episode at Doncaster in the Racing Post Trophy, together with Stepping Up and Austrian, both of whom displayed potential as two-year-olds.

It is nothing unusual to find Sheikh Mohammed involved in acquisitions, and not merely equine. In September 2005 he splurged $9.7 million on a colt by Storm Cat at the yearling sales in Keeneland. At the time it was the third highest price for a yearling in sales history. Also recently, the newspaper business pages have contained many stories relating to the purchase of the British corporate icon P&O by a Maktoum family-backed company. The 2005 season was, though, a disappointing one for his Godolphin operation, one which demonstrated that purchasing power may give you a head start but it can never guarantee success. Later in the coming 2006 season we would witness this theory borne out in dramatic fashion with the adventures of Marcus Tregoning's Sir Percy and Pam Sly's Speciosa, both purchased for no more than a pittance in Sheikh Mohammed's terms.

Despite the notable losses to Godolphin – and, thus far, disconcertingly, no confirmation yet of new arrivals from Sheikh Mohammed and the Maktoum family as a whole – Johnston's yard is flourishing at the end of yet another year with over a century of winners accumulated. Such consistent achievement ensures that Kingsley House remains a magnet for owners, many of whom entrust Johnston to purchase their bloodstock. Starting at the August sales in Deauville and continuing on to Doncaster, Keeneland, Goffs (in Ireland) and Newmarket, Johnston has lavished around £1.5 million on yearlings in 2005. Some are pre-ordered, and payment is guaranteed, but around half a million is spent speculatively on behalf of owners who may be prepared to back his judgement (they usually do). His assessments have to be sound. His reputation depends upon it, and Johnston knows too well that public perception is a key component of success.

There are, too, invariably arrivals of some 'second-hand' runners – older horses that have already run from other yards, and have possibly been in different ownership. There may be some hand-me-downs from the world's most powerful owners, who traditionally cull what they perceive to be those animals that are not going to be among the absolute elite towards, and sometimes well before, the end of the season, so as to allow for the intake of the next season's two-year-olds. Johnston has recently been the recipient of Shalapour. The four-year-old, bred and formerly owned by the Aga Khan had finished third in the 2005 Irish Derby when trained by John Oxx. He is now in the ownership of Swiss patron and Johnston stable stalwart Markus Graff. There are expectations that the newcomer could become a decent Cup horse.

Some of the yard's already familiar staying names will again take up arms for the stable in 2006. They include the Johnston stalwart Bandari, who boasts eleven victories, including the 2005 Hardwicke Stakes at Royal Ascot (run at York), and Golden Quest, who had been diagnosed with a knee fracture after finishing a half-length runner-up in the 2005 Goodwood Cup.

It was at this very early stage of my season visiting the yard that Johnston first articulated that primeval force which motivates him and provides his *raison d'être*. One assumes that what provides that drive is the search for those elusive moments of glory with a Classic victor, that tantalising moment when the eyes of all racegoers, and many beyond, are on you, feeding an ego. Not so, according to Johnston. 'It's fear that drives me on,' he says. 'Fear that the whole thing will collapse around my ears. That's why I can't take my eyes off the ball for a minute.' That revelation takes you aback slightly, as the foundations are seemingly cast in reinforced concrete. Yet, if you think about it, the advantages of large-scale production are only in play if investment – and by that I mean the horses sent by owners – remains high enough to support a workforce geared up to care for 200-plus charges. Johnston is adamant about this. If, for some reason, the horse numbers were allowed to dwindle significantly – say, to 150 – 'the whole thing would haemorrhage money', he claims. Later in the year we would return to that subject and discuss why it is imperative that the yard maintains a roster of at least 200.

But it is human turnover that engages Johnston's attention on this particular Sunday. The boss is preparing to make annual appraisals of his key personnel, and he sets the year's statistics before me. By now we have returned to the Johnstons' kitchen within the house that overlooks the office, and the entrance to the yard. Like many racehorse stables, that room is for more than breakfast and lunch; it is the centre of its galaxy, around which revolve the suns and planets, from the work-riders to the lads and lasses mucking out. Outside, on the wall of the nearest line of boxes, is fixed a board on which records of attendance, sickness and holidays are maintained in various colours. The implication is clear: there is no hiding place for the slacker or absentee. Is it healthy for staff relations for everyone to be aware of their colleagues' records? I had my doubts about that, as I did about the clocking-in procedure. Doesn't this reduce them to mere blue-collar workers rather than the skilled employees that most would prefer to be regarded? It could easily be a contentious area, but Johnston sniffs dismissively at such an assertion. 'We have this points system I copied from Kimberly-Clark (Richard Huckerby, one of his group of business advisers, worked there, together with Ron Huggins, who owned Double Trigger). They have a scheme called Save with Safety; it's about money for good attendance. They pointed out to me that it's not a coincidence that the same person gets injured all the time. It's not coincidence that the same person is sick, even if they are genuinely sick.' He claims that staff prefer it if a colleague's poor attendance record is made public. The staff approve, he adds.

Staff turnover is slightly disconcerting, though. His figures reveal that the yard has lost around 40 of its workforce in a year, out of just over 100. But within British industry as a whole, Johnston points out, the norm is 38 per cent. Yet it is evident that some of his yard managers are less successful at retaining staff than others. Like Sir Alex Ferguson, Johnston will attempt to find remedies for poor performances; he has plans to switch formations. There is an appliance of science in his methods. He searches diligently for ways of improving the management of the yard which he insists can only improve the number and winner ratio.

Then he recalls wryly that it was not always thus. Not when he and Deirdre, a vet in practice and a teacher, both in their twenties, set out on an expedition of discovery in the precarious world of horseracing. Nor many years before that when, as a schoolboy, Johnston first recognised where his destiny lay.

CHAPTER TWO

I just thought, 'I'll feed my whippets more, and work them harder.'
That's what I did, it worked, and my dogs were
fitter than everybody else's. I was only 14 at the time,
but it was through that experience
that I believed I could train racehorses.

What sculpts a man's character and ambition? What are the drives and instincts that shape us? Some originate within the genes; others are overtly, or sometimes subconsciously, implanted by peer or parental influence.

You can observe all those influences, with crystal-clear clarity, in the Johnstons' eldest son, Charlie. And you won't be left in any doubt as to how he sees his future. Though he is an engaging, thoroughly normal teenager, who can be heard listening to groups like the Kaiser Chiefs in his bedroom, not too many boys of his age make the *Racing Post* their first point of reference before departing for school of a morning. Charlie scans it avidly – reports, statistics, his father's planned runners. He is too young legally to have a wager, of course, but he frequently asks his father or mother to place a bet on his behalf. He rides work, is fully conversant with the mysteries of form, and has even appeared, confidently and impressively, before the TV cameras at the racecourse. When he has done so, he is regarded as almost as significant a celebrity as his parents. Short of pinning a label to his lapel stating 'Always Trying', therefore, Charlie makes his future intentions manifestly clear. And, in fairness to him, he would be far from the first trainer's son to take over the family business.

Yet his father is troubled that assumptions are already being made, by Charlie and by others, including me, that he is the heir apparent. In a quiet moment, just before the start of the turf season, we have somehow moved from the manner of Johnston's own introduction to the sport to discussing the bequeathing, one day, of his thriving multi-million-pound concern to Charlie. Or, indeed, his younger brother Angus. For the moment, Angus wants to design computer games. 'He's told us that he doesn't want to work with horses and doesn't want to be famous,' says Johnston. So, the plan, presumably, is that some years down the line Charlie will take over the management of the yard? 'Actually, we've talked about it for quite some time, half as a joke and half in earnest,' admits Johnston. 'We joked about the fact that from quite a young age Charlie was taking orders for yearlings for 2015! And so he was – and he still does, to some extent – encouraging the customers to still be with *him* in 2015.'

Why 2015?

'Well, I have talked, at times, about 2015 being the year when I would bow out. Then I would be 55. But I'm sure as every year passes and it gets nearer, maybe it becomes less likely that I'll quit then.' Few close to Johnston, who are aware of the tenacious grip he has on all activity in and surrounding the yard, would argue with that assumption. 'Anyway, whether I do retire then or I don't, it's certainly become quite a big problem at the moment, in relation to Charlie's schooling and what his future holds. We've felt that because he believes he's coming into this business, he thinks he doesn't have to do well at school, he doesn't need to do well at university, because his career's decided upon. Clearly, as in many things, I'm biased, and I believe that being a vet has been a tremendous selling point for me, and of fantastic value. If I'm honest, I think if he's going to take over this business he should go and get a vet degree as well. The problem is that he doesn't want to.'

As an outsider, it did appear to me that there were several backgrounds that made a man or woman suitable for enlistment to the training fraternity. Studying for five years at veterinary school was but one. Johnston won't yield an inch on this, however, as his son will no doubt discover. To him, that is a no-brainer, to employ the modern vernacular. It's exceedingly tricky to argue against the rationale of a character who first harboured aspirations to become a trainer when a little younger than Charlie, mapped out his own future meticulously, and who has since progressed relentlessly towards the summit of his profession. His eldest son's future is a subject to which we would return.

The factors that contrived to mould Johnston appear clear enough: a combination of his father's ownership and breeding of racehorses on a small scale (that interest having been stimulated by working with horses in the army in Palestine and North Africa) and his own fascination with all animals as a boy. Certainly, they were sufficient to provide the initial impetus. However, there was little about Johnston's background that indicated he would become such a dominant figure in what once was grandly branded as the Sport of Kings, though these days horrified traditionalists would contend that it is more the Plaything of the Parvenu. It faintly amuses Johnston that in doing so, over those 30 years, he has also managed to traverse the class divide.

Strange things, perceptions. Probably, few who have heard him speak so eloquently after a winner at Royal Ascot or Goodwood would question a reference in trainer and former England footballer Mick Channon's biography describing the rivalry between him and Johnston at the denouement of the 2003 season. Johnston is described by the author of that book, Peter Batt, as 'a middle-class ex-veterinary surgeon'. Johnston splutters into his coffee when I read him this extract, the reaction a mixture of astonishment and amusement. Jokingly, he suggests that his wife Deirdre possesses the more 'middle class' breeding of the pair of them. One suspects, though, that Johnston is not actually mortally wounded by the imputation (though he does remind you that as far as he is aware he is not, unlike the parrot in the Monty Python sketch, an ex-vet, he has not ceased to be qualified to practice). In a sense, it is a compliment to what he has achieved from relatively modest origins.

Unlike many of the training brotherhood, Johnston's christening gifts did not include a pair of silver binoculars and a subscription to the *Sporting Life* (now defunct, and still mourned by many of us) after he had entered the world on 10 October 1959, the youngest child of – and he places emphasis on the following two words – 'working-class' parents, Ronald and Mary. The couple already had two daughters, Lyn and Sharon. His father was born in Bridgetown, Glasgow, before his family moved on to Springburn. 'Both are now inner city areas, and are still not exactly upmarket, but then they were deprived areas, dominated by thirties tenement estates,' explains Johnston. 'It was pretty grim. Not quite as notorious as the Gorbals, but there wasn't much in it.' Mary Johnston's family hailed from Knightswood in the city.

Ronald Johnston had been evacuated to Aberdeen during the war and attended the high school there. 'He was bright enough to be sent there, and was given a bike for that achievement,' says Johnston. 'But my grandfather died when he was fourteen, and, as I understand it, without that paternal influence my father constantly verged on crossing the line and getting into trouble. The result was that he was packed off to the army, just after the end of World War Two, with a reputation for being a bit of a rebel.

He'd never been involved in school sports and had never been any kind of athlete before he joined the army, but once in the Service he boxed and won umpteen medals for running. Apparently, he was the Forces three-mile champion. The reason he joined the sports teams was simply because they got extra rations and less work.'

Boxing suited him eminently, it transpired. 'He was clearly from a very rough, very poor background,' Johnston adds. 'In fact, I believe quite a violent background. He was one of these small toughies. He was only five feet four inches tall but would fight anyone. He could take a drink and was a very aggressive guy, but never to us. If someone swore in front of us, he'd be liable to get hold of them and remind them how to behave. I'd call his attitude very principled, and I guess that's where I got it from.'

For all the imagery of the stereotypical hard-drinking Glaswegian who advanced arguments with his knuckles, Ronald Johnston was actually a pacifist by nature. He was also anti-establishment and, according to his son, disliked being in the army. He made it clear he was opposed to serving in Palestine and Tripoli. One facet of the army did appeal to him, though. When his unit was asked whether anyone knew anything about horses, he volunteered. 'My father claimed to be knowledgeable about them, but it wasn't true,' says his son. 'He also claimed to be able to ride when he couldn't. His only connection with horses was that his cousin, Jack Coneghan, who he'd grown up with, had worked with carthorses at a stable in Glasgow.' So Private Ronald Johnston went off to work in the stables as a groom. 'As I understand it, his regiment had a racehorse called Nonesuch,' Johnston recalls. 'He rode that in at least one army race. That was some achievement in itself because he was basically self-taught.'

After finishing his service in the army, Ronald Johnston moved down to London, with his brother, Jimmy, and held down various jobs, including waiting in hotels. But most significantly, he also worked in the airlines, as a steward for the British Overseas Airways Corporation. That was how he met Johnston's mother, in London. She was a stewardess with British European Airways. (The long-defunct BOAC and BEA were the forerunners of British Airways.) The couple married in 1951. Lyn was born in Woking in 1953, and Sharon arrived three years later, by which time Ronald and Jimmy had moved to Birmingham and bought a pig farm.

It was, however, always the intention of Johnston's father to return to Scotland. 'Apparently, my grandmother told my father, his brother and cousin that there were these great new council houses in East Kilbride and you could get one if you had a job in the area. They didn't work there, of course, but she had a friend who said you could beat the system just by *saying* you had a job, and they all gravitated back from England.' The Johnstons moved to a new council house in the then new town south of Glasgow, created in the fifties and sixties. It was there that Johnston was born and lived his early years.

'The thing I remember most about that time was becoming aware that my father was obsessed with horses and horseracing,' Johnston recalls. 'The younger of my two sisters, Sharon, was bought a pony and we both got riding lessons. I was about five at the time. As you can imagine, that wasn't exactly normal for your average kid on a council estate in East Kilbride. My father had always been a punter, and when he went to the bookie's on a Saturday I'd go along with him. Then we'd go along to my grandmother's house and sit and watch the races on TV.'

Throughout that period his father had various jobs. 'He worked as a night porter at a hotel in East Kilbride, and he even went back to night-school, because he thought about becoming a teacher. He was basically a very clever, intelligent guy.' At one time, Ronald Johnston also worked as a sales rep for S&H Stamps. 'If you remember, you used to get stamps with your petrol and so on,' Johnston says. 'There was Green Shield. My uncle Jimmy was Scottish agent for them, and my father was Scottish agent for S&H. Then he worked as a Scottish rep for Alba Televisions. When I was three he gave up the job and my mother took it. She remained doing that for many years, until Alba went bust. The main reason he gave up the job with Alba Televisions was that he was setting up his own business, which was loft insulation and television aerials. The former fell by the wayside, but the latter took off. He ran his own business, Ron Johnston Agencies, at 3-5 Duke Street, Glasgow, and was the sole representative for Pye Labgear in Scotland. Eventually, he sold it. But that's what would provide him with enough money to fund his hobby of owning racehorses. And, of course, that really spawned my interest.'

By the time Johnston was approaching seven, the family was on the move again. It was a defining moment in his life as he experienced his environment changing from the prosaic austerity of a new town to an exciting new world for a young boy to explore, albeit only 25 miles north of Glasgow. 'The two families tended to travel around together,' says Johnston, 'so when my uncle Jimmy moved to the holiday town of Aberfoyle and bought a hotel there, my parents, my sisters and I followed them up there. My father bought five acres of land, nearby at Gartmore Bridge, to build a house.'

The area, which is just south of the Highlands faultline, is popularly known as the Gateway to the Trossachs. Its historic and literary reference points have long entranced visitors from around the world. Notably, Sir Walter Scott was a frequent visitor to the area, staying in the old Manse house. He was a familiar presence as he rode along the forest tracks. It was this wooded location that he used as the backdrop for his novel *Rob Roy* and poem *The Lady of the Lake*, the 'lake' being Loch Katrine. He penned the poem in August 1810 while holidaying with his wife, Charlotte, and daughter, Sofia.

> *The summer dawn's reflected hue,*
> *To purple changed Loch Katrine blue,*
> *Mildly and soft the western breeze,*
> *Just kissed the Lake, just stirr'd the trees …*

Now located in the Queen Elizabeth Forest Park, it is an idyllic haven for any child to develop in, particularly one, like the young Johnston, whose curiosity in animals of all kinds was becoming apparent – although, as will become evident, not in an unduly sentimental kind of way. Even back in those days there was never any likelihood that he would understudy Dr Doolittle.

'I suppose, looking back, I was a bit of a loner, a bit different from the rest of the crowd,' Johnston recalls. 'Maybe it was because I'd arrived in Aberfoyle from the Big Smoke, or close to it, at East Kilbride. I was always rebellious, always questioning authority.' To which it may be asked, why wouldn't that surprise those who know him now? 'I also had different interests,' he adds. 'From childhood, I was always an animal person, probably more than my kids now, in bad ways and good. I was always trying to keep them: wild animals, like snakes and lizards, to chickens and dogs. Anything I could get hold of. I remember I did daft things. When I was eleven I went and bought a calf from the market for £1.50. I kept it in the garden shed and tried to rear it. But it died after about a week. It wasn't the brightest thing to do, but I learnt a lot from the experience. That's the difference between me and my boys. Angus has a couple of hamsters and both lads ride, but I had animals my parents didn't know I had. I kept wild animals and birds and fish. Or attempted to do so. I learnt the folly of that. They didn't survive because I tried to keep wild animals in captivity. I would keep minnows in a tank and find they'd died two days later. I went out and captured newts and snakes and slow-worms. I caught tadpoles and reared them to be frogs and toads. You could argue that a lot of what I did was not fair on the animals, but I learnt a lot from it. That was probably what led to me going eventually to vet school. I would also kill animals. Later, I'd go fishing, and hunting rabbits with my gun, or I laid snares for them. I'd shoot rabbits and feed them to my dogs. That didn't bother me at all.'

The young Johnston possessed a curious blend of traits: there was the pugilist, when required, but also, by preference, the philosopher. Academically, as he says, he was 'the best in class'; yet, like his father, he could look after himself. He would often get into scraps at school. 'I was often off school, though with my parents' knowledge. I spent quite a lot of time with my father. I'd go to work with him sometimes. I knew a few children in the village, but my closest friend, through my early school years, was my cousin, David, who lived in the same village. But when I passed the eleven plus and went on to high school, he failed. His parents sent him to private school in Edinburgh, so then I only saw him during school holidays.'

Johnston's sister Sharon, who is four years his senior, recalls her brother being doted upon by their parents. 'He was quite spoilt,' she recalls, affectionately. 'As the boy, he got treated differently from us girls. I remember us having to clear ice off paths in winter. I can't remember Mark ever having to do that. And when we were old enough to drive, we got old bangers. He was given an MG Midget.'

The Johnston children were the product of fiercely proud Scottish nationalist parents. Indeed, their mother, Mary, was for many years a member of the Scottish National Party, for whom she stood as a parliamentary candidate in Motherwell and Coatbridge. She also ran the trade union wing of the SNP. Ronald was also an SNP supporter. It was perhaps inevitable that through them Johnston should inherit a fervent love for his country. He rarely restrains himself from proclaiming that fact. 'He couldn't avoid having feelings like that,' Sharon opines. 'It was in our blood. Our parents had a huge influence on our upbringing. Other children would be taken out at the weekends to enjoy themselves; we'd have to do leaflet drops for the Scots Nats. Our parents were very committed to the cause. Meetings were held at our house. I'd go so far as to say that their views were quite extreme. At one time we thought our phone was being tapped. You don't grow up in a house like that without having strong nationalistic tendencies. Mark's got huge pride in where he came from. I'm sure that's why he gets an extra kick out of his winners at the big meetings down south.'

Those days lay a long way ahead. Yet even when he was as young as eight his father's all-consuming interest in the thoroughbred stirred the imagination of Johnston. The first race he can recall was Sir Ivor winning the 1968 Derby. 'By the early seventies, when I was in my early teens, I was very enthusiastic about racehorses,' he says. 'I had my bedroom walls decorated with pictures of the great horses of that era: Mill Reef, Nijinsky and Brigadier Gerard. Then my father bought a horse called Torso and put it into training with the ex-Irish jockey Paddy

Chesmore.' He was based at Drymen, eight miles from the Johnston home. 'It was placed God knows how many times but never won a race. But that's when I started to go racing.' When Chesmore died from a brain haemorrhage, his widow Sue took over the licence. 'My father went to Doncaster Sales and bought another horse called Sure Jumper. So for a while he had two in training. By the time I was fourteen I was also going to the stable to work at the weekends. That was the time when I made up my mind I wanted to be a trainer. When we went to the races to watch our horses, I used to sit in the back seat of the car and listen to my father and Sue in the front and think, "I want her job." I wanted to be paid for it, rather than watch someone else do it.'

There were also horses at the Johnston home, Ronald having become an amateur breeder, in a small way. 'It was his hobby, and he had a couple of mares,' says Johnston. 'He wasn't very good at it. He never bred a single winner. But it got me used to being around horses. I'd muck them out, and occasionally ride them. It meant we got some unusual gifts, though. For my tenth birthday my present was a horse. It was a two-year-old filly! The idea was that I could eventually ride it. I didn't. That ended up as a broodmare.'

Overall, however, the breeding project became more of a frustration than an inspiration to Johnston. 'By the time I went to vet school I was getting frustrated with the way my father dealt with these horses. We were on a hiding to nothing.' However, Johnston Senior's attempts at breeding a winning racehorse did result in one connection that would become important to his son in the years that followed. 'One of my father's home-bred yearlings, Yes Indeed, was broken by Sue Chesmore, but she didn't have a Flat licence. So it was sent on to a trainer who did – Tommy Craig, based on the coast at Dunbar. That's how I first came across Tommy, although I had no real involvement with him then as I was still just a schoolboy.' Ah, yes. Schoolwork. That was evidently far from a priority in young Johnston's existence, though he was aware that if he was to pursue his ambition such details like passing exams would have to intrude into his life.

Initially it was the greyhound track rather than the racecourse where young Johnston could more commonly be discovered – though he would insist, and subsequent events tend to support him, that he was not idling away his time. He was a watcher rather than a gambler. 'From my early teens I used to go greyhound racing more than I went horseracing,' he says. 'At one stage I went two days a week, at night after school. My dad would take me into Glasgow and we'd go dog racing: White City during the week, Shawfield at the weekend. I really believed I could train a greyhound, but my parents wouldn't let me own a dog of any kind. I didn't necessarily want a dog to race; it was just to catch rabbits and so on. In the end they relented and let me buy a whippet.

'I was fourteen when I got my first dog, and the first thing I did with it was to enter it in a show. Except I knew nothing about taking a dog to a dog show. Then somebody told me that a woman who lived near me, Flora Lindsay, was an ex-secretary of the Whippet Club of Scotland. If I went along to her, she would teach me how to show a dog properly. She agreed to help, and for six months I'd take it to shows, and we came away with rosettes.' There was an additional benefit from that contact. 'Flora asked me, "What school are you at? And what are you doing? What do you want to be?" I told her, "I want to be a vet." It turned out that *she* was a vet. Even better than that, she was a lecturer at Glasgow vet school. I'm not sure if, when the time came, she helped me get in there, but she was certainly supportive through all the time I was there.'

For the moment, though, Johnston concentrated on his whippet. Showing was all very well, but then he discovered there was a whippet racing club near where he lived. 'So I started racing the dog.' He laughs at the memories. 'It was like going out and buying an Arab racehorse. My bitch didn't have a racing dog in eight generations of her pedigree. It was all very amateurish. You're only talking about a club with ten dogs in it, but mine became Scottish bitch champion. Then I bred some very successful dogs by crossing her. There were all these guys in the club who had been training dogs for twenty years, whatever, and I believed I could train dogs better than them.' His training philosophy was simple enough. 'I just thought, "I'll feed my whippets more, and work them harder." That, essentially, was all that was contained in the Mark Johnston Book of Training Whippets. That's what I did, it worked, and my dogs were fitter than everybody else's. I walked them three and a half miles in the morning before I went to school and I fed them as much as they could eat. Just as importantly, I took them out on Saturdays and Sundays when they weren't racing, walked them for about twenty miles and let them chase everything that got up and ran. They were as fit as the proverbial butcher's dog. I worked after school, washing dishes in a hotel. It wasn't the 25p an hour I earned that was important; it was to get the steaks off the plates. That's what I fed my dogs on. It was through that experience that I believed I could train racehorses.'

His sister Sharon recalls that first whippet well. 'She was called Flip, as in flip side of the coin. He'd actually wanted another of the litter, and ended up with her. But she did well for him. Mark went on to breed from her a couple of times. He wanted to keep the puppies. But, remember, he was still at home, and our parents put their feet down and told him, "We're not having a house full of dogs." So Mark, clever little blighter, agreed that no, *he* wouldn't keep the offspring. He gave the rest of the pups from the litter to all of us as presents. That's how he kept them. We had about seven at one time.'

Though Ronald Johnston was essentially devoted to his equine interests, he began to accompany his son to dog races. 'It didn't always go according to plan,' says Sharon. 'They left some of the dogs in a car once while a race was on, and came back to find the interior of the car entirely ripped up, and I mean ripped up. Another time, Mark left a couple of bitches for half an hour and came back to find they'd nearly killed each other.' It was all part of the education process for Johnston. 'You could say it was quite a sharp learning curve for him,' Sharon adds.

In the meantime, another person had entered her brother's life, one who, had not equine pursuits preoccupied her, could well have trod a very different stage.

CHAPTER THREE

I suppose it was when I was fourteen that the attraction started,
as I used to notice him driving up and down the road in his sports car.
But from the moment I met him it was clear that all he ever wanted to do
was become a racehorse trainer – Deirdre Johnston.

It doesn't require too much of a leap of the imagination to wind the years back a couple of decades or more and see her portraying Sally Bowles at the seedy, sinister Kit Kat Klub in 1929 Berlin.

Deirdre Johnston, that is.

Lest there be any misunderstanding, it should be stressed that this thought comes to mind after Deirdre reveals that she often used to tread the boards. 'When I was young, I used to do a lot of amateur dramatics,' she says. 'I played the lead in *Cabaret*. I was also in Gilbert and Sullivan productions, and *The Boyfriend*. I did everything – singing, dancing … I never thought about it, but Mark often says that I should have studied drama at college.' Even if her husband is a trifle distracted by the affairs of the yard, you can be assured of a *wilkommen, bienvenue*, welcome, with the effervescence of Liza Minnelli, whenever you visit Kingsley House. Today, Deirdre performs the role rather well of refusing to turn a drama into a crisis.

The Boyfriend, the real one who was to become her husband, first entered her consciousness when she was ten. He was by then fourteen. 'Deirdre's grandparents lived in Aberfoyle,' Johnston explains. 'When they died, the house was kept on as a holiday home and Deirdre, her sister and their parents would stay there for a month in the summer. That's how we met.'

Deirdre continues the story. 'For a time, I didn't know him that well. We only really started going out when I was approaching fifteen. By that time Mark was just about to start further education.' A fond smile spreads across her features. 'He had a reputation for being quite wild and boisterous, and I remember my uncle didn't think that he was at all the kind of boy I should be socialising with.' In fact, at one time he was thrown out of the garden by Deirdre's mother 'for swearing'. Whenever Johnston and his cousin and friend David were together, the former was considered to be the rough one of the pair.

Though today his memory conveniently fails to recall such an image, the teenage Johnston certainly appears to have had an impetuous, self-willed side. His sister Sharon recalls the occasion when Mark and the boy next door discovered a can of liquid and endeavoured to determine what it was. They decided to put a match to it, the liquid turned out to be paraffin, and they managed to set fire to the toilet of a nearby station at an old disused railway line near where they lived.

Deirdre was brought up on the outskirts of Glasgow, though her family hailed from further north, in Stirlingshire. Both parents came from only a few miles from Aberfoyle. Her mother was a farmer's daughter, from Thornhill, while her father is from Stronachlachar, on the banks of Loch Katrine. 'Strangely enough, they were both from the area that I ended up in,' says Johnston. 'My family were city people living in the country. Deirdre's family, who are Fergusons, would be what we call Teuchters (pronounced 'tooch-ters'), or semi-Highlanders.' He reveals this fact in a somewhat mischievous tone; I discover later that it is a somewhat derisory term. It has been used by Billy Connolly and other prominent Glaswegians at the expense of those who hail from the Highlands. 'English people tend to think of Scots as all being alike, but there's a great difference, depending on your origins,' Johnston explains. 'For example, Deirdre's father, who was from the borders of the Highlands, a countryman who happened to live in the city, would always wear the kilt as formal dress. My father wouldn't dream of wearing one.'

Deirdre's affinity with horses began early in life. 'I started to ride when I was five,' she recalls. 'My parents weren't horsey at all, but I talked my dad into paying for me to have riding lessons and managed to persuade them, by the time I was thirteen, that I should have a pony. My sister and I shared it, and we used to take it out to Aberfoyle in the summer. Eventually I would keep it in Mark's field.

'I suppose it was when I was fourteen that the attraction started, as I used to notice him driving up and down the road in his sports car. But from the moment I met him it was clear that all he ever wanted to do was become a racehorse trainer. I always thought that was absolutely great because I had it in my mind that all I ever wanted to do was work with horses. But my father said, "No, there's no money in it. You just concentrate on your education."' Deirdre did. Her future husband did anything but.

Johnston met up with Flora Lindsay again recently. It will be recalled that she was the lecturer at Glasgow University Veterinary School who had advised him on how to show a whippet. 'Her husband died while we were in South Africa on holiday last winter, and I attended the funeral when we came back,' says Johnston. 'It was full of ex-lecturers from vet school. They must have all remembered what a bad student I was.' That is more than false modesty; it does appear very close to the truth. 'But Flora kept defending me, saying things like it was more to do with what was wrong with the course, that they didn't recognise talent when they saw it. "Look at what you've achieved," she told me. "It proves you *weren't* a bad student." That was nice of her. But the truth was that I was a bad student. I scraped through by the skin of my teeth. I wasn't a very good student at school, either. I was hardly ever there. I had a terrible attendance record. I got low grades in all my exams, my Highers. I got four Cs when I needed two As and three Bs to get into vet school.'

Johnston actually left school at sixteen and sought out a further education college where he could obtain higher grades in the subjects required. 'The best further education college at the time in Glasgow was called Langside College, in the south of the city,' he says. 'I told them I had four Cs and needed two As and three Bs because I wanted to be a vet. The guy looked at me as though I was completely crazy and said, "Choose another career." I was so down and depressed at that. Then I went to a place called Glasgow Cardonald College of Further Education, which was full of immigrants who didn't have the best English. They were trying to get an O level or two. I told them the same story, how I wanted to do Physics, Chemistry, Maths and Biology because I wanted to get into vet school. They weren't really interested in what my ultimate aims were. They just said, "Sign here, start on

Thursday." I was almost *more* depressed at that. I started thinking, "What are these guys going to teach me?"

'Strangely enough, there was another guy, my age, in a similar position, except he wanted to study medicine. At the introductory stage, in the Physics class, everyone was asked by a lecturer, a bit of a character who reminded me of the actor Danny DeVito, what they wanted to achieve and why. We two were both sitting together and said we needed As. The lecturer quipped, "So, what are you two doing at a dump like this?" Well, we both did get As. I should go back and thank that teacher. He was excellent.

'I had an offer of a place at vet school the first time, when I got four Cs in my Highers. But the second time, I didn't get an acceptance. Fortunately, I got in on a last-minute place.' And got his head down to some serious studying, presumably? Johnston shakes his head. 'When I say "bad student", I mean it. Yes, I know I have a reputation now as a workaholic, but I'm certainly not one by nature. When you end up working for yourself, there's no option. But I've always had a short attention span. I get bored very quickly. That's why I was never going to make a good student.'

'He was terrible,' Deirdre confirms. 'He just wouldn't do any work at all. I'd be working for my own O levels and Highers, and I'd go to the university reading room with him, sit over him and get him to learn while I was preparing for my exams.' He still possesses a reputation for being something of a 'last-minute Johnston'. 'He's never really changed in that respect,' Deirdre continues. 'When, years later, he used to write his *Racing Post* articles, he'd do them at midnight the night before he had to submit them. Until he actually has to do something, he won't. His exam revision was just like that.'

Just listening to his litany of failures, you wonder how he stayed the course on what is a marathon trip of a subject. Johnston admits, 'I failed Chemistry the first year, and the re-sit too, and the rules were that you couldn't stay on the course. I had to appeal in order to be allowed to continue the course. I had a year of re-sitting just Chemistry. Then I had re-sits in my second year, in Anatomy and Physiology, and in my third year, in Pathology and Parasitology. In my fourth year there were no degree examinations but there were a lot of class exams. You had to pass them in order to be allowed to sit your finals at the end of the last year. Most of them were oral exams. The system was that if you didn't pass them, you had to keep re-sitting them until you did. I had heaps of these things. In the last year I was absolutely convinced that I would have to do re-sits again. Yet my finals were the only time I passed at the first attempt! That was a huge shock to everybody, most of all me. I and a friend of mine, who had started at the same time and had also done re-sits, looked up records to see if anyone in the history of the course had done re-sits every year but had passed finals at the first attempt. It had never happened. We decided it wasn't possible for us to pass.'

His arrival on that dreaded evening when the results were posted at the main university building, at six p.m., was, Johnston recalls, 'one of the worst moments of my life. I arrived at 6.30 to avoid the crowd. They were presented in a certain way. One list read: "The following people have satisfied the examiners …" That meant you had passed. You'd got your degree. Below that, another list read: "The following people have passed medicine …", or surgery, or pharmacology, which meant you had failed something so you hadn't got your degree. Naturally, I started at the bottom. I wasn't on the pharmacology list, I wasn't on the surgery list, I wasn't on the medicine list. I said to myself, "Shit, I've failed them all." Then somebody said to me, "Look, your name's up here." I couldn't believe it. I couldn't believe that I'd passed at the first attempt.'

Commitment clearly hadn't been his byword. Skipping lectures almost became a fixation. 'I missed a huge amount of them,' he concedes. 'I was always swanning off doing ridiculous things. To some extent, that's the nature of vet school. There were around 70 of us who started together on the course, went to all the same classes and finished together, so we knew each other pretty well. We had more parties than other faculties, and we'd have these AVS weekends – the Association of Veterinary Students – where two bus-loads of us would go down to London and run riot for a few days.

'I simply got fed up with lectures, or sitting there in a histology lab looking down a microscope. I thought that was as boring as hell. One day, I and a friend of mine, Gordon Lonsdale, who I shared a flat with, were sitting in an anatomy lecture. There were all these glass windows looking out on to the Campsie Hills. There was snow on them. We thought, "If there's snow on the Campsies, think what it must be like up north. Let's go for a drive looking for snow." So we did. And not just the once. We'd sneak out and just set off for some crazy places, like Thurso. We'd just drive around looking for snow. We did several trips like that, mostly to the north of Scotland, but also to the Lake District and Hadrian's Wall.' Or further afield. 'One time we were supposed to be going to a Meat Inspection lecture,' Johnston recalls. 'We had to get a bus to the abattoir. We stopped for a pint or two and decided that we didn't really want to go to the lecture. So, after arguing about it for a while, we decided to go to Paris instead. That's what we did, hitch-hiking. We arrived, spent a day there, sent postcards to folk in the class, and returned about six days' later -- it was just to show we could do it, I suppose.'

It was Gordon Lonsdale who apparently had a hand in his friend's entry in the Glasgow University Veterinary School yearbook (1978–83) in which the student Johnston is described thus (my words in parenthesis):

An intensely private person about whom, until now, little or nothing was known … Mark's scruffy barrow-boy appearance initially failed him as a playboy while attempting to set up the James Bond Club, a renovated outhouse in Aberfoyle. ('This was my cousin's restaurant that we all used to trek out to,' Johnston explains.) Mind you, the club, dedicated to good dining and not-so-good women, obviously taught him something. He developed a rapport with the young, high-spirited girls of Park School, in particular with the daughter (Deirdre) of an eminent Bearsden Gas consultant (her father was an anaesthetist).

With time came generous sponsorship from, to name but one, the Clydesdale Bank, and no expense was spared: women, cars, sheepskin coats, even velvet pointed shoes were provided. Who could ask for more? 'Well, Quantreau (sic) would do nicely.' Over the years, the Spanish Orange Liquor (sic) Industry has been given a much-needed financial boost thanks to Mark's faithful support. Consequently, many of us have had to reluctantly support Mark, certainly more colourful than the mediocre meritocracy that has now classlessly overtaken the year.

Meanwhile, Deirdre was completing her schooling, uncertain as to which direction to take. 'When I finished school, I had a choice of what to do next. I had a place at St Andrews University to do English and History, and another at the I. M. Marsh College of Physical Education in Liverpool. I could have gone into teacher training in Glasgow. But my parents were very keen on Dunfermline College of Physical Education. There were very few places; it was hard to get in, and very prestigious. So that's what I did. I'd got all my exams in the fifth year, so I spent the sixth year having a nice time, and doing lots of sport, lots of singing.'

Her relationship with Johnston had continued to flourish, even when he went off to university. 'I was at school in Glasgow, not far from where he was at university,' she says, 'so I saw him nearly every day.' But theirs was a romance that evolved, punctuated by break-ups. As Johnston recalls, 'It was a relationship that was on for six months, off for six months, on for eighteen months, off for two years, and finally we got back together when I was in my final year at vet school, and she was in her third year of a four-year course at teacher training college.' It was when Deirdre went to college in Edinburgh that she and Johnston had their most serious parting of the ways. 'I didn't really know Deirdre until it became quite serious,' says Johnston's sister, Sharon. 'Then they split up, and that's when I got to know her well. I felt a bit sorry for her. Mark was doing his exams at the time, and was a pain in the butt. Fortunately, they eventually got together again.'

Though this was a period punctuated by constant duelling with the demands of academia and the angst of relationship difficulties, Johnston's eyes were fixed firmly on his guiding star, which would lead him to his kismet. 'He talked about his ambitions a lot,' says Deirdre. 'He always knew exactly what he wanted to do. He told me he was going to be a millionaire by the time he was 24. I believed everything.' She laughs, and adds, 'He lied. No,' she says quickly, 'I never had any doubts. He must have been very convincing. He gave off a great air of confidence. He didn't strike me as a dreamer. He was very practical.'

Despite struggling through veterinary school, Johnston was steadily preparing himself for a training career. Every spare minute away from his course was devoted to enhancing his knowledge of horses. In their first year, students had to gain work experience, during their holidays, of how veterinary practices worked. Johnston spent time with a small-animal veterinarian in Edinburgh. In the second and third year, it had to be somewhere that specialised in lambing, dairy and pigs. 'So I looked through the *Directory of the Turf* to find somewhere where I could do those things and there'd also be racehorses. I found a place – it's now the Collin Stud – at Stetchworth in Newmarket, run by a woman named Hermione Bartholomew. She called herself a dairy farmer, although it turned out she only had thirteen Jersey cows. There was an old gelding in the field that she'd "rescued" from Cambridge market. It would have otherwise gone to the knacker's yard. She said she didn't know its background. I looked at it, and noticed that its legs had been pin-fired. I thought, "It looks like a thoroughbred, and if it's been pin-fired it must be broken." So I put a saddle on the horse and rode it. Hermione said, "Oh, you ride fine. Why don't you go and ride out for (the Newmarket trainer) John Winter?" She knew John well and arranged for me to ride for him during the fortnight I was there. I wasn't very good, but I coped, well enough to think that when I got home I'd phone Tommy Craig and ask him if I could go and ride out for him.'

Few would have argued with his modest self-assessment of his riding abilities at the time. His sister Sharon recalls one worried phone call from her father. '"Mark's having problems with his horses," he said. "He gets on them and they're running away with him all the time." Fortunately, he didn't have to pursue riding as a career. He discovered that training horses was all about using your mind, and he had a brilliant one.'

Johnston continued to ride out over the next four years, when he was home, even though it was about 70 miles each way from Aberfoyle to Craig's Tilton House Stables at Westbarns, Dunbar, which meant that he had to leave at four every morning. Craig's uncle was George Boyd, the only Scottish-based trainer to train a Classic winner, the 66–1 shot Rockavon, triumphant in the 2,000 Guineas in 1961. Craig was head lad to Boyd until the latter retired in 1969, and he then inherited the stable. 'Tommy was always a small, struggling – probably gambling – trainer, but I probably learnt as much about training racehorses there as anywhere else,' admits Johnston. 'Tommy trained on the beach. It gave me the confidence that I could do that too. I didn't feel that, when the time came, I would necessarily need any grass gallops.' Considering how Johnston's career developed, that belief was remarkably prescient. The pair have remained in contact. 'Tommy and I still speak once a month and we have met up in Dubai occasionally. He also persuaded one of his ex-owners to have horses with me.'

Craig was not Johnston's only influence. After vet school, there would follow a three-and-a-half year period spent in general veterinary practice. Johnston worked at three: in Newtonstewart, between Omagh and Strabane, County Tyrone for six months; in Yarm, a few miles south-east of Middlesbrough, for a year; and then in Braintree, Essex, for eighteen months. During his holidays, Johnston travelled widely to work at racing yards. He went to Charlie Milbank in France, the late John Russell in California, and Alan Bailey in Newmarket.

Yet, before then Johnston recognised that he may have to adopt unconventional methods if he was to gain a foothold in the sport. Back home, his father had been still resolutely attempting to breed racehorses, without conspicuous success. And from somewhere an idea formulated in Johnston's mind.

The scheme yielded evidence of two qualities that would later come to the fore: Johnston's ability to market himself, and the tendency to fight his corner, even if all the warnings suggested he would end up bloodied and bruised.

It was early 1983, and remarkable as it may appear today, the future of the Grand National was in jeopardy. That year, it was sponsored by *The Sun* newspaper, but there was no certainty about its future. Reports at the time suggested that £4 million was needed to save the racecourse from closure, and a campaign to save the marathon steeplechase was launched.

For one young veterinary student, determined to machete his way through what appeared to be the impenetrable forest of horseracing, in search of a clearing of opportunity, it was the ideal chance to publicise himself. He was then aged 23 and in his fifth and final year of vet school. 'I was forever trying to do things to get into the horseracing world,' he says.

He had a three-year-old colt, by Scallywag. Johnston had bred him from the 10-year-old mare, Kimbo, which had been bought at Ascot Sales by his father. 'I had broken him, but he was doing nothing. Going nowhere. At that stage in his life my father couldn't afford to put him in training.' However, the colt, which he had named Mister, was a good-looking animal by a sire who stamped his progeny with his imposing physique. Scallywag had needed a specially enlarged starting stall when he ran third to Crow in the 1976 St Leger. So Johnston offered his three-year-old dark grey colt, which had a 'Lucky Seven' on its flank, to be auctioned on behalf of the appeal before the big race. 'It was a bit of a brainwave. I had this idea that we would do our bit by giving this horse to be auctioned, with the proceeds going to the Grand National campaign. That way, I'd have done something for the National and my horse would go into training. That was what I most wanted. I offered it, and the campaign people accepted it.'

Before the auction, the colt went to Ken Oliver's stable in Hawick. Oliver predicted it could fetch between £5,000 and £10,000. 'I was in practice in Edinburgh with a small-animal vet at the time,' Johnston recalls. 'I got the day off to go down there to be interviewed by the BBC.' The story also featured prominently in local and national newspapers. An earnest Johnston told the *Glasgow Herald*, 'We will feel really proud when we see the colt paraded at Aintree in front of all those people. It will be a big wrench for me. I've fed him three or four times a day since he was a foal.' He added, 'I have no prospect of being able to afford the training fees, so I decided to do the best thing for the horse and help the National appeal at the same time. The money is going to a good cause. I want to see the National saved.'

Half an hour before the big race, Johnston, who was accompanied to Aintree by his father, proudly led his colt into the winner's enclosure to be sold. To his delight, expectations were exceeded – *and* the horse stayed in Scotland. The highest bidder was Arthur McCluskey, a director of a Glasgow kitchen furniture contract firm, who paid 10,500 guineas (£11,025), the equivalent of around £26,000 today. McCluskey presumably hoped that the colt would turn out to be as good as the brilliant hurdler The Grey Bomber, also by Scallywag. This latest acquisition was to be put into training with Michael Cunningham in Ireland. It was an emotional day all round. It was the year when the National was won by Corbiere, trained by the First Lady of Aintree, a tearful Jenny Pitman. The following year, Seagram stepped in to sponsor the National, and since then the event has thrived, despite the 1993 void race and 1997 bomb hoax.

That wasn't the end of the affair for Johnston, either. Scallywag was owned by the De Rothschild family, and Mrs James de Rothschild rewarded the student for his generosity by offering him a free nomination to the sire.

Before he could act on that gesture, Johnston found himself embroiled in controversy. A correspondent to the *Glasgow Herald*, one Ian Turner from Kippen, Stirlingshire, protested in a reader's letter that Johnston's support of the Grand National condemned him as being 'no animal lover' and that 'his desire to see the continuation of the Grand National, and therefore the cruelty that is part of it, demonstrates to me that he has no time for the feelings of horses'. The family rallied around Johnston. His cousin, Jill, was moved to pen a supporting letter to the newspaper in which she condemned Mr Turner's views. This would, no doubt, have been welcomed by Johnston, even if everything we have learnt since has confirmed that he is not a man who has ever required too much support, even when intruding into highly contentious territory.

He was soon to demonstrate that. Now in practice in Yarm, he responded to a newspaper item regarding an animal rights group petition and protest against performing animals which took place outside the Austen Brothers' Circus in Middlesbrough. The members of the Cleveland and South Durham Animal Rights Group were convinced that the circus animals – including elephants, camels and horses – suffered needless cruelty, painful travelling, life imprisonment in travelling cages and domination by fear or force. Johnston couldn't restrain himself. He was quoted in a follow-up article as stating, 'I was called out to the circus at the weekend to treat a horse, and was amazed at the conditions. They were fantastic. The animals were in excellent health, very happy and contented. There was absolutely no cruelty and I was annoyed that demonstrators had implied the circus was maltreating animals.' He added that circuses were a healthy way of keeping animals fit, and they would be happier than animals roaming around in a field. It would not be the last occasion when Johnston would enthusiastically thrust a stick into a hornets' nest.

What no one contested was that his contribution to the Grand National campaign was an astute piece of initiative. 'I got a bit of fame out of this, in a small way,' he reflects. '*And* I got given a free nomination to send my mare back to the stallion Scallywag. The colt was born, and when I qualified as a vet I took the mare away with me, with her foal, down to where I was living at Yarm.'

That may have been the end of that episode, but then Johnston noticed in the *Sporting Life* that someone had paid a record sum for a Scallywag yearling at Doncaster's National Hunt sales – 28,000 guineas. 'The purchaser's name was Edward Stenton. I tracked down his number, phoned him and said, "You paid 28,000 guineas for a Scallywag colt. I've got a Scallywag colt. Do you want to see mine?" It turned out that he was a life insurance salesman and a bit of a crank, an oddity, who had horses in training. Anyway, he came to see my colt. He never bought it, but I stayed in touch with him.

From Yarm, Johnston moved on to the practice in Braintree, Essex, the prospect of establishing a niche in horseracing still nagging away at him. 'I was looking for any way to get into the sport, and the most obvious way was to look for a yard to start training,' he says. 'I looked at a yard to be let, at Tupgill, Middleham, and another at Wetherby, which Richard Whitaker got. I made stupid offers, knowing, really, that I wouldn't get them. And I was also applying for jobs.' There was no limit to his search parameters, or his audacity. 'I was just looking for a job in the racing industry, in any shape or form. I wrote to trainers, and owners. I applied to be racing manager to Fahd Salman. I didn't get it, obviously. I phoned Martin Pipe and asked if he needed an assistant. There was nothing advertised. Nothing came of it. I also applied for a job with Sheikh Mohammed, in 1985.' And the response? 'I wrote twice and then I went and handed him a letter at Newmarket October Sales. I didn't get a reply.'

One contract was sealed that year, though, a lifelong one: Mark and Deirdre were married on 8 June. The happy couple were 25 and 22, respectively. Johnston had taken some persuading to go down the conventional route. 'He would have been quite happy for us just to live together,' Deirdre says. 'But I told him, "I'm not doing that. If you want me, you take me lock, stock and barrel." Then he didn't want to get married in a church, because neither of us were particularly churchgoers, but I said, "Well, I'm not doing it any other way. I want the white wedding, the whole works." So he left it to me to organise. I was delighted.'

The wedding took place near Aberfoyle. 'We had strolled around, found a church we liked, at Brig o' Turk, and asked the minister if we could get married there,' Deirdre recalls. The little Trossachs church, situated on the western shore of Loch Achray, is a popular venue for traditional weddings. Deirdre was determined to ensure that their day would not be forgotten. 'I wanted it to be a fun occasion, and for everybody to have a really good time. I got buses to take everybody from the hotel to the church, we had the service, and then the buses took the guests to the end of the loch. I'd got special permission from the water board for us to go on a steamer from one end of the loch to the other. The buses were allowed to drive around the private road while we were on board. So we had a band and champagne on the steamer, and then were driven back to the hotel. At the end, Mark said he was really glad we'd done it, because he'd had a brilliant day. In fact, we watched our wedding video the other day for the first time in about ten years.'

Deirdre had done far more than tie the proverbial knot; she knew that, in doing so, she had bound herself to a man empowered by an all-consuming conviction in his own potential. She was buying into a belief just as much as she was taking his hand in marriage. 'At the time I knew nothing about racing,' Deirdre maintains, 'I just knew about horses. But I just believed in him, believed in him completely, and in what we were trying to do.' Her faith has been a crucial component of Johnston's development. As Johnston's sister Sharon confirms, 'Deirdre's been a huge part of what he has achieved. Mark would have been a success anyway, but maybe not to the same degree.' You could probably threaten Deirdre with burning at the stake and she would never confess to a scintilla of scepticism about her husband, even back then, amid much uncertainty, as Johnston desperately sought the keys to what increasingly appeared to be a closed shop.

Then, not long after they'd got married, Johnston chanced upon an advert in *Horse & Hound*. It read, 'Racing Yard: 20 boxes. Three-bedroomed house. Lincolnshire. Offers over £95,000.' Johnston rang and asked for details to be sent. 'That night Edward Stenton, the fellow

I had spoken to about my Scallywag yearling, phoned me about something completely different. I knew he came from Lincolnshire, so I said, "Oh, I've just sent for details of a racing yard in your area." He said, "Who's selling it? It's not Moore, Mason and Bell (estate agents), is it?" I told him it was. He said that he knew them and that he'd find out more about it. The following morning he rang and said, "Don't panic, but I've made an offer for you, on your behalf. I've found out that they (Mawer, Mason and Bell) are owed £33,000, so I've offered them that. You'd better come and see it."'

CHAPTER FOUR

Val, just making conversation really, said chattily to Willie Carson,
'So, what do you actually weigh, Willie?' He looked her up and down
before replying in that familiar tone, 'A lot less than you, love.'

The arrival of Mark and Deirdre Johnston, two staff and twenty horses at their first training base, Bank End Stables in North Somercotes, Lincolnshire, was akin to decamping to the Russian steppes or the landscape of some distant planet. Johnston recalls ruefully that the stables, fifteen miles down the coast from Grimsby, were located in 'the coldest place on earth. Well, virtually. It's certainly the coldest place in Britain. The wind blows straight in from Russia.' The area was not for anyone with agoraphobic tendencies. 'It was all reclaimed land,' Johnston recalls. 'Completely flat for miles around.' But it was an experience he and Deirdre could tolerate. This was just base camp on what he expected to be a long and arduous route to the summit.

Johnston clearly enjoys reminiscing about those days, ones when he dauntlessly dipped his toes into the lapping waters of his new profession and discovered that they were warmer than he'd anticipated. 'The stables were only a mile from the beach, which was used and still is, by the Ministry of Defence, as a bombing range,' he says. 'They were actually firing missiles, and you had to ensure you didn't stray beyond the MoD marker points. We used the shoreline for gallops. There were telegraph poles two furlongs apart, which was very useful. I used to climb up one to get a better view of the horses working.' Both he and Deirdre maintain that they spent some of their happiest days there, despite there not being an immediate welcome within the neighbourhood. 'All the local farmers had this suspicion of strangers,' Johnston says. 'If you came from west of Newark they looked at you as if you had two heads. They were very insular people. But we went there, in the autumn of 1986, because it was available. And, eventually, cheap.'

Their first view of the yard wasn't the most propitious sighting for a prospective buyer. 'We drove up there one Sunday, and the whole area was enveloped in fog. But we could see enough to tell us that the yard was a mess, and completely overgrown with weeds. It looked a complete disaster area. But Edward Stenton was rushing me into it. We'd only been there an hour and he was saying, "Do you want it, or don't you?" Well, I'd been looking for a yard for ages, so there was only one answer. "Yes, we want it." We drove away, and Deirdre was reading out the agents' details. "Neatly laid-out gravel yard", it read. So we went back after he'd gone and found, yes, there was the gravel all right, under all the weeds and grass.'

'It was a mess,' says Deirdre, 'but it was great. Hopefully it was going to be cheap and it was what we wanted, so to us it was fantastic. We were determined to get started, no matter what. We'd been to look at places for rent, but it seemed an awful lot more sensible to buy somewhere. There were a lot of good things about it. It had the beach to work the horses. I had no idea how we were going to train them, but it all sounded good to me.'

It transpired that the yard had been owned by Kate Bull, who had trained there but had gone bankrupt. The estate agents were selling the property for the building society, which had repossessed it. According to Johnston, 'it was cheap, shoddy and only three parts finished, and dilapidated. However, a coat of paint would make a big difference to its value.'

That first viewing was around April 1986, and the purchasing saga continued throughout that summer as they attempted to negotiate a price they could afford. 'Edward (who was acting as a go-between) would phone me and say, "Oh, it's accrued interest, it's up to £40,000," then, "It's up to £45,000." Eventually it was up to £50,000.' By then it had got to the stage where the Johnstons thought a deal was never going to materialise. So they planned a holiday. 'Deirdre wanted to visit a college friend in Canada. We had £1,000 in the bank. So we said, "Oh, stuff the yard. We'll go and spend the thousand quid on a holiday to Canada." I went to the travel agent to book it. I came home and Deirdre was standing at the back door. She said, "I don't know whether to laugh or cry. We've got that yard in Lincolnshire for £50,000."

'Edward said he would get us a mortgage. He arranged an endowment mortgage for us, probably the worst kind of mortgage you could have had at that time. Still, needs must … It was a 90 per cent mortgage, so we needed a 10 per cent deposit – £5,000. We phoned Deirdre's father and Deirdre told him we'd just spent £1,000 at the travel agent's. He said, "You'd better have your holiday. It'll be the last one you'll have for a long time. I'll give you the deposit." So we borrowed £45,000 and the yard was ours. Everything was fine.'

Well, not quite. There was the small matter of some working capital. 'I went to the Midland Bank in Braintree where I had £200 on deposit, and I took along with me two little business plans, cash-flows really, written on graph paper,' recalls Johnston. 'I'd bought a book on business which explained how to do it. One business plan was for a vet practice; the other was for a racing stable. I showed the manager photographs and particulars, and told him, "I need an overdraft. I need working capital." I added, "Everybody says I should be starting a vet practice. Here's the cash-flow for that. But the truth is that I want to start a racing stable. Here's the cash-flow for that." Fortunately, we got on, because his daughter had a pony and our practice looked after it. The manager explained that it was out of his area, but he'd forward the details to the Midland Bank in nearby Louth and get back to me in a week.'

The bank representative in Louth was not impressed. His verdict was, 'It's not very nice, it's damp, and it's in a mess,' and he declined to authorise a release of funds. Johnston was dumbfounded. The blood drained from him. Surely he and Deirdre weren't to be frustrated after all these protracted negotiations? 'But then the local manager had a thought. He told me, "I cannot believe you've bought a twenty-box stable, with a three-bedroom house and a flat, all for £50,000. So *I'll* lend it to you." And that's what he did. He also gave us a £15,000 overdraft facility, which over two years increased to £30,000. I just kept phoning him up and saying, "I need a bit more, I need a bit more." He'd say, "OK." That's how we existed.' Hand to mouth, and overdraft to empty wallet. 'The mortgage company we never spoke to. I worked on the basis that as long as I made the repayments of £60 a week, they wouldn't ask me any questions about whether the business was doing well or badly. The only person I had to convince was the man giving me the overdraft.'

That early business truly was organised on a no-frills basis from the outset. 'I bought an old horsebox in Perth, which had been constructed *circa* 1961,' says Johnston. 'We called it Thomas the Tank Engine. In October we crammed all our furniture in it and moved to Lincolnshire, although Deirdre stayed with friends in Essex until Christmas that year. She had to work a term's notice, and would teach during the week then drive up to Lincolnshire at the weekend.'

Deirdre was teaching in Chelmsford at the time. It had never been her vocation, but after she left college her naturally gregarious character and ability to communicate meant it suited her. 'At the time we got married, Mark was in practice in Essex, and I needed a job. I just looked around for anything that was available. I'm not the sort of person who likes sitting round, doing nothing. I've never been on the dole. I hadn't really wanted to teach, actually, but a job came up in a school in Chelmsford, I applied for it, I got it, and that's how I started teaching. I taught there for just over a year.' Yet even while she was there Deirdre was preparing for her life ahead. 'I went to Newmarket and spent two or three days with trainer William Huntingdon's secretary to learn about that side of the business. All along we were preparing for this moment.'

Finances were severely restricted after the move to Lincolnshire, and it was decided that Deirdre should continue teaching. 'There didn't seem to be any permanent jobs around there, so I wrote to all the schools in the area saying I'd be available on supply. I spent two terms doing that before I was offered a full-time job in Cleethorpes, teaching English and Drama. Now, remember, I wasn't trained to teach. I wouldn't have been allowed to do that in Scotland. But I needed the job, and I needed the money.' And it was a satisfying experience? She pulls a mock-grimace. 'It was really hard. It was a very tough school, and basically I got that job because I was able to keep the kids sat in their seats and learning something. No, I did enjoy it, actually. I enjoyed it a lot more than I thought I would.' Deirdre assisted her husband when work permitted, along with, for that first year, Deirdre's sister Donna and her husband Peter, who lived with them. Peter would drive the horsebox;

Donna would help with the mucking-out at weekends. 'Donna was a pharmacist,' says Deirdre, 'so she would go away to where she was working at Bawtry on a Monday morning and return on a Friday night. We had two staff, one in a little flat next door and one in a Portakabin.'

Meanwhile, the rookie trainer was undergoing a process of self-education. He had watched and listened, and devised his own ideas which he was eager to put into practice. But that couldn't happen until he'd overcome the not exactly minor complication of obtaining his licence to train from the Jockey Club. As may be imagined, racing's ruling board doesn't exactly dispense such an entitlement with abandon. It's not like learning to drive. You don't just stick 'L' plates up, go out with a qualified trainer and at some stage take your test. What always helps, though, is the possession of a noble racing name, or a close connection with one. Dunlop? Hills? Harwood? That'll do nicely, sir/madam. But Johnston was a mere commoner, an innocent in the game.

As soon as it was confirmed that the yard was his, he phoned the Jockey Club. It's something he has done many times since, though on that first occasion he had to search for its number in the *Directory of the Turf*, an annual volume he regards as 'my indispensable bible'. 'I asked for application forms for a trainer's licence. Frankly, I just wanted to see the forms, see what was involved. I had no idea at all. The girl put me through to Licensing, and I spoke to Kevin Dwyer, secretary to the licensing committee. He said to me, "What experience do you have?" Well, I wasn't expecting that, so I said to him, "I'm a vet in practice." He retorted, "Just because you're a vet doesn't mean you can train a horse."'

Now, some may contend that an understandably sceptical Mr Dwyer, who was then not to know Mark Johnston from Mark Twain, and certainly could not have imagined that he would achieve what he has done since, had a point. It will surprise no one that Johnston viewed things differently. 'It was like a red rag to a bull,' he says. 'I was absolutely fuming. My first instinct was to say, "Stuff you, I'll go and train in America," and put the phone down. Working in the USA had always been in the back of my mind anyway. As a student, I thought it would be very easy there, in comparison to here. I'd just been told I'd got this yard, I was in total disarray, and this guy does that to me. Yet he actually did me a huge favour because he made me realise what I was going to come up against. I suddenly realised it wouldn't be straightforward.'

Johnston knew that, as a man who had no experience other than riding out at yards here and abroad, he needed to establish a strong supporting case for a licence and he would require some substantial backing before he put his application before the licensing committee. 'What an uphill struggle that was,' he recalls. But Johnston laboured tirelessly to organise it. 'For a start, I knew I needed a minimum of twelve horses. I needed to gather as many potential owners as I could. So I visited, wrote to or phoned everybody I knew who had racehorses and asked them to send me a horse, or at least to write me a letter which I could show to the Jockey Club, saying that they'd send me one. I got twenty promises from people who would send me horses, and they were invaluable when I went to the Jockey Club. In fact only two materialised. One was Paul Venner, owner of Baileys Horse Feeds, although another three or four became owners later, once I was up and running. He personally, along with his partner George Knowles, and his company, sent us horses. We repaid him with a Classic winner seven years later. The other was Brian Palmer, founder of the electronics firm Hinari, who became my business partner when we moved here to Middleham. Half our horses were owned by those two, and there were others' bits and bobs.' Interestingly, the yard's complement of horses included the Scallywag colt Johnston had bred, which by now had been named Rapscallion. 'We sold a half share to Paul Venner on condition that we buy half of another horse from him,' Johnston says. (Sadly, that Scallywag episode wasn't to have a glorious denouement. The horse showed nothing on the Flat in three races, and after one hurdle race for the Johnston yard, when he pulled up, he moved on to John Jenkins.)

Yet, as crucial as that backing was from those owners, it was the support of Major Michael Pope, then president of the National Trainers' Federation, which probably propelled things Johnston's way. 'I went to see him and told him all about my background. Probably it was my connection with Tommy Craig, the trainer I'd ridden out for in Scotland, who was my mentor and who had taught me the little bit I knew, that made him positive towards me. I think Michael Pope felt the industry owed Tommy a debt because he had been warned off for a year for using anabolic steroids on his horses in the mid-seventies, at a time when they were in common use. The major thought that Tommy had been made a scapegoat for all the other trainers who had been using steroids, and the industry owed him a favour. I was lucky to get that favour. The backing from Tommy Craig wouldn't have pulled much weight in itself, but the support of Michael Pope did.'

There was one other significant difficulty. 'The Jockey Club wouldn't accept that our gallops were the beach,' says Johnston. 'Fortunately, we found a local farmer, Cliff Dawson, who had 2,000 acres. He was master of the local hunt and point-to-point. He was prepared to confirm that we used his land as gallops.'

Finally, the moment that would decide the future course of events for the Johnstons arrived – an appointment with the licensing panel. It was February 1987 when one rather anxious would-be trainer arrived at Portman Square, then home to the Jockey Club, an anonymous building between Park Lane and Oxford Street, a location traditionally visited with great apprehension by trainers and jockeys. Serious disciplinary cases were referred there before the move to Shaftesbury Avenue. 'I sat before them and they asked me strange questions like, "Have you ever saddled a winner?" I thought, "They know I haven't got a licence and have never had a runner, let alone a winner. Do they mean do I know how to put a saddle on a horse?" Did they really think it was going to take me more than half an hour to learn how to do that? So I said, rather lamely, "Is that important?" Anyway, I managed to negotiate my way through the interview. They sent me out so they could consider my case. When they called me back in, the chairman of the panel said to me, "We think you should have a jumps licence. Start just in the winter." Now, where I got the inspiration for this I don't know, but I said, "No thanks. I'm going to give everything to this. I can't do it part-time. I need a licence for twelve months of the year. Give me a combined licence or no licence at all."' The panel were almost certainly not familiar with what could easily have been interpreted as impertinence. Had they been, Johnston's ambitions could have been consigned to obscurity there and then. 'They sent me back out again, called me back in, and basically said OK. Where I got the balls to come out with that I don't know. But thank God I did.'

So Johnston now had a yard, owners, horses and a licence. But one important consideration remained: could he train them successfully?

The first runner from the yard of M. S. Johnston, as he registered himself early in his career, was over the jumps. It was a momentous occasion for the family. 'We all went,' Johnston recalls. 'Even my dad came down from Scotland.' When that chestnut nine-year-old, General Billy, approached the tapes under jockey Richard Rowe to set off in the last race at an emptying Towcester at just after 4.30 on 17 February 1987, there was no indication that those were to be the first strides of an illustrious career.

The race was a two-mile-five-furlong handicap hurdle worth £1,671.30 to the winner. Not that the prize was of any relevance to the novice trainer. His 16–1 shot finished ninth of 21, but it was an announcement that Johnston had arrived, albeit rather anonymously and at the periphery of his chosen profession. The *Raceform* comment was a perfunctory 'n.d.' (never dangerous). 'We thought it would win,' Deirdre recalls, 'and we were devastated when it didn't. We thought the jockey hadn't given it a very good ride. He'd obviously thought "small trainer, don't know him", and hadn't really tried. We were very put out.' The suggestion that anybody connected with the yard was not trying was to be the exception rather than the rule where Johnston runners were concerned over the years.

A week later, the yard dispatched its second runner, Rosie Oh, to a novice hurdle at Huntingdon. She was ridden by a conditional jockey named David Hood (now the public face of bookmaker William Hill). She was the stable's first placed horse, finishing fourth. 'It was all so exciting, just having a runner,' says Deirdre. 'We all wanted to go to the races, although sometimes I couldn't go because there was no one else left at home. That was the problem with having so few staff.'

By then the Flat season was fast approaching. Although later in his career there would be victories over National Hunt obstacles, including Newcastle's Fighting Fifth Hurdle, Johnston had always believed that the Flat would be his forte. It was where serious money was invested in bloodstock and decent prize money was won, or relatively so anyway.

Much though he respected the prowess of jump doyens such as Pipe, Stephenson and Richards, he aspired to compete among names like Hannon, Hills, Dunlop, Cumani and Cecil.

With the Flat in mind, Johnston had bought two horses for Brian Palmer at the breeze-ups (where horses are worked on the racetrack in front of prospective buyers). 'At the time, Brian wanted to promote Hinari, the fastest-growing electronics company in Europe, and he wanted to do it through racing,' says Johnston whose uncle Jimmy had introduced Brian Palmer to horseracing, having worked for him. The colt was named Hinari Video and the filly became Hinari Hi Fi. 'As you can imagine, I was pretty naive in those days about entries and declarations, and Brian Palmer had even less understanding. He said he wanted to entertain his customers at Haydock on 22 and 23 May. He told me back in April that he'd like both horses to run there in the maiden five-furlong two-year-old races on each day. I said "OK" and duly entered them. That was it. Never mind what the opposition was. We thought from their work that Hinari Video was our star horse of the two.'

At the time, Johnston didn't even have a regular work-rider. 'So I rang Tommy Craig and he recommended Mark Beecroft, who was based in our area. Tommy said, "He's good, but he's struggling. He'll come and ride out for you."' The horse worked on the beach at home, and then Johnston galloped both horses on the racecourse at Beverley. 'I told Mark Beecroft that he'd be riding work on Hinari Video because the colt was the better of the two, and then I asked him whether he could organise a jockey for the other one.'

R. P. 'Bobby' Elliott was booked. The phone call from Johnston was to transform his life. At the time, the young trainer had never heard of Elliott. 'When he came to ride the horse, Bobby Elliott made some comment to me about how he'd ridden Hinari Hi Fi's sire, the sprinter Song. I looked Elliott up in my *Directory of the Turf*. There he was, best horses ridden: Brigadier Gerard and Song. I later discovered he was Joe Mercer's sidekick for quite a long time, through various yards that Joe was in. When Joe was away, riding in India, Bobby was writing to him and telling him that Major Dick Hern's yard had this superstar, Brigadier Gerard, in the yard.'

All went well until just before the first of Brian Palmer's horses was due to run at Haydock. Mark Beecroft was to ride them both. 'Unbelievably, about four days before the meeting, he told me he wasn't available,' Johnston recalls. 'So I booked Rae Guest to ride the filly on the first day and Willie Carson to ride Hinari Video, whom I regarded as my winner.' In the event, Hinari Hi Fi finished twelfth, though not far adrift of the winner. Johnston professed himself 'delighted' with Rae Guest.

In the paddock before Hinari Video's race the following day, Carson was in typical impudent mood. 'Willie, as I later learnt, could be very dismissive,' says Johnston. 'Now, you have to remember that the owner, Brian, and his wife, Val, knew nothing about racing. Val, just making conversation really, said chattily to Willie, "So, what do you actually weigh, Willie?" He looked her up and down before replying in that familiar tone, "A lot less than you, love."' Followed by the famous cackle, no doubt. 'That was our introduction to Willie Carson,' Johnston adds, 'a great rider who always came across as super-confident, but a horrendous personality until he retired. He was very stubborn and difficult to work with. And you always got a smart reply. That's probably because he is a smart guy, very streetwise, and well able to market himself. It was only once he retired and started working in the media, appearing on *A Question of Sport* and as the BBC's racing pundit and so on, that he developed a more positive side to his personality.'

Later, Johnston was to employ, and enjoy conspicuous success with, another jockey whom he regarded as equally competent and intelligent. That was Jason Weaver. However, the two men could hardly have been more opposite in terms of their out-of-saddle manners. 'I used to try and tell Jason this. Willie used to ride a horse and come in, having got beaten, and he'd say something along the lines of "Oh, if I'd done this or done that, I'd have won. I just didn't know such and such about the horse, but next time, I'll know better." You see, the owner is then instinctively made to feel that he or she wants Willie Carson next time. It's a very clever way of making sure he gets the next ride. Blame yourself just a little bit. Not too much, just a little bit. And maybe bring the trainer into it too. In contrast, Jason would never blame himself. I think that's a fault. Even if Jason knew he was wrong, he'd never blame himself. You see, where owners are concerned, it's generally the jockey who gets the blame. Even if they've no idea, these naive owners will always have a pal in the pub or club – or, as I well remember one owner, Val Rowland, saying, "the man who filled my car at the service station" – prepared to tell them that the jockey made a balls of it. Everyone's got an opinion on jockeys. If the jockey's done the least thing wrong, it's far better for them to say, "Oh, sorry about that. Next time he'll win." And the owners won't want anyone else to ride.'

In the race at Haydock, Hinari Video finished towards the rear, like his stable-mate had, in tenth. Carson's faith was unshaken, as Johnston recalls. 'Willie came back and said, "Teach it to come out of the stalls, take it up north, and it'll win next time." I asked him something else. "Has he run green?" – something like that. He repeated, rather impatiently, "Teach it to come out of the stalls, take it up north, and it'll win next time." That was typical of him. Then Willie added, "I pushed the button today, so give him a couple of weeks off before you run him again."' The horse had more time than that to recover as he came home with slightly sore shins. Also, in those days entries had to be made three weeks in advance. Hinari Video was entered to run at Carlisle on 1 July.

Meanwhile, the filly, Hinari Hi Fi, was declared to run at Carlisle on 1 June. 'We thought "stuff Mark Beecroft" and booked Rae Guest to ride Hi Fi,' says Johnston, 'but the day before the race he told us that he wasn't well and couldn't ride the following day. It was late on in the day and we couldn't get a jockey. We were really scraping around, phoning everybody. Then I thought to myself, "What about that guy who rode her in the gallop at Beverley?" I phoned Bobby Elliott at home and asked if he'd be available. He of course said yes, because he was always available, although I never realised that. It was his only ride of the day. He rode Hi Fi and she finished fourth. We were very pleased with that.' Afterwards, Johnston told Elliott that he needed a jockey to come down to Lincolnshire and ride out. '"If you could do that," I said, "you could ride our horses. I've got another one running soon." Bobby agreed. He came down within a few days and rapidly became our principal jockey.'

At Carlisle a month later, Elliott rode Hinari Video in his second outing. The horse won convincingly. The Form Book report was 'Made all. Clear 2f out. Stayed on.' That might be a tactical template for so many Johnston winners, to the present day. 'We couldn't quite believe it,' recalls Deirdre. 'I was teaching my last class of the day. The race was at 2.30 and I finished at 4.15. I couldn't wait to get out and phone. I ran out to the phone box to discover that it had won. I put the phone down, ran back to the staff room and screamed, "We've won! We've won!" My colleagues just sat there and were obviously thinking, "What an odd woman." Then I thought I hadn't heard right, so on the way home I rang again, just to check. When I got back, I switched on Teletext, and it was still on when Mark got back four hours later. It was just fantastic to see his name up there.' Elliott remained with the yard until the end of 1996, when he left to work for Michael Dickinson in the United States. He returned to Middleham, to work for Johnston, before setting up as a trainer in his own right near Southport in Lancashire in 2003 – at the age of 62 – with the support of wealthy owner, Peter Grayson. He returned once again to Middleham in 2005, and currently rides out for Karl Burke and Patrick Halslam.

'He's a fantastic work-rider,' says Johnston. 'As good as I've ever seen. He made an invaluable contribution to the yard.' In that first year, 1987, Hinari Video was the stable's sole winner. That tally increased to five the following year. It was a modest start, but the portents were auspicious.

CHAPTER FIVE

I can't say I was satisfied with that first year. But for me, at 27,
it was a huge achievement just to have a trainer's licence.
That was an ambition I'd been thinking about for fourteen years.
I'd achieved the number one goal. For a while, nothing else mattered.

Watching Mark Johnston reminiscing about those intoxicating days of 1987 and 1988, when placing every winner gave him an almost spiritual uplift, is like watching a bon vivant stumbling across a long-forgotten cellar of vintage wine. The trainer rattles through those early victories. In addition to Hinari Video, there were Hinari Disk Deck and Hinari Televideo (both for Brian Palmer, and both partnered by Bobby Elliott, at Beverley and Ayr respectively), and Just Precious for Paul Venner (won handicaps at Beverley and Doncaster, ridden by Greville Starkey and Ray Cochrane). And there was Craft Express, again in the hands of Elliott, at Catterick. 'That was owned by a guy named Tony Fair,' Johnston explains, 'although it ran in the name of Val Rowland, a vet client when I was in practice in Essex, who had bred it.' He can recall every triumph, every jockey, every owner. In contrast, he concedes, 'I couldn't name half the winners we've had in the last couple of years.' Craft Express, under the same jockey, went on to win the Tote Portland Handicap at Doncaster the following year. 'Remember that year when a lot of horses fell in a hole?' Johnston reminds me. 'One slipped up and two were brought down. He missed all the trouble and won.'

Ah, nostalgia, guaranteed to inject an emotional supplement into a past life. It makes the good times feel even better, the tedious and troubled times bearable. 'I suppose that fifteen years from today we'll look back on our great days now and think, "Oh, we had great fun,"' Johnston says. 'But Bank End in 1987 and 1988 really was a great way to learn. I trained there for two years, having bought the place for £50,000 and run up an overdraft of £30,000. Yet we sold it eventually for £130,000 and walked away with £50,000. It clearly wasn't a sustainable business, but that never worried us. Life was so different then. All we knew was that this was what we wanted to be doing and we had enough cash-flow to be able to eat. We made a lot of friends in the area. There are still people there we go and visit.' Deirdre agrees. 'It was a fun period,' she says. 'We made a lot of friends, some of whom we still have now, and some helped us out. It must have been tough, but looking back, it seems easier. Now it's such a way of life. Every day you're racing and riding out. Then, we didn't have that many horses. There were only three in a string. We always look back on it fondly.'

Johnston can relate stories aplenty about those two years at Bank End. 'I remember one winter's day I was up at five a.m. to feed the horses, and it was snowing. There was a girl living in the flat which was part of the yard, and my then brother-in-law and I built a wall of snow against her door and above her windows before she got up. For a minute she thought it had snowed so much it had buried her flat!

'At night, we'd play games like Trivial Pursuit while drinking bottles of lager until it was time to feed the horses at nine or ten. There was one guy, Robin, who was Grimsby Council's clerk of works and who helped out with supervising the concreting and bits of building work we were doing. One horse was called Bestbuybaileys. He'd stand in the corner of his box and wait for his food, then charge at the door when you entered. The penalty for losing the game was to feed Bestbuybaileys!'

If it sounds like the script for *Carry on Up the Humber*, you wouldn't be too far amiss. Such behaviour would be unthinkable now. 'Then we had time to do stupid things like that,' Johnston says. 'It was a very different atmosphere to today. There was nowhere near the same pressure.' Which, if you consider it, is a curious observation. Certainly Johnston's reputation demands consistent success now. But wasn't there an urgency then for the yard to demonstrate that it could produce winners? As a virtual unknown, questions would soon begin to be asked about his prowess, wouldn't they? 'Sure,' he responds. 'I know that people who have small yards now look at us and think, "Well, what the hell has he got to worry about? So many winners already this year. Why's he walking about with a face like a fist?" Yet I look back and realise that it was much easier when you have one winner a year. We could go months without a winner. It didn't matter. I don't remember it worrying me that much. Things were rolling along much as we'd planned. It was very different from all this.' He ponders the question further, then adds, 'No, I can't say I was satisfied with that first year. But for me, at 27, it was a huge achievement just to have a trainer's licence. That was an ambition I'd been thinking about for fourteen years. I'd achieved the number one goal. For a while, nothing else mattered.'

What still mystifies many, though, is how the grounding of a veterinary qualification and riding out for a quartet of trainers, scrutinising how they operated, could satisfactorily prepare Johnston for this moment. There are, after all, more familiar roads to success as a racehorse trainer than the one Mark Johnston travelled. For many, the secrets are handed down from father to son, or daughter. John Dunlop's elder son Ed and younger son Harry, who has recently set up on his own; Peter Easterby's son Tim; Barry Hills' son John – these men spring readily to mind as examples of those who have succeeded an illustrious parent. As, indeed, Charlie Johnston may do one day. You could have entered the industry through the traditional method of becoming a pupil assistant with an established trainer, or by garnering experience over several months, years even, working in a yard. Or, like, say, most recently, Pat Eddery and Walter Swinburn, you may have been an experienced jockey first, and/or been involved in the bloodstock industry. Today, it is also necessary to attend one of the courses that are now mandatory for all racing professionals.

Johnston was blessed with none of these advantages. For all his words at the start of this book – 'There are times when I think, "Anybody could do this job, it's not rocket science"' – it is still extraordinary that an essentially self-taught man transformed himself from a novice to a Classic-winning trainer within seven years. It may not be rocket science, but it's not exactly basic domestic science either, is it? Nurturing half a ton of sometimes capricious, injury- and sickness-prone, highly tuned equine athlete to the pitch of fitness is not comparable to bringing an egg to the boil. You can't exactly buy yourself a *Teach Yourself in Two Weeks* handbook or *Training Racehorses for Dummies*, can you? So how, back in those days when he was blessed only with basic facilities and limited knowledge, did he penetrate a world that has always been full of mystique, one containing as many enigmas as the tomb of an Egyptian pharaoh?

In simple terms, it was down to a self-belief that could be occasionally scratched and slightly dented but would never suffer irreparable damage. As far as Johnston was concerned, he may not have been a Grade A genius with the Form Book or a Lester Piggott in the saddle, but he understood horses. Johnston knew how they were put together, how they might fall apart, and, most crucially, how to get them to run to their optimum. He refused to genuflect before conventional wisdom, even when there were many surrounding him prepared to impart the advice, 'That's the way it's always been done.' 'I remember our first head lad when we came here to Middleham, Declan (Condell), talking to me about shins and bandages and claiming that so-and-so was saying something, with which I profoundly disagreed, and that he must be right because "he's been training for 50 years",' Johnston recalls. 'My attitude was that he had probably been training badly for 50 years.

'It's true that there's a terrible lot of arrogance within the medical profession, including on the veterinary side of things. But the fact was that I knew a lot about animal husbandry, and still do. I think that's vitally important. I try to get that across to my son, Charlie. My horses weren't going to be sick, ill, undernourished or under-cared for. I may have been naive in many ways, but I did know how to look after my horses.' That's why the manner in which he was treated when first applying for a licence still irks him today. 'If you know how to look after your horses, to my mind, the Jockey Club haven't any right not to give you a licence. You are qualified to do the job. I was not going to bring racing or the Jockey Club into disrepute. Instead of that, they ask you stupid questions like "Have you ever saddled a winner?"'

Talk to him about his training skills, and Johnston will invariably return to the whippets he bred, showed and raced. He recalls how his sons started to show some interest in greyhounds the previous year, and that he and Deirdre were considering buying one for them. Kevin Wilde, a major breeder who has owned and trained many greyhounds, and who is also one of the Johnstons' patrons, agreed to help them select and purchase the animal. Wilde owned Sunderland and Newcastle greyhound stadiums before selling out to William Hill in September 2002. He has horses in partnership with John Brown of Hill's. 'Yet it never occurred to me that anyone would train the dog other than me,' says Johnston. 'Conversely, it never occurred to Kevin that I would train it. He thought that was the most ridiculous suggestion under the sun, the most stupid thing I could possibly have said.' Johnston looks at me pointedly and adds, 'Where Kevin was concerned, it was the equivalent of you saying to me, "Buy me a racehorse and I'll train it myself." Yet, frankly, I *know* I can train a greyhound, far more than I knew I could train a racehorse. I *believed* I could train a racehorse in 1987 because I'd thought about nothing else for fourteen years beforehand, about how I was going to train it better than anyone else who was training racehorses at the time. I really believed that. Today I believe I train them better than most, or I wouldn't have got to where I am. But back then I thought I was going to be miles better. I thought I was going to break all records. I always had fixed ideas about how I was going to do it better. When I was riding out for Tommy Craig, and for John Winter in Newmarket, Charlie Milbank in France and John Russell in the US, it wasn't because I wanted to improve myself in the saddle. I was a very bad rider. All the time I'd watch what they were doing, and all the time I convinced myself I could do it better.'

While for those who had grown up around a yard, or who had worked for a lengthy period in one, it would be just a relatively simple matter of continuing existing practices, Johnston was never in that position. It proved to be both a disadvantage and advantage. He was forced to go back to basics, to formulate his own ideas on how he would train. 'Some of my theories were, no doubt, completely wrong,' he says. 'Everybody who watches *Channel 4 Racing* and reads the *Racing Post* probably thinks that every horse has its "pipe-openers", and gallops a week before a race, then gallops the day before it's going to race. That's what I did, too, from reading the *Sporting Life*, or seeing what happened in the few racing stables I'd been in. We don't do any of that now. I always had ideas about how I was going to do it differently. How my horses were going to be out for two hours, and work hard and eat more. I based that on my whippets. I had young, naive ideas that everyone else was daft. In fact' – and he stresses these words conspiratorially – 'there was a little bit of truth in that. To this day it's not entirely wrong to say that everyone will cut corners. So, if horses should work for two hours, they'll work them for an hour and a half.

'A lot of my ideas came from watching people train whippets and greyhounds. The biggest joke in the world was seeing old men or kids out walking their racing greyhounds. My thinking was, if those dogs couldn't walk faster than old men or children, if that's as much exercise as they did, what chance did they have of winning a race? I sort of thought the same about racehorses, that trainers probably didn't work them hard enough. Yet, over the years, my thinking has changed on that. Having worked with racehorses now for nearly twenty years, it's staggered me how little work a fit horse can get away with. It's unbelievable how little work you have to give them. I now realise that there is a balancing act between fitness and freshness. You have to walk that tightrope. Just more and more work isn't the answer.

'I don't think I've revolutionised training. I probably started off with some quite extreme theories about how I was going to change the way people trained racehorses, and gradually, through trial and error, I learnt I didn't need to change things that dramatically. What made me different from many trainers is that I was open to new ideas.'

It is a subject we would broach again.

In the summer of 1988, with such thoughts already evolving in his receptive mind, he and Deirdre decided the time was ripe to move on from Lincolnshire. The lure of greater success was increasingly seductive, and that would require scope to develop and expand, which would be impossible at Bank End. As Deirdre explains, 'We realised fairly quickly that the yard was way out on a limb. You'd think you were almost there when you left the A1 but there was another hour's driving, the road got smaller and smaller, and it wasn't practical. But it had served a purpose. It got us going. There were no regrets at all.'

CHAPTER SIX

In those days there were lots of tears and panic. I don't know whether Deirdre's always had faith in me. I think there were times when she felt it was a bit of a roller-coaster that she was caught on, and she never got any say in the matter. In the early days, she agreed with me that there was nothing to lose. She became very frightened when she felt there was a lot to lose.

Just many of the inhabitants of Longbridge or Cowley tend to work in, or know someone who works in, vehicle manufacture, the likelihood in Middleham is that they'll have some involvement with the Johnstons' satellite stables within this rugged idyll situated between the rivers Cover and Ure. Or, if not, one of the other fourteen training establishments based here. Eight of them are located in Middleham; the others are at nearby Coverham. It is the blue and green livery of the Johnston yard that dominates, however. If nearly 120 staff make their living at his various yards, the wives, husbands, children and auxiliary workers who directly or indirectly take an interest in Mark Johnston's fortunes probably quadruple that number.

No one would have thought on such a scale when, in November 1988, the Johnstons, a few staff and thirteen racehorses arrived here, fired with the optimism of gold prospectors to create, as Johnston puts it, 'something unique'. The locals smiled knowingly. They had seen it all before. And the reaction was understandable. Johnston can laugh now at the response from the townsfolk. 'The local reaction was that they thought we wouldn't last five minutes,' he says when we meet up again early in 2006. 'They thought I was a complete nutter, that I didn't know what I was doing.' The reason for that scepticism was twofold. The Johnstons' predecessor, George Dawes, who had won the pools and then installed George Moore as his trainer, had gone bankrupt. A similar fate had befallen trainer Ken Payne before that. 'They thought we were next,' says Johnston, who had bought a dilapidated 34-box yard that offered nothing but potential.

But in part the locals' suspicion was provoked by Johnston arriving with business partner Brian Palmer, who had founded a company called Hinari. You can just imagine the knowing rumours circulating. A Japanese company, wasn't it? Something big in Tokyo or Yokohama. They made electrical goods, didn't they? Well, not quite. 'He'd just made it up, to sound Japanese, because electrical products from the Far East were the big thing at the time,' Johnston explains. 'Now Brian actually *does* do a lot of business in the Far East, and I think he probably brought some Chinese people here at one point early on. The locals used to nod knowingly, and say, "Have you heard about Kingsley House? The Chinese have bought it." They thought I had Oriental backers. They didn't want to sell us newspapers or do anything for us because they all thought we'd go bust in five minutes and we wouldn't pay our bills – particularly as all the previous people had gone bust!'

So, why Middleham? For all its magnificent history and tradition of Classic winners stretching back to the late eighteenth century, when John Mangle produced no fewer than four St Leger victors; for all that it was believed locally that the High Moor gallops on the site of what was once the racecourse offered the advantages of 'altitude training', back in the late eighties no scent of conspicuous success permeated the area. Given the bankruptcies of his two predecessors, it didn't appear the wisest investment for the prodigiously ambitious Johnston and his equally committed wife. Why not Newmarket, or Lambourn, or in the wealthier south of the country?

The decision was essentially financial. When the Johnstons opted to move on from Lincolnshire, they had a budget of over half a million pounds. 'Brian Palmer matched our net profit of £50,000 on Bank End when we sold,' Johnston says, 'and he ended up lending the business a further £125,000. So we started off with £225,000, and borrowed another £400,000. To us, then, it was a huge amount.' They had considered relocating to Newmarket. 'The Jockey Club was leasing sites in the Hamilton Road at the time, for trainers to build their own yards, but we thought for the money we had, well, all we'd get was a bungalow and 40 boxes. We had this idea to build something unique, a yard with every facility, including a swimming pool. I had all these great ideas about veterinary and other gadgets and things I wanted to include. We did look at Hamilton Road, but couldn't afford it. We just couldn't do it there; it was too expensive. We also looked at Malton. We looked at buying a farm around the York area because we had decided that York was the most central place in the country to train. We looked at Epsom too, and Hambleton, near Thirsk, where Kevin Ryan is now. We fancied that a lot. But we ended up buying this.' Kingsley House, the Deanery up until 1955, was once the home of Charles Kingsley, author of *The Water Babies*. It was actually recommended to Johnston by Bobby Elliott, who lived at nearby Leyburn. 'Now,' Johnston asserts, 'I've got no desire to be anywhere else. People promoting Middleham will tell you that we came here because of the best gallops in the world. The truth of it was that we came here because it was the cheapest.'

From those early days, Johnston made an impression with his training philosophies, and raised a few eyebrows. 'When we arrived here we worked our horses considerably harder – and, for that matter, we still do – than the average Middleham trainer,' he says. 'Though it wasn't exactly unheard of, they'd all got into this habit of believing that you couldn't take a horse out on a Sunday, or take all the horses from Middleham village all the way up to the High Moor, but we started doing those things. They thought we were crazy. Then I started taking two-year-olds, and they said, "You *definitely* can't take two-year-olds all the way to the High Moor." The fact was they couldn't be bothered. They maybe didn't have the staff. In fact, it's *good* for the two-year-olds. There's a lot of that kind of thinking in racing. I'm sure a lot of unsuccessful yards convince themselves that certain practices aren't the thing to do because it's not the convenient thing to do or the economic thing to do. But if you look at Michael Stoute, Luca Cumani, John Gosden, they don't cut corners. Mark Prescott doesn't either. I'm a firm believer that training racehorses is about not cutting corners. That was my strong belief from the start.'

Johnston also found the industry hidebound with customs. In those early days, he deliberately sought young stable staff in the knowledge that they wouldn't arrive with preconceptions about how to train horses. 'The older fellows all thought they knew more than me,' he says.

'Probably still do, a bunch of them here now, but they don't get much say in it now.' He pauses to review what he's just stated. 'No, that's not true. Everybody gets more say in it than they did in those days. But the truth remains that I found that the best staff were the youngest staff. They were open to new ideas.

'Out in that yard there's approaching 120 staff and there's probably about 25 of them who think they know more about horses than I do, that I run this business from an office and my success is based on knowing how to run a business. If you asked twenty trainers who are less successful than us, probably nineteen would say the same, that I know more about running a business than they do. That's crap. Yes, when it's all going well I can sit there reading my emails and run everything from my office. If it goes wrong, I have to get out there and get among the horses. At the outset, I had to know about horses.' Knowledge is strength? He nods. 'I keep trying to drum this into Charlie, who thinks he can come and take over this business. As my dad used to say to me all the time, "There's money in muck, as long as you know about muck." You can make a successful business in any field, but make sure you know about it. Charlie doesn't realise that you have to know about horses. He thinks if you know about form, and betting, then that's more important. That's why I went down the route I did. Some of it was luck, because when I was fifteen I didn't realise entirely that I needed to know so much about horses. I look around me now and there are a few successful trainers around, but I wonder, "How much do they actually know about horses?"'

The peak complement of horses in Lincolnshire was twenty. A total of thirteen made the move to Kingsley House, and in their first year there that tally rose to 27 charges. It was promising, but Johnston knew that the priority was new patrons. As Irish trainer Willie Mullins once opined, 'I'd rather have a good owner than a good horse.' One of the latter can lead to several of the former. Word of mouth is an important vehicle of communication. Yet Johnston was aware that he had entered a highly competitive marketplace in which he would have to sell himself. And if that meant doing so as brazenly as a Paris street-walker, so be it.

When Johnston arrived in Middleham, for all the town's horseracing associations, there was little then to commend it to prospective owners. It was about as sexy as Nora Batty's stockings. There were few local owners, and there was no particular reason why anyone should send a racehorse to Middleham to be trained. Johnston needed to offer them one. 'I needed winners, but I wanted quality as well,' Johnston says of that initial period. 'I wanted to win televised races because I was desperate to be interviewed on telly. Not because of my ego, but to publicise the yard. I knew what I was going to say; I had it planned maybe for six months before I appeared. I'd go out and deliberately stand in the right place so I'd get interviewed.

'I remember the day very well when Just Precious won at Doncaster in our second year of training, in September 1988, just before we moved to Middleham. *Channel 4 Racing*'s Derek Thompson interviewed me, and I'd prepared myself fully. I knew I had to talk about owner Paul Venner, and his company Baileys Horse Feeds, and the fact that we fed the horses with that; I had to mention Hinari too because they were our biggest supporter; and I had to talk about our impending relocation to Middleham and our plans there. I had this list of things, and I had to answer his one question and get everything into the answer somehow. It was the best advertising I could get. I was *desperate* to get on telly. I *had* to sell myself on telly. All my interviews those days were like that. I think I was far better at doing interviews then than I am now, because now my mind is invariably on something else.'

Johnston is quite emphatic about which interviewer he preferred, and who was the best from his perspective. 'In those days, the best person for me to do an advert for Mark Johnston Racing was Derek Thompson. Despite all the stick he gets, he's the most professional of presenters. OK, he makes a few gaffes, but if he's interviewing Mark Johnston, he's trying to get the best out of Mark Johnston. He'll ask all the right questions, and will present it in exactly the right way to put his interviewee in the best possible light. Generally, he makes an excellent job of it. The others with most knowledge of racing who are also excellent to be interviewed by are Brough Scott and Clare Balding. John Francome is great when he talks to you, genuinely quick-witted. But to do an interview with John McCririck is a nightmare, because all he wants to do is present John McCririck as loudly and flamboyantly as possible. He doesn't give a shit how the guy being interviewed comes across. You won't get me doing an interview with him.'

At one time, Johnston would indulge his interrogators their faults. These days, he is not so generous. 'Some of the questions you get asked, they drive me insane,' he says. 'There's one guy, northern-based, who used to ring me every Sunday and ask me basically to tip a horse. I just don't like his interview style. He asks stupid questions that I don't think warrant an answer. He's got no diplomacy, so he says the first thing that comes into his head, while others would think about it. At Hamilton once, he said what a lot of people think, that we don't have winners first time out, that our debutants "need a run". So, I actually went and found a data section from the *Racing Post* and showed him three ticks against "training winner first time out". It's true that most trainers' two-year-old debutants improve for the run. Others maybe improve more than others in that they're often green first time, if, for instance, they've never been off the bridle, or hit, at home. Despite that, our first-time-out record is more than respectable. In fact, ours is better than most trainers'. Ours is probably 14 per cent; the other trainers in the race are probably around 4 per cent. And this fellow's got the cheek to say he's surprised that we won first time out, and probably at odds-on favourite.'

These days, Johnston doesn't need interviews, or certainly not as much as he did at the start. 'I didn't particularly enjoy them because I wasn't particularly outgoing in nature,' he says. 'I just knew I had to do it. It was one of the necessary evils if I wanted to get on. Another was phoning up potential customers, and I found that the most difficult thing in the world.'

That first year at Kingsley House, Johnston put together a brochure of the yard. He smiles wickedly at the thought of it. 'We called it our Spanish Holiday Resort brochure, because it was a bit of a con. The photographs weren't of this yard, or if they were, they were of selected, more prepossessing bits of the yard. The building site was kept well in the background. That wasn't our swimming pool, or our horse-walker, and those boxes weren't actually finished yet.' He trawled through the owners' names in his faithful *Directory of the Turf* and dispatched the brochure to everyone who had more than one trainer. 'We worked on the basis that there was no particular loyalty there.

'My uncle Jimmy, who took a close interest, advised me: "After you've sent out the brochures, follow them up with a phone call," but I really didn't want to do it. We had zero success, if I remember rightly, although some positive interest did come out of it within the year. The most notable owners who are still with us are the Kennedys' Greenland Park Stud, in Berkhamsted. Robert Kennedy told me, "Well, I've got no intention of sending anyone else a horse at the moment. I'm happy with the trainers I've got, Peter Calver and Ian Balding." But he added, "I think it's really fantastic that you thought to follow up your brochure." A year later, he sent us a horse. And the family are still here with us. (Sadly, Robert Kennedy died in July 2006, aged 85). In fact he gave us our first Group winner, in 1992, with Marina Park.'

Today, the modern equivalent is a list of horses for sale on Johnston's website, www.markjohnstonracing.com. 'Well, it's a bit different. There's no cold-canvassing now. But I wouldn't say that we'd never do that again.' Also, whenever he is attending bloodstock sales, he faxes back details of all his purchases to the office at Kingsley House. All his owners are immediately circulated with the details. Now success is the greatest selling tool. It was not always so.

Johnston insists that creating a positive image is crucial. 'Take the guy down the road who's never had more than twenty horses and blames it on the horses being not much good. It's nothing to do with the horses being poor. I've always said that it's easier to win races with moderate horses than good ones. It's that he's not proving himself a good trainer by getting the best out of them – and, just as important, being seen to get the best out of them. He's not selling himself.

'At a very early stage, in Lincolnshire, before Brian Palmer got involved, I knew none of the business-speak, the jargon. Brian came along and was immediately saying, "We've got to look at our unique selling points" – the USPs, as he called them. "We've got to get them across to potential customers. What's unique about our business that we can sell to the customers?" When we came to Middleham, they loved to laugh at everything we did. Yet all we did were the most obvious things in the world. We were concerned with making our horses and our staff look smarter than the others. It was the maxim "If you can't be better, look better." Our rivals stable staff thought that was funny.

'I remember there used to be a guy called Adrian Lee, who was based in Exeter Road, Newmarket. He now trains in Saudi Arabia. When he started everything was green. It was a small stable, but the horses wore green blankets, the staff wore green jodhpurs, and he wore green chaps. Everyone mocked him and called him the jolly green giant. Everybody thought it was a joke. He didn't do particularly well, and they laughed louder and louder. A few years on, along comes Godolphin and everything's blue. Nobody laughs at them. Some of what that guy did was absolutely right, just as it was absolutely right for Jack Berry to have all his horses in sheepskin nosebands, and all plaited, and for him to wear a red shirt. It created familiarity with his operation. It was branding. It was salesmanship. We were doing that from a very early stage.'

The move to Middleham, and a considerably larger yard, offered new opportunities, and the graph of winners soon showed a healthy upturn. But it was not too long before the headstrong Johnston felt a hefty tug on the reins. Business truths began to dispel the aura of optimism. 'When we came to Middleham, in partnership with Brian Palmer, he largely pushed it all through financially. But then came my biggest eye-opener. I couldn't forget it.' The arrival of a new bank manager after the Johnstons had been *in situ* at their new base for about eighteen months brought with it an icy blast of realism. 'We thought that winners-wise everything was hunky-dory. It was going great.'

And in many ways it was. After that sole winner in their first season and five in their second in Lincolnshire, the tally rose to fifteen for 1989, their first season at Middleham. In that year the yard secured its first victory at Ascot, with Hinari Televideo, and for the first time a Johnston horse gained so-called 'black type' (in a sales catalogue, the form of any horse that has won a Group race or a Listed race is written in bold type). A Listed event, the Cock of the North Stakes at Haydock, was won by a Bobby Elliott-partnered Lifewatch Vision. The following year, 1990, the total of Johnston winners rose to 27.

'The winners were flowing,' says Johnston. 'Everything was going the right way. But interest rates were going through the roof. We were paying £70,000 in interest. We hadn't budgeted for that. We were losing money. The bank manager came and sat in the kitchen and gave me a lecture, telling me that we should raise our fees. That just annoyed me so much. I thought, "Who's he to try to tell me about the job?" We were all about filling the place with horses and getting winners, because if we didn't do that it wouldn't matter what we charged, we wouldn't have any customers.'

The Bank End Stables had, of course, been financed by a mortgage and an increasing overdraft, on which interest was paid. Now, things were on a different footing. 'When we came here,' says Johnston, 'we didn't have an overdraft any more. It was a business loan which had monthly repayments, but I still thought of it as the same. "Got to make the repayments" – that was my only thought. I'd also got a £100,000 overdraft facility, so as long as I didn't go over that, it would be fine. Everybody'll be happy. I couldn't have imagined that anyone would come and sit in the kitchen and tell me how to run the business.'

The real shock came when Johnston realised that the bank not only wanted him to make the repayments on the loan *and* stay within the overdraft limit, but demanded that he present accounts to show that he was making a profit. 'I thought, "Why? What business is it of theirs whether I'm making a profit or not? I'm eating, I'm living, I'm getting around, I'm training winners, and I'm meeting the repayments." I couldn't understand that they could threaten to call in the loan or cancel the overdraft if I didn't make a profit. I thought, "How can you be expected to make a profit as well?" I now realise that is exactly what they expected. When you've built up a property and capital outlay as big as we now have here, if you were to go to the bank you would be expected to show quite a significant profit. Nobody'll be happy with the break-even, and meeting the repayments.'

He may have entered the business with a solid knowledge of equine physiology and grand plans to assert himself in the sport, but nothing had prepared Johnston for this. Profit was not then in his lexicon. 'I've always been driven to make money,' he says, 'but only as a means to provide for us. Becoming wealthy from racing never really entered my head. At the beginning, all I thought about was avoiding the downside. When we set up Bank End Stables, we had considered the negatives, not the positives. We didn't say that we could make it to the top, we just took the view that the worst that could happen was that we ended up back as a teacher and a vet.'

Johnston tells of how, recently, through an owner of his, he agreed to go and scrutinise a property in Newmarket that some property investors had bought. It was being used as a stable. 'I was asked to advise them on what they should be doing with it. I told them the sort of thing that I had been told, and didn't listen to eighteen years ago. I said, "Forget it. It can't make money as a racing yard." You see, I blithely ignored most of the financial advice I was given initially. I went through a terribly risky time, without even realising it. We had some pretty sleepless nights. We needed money more than at any other time in our business life but we couldn't get it in.' The explanation for that was simple enough. 'People didn't pay us,' Johnston states. 'We had huge debts through bad payers. We were no good at collecting the money even though we needed it desperately. We tried chasing people up but we weren't very good at it. I was pretty naive about running a business.'

There is a commonly held belief that training is one of the safest businesses in which to operate. Weatherbys, which collects entry fees and distributes prize money and trainers' and jockeys' percentages, have a so-called 'Forfeit List' of owners who are non-payers of their training fees. According to Johnston, it is 'absolutely toothless'. 'There's nothing to make you pay up,' he adds. 'Maybe there shouldn't be. I wouldn't be one of those who thinks that Weatherbys should handle bad debt problems. I think that trainers should deal with them. But it was a serious problem for us at one time. Some of the people with the best horses we had didn't pay us. And, of course, you're scared to put too much pressure on because you fear they may take the horses away. And we needed winners to raise our profile. Another way is to refuse to let them have their horses, but then you have to go to court and fight it. It costs a lot of money, and the Jockey Club don't help at all. All the customer has to do is dispute the debt and the Jockey Club say it's a matter for the courts.'

'It was a horrendous time,' Deirdre confirms, 'very worrying. I'd never done accounting before, yet here I was doing cash-flows and reconciling bank statements on a daily basis so that we knew where we stood. At one stage we couldn't pay our own bills. We had to sit on them until some more money came in. It was frightening owing money, feeling under pressure to pay and not having any money. We'd gone into business with Brian Palmer, and that gave us loads of confidence. But it was only when things got tough that we suddenly realised how much money we'd borrowed, and if we didn't get more horses in training ...' Even now, she shivers at the memory. 'I just don't like being in debt. Don't like it at all.' Perhaps her husband should have taken note of Mr Micawber in Charles Dickens's *David Copperfield*. As he put it, 'Annual income twenty pounds, annual expenditure nineteen nineteen six, result happiness. Annual income twenty pounds, annual expenditure twenty pounds ought and six, result misery.' Deirdre pauses, then says pointedly, 'I think you can say that Mark's come round to my way of thinking on that.

'When we arrived here, Mark thought we must have good facilities, but Brian went even further than that. It was Brian's idea to do everything big and bold. That included the house. We'd just moved into it the way it was. It didn't have a damp course or any central heating. But that didn't matter to us. We were prepared to leave it. Brian insisted we did it up, and looking back, thank goodness we did because I think we'd have been a bit frozen, but it did mean we spent a lot more initially than I thought we were going to.'

The Johnstons found themselves in a dilemma. It was essential that they renovate the yard and the house, and expand; the problem was doing so when income could never be guaranteed. Early on at Middleham, they came close to going bust. 'We had already rented boxes from Chris Fairhurst, in the yard that Kate Milligan is now in. But we needed more of our own,' says Johnston. 'We wanted to build thirteen more loose boxes here at Kingsley House, which took us by that time to a total of 57. We had a verbal agreement from our Barclays Bank manager in Leyburn that we'd get the money, and had already started building. We were up at wall-plate level. It wasn't the builder we needed to pay at that stage – he'd already been paid – but the Inland Revenue. It's well known that they won't wait.

'Just at that moment, our bank manager told us that his regional office had apparently rejected the request. We couldn't have the money, which was around £20,000. We were in real trouble. At the level we were operating at then, we had five days to find an alternative to pay the Revenue. Having paid the builders, we were bang up to our overdraft limit. To this day, Brian Palmer has never told me how he thought we would get out of it. His attitude at the time was, "We're going out of business." It had been suggested that we'd borrow money from Deirdre's father. But Brian said it was against his principles to borrow from family and friends. Fortunately, Deirdre's father stepped in behind the scenes. While all the arguments and discussions were going on with our bank, he quietly put the money into Deirdre's own Midland Bank account in Leyburn. Deirdre wrote out a cheque for the Revenue. We told Brian what we'd done and went to see the bank manager. Now we were in the driving seat. Brian gave them a ticking off, saying how embarrassing it had been, and how Deirdre had had to step in, with her own private money, to pay the Inland Revenue. The truth was that if Deirdre's father hadn't ridden to the rescue, we would have been in serious trouble.'

Johnston concedes the whole affair was like an army camp reveille; loud, unwanted and unpleasant, but necessary to rouse him as to the realities of commercial life. 'I was just sitting here, watching it all go by,' he admits. 'Fortunately, we got through that period. We were bedding down those boxes, and staff were moving horses from the Fairhurst yard, literally as the doors here were being screwed on. It enabled us to turn the whole business around. That was a defining moment, moving from 44 to 57 horses: from losing money to breaking even. We paid her father back within three months. It's been steady progress ever since.'

Still, it was a time when Deirdre's faith in her husband's financial acumen took something of a bruising. 'In those days there were lots of tears and panic,' says Johnston, with a grimace. 'I don't know whether Deirdre's always had faith in me. I think there were times when she felt it was a bit of a roller-coaster that she was caught on, and she never got any say in the matter. In the early days, she agreed with me that there was nothing to lose. She became very frightened when she felt there was a lot to lose. No, at that time, I'd say she wasn't confident at all.

'It sounds daft, but I still had this idea that all we had to do was make our regular payments. Profit wasn't really an issue. From the very early stages we'd done very regular, disciplined management accounts, with profit and loss, but although I used to get a balance sheet I never looked at it, or really understood it. It never really occurred to me in those days that we were probably insolvent. We'd over-value everything to bolster the balance sheet. We used to put in huge amounts for tack and equipment, anything to keep it up so it matched the borrowings.'

Deirdre's father wasn't the only positive factor to intervene in the early 1990s, for the cavalry also galloped in, bearing a familiar livery that had dominated the turf worldwide since the mid-seventies. The arrival of the Maktoum family as owners was a defining moment in Johnston's career. As a result, the yard benefited not just from superior bloodstock, but patrons who didn't require reminders to pay their bills promptly.

CHAPTER SEVEN

The Maktoums had arrived, and suddenly we had customers to whom we sent
a bill saying 'please pay within 30 days' and they paid sooner!
Bad debts became a thing of the past. It helped solve our cash-flow problems.
Now we could pay the staff without worrying about it.

Seven years had elapsed since a rather gauche Mark Johnston, still in veterinary practice in Braintree, had made his approach to Sheikh Mohammed, asking to be considered for a job. That plea for employment was in vain. Now he sought the Sheikh's patronage, and that of his family.

'The next time I wrote to Sheikh Mohammed was in early 1992,' says Johnston. 'It was around the time there was an item in the press saying the Maktoums were going to have more horses in Germany.' In hindsight, that was probably nothing more than bluff by the ruler of Dubai. Germany has many sporting and cultural attributes, but premier status as a horseracing nation is not one. 'It was a bit of a dig at British prize money,' says Johnston. 'It was atrocious in Britain then. Anyway, I wrote to him and said, "I appreciate all the reasons why you're abandoning British racing, but there is another option: cut costs and have the horses trained cheaper. We can do that, and to the same standard, in Middleham."' It was typical Johnston audacity. He believed that nothing would be gained by reticence.

At the time, the Maktoum family had their horses assigned to a range of trainers, many in Newmarket with the likes of Henry Cecil and Harry Thomson (inevitably known as 'Tom') Jones but also elsewhere: with John Dunlop at Arundel, Major Dick Hern at West Ilsley and Barry Hills and Peter Walwyn at Lambourn. Johnston looked on covetously.

'I got a nice letter back from Anthony Stroud (Sheikh Mohammed's racing manager at the time) just saying that they weren't planning, at that stage, to have any more horses in the north. At the time he had horses up here with Bill Watts (in Richmond).' Watts, whose triumphs included the 1972 1,000 Guineas with Waterloo and the 1985 Arlington Million with Lord Derby's mighty Teleprompter, would retire five years later because of what he deemed 'the financial state of British racing'. But at the time, Watts's Hurgill Lodge Stables was considered one of the Yorkshire power bases.

Johnston remained undaunted. Around the same time he cooperated in a lifestyle feature for the *Sporting Life*. 'There were the usual daft questions, like "Are you superstitious?" One question was "What's your favourite colour?" I said, "I'd like it to be maroon and white (the colours of Sheikh Mohammed's silks), but it isn't yet." I couldn't resist it. A short while later I happened to see Simon Crisford, who was representing Sheikh Mohammed (Crisford is now racing manager of Godolphin), at Sandown. I didn't really know who he was then; he must have just started working for them. He said, "We saw the item in the *Sporting Life*. We all had a good laugh at that."'

That is perhaps where Johnston's transparent attempt to ingratiate himself with the country's most powerful owners could have ended, in laughter. Or so a less self-assured character might have assumed. 'I was sitting in the kitchen one day at the end of 1992,' Johnston continues. 'The office used to be next door. Our secretary put her head round the door and said, "It's Anthony Stroud on the phone." In a strange way I was expecting the call. I felt I knew what he was going to say. Anthony just said, "We wondered if you had room for one horse?"'

Kingsley House certainly did have room for this particular horse.

'We were overjoyed. The filly was called Pearl Kite and was by Silver Hawk. Later, she became a successful broodmare. She ran in the name of Saeed Manana in 1993 and won at York on her only outing that year, on 1 September, ridden by Michael Roberts.' Johnston will always remember that race, the Wachenfeld German Wines Maiden Stakes, as a significant breakthrough. It was akin to joining a masonic society, although he was aware that he still had to win the full approval of the brotherhood. The response, it must be said, to that triumph, was not exactly tumultuous, Johnston adds. 'I went to the yearling sales that year and none of the Maktoums or their representatives spoke or said anything to me. I didn't know if we were going to get any more horses.

Then, one day, we were sitting there having our dinner and we heard the fax machine whirring next door. The fax was headed "Darley Stud". It simply said, "Your yearling allocation is …" and the details of four horses came shunting out of the machine. The whole yard was celebrating. From 1994 onwards, the (Maktoum) family started to send a reasonably significant number of horses to Kingsley House. There were six of their horses here in 1994.'

Johnston had broken the spell. The coming of the Maktoum family not only provided an injection of class, more than that it yielded a much-needed cash-flow. 'Suddenly we had customers to whom we sent a bill saying "please pay within 30 days" and they paid sooner! We couldn't believe it. That was just great. We could pay the staff without worrying about it. It was an education for us. It helped solve our cash-flow problems and made us treat problems differently from ever before. We've learnt over the years. It changed the way we paid people and changed the way we expected to be paid. It was fascinating how it just turned things around. Bad debts became a thing of the past.'

Profits now became his quest. Which, you suggest to Johnston, could be perceived as a clash of ideals. Now, nobody would have contended for a moment that Johnston was about to metamorphose into Michael Douglas's Gordon Gekko in the film *Wall Street*, a character who at the end of the eighties famously espoused the philosophy 'Greed is good'. Yet, for a man born into a socialist household and whose leanings earlier in his life were decidedly left-wing, surely 'profit' was a tricky concept to deal with?

And while we were on this tangential lay-by, just how comfortable had it been for him to become a fellow of an industry some would have us believe is among the worst of exploitative employers? 'Feudal' is but one of the adjectives that have been flung around. The *Racing Post*'s Paul Haigh, for one, wrote at the end of last year that 'the structure of racing is so steadfastly anachronistic … with owners at the top, trainers who are little gods … jockeys who are lionised but regarded as social inferiors by many, and then at the bottom the mass of stable staff, whom we never really register, who get up before dawn has cracked to work for weekly wages that wouldn't pay a poshie's dinner bill'. It was an issue that came particularly to the fore in 2003, when the *Racing Post* ran a campaign against racing staff's perceived poor wages and conditions. Johnston, who was writing a weekly column for the paper at the time, resigned on principle, so infuriated was he by the nature of the campaign.

That, too, is a debating point we will return to. For the moment, Johnston claims there was no conflict of philosophies. 'There was a strange contrast within my upbringing,' he says. 'My father was in principle a communist, but was, in practice, nothing like one. Today, I don't believe I'm that different from everyone else. Politically, you've got this natural progression from when you're a teenager and you're the most left-wing, most rebellious of your life. As you go through life you become more conservative, with a small "c". You move to the right, probably, and become less rebellious.' However, Johnston stresses that 'I never agreed with Margaret Thatcher's belief in a free economy, that if an oil rig's cheaper in Japan then close the shipyard in Glasgow. I would say that's only true if you take into account what you would have to pay the unemployed workers here. Then, sure, buy in Japan. But if it's cheaper for the country to insist that the oil rig is bought in Britain, because it will save us paying unemployment benefit, then I'd rather pay those shipyard workers to build ships than pay them to do nothing and buy the ship elsewhere. But you also have to understand that if you make your oil rigs 20 per cent more expensive than elsewhere, nobody will buy the British one. That's a sad fact of life.'

Johnston has recently been reading *Man and Boy*, the novel by Tony Parsons. 'The theme is that, given the opportunity, there's nobody more selfish than a socialist in his desire to get more than his fellow man. Nobody is greedier. That's one of the more upsetting realisations about politicians.' He then adds, 'I must read *Animal Farm* again. That's the greatest book in the world. It's so completely true that some animals are more equal than others. They're willing to fight for equality, until they can have more for themselves. That's the most upsetting thing.'

So where does he stand today? Basically, Johnston is positioned squarely behind one basic piece of philosophy: he didn't write the rules. Had he done so, they might have appeared slightly differently on the page. 'But I'm comfortable that I'm fair within them as they are. I'm not running a staff benefit. No business can afford to be that. But I believe

I'm running one that greatly benefits my staff. I always go back to the principle of Always Trying. From the outside, people will think it's all about my horses always trying. The reality is that it's all about people trying. The expanded phrase is that 'everybody should be always trying to do the best for the business and the best for themselves'. He adds: 'It's my business, and at the end of the day, obviously the principal gain is for me and my family. I employ a lot of people to help me with it. No, we'll not all get paid the same. Everybody's at a different level, but that doesn't mean they're not doing the best for themselves, or we're not doing the best we can for them. Or we're not paying them a fair wage for the job.'

Now in one of his fiercely provocative moods, a thought strikes him. 'A socialist friend told me recently how he was stopped in the street and asked to sign a petition demanding a minimum wage of £8 an hour. He joked with them and said, "I'd love £8 an hour! Where do I sign?" As that friend said, where do you get the balance? It's all very well saying "Yes, put the minimum wage at £8 an hour" and then complaining because the call centres are going to India, where they'll do it for £2 an hour. Are we in a global economy or a goldfish bowl economy? I like to think I can see both sides to it.'

He returns to his personal circumstances. 'I don't think we need to apologise for making a profit, or be at all ashamed for doing so. It's essential. The day we stop making a profit, we'll shut. Yes, this (he sweeps his hand round) makes money. It has not failed to make money now for over ten years. If it wasn't doing that, I'd be doing something else. Why *shouldn't* it make money? I'd love to have that debate with (John) McCririck. He's forever knocking trainers for their champagne lifestyles, saying that training fees are just putting petrol in the Mercedes. If we're successful at it, we should expect to make money from it. Just as he does in his job.'

I related to Johnston how, a few years ago, I was offered the opportunity to interview the late Lord Howard de Walden, who owned (his family still does) a sizeable plot of London and whose apricot silks were once a familiar sight on the jockeys who partnered such racehorses as the 1985 Derby victor Slip Anchor and that magnificent miler Kris. During the conversation I asked him about the qualities of his racehorse trainers. The peer was drily dismissive. 'Well, they drive around in their expensive cars, but they're just glorified grooms, really, aren't they?' he replied.

Johnston smiles, then argues that, apart from their knowledge and experience, the risk element for trainers is as significant as it is for any entrepreneur. The business can succeed or it can crash and burn, just like any other small to medium concern. 'Though we've made money, there's been huge amounts of risk along the way,' he says. 'Now it's established, and there's so much invested in it, you just have to compare that return with sticking that investment in a deposit account and doing nothing all day. This has *got* to bring a return. Sometimes I look at it and I wonder how trainers further down the scale survive. There must be an awful lot of them still applying my Bank End principles: eating and existing, making the repayments, and that's about it.'

We return to that initial period at Middleham. Despite those first three years being fraught with the avoidance of privation, Johnston was quietly achieving what he had planned from the beginning – to accumulate an ever larger complement of horses, and to become synonymous with winners, preferably consistent winners who would capture the imagination of the media and public. He achieved that with Lifewatch Vision, who won seven races in all for the yard before moving to Dermot Weld, and Quick Ransom, who cost only 6,000 guineas as a yearling but included the 1992 Tote Ebor at York among his nine wins.

But if they were willing and able foot soldiers, it was Marina Park, bred and owned by Robert Kennedy, owner of Greenland Park Stud, who became the first standard-bearer for the stable and led the Johnston name into a battle for recognition from which the trainer would ultimately emerge triumphant. The first horse Kennedy had sent to Johnston was Key Point, a horse with knee problems which it was believed could be solved by sessions in the swimming pool. Key Point never made it to the racetrack, but for many years he was ridden by Deirdre, who evented him and used him as a hack. Marina Park was a different story. The daughter of Local Suitor won four of her twenty starts and was later a multiple stakes winner in California. She claimed the Group 3 Princess Margaret Stakes, partnered by Dean McKeown, at Ascot in 1992 before proceeding to be placed third to Zafonic, beaten less than two lengths, in the Prix Morny at Deauville, and a close second to Forest Wind in Newbury's Mill Reef Stakes. She raised the stature of the yard, which soon became recognised for nurturing quality. And the relationship between Johnston and Kennedy continued to flourish. A decade later they combined for another Group 3 success with Fight Your Corner – an apposite name, given Johnston's sorties into many controversies in the years ahead. The son of Muhtarram won the Chester Vase, having won three of five starts as a two-year-old. The colt was bought by the Maktoum family before the 2002 Derby, in which he finished fifth.

At the same time as Marina Park was beginning to fulfil her potential in 1992, a remarkable filly named Branston Abby arrived at the yard. The then three-year-old sprinter was already the winner of two races, and would end her career four years later with 25 victories from only three short of a century of runs between 1991 and 1996 (and she was placed in another 24 of her races). It was a post-war Flat record for a filly or mare, though her first two wins were for other trainers. A 25 per cent winning strike rate is exceptional at any level, and Branston Abby's appetite for racing was voracious. That record is testimony to both her exceptional character and Johnston's placing of a horse who succeeded in winning ten races in Listed company, and who became an experienced world traveller. Evry, Munich and Sha Tin were among her stop-offs. Sadly, she did not enjoy a lengthy retirement. The mare died in 1997, having suffered from acute grass sickness (the disease which also killed Godolphin's Dubai Millennium) when in foal to Mark Of Esteem at Chippenham Lodge Stud in Cambridgeshire. She is buried at Kingsley House.

In the 1990s, too, Johnston would prove himself an adept trainer of handicappers, despite his protestations in later years, to which we shall return. Star Rage, like Branston Abby owned by David Abell, won nine Flat handicaps in 1994 alone, equalling the twentieth-century seasonal record. By the end of his career, which spanned an astonishing ten seasons, the versatile son of Horage won 28 of 137 starts on the Flat, on turf and the all-weather, and over hurdles. The zenith of that latter career came in late 1997 when Dean Gallagher produced the gelding with a finely judged run to secure the Fighting

Fifth Hurdle at Newcastle. It was also at Gosforth Park, too, on 25 June 1993, that a colt made a tardy start from the stalls before eventually striding home by seven lengths in a six-furlong juvenile event. Even at his most sanguine, Johnston could not have imagined that his first Classic victor, yielding a success that was to transform the yard's prosperity, was taking his first tentative steps.

CHAPTER EIGHT

You know, I wrote a long letter to Paul Venner, stating all the reasons
why Mister Baileys should run in the Derby. He didn't want it to run. I
suppose I was dreaming of Nijinsky and Triple Crowns, and the Derby being
the most important thing in the world. It wasn't.

Early in the Flat season of 1993, Mark Johnston stopped for a brief chat with Sally Hall as they passed on the Middleham gallops where the two-year-olds were placing their first skittish hoof-prints. He can still recall her words. 'She said to me, "What's that horse by … that one there with a big white face?" I told her, "Robellino." She said, "I like him. I think I'll send a mare to Robellino."' Johnston knew that Hall, niece of the legendary Sam and a successful and knowledgeable trainer in her own right, kept a few brood mares at her nearby Brecongill Stables.

In late June that season, Johnston happened to see Sally's partner and assistant, Colin Platts, at the meeting at Newcastle where the same bay juvenile, named Mister Baileys, was due for his introduction to a racecourse. 'Colin said to me, "Is that Sally's Robellino colt?" I nodded. "Yes, that's the one." He just said, "I'll back it."' Sally Hall proved to be an astute judge. As Johnston will readily concede, her assessment was possibly better than his own at the time. 'Sally had picked that horse out just from seeing it cantering past her,' he says. A victory in that Newcastle maiden, by a scintillating seven lengths after dwelling at the stalls, was the beginning of a sequence that would enhance the lives of many involved. Not least Johnston's own. After nearly five years of a burgeoning career at Middleham, the accelerating output of winners had still not entitled him to be granted membership of the major league of trainers.

'Strangely enough,' Johnston adds, 'we had a two-year-old at the time, named Legal Fiction, who I thought was better, but from a very early stage Dean McKeown (then the yard's principal rider) kept telling me that Mister Baileys was the best we'd got.' Deirdre, who is a sound evaluator of bloodstock, was also convinced by Mister Baileys' potential. 'Although he was quite cheap,' she says, 'we all really liked him, and we knew the owner did. We were all really excited, but we had no idea to begin with that he was going to be that good. I never rode him at home. Back then I wasn't good enough to ride two-year-olds in their work. You just can't take risks. I never rode Mister Baileys or Double Trigger. I had to work my way up, just like everybody else. I only get to ride the good horses now because I've served my apprenticeship. But it was great watching him. We were pretty sure, by the time he ran at Newcastle, that he would win his maiden. We were pretty bullish about it.'

Mister Baileys' progress from a horse who cost his owner, Paul Venner, a relative pittance of 10,000 guineas to one of the nation's top milers is a parable that heartened every small owner in the land, just as Pam Sly's Speciosa did in 2006. It is also testament to his trainer's ambition. Recollecting the events of that period exposes Johnston at his most emotional; at his most candid, when his judgement subsequently comes under question; and at his most vindictive, towards anyone who dares to diminish his charge's achievements. He has never been cowed from hitching his wagon to a star, as the American poet Ralph Waldo Emerson expressed it.

'Mister Baileys went from winning that race at Newcastle to a Newbury conditions race where he got beat, boxed in during a five-horse race and only finishing third, but we thought so much of him that he went straight from that defeat to running in the Champagne Vintage Stakes at Goodwood,' recalls Johnston. 'He won that, went to the Gimcrack, where he was sixth of eight, but then won the Royal Lodge at Ascot. Three of his five two-year-old starts were Group races.'

The winter that separates a racehorse's two- and three-year-old careers can be insufferably long, particularly when you have care of a Classic contender. For Johnston, it was worse: he had never been there before. But throughout, his belief in the colt remained unswerving. Other arbiters were not so certain about Mister Baileys' Classic credentials. *Timeform*'s much-vaunted *Racehorses* annual for 1993 damned his charge with faint praise. 'Mister Baileys represents the best chance for northern success in the Classics for several years, even if he cannot yet be regarded as up to Classic-winning standard,' it said. Having accepted that ringworm had afflicted the horse around the time of the Gimcrack, the piece concluded, 'very much the type to train on'.

In the spring of 1994 Johnston had the traditionalists muttering their disquiet when he dispatched Mister Baileys directly to the Guineas, with only the benefit of a racecourse gallop. That was presumably one of several explanations why, on the day, Mister Baileys started at 16–1 for the first colts' Classic. It was absurd in hindsight, but back then? 'There were only two horses in the Guineas that year,' Johnston says. 'I believe the most important thing in looking at the form of a horse at Group level is what it did in its last run, and at what level. Look at that 1994 Guineas, and there were only two horses in that race who had won a Group race on their last start. One was King's Theatre, trained by Henry Cecil, who was favourite. The other was Mister Baileys, trained by Mark Johnston, who was 16–1. I guarantee that if you had reversed the trainers you would have reversed the odds. Mister Baileys had all the credentials. He'd won the Royal Lodge on his last start. In hindsight he should have won the Gimcrack. He was the best horse at York.' I suggest to him that punters will always favour Newmarket- or Coolmore-trained horses, particularly if they are Dettori- or Fallon-partnered. He accepts that point, then adds, 'But 16–1 was a bit barmy.'

Maybe it was also Mister Baileys' jockey that deterred some punters. Dean McKeown had ridden the colt in his first four races, but Frankie Dettori was in the saddle when the colt won the Royal Lodge. Johnston had initially planned that the pairing should remain intact at Newmarket. The gifted young Italian jockey, who was already beginning to impress himself on the public's consciousness with his flamboyance and garrulous repartee in front of the cameras, opted instead to ride the Lord Howard de Walden-owned, William Jarvis-trained Grand Lodge. Jason Weaver was the beneficiary, though, only a year out of his apprenticeship, there was concern in some quarters over whether he possessed the experience. Johnston was not among them.

After the move to Middleham, Bobby Elliott had continued to partner the majority of the yard's horses, then McKeown had increasingly assumed that role, although occasionally John Carroll,

Richard Quinn, Tyrone Williams and Michael Roberts were booked. In the summer of 1991 Joe Fanning had ridden his first winner for the stable, in a seller at Catterick, but he was many years from assuming his current relationship with the yard. So it was Jason Weaver, who had begun his career with Luca Cumani as a sixteen-year-old and had been champion apprentice in 1993 with 60 winners, who entered the picture. 'Jason had just lost his claim, and he just appeared at the door one day,' recalls Johnston. 'He asked if he could ride out.' The association proved immediately fruitful. He rode eight winners for the yard in the remaining months of the season. His first winner for the Kingsley House trainer was at Musselburgh on 20 September 1993. Five days later, while a trio of the stable's luminaries headed for Ascot, Weaver was dispatched to Redcar to partner a two-year-old debutant. The colt's name was Double Trigger. It was a partnership which, like white-water rafting, would frequently be exhilarating but always liable to strike rocks.

The style and positive attitude of the Nottingham-born jockey was sufficient to impress Johnston to offer him a retainer, starting the following season, although Johnston concedes, 'Despite the fact that we had retained him, some of the owners of the best horses were, at first, not prepared to have him ride their horses.' In the spring of 1994, therefore, Johnston might have been expected to summon an experienced, Classic-winning jockey after Dettori had declared his allegiance to the connections of Grand Lodge, but Johnston eventually opted for Weaver. 'It was very much a last-minute decision,' he says. 'By the time the Guineas arrived, Jason was doing very well for us (he had already ridden 31 winners for Johnston that year before the Newmarket Classic). And you mustn't forget that Frankie was not then the big star that he is now. He was pretty big, but not a champion.'

The day itself is still imprinted indelibly on his brain. 'We *thought* we'd win,' he says. 'We certainly weren't going there to run down the field. I was supremely confident about it. The horse was there very much on merit. I remember there was one of those tipping lines, run by a guy called Cliff Woof, at Newmarket. Every week they would feature a trainer. It's not something I would get roped into now, but I did an interview for them on the morning of the race. I had nine runners that day. We hadn't been having a particularly good spell in the run-up to the Guineas, and I was asked, "What do you think is your best chance of the day?" I replied, "Our best chance is Mister Baileys in the Guineas." Yet I had other runners that day, like Double Blue, who were strongly fancied. I won a case of champagne for the longest-priced nap of the year!'

As it turned out, Weaver's acumen in the saddle, as he allowed Mister Baileys to forge into a lead on the far side with over three furlongs remaining, could hardly have been bettered by Dettori, Lester Piggott and Sir Gordon Richards combined. 'It was a very typical Jason Weaver ride,' says Johnston. 'It was something that you'd normally see Jason do in lower-grade fields where he'd coast up front, then kick with quite a way to go and get them all in trouble. My most vivid memory of it was Mister Baileys not really being called in front by the commentator, although my vision of the race from the head-on stand was that he was in front. That was probably because most people's eyes were on the favourite, King's Theatre, and he was on the stand side. Then, just as they entered the dip, I saw that not only is Mister Baileys in front, but that he had opened a gap, and the other jockeys were having to go for their whips. From two furlongs out until they passed the line I had no doubt that we were going to win. But, then as I ran down the steps, I suddenly thought, "Shit, have we done it?" Ironically it was William Jarvis, trainer of Grand Lodge – although I had no idea where his horse had been placed (he was a short head second) – who was the first to say "well done". I just turned to him and said, "He *did* win it, didn't he?" I waited for Mister Baileys to come off the track, but he wasn't there. I really started to panic, thinking something had gone wrong with him. But this was the first year when they had this idea of holding the winner out on the course, and bringing him in last.'

Back home at Middleham, there is a photo of an unusually animated Johnston, fist in the air (the one in use, that is: the other arm was encased in plaster, his wrist having been broken in two places after being kicked by a horse). He can be quite inscrutable when one of his horses wins, although one suspects that beneath that exterior the pulse is always quickening. 'Maybe I wasn't quite so much in control in those days,' he says. 'I got much more excited.' It was the ultimate sensation. Euphoria, relief, vindication ... so many feelings surged through him at that moment. That is why today he can insist, 'I remember that even more than Attraction's victory. In fact, for all that she achieved, and Double Trigger and others, nothing will ever surpass Mister Baileys' victory. It wouldn't mean so much now, among so many other big winners. But at the time it was fantastic. We won the next race as well, with Double Blue, but I was almost oblivious to that.'

Fortunately, Deirdre hadn't been. 'I had to do all the saddling because Mark had that broken arm,' she recalls. 'So for me Mister Baileys' victory meant: you saddle it, you win it, Mark and the owner go and collect the prizes; I just had the next one to saddle for the handicap, Double Blue. That's normal for me.' She laughs. 'It's the same at Royal Ascot. But I don't mind. I like something to focus on straight afterwards. Sure, I get excited, but I don't need to be in the limelight; I don't need to be on the podium. I'd much rather be back with the horses. I love that bit. I love thinking I've actually made my contribution.' And, on this occasion, played her part in the yard's first Group 1 winner. 'It was like we'd really won a big, proper race. We lived on it for weeks afterwards … just kept watching the video. Before then, most of the big races we'd won had been handicaps, and the odd Group race. It was strange how people's attitudes changed. Michael Stoute had never spoken to me before. I went to Lingfield a few days later, and I remember it vividly. He said, "Congratulations on winning the Guineas." I thought, "Wow." He didn't even know who I was the week before. We felt we'd climbed one huge rung up the ladder.'

And her husband's self-belief, as powerful as Billy Graham's at the lectern, right from those early days, had been vindicated. 'I was pleased most for Mark,' she says. 'When we'd come to Middleham, here was this guy who told everyone he'd train Classic winners, and everyone laughed. Not any more. Now it was, "Oh, gosh. He's actually done it."' After that, he was suddenly regarded as more of a threat to the training hierarchy. 'It really did change people's attitudes,' Deirdre continues. 'But there were several things that made us a bit different, not just because it was a smallish trainer winning it. We'd done it with a cheap horse. We'd also done it with a first-time-out horse, which was breaking the trend. In those days, most people still gave them a prep run. It made it more of a training performance.'

That victory also advanced the career of Jason Weaver, who would proceed to ride over 200 winners that season, and trainer Johnston, but the triumph was gratefully received by Paul Venner too. That one minute and 35 seconds of action on the Newmarket Rowley Mile was appropriate reward for the faith of Johnston's first owner. 'Paul will always be one of the most important owners we've ever had, or ever will have,' insists Johnston. 'He was the only one who backed us from the start, from day one. I've always been hugely grateful for that. In fact, when we first started, I think he was the only one paying us any money! Everything else was borrowed or leased. Mind you, he'd not always had *complete* faith in me. We went to the sales, in the October before we'd moved into our yard in Lincolnshire, and I bought a filly by Sharpo for him. I naturally assumed I'd get it. But when the box arrived, it wasn't my filly inside but some other bloody thing, by Junius I think, which Gerry Blum had bought. But Gerry was his number one trainer, and he had the pick.'

The ensuing developments in the career of Mister Baileys will always prompt his trainer towards some self-recrimination. 'Originally, we thought he was a mile-and-a-half horse,' explains Johnston. 'Though the fact that he was by Robellino out of a Sharpen Up mare (Thimblerigger) should, maybe in hindsight, have told us that he wasn't. I'm sure now that he wouldn't go for the Derby. He probably wouldn't have run in the Dante either. But if he had, we would have learnt our lesson, and come back to a mile. He would have run next in the St James's Palace Stakes. That's what happened the next time I had a similar horse, Bijou D'Inde. He went the Irish Guineas, St James's Palace route.' I put it to the trainer that he wasn't to know. That the same radical thinking that had brought Mister Baileys home without a preparatory run was justifiably applied to the belief that he could stay the Derby distance. 'No,' Johnston states firmly. 'It was an error. It was my inexperience.

'You know, I wrote a long letter to Paul Venner, stating all the reasons why the horse *should* run in the Derby. He didn't want it to run.' Maybe the trainer had been influenced, albeit subconsciously, by those photographs of equine legends he'd had pinned to his bedroom wall in his youth. Johnston quietly agrees. 'I suppose I was dreaming of Nijinsky and Triple Crowns, and the Derby being the most important thing in the world. It wasn't. Maybe going to the Dante as a Derby trial was a sensible move, but I should have seen the writing on the wall at York. I really should have learnt from that.' Apparently cruising three furlongs out in the traditional Derby trial at the Knavesmire, the fuel tank warning was flashing red by the final furlong. Mister Baileys finished third of nine behind Erhaab.

In the Epsom showpiece event itself, Weaver opted for an audacious strategy, bursting clear four out. A catch-me-if-you-can tactic designed to outwit the opposition. But was it the correct one on a horse that was not proven to stay? Willie Carson, then 51 and riding his 26th Derby, on the favourite Erhaab, was wise to the move anyway. He was quoted by Jim McGrath in the *Daily Telegraph* thus: 'When the field of 25 straightened up, the first sight I got was of the green and gold colours of Mister Baileys, who appeared to be a furlong ahead of us. It was the first time I had to pick Erhaab up, and he instantly quickened.' McGrath added his own impressions:

> Yet, even two furlongs out, Mister Baileys was still galloping at a furious pace, with Colonel Collins and King's Theatre in pursuit. Erhaab still had almost ten lengths to make up on the leader. A furlong out, he looked certain to gain a place, but then, 100 yards out, he put his head down, changed legs and produced another surge of power to overhaul King's Theatre and record a great victory by a length and a quarter. King's Theatre ran his best race of the season by holding on for second, a length and a half clear of Colonel Collins, who just failed to last home. Mister Baileys, the 2,000 Guineas winner, underlined his class by holding on for fourth, just ahead of Piggott on Khamaseen. For the crowd of 103,406 it was a happy result as the winner was the 7–2 favourite.

First in the Guineas, fourth in the Derby. Johnston may have preferred the results to have been reversed, but they remained valiant efforts. 'Paul probably enjoyed the race more than I did,' reflects Johnston. 'He thought for a long way that we were going to win. But he had no regrets. He's very good at making the most of things, and Mister Baileys certainly did him no harm from a business point of view. It was great publicity for his company.'

Weaver has long claimed that one of his greatest moments came when he drove Mister Baileys five lengths clear of the pack coming out of Tattenham Corner. Johnston doesn't concur with that. 'I'm not sure it did him any favours being asked to go for home so early,' he says, before adding, somewhat provocatively, 'You had to wonder, if Lester had been on Mister Baileys, would there have been a different result? Lester was so much the master of Epsom, and it's a very difficult course to negotiate. But I'd have to qualify that by saying that Jason was a fantastic jockey, and it was probably the best relationship I had with a jockey.'

It was virtually the end of Mister Baileys' brief but intermittently explosive career. 'After that he got a tendon injury,' Johnston explains. 'We patched him up and ran him in the Sussex Stakes, where he finished fifth,' but the colt was then retired to stud, bearing the badge of honour of Middleham's first Classic winner since 1945. His stallion duties are now over. He was retired from those pleasures of equine retirement once he'd failed to get any mares in foal at Chris Harper's Whitsbury Manor Stud in Hampshire. He had arrived at Whitsbury in 2000 after a 45-share syndicate purchased him from the Vinery Stud in Kentucky, where he stood his first five seasons. It was suspected that infertility was caused by a near-fatal bout of grass sickness. But from five crops of racing age, Mister Baileys sired 76 winners, including five stakes winners, from 124 starters who amassed earnings of $3,792,292. Mister Baileys is now back with Venner, in retirement at his home.

For all the dramatic denouement of that Guineas triumph, Mister Baileys' critics couldn't find it in their hearts to bestow any plaudits, despite Johnston's horse establishing a new track record. Could his trainer give a damn? Well, yes, he could, and he still does. In his *Racing Post* column of 5 May 2001 he explained that he would be 'rooting for Rumpold, a son of Mister Baileys in today's 2,000 Guineas':

He has, arguably, got the best form … but a Rumpold victory would be even greater for Mister Baileys. To sire a Guineas winner so early in his career at stud would perhaps gain him some of the recognition he should have received for winning the race himself in 1994.

That Guineas was rated by most 'experts' as the worst of the decade, but I have always felt that that was a very unfair assessment. It could not have been rated as poor on the basis of the time as Mister Baileys set, and still holds, the record for the 2,000 Guineas, and it could not, surely, be rated as poor based on the quality of the field: Mister Baileys beat the likes of Grand Lodge and Distant View. No, it was rated as poor for one reason and one reason only: because 16–1 shot Mister Baileys won it. If Rumpold wins today a few 'experts' might just gain enough courage to review their assessment of the 1994 race.

Moreover, in the *Racing Post*'s book *100 Greatest Races*, under the title of 'the greatest race I ever saw', Johnston nominated his 1994 2,000 Guineas winner.

Today, he maintains that Mister Baileys' detractors are talking 'absolute piffle'. 'It was ridiculous to say he was the worst Guineas winner of the decade. They're basically saying that it was a bad Guineas. But it wasn't. If the top three milers hadn't run you may have a case. But they did run. Mister Baileys won it, Grand Lodge was second, and Distant View was fifth. The best horses were all there, there was the usual size of field, and it was a track record. Mister Baileys was among the top three milers of that year. Grand Lodge won the St James's Palace Stakes, Distant View won the Sussex Stakes. My horse would also have been in the top half dozen of the mile-and-a-half horses of that year too. It's like when they say that Kris Kin is the lowest-rated Derby winner. It can't be. You can say time doesn't matter, but that's not true. If Kris Kin met Sea-Bird, based on time, he'd beat Sea-Bird by something like 35 lengths.' He shakes his head in annoyance. 'Nostalgic rubbish. Sure, when I was Charlie's age I was talking about horses as being horses of the decade or century, whatever. But not now. It's nonsense. You cannot really have a bad year. It can't be the case that 2006 three-year-olds are not as good as those of 2005. You can argue, a bit, that the best ones don't compare. But not a whole year. Only if, at the end of the year, the Guineas winner is rated tenth can you say it was a bad Guineas.'

Doubts may have been expressed about the merits of Mister Baileys' performance, but there were no such reservations about his jockey. That season, as his partnership with Johnston prospered, Weaver became one of only seven jockeys in British racing history to ride a double century, and finished runner-up to Frankie Dettori in the jockeys' championship. Weaver was at the zenith of his powers when partnering Double Trigger to victory in the 1995 Ascot Gold Cup, and when claiming another Group 1 at Royal Ascot the following year, driving Bijou D'Inde to victory in the St James's Palace Stakes. 'He was a fantastic rider,' says Johnston. 'He wasn't around long enough to become recognised as one of the true greats. If he'd stayed around, I'd say he would probably – probably – have been champion several times.' He is prepared to state that despite the pair separating twice. Breaking up may be hard for lovers, but for jockeys and trainers it is an occupational hazard. 'Of course there were huge frustrations at times, but then you get that with all jockeys. In fact, you get it in every walk of life. When you get a successful jockey–trainer partnership – and we'd had around 70 winners together that first season – you want it to continue. But he decided to go his own way, and I don't blame him for that. People have to think for themselves and make those decisions. But the second time, did he jump or was he pushed? I don't know. Probably there was something wrong on both sides.

'It was September 1997, and we had our good miler Fly To The Stars, who we wanted to run in Turkey, in the Topkapi Trophy at Veliefendi. We also had Land Of Dreams running in the Flying Childers (the Group 2 two-year-old event) at Doncaster on the same day. I wanted Jason to go to Turkey, basically because there would be no problem getting another jockey for Doncaster, but we couldn't easily get one for Turkey. At least that was my official reason. It's always been my view that you pay a retainer so that the jockey is available to go where you want him to go. The jockeys, however, tend to see it differently. They see it as giving them the right to the best rides. Jason insisted he wanted to go to Doncaster. I told him, "We pay a retainer so that you're available to go where we want to send you. You either go to Turkey or the deal's off."' Weaver refused to go, and the deal was indeed off. In the event, Fly To The Stars finished third in Turkey, under the Irish-based rider Warren O'Connor. Land Of Dreams won the Flying Childers impressively, having been held up off the pace for a late run by Darryll Holland. 'I think I was fully entitled to do what I did,' says Johnston. 'Having said that, I did have some underlying sympathy for Jason. The truth was that I particularly wanted Darryll Holland to ride Land Of Dreams. She was a sprinter, but a hold-up horse, to some extent, and Darryll is a lot better at executing that.'

Ultimately, continuing weight problems persuaded Weaver to quit the saddle at 30, in 2002, after a fourteen-year career. Johnston told the *Racing Post* at the time, 'I could see the beginnings of Jason's weight problems when he was retained by us. It's very sad for him; we had a great association. Of our six Group 1 winners, Jason rode five of them and, particularly in the 1994 season, we never had a better association with a jockey. It was tremendous.'

That year, 1994, was the first in which Kingsley House sent out a century of winners. 'It's incredible how fast the progression was,' Johnston says. 'One winner in 1987, five in 1988, then 15, 27, 46, 76 ... so clearly we were getting there fast. But that Guineas win enabled us to make another huge jump. We bought another yard on the back of that. There's been a lot of landmarks along the way, but that was the most important.'

Though by then, financially speaking things were on a much better footing, it was still clear that Johnston's financial education required some remedial work. 'Brian Palmer had lawyer Joe Friel, his mentor and adviser, come down here in 1993 when we were discussing whether to expand the business by buying or renting,' Johnston recalls. 'We were really chuffed with ourselves. We were really flying at that time. The first Arab horse had arrived. We could never have imagined the business would grow so fast, and we'd had 70-odd winners. I can still never forgive Joe. His first words to me were, "Well, Mark, I see you're still stumbling along the bottom." It was such a shock to me, because I thought we were doing so well.'

Johnston was provoked into action. 'My response was to construct another ten boxes, at huge expense, to take the full complement up to 67. We were looking for space anywhere.' After Mister Baileys' 2,000 Guineas triumph, Johnston rented another twenty boxes from Chris Thornton at Spigot Lodge. 'By the end of 1994 we were in such demand that if we didn't get another site we were out of Middleham.' By the end of 1994, only a few years on from that awkward episode with Barclays Bank, Johnston had bought Warwick House from Patrick Haslam. 'We paid £240,000, I think. We were getting into further debt, but now it was not a problem. The situation changed dramatically in the two years which followed that period when we had those financial problems, and we've continued that expansion,' he says. Since arriving at Middleham, Johnston has outlayed more than £1.5 million on creating one of the most up-to-date yards in the country.

Complacency could have set in, like dry rot, once a century of winners began to become an annual occurrence. It is not unknown in the industry for once distinguished houses of excellence to crumble. But Johnston has constantly sought to expand his realm. By 1999 he would have 147 horses under his care, sufficient to compete with the leviathans of horseracing. And Middleham had once again become a significant contour on the equine landscape. There, on that sun-kissed plateau, is where Johnston has remained to the present day, continually returning with the spoils of ambitious campaigns here and abroad. Although in the 2006 season he had to retain his nerve as never before as misfortune blighted his plans in the spring and early summer.

CHAPTER NINE

*Those small struggling trainers out there who are blaming the fact
that that's what they are because I've got better horses are talking absolute
crap. What makes a good trainer is making the most of what he's got.*

A quiet Tuesday afternoon in late February 2006. A period of deceptive calm before the turf Flat season bursts upon us. Debbie Albion, Mark Johnston's administration secretary, knocks lightly on the door of the family living room where we have been discussing Mister Baileys and those early days at Middleham, and Johnston has been musing over which horses will represent the yard in this year's Classics, and planning campaigns for his other three-year-olds. The room has a slightly obscured outlook over the moors where lambs are already in evidence, despite winter over-extending its stay. But you get the impression that there's not a lot of admiring the view done here.

Johnston confirms that not a lot of living takes place here either. They rarely gather in front of the TV, though he will study re-runs of races. *Taggart*, the series about Glasgow detectives, is the last entertainment programme he can recall watching. It is essentially a trophy room, in which the big-game hunter's 'kills' are exhibited. Paintings of the yard's major winners adorn the walls. They include Double Trigger and Mister Baileys. On the tables and shelves, equine sculptures, cups and other memorials of victory stand testimony to the trainer's career. Pride of place on the table where we sit is the winning trainer's prize for the 1999 Dubai Turf Classic, won by Fruits Of Love, and a small trophy, so discreet you'd almost miss it, for the trainer of the 1994 2,000 Guineas victor.

Debbie, originally from Lancashire, is a no-messing, tell-it-like-it-is kind of woman. What you could call forthright charm. She has worked for the yard for thirteen years, apart from an absence when she left to join a building firm. Her affinity with Middleham was too powerful to resist.

She returned, and brought with her the owner of the company – as an owner. She apologises for disturbing us, but she thinks Johnston would like to know that ten more horses have been consigned by Gainsborough Stud. 'Just been speaking to Bruce (former jockey Bruce Raymond, successor to Joe Mercer, who had retired at 71 as racing manager of Gainsborough Stud). Five colts, five fillies by the tenth of March.'

One is not often in the vicinity when a trainer receives such a gift – ten two-year-olds from a source that is a metaphor for quality. Johnston doesn't punch the air. He doesn't drop to his knees and prostrate himself before the gods of outrageous fortune. Instead, there is a quiet 'Oh, right, thank you', as though he's just been told his lunch is ready. I can, however, just detect the merest hint of satisfaction.

Some uncertainty had surrounded the future of Gainsborough Stud, based at Newbury in Berkshire, following the death in Queensland on 4 January of Sheikh Maktoum bin Rashid Al Maktoum (more commonly known in racecards as just Maktoum Al Maktoum). He was 63, and had suffered a stroke. However, once the 40-day period of mourning was over it was decreed that Maktoum Al Maktoum's 70 horses would run in the name of Gainsborough Stud, in those familiar royal blue silks with white chevrons and light blue cap. The Sheikh was the first son of Sheikh Rashid bin Saeed Al Maktoum, the ruler of Dubai, and in his twenties he played a leading role in the formation of the United Arab Emirates. He had been appointed its first prime minister. Johnston had trained for him the Group 1 winners Princely Heir, Lend A Hand and Shamardal, and the Group 2 victor Land Of Dreams.

It is a month before the start of the season, and there is an intake of 93 two-year-olds on the roster. It brings the yard's full complement to 220 horses. Johnston is unable to confirm that fact precisely, although he can be guaranteed to quip, if the question arises, 'I'd miss one if it wasn't there ...' (And to think that only two or three months earlier he was sweating on whether there would be a full house.) His two-year-olds are spread across a wide span of ownership profiles, from the Maktoum family to those who outlay a rather more modest amount in order to belong to the increasingly popular syndicates. Sir Alex Ferguson fronts one such enterprise, the Right Angle Club, and they were soon to boast a winner. There are individual owners too, including celebrities.

Sir Clement Freud has a two-year-old with the yard; so, too, does Jim McGrath of *Timeform* and *Channel 4 Racing*. According to the author's reckoning, Sheikh Mohammed alone has dispatched him 21 two-year-olds. Johnston nods to confirm this. 'I'm very happy with that,' he says.

The question is, though, how many potential Group winners are there among his assigned number? Unfortunately, unlike the American football system, you don't get to pick your own from Sheikh Mohammed's draft. And certainly, unlike the NFL, if you're the weakest team (which Johnston is not) you don't get first pick. He pauses before explaining, 'You have to say that if you take all Sheikh Mohammed's operations as one, and he graded all his horses into divisions, I'm not going to get his division one horses,' he says. 'There's no possibility of that. *They* will go to Godolphin.' His tone is not one of discontent; it is simply a statement of fact. 'I don't know where we come in the pecking order,' he adds. 'Probably quite low down in terms of the quality he sends us. Now I don't know that for sure. I don't know how they see it. But certainly never division one. In fact, we probably get better quality horses from Gainsbrough and Shadwell (Hamdan Al Maktoum's stud in Thetford, Norfolk). They're probably more evenly spread among their trainers. Of course you always want the best quality you can get, but, on the other hand, we do very well from Darley Stud (Sheikh Mohammed's operation in Newmarket). Financially, they helped us turn this business around. They send us so many horses, and they pay so well.'

Some Godolphin 'rejects' have helped the Johnston stable make a splendid start, even before the turf season has begun. 'With some of these three-year-olds which have come from Godolphin – they're not stars, otherwise they wouldn't have sent them – we can say, "Let's get on and run them, see what they can do on the track."' Three winners already in maiden races on the all-weather – Soho Square, Orvietan and Rebellion, in the colours of Jumeirah Racing, generally the Sheikh Mohammed horses of whom least is expected – vindicate that policy. Indeed, the strains of 'Auld Lang Syne' had barely faded when the yard recorded its first winner. At Southwell on New Year's Day a six-year-old mare named Spitting Image has opened the year in tremendous style over what is the toughest test of stamina on the sand, two miles. This is already the best all-weather campaign the yard has enjoyed for a while, which is partly because, as Johnston explains, 'We got disillusioned with it. We thought it was such terrible racing. It was once a big part of our year, January, February and March. But to be honest, I lost interest in it. But this year we did see it as an opportunity.

'The horses we have staying in training (after their two-year-old careers) are mostly colts and geldings and it's always been our policy to just walk and trot them here in November and December. It's when we tend to have a lot of staff away anyway. Those horses aren't doing proper cantering until the New Year. This December, though, we were flush with staff, and Jock (Bennett, his assistant) started cantering the colts on something like the sixteenth. They didn't miss a day. Some even went out on Christmas Day. They went right through. Deirdre and I were on holiday in South Africa all that time, and when we returned we had all these colts that had been cantering. I thought, "What do I do for two months?" These horses were going to be ready to run by the end of January, and we were not planning to run them until the end of March. They were ready early, by mistake almost. With the influx of sixteen Godolphin horses we had a lot of middle-distance maiden three-year-olds who were all looking to be running in the same races, and they were all fit. If we had waited for the turf, we'd have had five horses for every maiden race. So I thought, "Let's get some of them out and qualified for handicaps, or whatever."' Johnston phoned a few owners, two in particular – John Ferguson, current manager of Sheikh Mohammed's Darley Stud, and Gary Coffey, manager of Newsells Park Stud – and told them their horses were ready to run. Did they want him to run them? Both Ferguson and Coffey agreed. 'Circumstances meant that we had these horses fit to run,' Johnston says. 'But if we'd been sitting there in November and December and thinking about running those horses on the all-weather in the winter, it would have been very depressing. Even the all-weather masters like David Barron would agree how depressing it is.'

The debate over the ever-increasing all-weather cards, and racecourses, is one that has long simmered. The waters would foam again once the converted began to preach the benefits of Kempton's newly developed track, despite attendances which suggested that the public was not so convinced. Some dismiss all-weather racing as betting fodder. Good heavens, they contend, the evening cards at Kempton Park are even staged at 'greyhound-style' intervals, at times like 7.28 and 7.56, so as to finish by 9.30, the time the betting shops close. It is not for the true aficionado of the sport. For Flat enthusiasts suffering withdrawal symptoms, it is, of course, a variation that adequately provides them with succour through the winter, when otherwise horseracing would be frozen off. Yet those cards which gave opportunities to lesser horses and kept jockeys in work in the 'close season' no longer simply complement the action on turf tracks. The meetings are becoming increasingly prevalent.

The tracks are constructed, in the case of Lingfield and Wolverhampton, of Polytrack, which comprises polypropylene fibres, recycled rubber and silica sand covered in a wax coating. At Southwell the track is laid with a substance called Fibresand. Kempton has now joined them, to be followed by a new course at Great Leighs in Essex. Kempton, thankfully still home to jumping, most notably the King George VI Steeplechase on Boxing Day, has also installed floodlights. In days to come we will, no doubt, go for a night's racing at the Park instead of dog racing at the 'Stow. Newbury contemplated following suit. Even the 'headquarters' of Flat racing, Newmarket, has considered an all-weather track.

'When all-weather racing first came along, I was a great enthusiast and great supporter of it,' Johnston admits. 'I'm a great fan of initiatives like the Dubai World Cup.' He laughs. 'I'd go racing on *any* surface for $5 million. The problem now is that I'm much less of a fan of it because what we're seeing is that it's all part of a general process of "dumbing down" British racing, and taking us away from what's made British racing so popular and so good. I'm horrified by that. All-weather racing should be run *as well as* turf, not *instead of* turf. It worries me terribly that it's creeping in. People are starting to get so enthusiastic about Polytrack; they're saying it's a better surface to run horses on than turf. To my mind, that's absolute nonsense. The Polytrack is a magnificent all-weather surface. It is superior to most other all-weather surfaces, but it is not superior to turf and never will be, in terms of injuries to horses. Turf is a much better surface for racing horses. It will be a very sad day if everything graduates towards going left-handed towards mile-round dirt tracks. A very sad day. It's getting more and more like greyhound racing.'

Indeed, the fear of the Polytrack-phobes is not so much the existence of all-weather racing but that it is creeping into the sport like an alien life-force. Dog racing, but with bigger 'dogs', the cynics may submit. Johnston is heartened by the fact that he is not alone in his concerns. One of his principal rivals, Mick Channon, maintains, 'How many of these tracks do they want? Fifty? If the trend continues and our racing becomes like that in America, there will be more people leaving our sport than ever before.' Its advocates would claim that all the fears are unwarranted, that its opponents are backwoodsmen. There are many punters, owners and trainers as happy as sandboys. For them it merely provides a betting medium and opportunities for moderate horses. 'That's the problem,' insists Johnston, 'it's poor racing. Now, there's no problem with that *per se*. There is a place for poor racing, but not at the expense of better racing; just as there is a place for all-weather but not at the expense of turf. Everybody recognises that better racing is more popular. That's what people want to go and watch.'

Sometimes it's possible to question that assumption. In summer, huge crowds gather at York, Chester, Newmarket and other venues. But are racegoers attracted in their thousands regardless of the quality, principally because alcohol is available all day and, for them, one race is as authentic a betting vehicle as another? Or are they truly entranced by Group races and valuable handicaps? Probably something of both, in reality, but Johnston is more convinced by the truth of the latter. 'A great example is a track like York. Generally, it offers excellent racing and gets huge crowds. Compare them with the one or two days when, to my mind, racing is below the standard that a course like that should be staging, when the prizemoney is poor, and you'll find that the turn-out is completely different. Good racing and top-class horses bring in people. That's what we should be promoting. We should be selling that idea. It's good to see initiatives like the Winter Derby and some of the things Lingfield have done. But that's just one meeting stuck in the middle of nowhere, backed up by all this dross.'

It is a discussion that will crop up again, although intriguingly, around that time a Johnston three-year-old, running for only the second time in its career, was backed down from 7–2 on favourite to 11–2 on ('nonsense' is the response of his trainer at those prepared to invest at those odds) for a modest race on the all-weather at Wolverhampton. In hindsight, it would be realised that the price that day might well have been generous. Soapy Danger, as the colt is curiously named (until you look at the breeding: by Danzig, out of On a Soapbox), won comfortably. There will be considerably more to come from him before the season is out. Johnston merely observes, 'We've nicknamed him Sloppy Danger, because he just slops about on the gallops; he's not interested in anything. He could be quite good, because he's never disgraced in a gallop whether he works with good or bad horses. But he never shows any flair. He never beats the others by five lengths.' Another of his charges, Royal Island, finished only ninth on the sand of Wolverhampton in mid-February. But that did not unduly concern Johnston, who had also run the horse on snow at St Moritz to prepare him for the Lincoln.

For any intrepid British trainer, the Swiss village, 6,000 feet above sea level, is far more than a chic playground for the well-heeled and the celebrity A-listers, who this year, in no particular order of celeb seniority, included Liz Hurley, Britt Ekland and the Earl and Countess of Wessex. The tri-annual race meeting, staged on a thirty-foot-deep frozen lake, provides inviting prize money and an opportunity to seek fitness before the turf Flat starts at home. The programme includes Flat races, trotting events and 'skikjoring', which is like water-skiing but with a horse replacing the motor-boat and ice instead of water. Fur coats and snow boots are *de rigueur* among the 10,000 spectators. With hospitality marquees all round, Johnston likens it to 'a posh point-to-point, with furs instead of Barbours'. Royal Island, owned by the Swiss Markus Graff, made the three-day road journey from Middleham for the Grand Prix von St Moritz. Johnston scoffs at the perceived dangers. 'They get a good grip on the surface and I've never seen a horse slip up,' he told Alan Lee in an article for *The Times*. 'They used to wear purpose-built steel shoes, which were very heavy, but this year they have approved American dirt racing plates with a toe grab. The biggest challenge is the kickback of snow and ice, which is why I ran Royal Island on the all-weather in England first.'

The target at home for this early bird is the first major handicap of the season, the Lincoln in late March. It is a race which, yes, was once run at Lincoln before moving to its home for many years, Doncaster. This year it is relocated to Redcar while Town Moor undergoes renovation.

Meanwhile, back at Middleham, the newcomers for 2006 have been arriving at irregular intervals, which doesn't help preparation and plans for the season. 'This year they were very slow to come in,' says Johnston. 'In fact, as you know, at the end of 2005 I was panicking that the numbers were so far down. I couldn't see how we were going to fill the place. Now we're jam-packed.' The uncertainty had mainly surrounded the Maktoum consignments. 'John Ferguson, manager of the Sheikh's Darley Stud, came up here around that time and told us that we weren't getting any for the time being. He said, "No, we're pooling them all at our base in Hamilton Road (in Newmarket), and we'll allocate them in April." He told me, "Come and see us at the breeze-ups, and we'll tell you then what you're going to get." Then he said, "Come down when you're at the December Sales." At the time we were overstaffed and had lots of empty boxes. I told him that. He told me again he would allocate them in April. The next thing I know, ten came the following week. Then another ten three-year-olds, those ex-Godolphin horses. Then another six. The upshot is that Darley Stud has 48 horses of all ages with us. That's about twenty more than last year.' And now, as Johnston has just been informed, ten more horses from Gainsborough Stud.

I try to conjure an image of those 220 equine athletes. Even though they are spread across three yards, it is still a mind-boggling figure. On every visit, the stable's work carries on around me, every facet seemingly working smoothly and in harmony. Yet we are not speaking of cartons of tea, or lengths of iron ore; we are talking of fragile, occasionally fractious beings of flesh and blood, all with their own idiosyncrasies and temperaments. Some are biddable and comply quietly; others are stroppy characters. Some have special needs. Each is the property of owners who have different expectations and demands, and each is in the care of stable staff and work-riders. Tally the owners and staff and their families together and you probably have a population the size of a small town all of whose lives are influenced by Johnston's progress. That's before you even mention the punters backing them. It is not easy to imagine anyone coping with such an awesome responsibility.

'Back in 2003 (when the yard enjoyed a summer of saturation when it came to winners), I remember thinking there was no limit to the number of horses we could train,' Johnston recalls. 'We'd just added another yard manager. No problem at all. Then 2004 was arguably our best-ever season. Even better. Yet it was driving me mad.' Couldn't you maintain overall responsibility, delegate, and sit back and enjoy the fruits of your labours? Isn't that what successful businessmen do? He looks at me as though I've just asked him to recite the benefits of the Act of Union. 'Planning the horses' work, planning their entries, what they're going to eat … my belief has always been that the day I stop doing that is the day I stop holding the licence. I have to do the list (of proposed work for each horse) at night. I used to say, "I haven't got anyone good enough to delegate the list to."'

Things came to a head at the end of 2004. Johnston was discussing his concerns with Ian Harland, one of his owners, who was also head of a major accountancy practice. Harland handled the buy-out of Brian Palmer in 2001. 'Ian came in to do an official review, not just of the business but of our whole lifestyle and plans for the future. He asked me, "What is the worst thing about your job?" I said, "Doing the list." At that stage we had around 180 horses, and I'd get my vet diaries at seven o'clock at night, read them over dinner, then go straight out into the tack room. I wouldn't be finished until midnight. Everyone else had gone to bed. If I'd been racing, I might be there until one in the morning. It was like that day in, day out. I said to Ian, "You can't delegate this job." Yet at the same time I also realised that was the limiting factor. The more horses you have, the longer the list takes.

'Ian gave me a little lecture about McDonald's. He said, "If you go to them anywhere in the world, the standard of food is exactly the same. Do they employ brilliant, capable people or sixteen-year-old spotty kids who can't get a job anywhere else, and pay them the minimum wage?" I said, "The latter." He said, "That's because the systems are so good they can't get it wrong. If you think you can't delegate things, the system you've put in is not right. Go back and re-design the system so that you can delegate and still have the input you want." That gave me a new lease of life. I realised that was what I enjoyed about the business, as well – designing the system.'

Johnston altered things, radically. He promoted 'Jock' Bennett, who had formerly worked for Bill Watts, from yard manager to his assistant. 'His one and only job in the afternoon is to do that list,' says Johnston, 'although I still keep tabs on it all. So now, when you say 93 two-year-olds is a lot, I can tell you, "No, it's not." I'm more in touch with them than I was in 2003 and 2004.'

We turn to his two-year-olds. They have already been evaluated, according to their suspected relative precocity, although it is by no means an exact science. Like a school headmaster grading his pupils, I suggest; not so much an eleven-plus as a two-plus. Johnston nods, patiently. 'We sat down, just about three weeks ago, Deirdre and I, and we put the pedigree for all of them into alphabetical order. Then we have lists of our two-year-olds in date of birth order. We go through that, going through pedigree, conformation and age. We try to sort them into four groups for each quarter of the season, when they're likely to start their racing careers. Group 1s are those suspected to be the earliest runners, Group 4s those who will mature more steadily.' However, he stresses that 'this is just a preliminary stab at it'. After that the yard managers who look after the two-year-olds are asked to go through the same process. 'If a horse matches my assessment, that's fine. If not, we have a debate about where it should be. The yard managers could have more feedback from the work-riders, which means they may try to push a horse forward to an earlier group.' The process must give rise to much heated debate. 'There are disagreements,' Johnston says. 'I might say, "Don't be ridiculous. That colt's by Generous, or by Lomitas. He's not going to be a Group 1." But I'll compromise. "He's not a four, he's a three."'

The two-year-olds are then worked against one another within their groups. 'But even a Group 4 horse will get some fast work now, or if not now, in the next few weeks,' Johnston points out. 'We still give them work in case something bounces out of it. Horses can jump from one group to another. At the moment, we've got fifteen in Group 1, and we'll start looking for some early runners among them. Once you've got your first winner, everything starts falling into place. But I have to say that value comes into it as well. To be quite honest, you're not going to put a

150,000-guinea horse in Group 1 and send it out to Redcar or wherever in the early weeks. You're not going to use it to test the water of how good your group is. You're going to send out one or two cheaper ones. Over the years we've had very few March and April two-year-old runners. But this year we've got a few earmarked to run early, on pedigrees, conformation and value. If they're no good this May, they're not going to be any good next May.

'I don't emerge with the two-year-olds at a particular time of the year,' Johnston continues, adding with gentle mockery, 'It's not like Henry Cecil making his annual appearance at Warren Hill. No, there's no particular date. We just start breaking them; then it's on to an expanse of land below the Low Moor gallop where they do figures of eight and learn steering and braking. They used to just canter on the grass, then go on to the main all-weather gallop, do one furlong, then three, then build up to five. This year, for the first time, they've gone on to a little two-year-old gallop. The problem is that it's only three furlongs long and, though it's better in many ways, it's not as testing for them as in past years. I'm not absolutely convinced that they've done enough to be fit for their first race.' He suddenly senses that he is drifting towards finding excuses. He snaps out of it. 'It shouldn't matter, though,' he adds. 'If the yard managers say to me they're not a very good bunch in three weeks' time, I'll still jump on them from a great height. It's absolutely impossible. They can't be "not a good bunch".'

Racehorses, though, could be considered perishable goods. Like fruit, you have to enjoy them when ripe. Is Johnston ever concerned that early opportunities, easy pickings, are being spurned? 'They're ready when they're ready,' he says. 'There will be times I start panicking, of course. Are we ahead of or are we behind previous years? I will go back through the records of gallops and see what we were doing in previous seasons.'

Johnston recalls that the earliest he has ever galloped a two-year-old was on 4 January. That horse was Starstreak, one of the yard's early good horses in 1989. 'He was runner-up in the Gordon Stakes at Goodwood and won the White Rose Stakes at Ascot. He beat a short-priced favourite of Sheikh Mohammed's. That was when we thought, "We've made it."' He smiles at the memory. 'At that time I was doing everything possible to try to get the Maktoums as owners, to try to get noticed. I don't think I cracked it with one horse, but there have been milestones, and I remember thinking then, "Sheikh Mohammed must have noticed me *now*." Probably he didn't notice me at all.

'Starstreak was a big, scopey, middle-distance horse. It didn't do any harm, but in later years I learnt that there wasn't an awful lot to be gained from galloping them so early. So, as each year went by, our gallops probably grew later and later. But the gap between doing a good gallop and running in a race has got shorter and shorter. Everything they're doing in January, February and March is just education. You're not really trying to find out how good they are.'

Experience has definitely taught Johnston that appearances can be deceptive. He tells the story of Russian Valour, a horse he'd bought by Fasliyev. 'It was around Easter time 2003, and I noticed this big boat of a horse. I kept seeing it go up the road. It was such a big, plain, common, heavy lump. I'd be thinking, "It's in the wrong string. What's that rider doing with an older horse mixed in with the two-year-olds?" Then I realised that it was Russian Valour. It was a Sunday, and the Always Trying partnership, a syndicate of about twenty people, were coming to see their horses. Everything had worked. We were really chuffed with a horse of theirs called Always Flying, but I had to find a horse to work with it. I thought, "Let's put it with that big Fasliyev thing that's never galloped before. That'll make it look good."As you can imagine, Russian Valour absolutely floored Always Flying. 'Manny' Mercer was riding – just couldn't hold him. Russian Valour ran away with him. We were stunned. A week later we repeated it to make sure that it was right. And it was. Another week later, we ran him. Two weeks, from doing a decent gallop to running in a race. He went on to win the Norfolk Stakes at Royal Ascot in an excellent two-year-old season.'

Celtic Silence provides a similar example of the engine under the bonnet being far more powerful than Johnston had suspected. 'When the colt came from Peter Savill I thought he was a typical late-developing slowish horse. Nothing special. Kevin Darley thought that too. He always says he knows a good horse as soon as he sits on it. Quite by accident, I threw him in with some that had been doing far more work and to my mind were far more forward. I thought it was a mismatch, that they would burn the legs off him. Quite the opposite. He burnt the legs off *them*. I knew we had a good horse. I told Peter he was quite useful. Peter, who always wants to be involved in these things, said that there was an auction race at Ayr at the end of May, and if he won that he wanted to run him in the Chesham. He did win, first time out, and then won the Chesham.

'So, quite simply,' Johnston sums up, 'I don't know which are going to be the good ones. At the sales, there are always ones you're delighted with. "I got a bargain there." And others, you think, "I shouldn't have bought that. I paid too much."'

One horse that always stands out was bought at the sales in 1994. 'I bought 28 yearlings for a total of 200,000 guineas, which was a lot of money for us then. One was a colt by Cadeaux Generaux, a big heavy thing. The year before I'd had another Cadeaux Generaux, from the Duke of Roxburghe, who was in his early days with us. It was big, plain and slow, and we sent it home without running it. This yearling looked exactly the same. To rub it in, Deirdre said to me, "Oh, that Cadeaux Generaux that you bought, did you see that his half-brother has won over hurdles again?" I actually thought I'd bought a big brute of a jumper – until Easter.

'The horse was owned by Stuart Morrison, who's very patient and easy-going. He'd had Quick Ransom just before this. He very rarely comes to see his horses, but this time he came down because it was Easter. Now, it wasn't the end of the world. He didn't have any great expectations. He'd just given me the money. Never even saw it until that day. He'd just told me, "Buy me a horse." When he came to see it, Anthony Stroud was here for Sheikh Mohammed (at that time Stroud was the Sheikh's racing manager). Stupidly, I worked Stuart's with Sheikh Mohammed's. I thought the Sheikh's was so far ahead that I warned Stuart: "Don't worry, yours is a big, backward horse. He'll not be able to go with those horses. Don't worry that they're better than he is. He just needs more time." I was completely wrong, of course. That horse was Bijou D'Inde (the 1996 St Jame's Palace Stakes Winner). Yet, after I'd bought those 28 yearlings, if I could have given one back it would have been him. So you just never know.'

The previous day, Johnston tells me, Sheikh Mohammed's assistant manager had visited. He asked him if any of the two-year-olds were making a significant impression. 'I said no, there was nothing standing out of all the two-year-olds, although Deirdre and the work riders would have more feel for what was making an impression. Certainly, nothing was doing enough for me. Actually, that wasn't quite true, because the odd horse has started to stand out for me. There's one called Tartan Tie, by Grand Lodge. I just see it all the time, and I think, "What's that?" It just stands out. You think, "That's a nice horse," and you check to find out. There's another called Schermuly, by Fruits Of Love. They stand out from the string but they shouldn't do. You think, "It's a Fruits Of Love and a Grand Lodge – they shouldn't be that far forward to look like nice horses." You expect the sprinting horses, the mature ones, to be standing out.'

Johnston respects the fact that his riders are frequently better arbiters of talent than he. Deirdre, he believes, is also a sound judge. 'She likes nice, big, strong, smooth horses,' Johnston says. Yet he retains some scepticism about his riders' verdicts. 'Even the professional jockeys get it wrong at this time of year. They equate pulling hard and *wanting* to run fast with being fast. I don't think we've ever had a runner in the Brocklesby (the first juvenile race of the season), but if a rider comes in and says "This'll win the Brocklesby", it's probably useless.'

Johnston admits that even after all these years he is still stirred by the prospect of a star in the making. 'Now when I get excited it's when there's a horse out there and I desperately *want* it to be good. I've got a Monjeu out of Coyote (it would be named Eradicate). He cost 160,000 guineas. I thought he was a beautiful yearling. I *want* him to be good. Now, if I put him up against some wee thing they say could win the Brocklesby and I suddenly discover that this big, middle-distance horse can floor this little fellow and he does it just by lengthening his stride; he stretches, and he looks like he's going slow, and the riders think he's slow because he's big and he's comfortable, and he just outclasses this little horse who's trying to run so fast – *then* I get excited. I think, "I might have a champion horse here." The ones that excite me, jump out at me, are the ones that get a bit behind in the gallop, then they just pick up, lengthen, and they're there. It's as if their stride's one and a half times more than the stride of the horse next to them, without putting in more work. But then the gallops don't always tell you which is the exciting horse. It's the races.

'A trainer, I think it was Bill O'Gorman, said recently, "Anyone who doesn't know how good his horse is before going to the races is not doing his job; you should know how good it is *before* it goes there first time." I don't agree with that all. I didn't have a clue that Double Trigger was good. He was a clown at home, and never did a decent gallop. Attraction didn't sparkle on the gallops either, although she did enough to suggest that we'd win races with her.'

So, determining the promise in a racehorse is far from an exact science. 'This morning,' Johnston continues, 'we worked a few two-year-olds on the gallops. Say you put this little two-year-old in, and think, "He's my sharpest two-year-old. He might be my first runner." If he works well, that means everything is working out fine. Your suspicions have been correct. But what happens if you work him with two others and they beat him? Do you start again and re-plan because that has thrown everything? Of course not. The same applies when you start running them. If you predict this is a good one, this will win, and he finishes tenth, that doesn't just mean *he* was wrong. The problem is that it affects everything that's worked with him. What about the horse who worked half a length behind him? Was he useless? Were others? No, they can't be. But what it means is that you're back to the drawing board.'

The trainer has an anecdote which he often tells to remind people of how a handful of early runners can damn a whole season's intake. 'He's sick of me reminding him, but at the start of last season we made a very slow start with the two-year-olds. Jock Bennett had remarked on more than one occasion, "I don't think they're a very good bunch." Well, I jumped down his throat. I said, "Jock, you can have ten who are not a good bunch, even twenty who are not a good bunch, but you cannot have a hundred who are not a good bunch." It's surely not possible for a whole generation of two-year-olds to be inferior to the previous year's. It just can't be the case. The best one may be inferior to last year's best, and the worst one may be too. But the average of three thousand horses has to be the same. It's the same with us. If we have a hundred two-year-olds, they can't all be bad. Neither can they all be superstars.

The question we have to answer is: are we running the right ones?'

Rather than just dismissing a whole group of horses, which have originated from a variety of different sources, as below par, or attributing indifferent work and poor runs to 'the virus', Johnston insists on applying logic. 'Maybe that's one of the things that has helped make us successful. If there's a problem I don't believe in screaming, like the naughty kid in the playground, "The big boy done it and ran away." I don't try to find something, or someone, else to blame. That's why it can never be the case that you've "got a bad bunch" this year. Something I always try to drum into the yard managers is this: good horses don't win more races than bad horses. It's completely ridiculous to think that. It's actually quite the contrary. So, all those small struggling trainers out there who are blaming the fact that that's what they are because I've got better horses are talking absolute crap. What makes a good trainer is making the most of what he's got.'

Johnston's eyes demanded that you concur with his rationale.

'What absolute crap that was in the *Racing Post* when they published a list of the hundred greatest training feats,' he continues. 'How the hell do they know? It's absolute rubbish for them to assess something that happened a hundred years before they were born. That was the case with some of the trainers featured.' I suggest, as an advocate for the defence, that it was not a definitive list; it is not to be taken too seriously. But Johnston is unmoved. 'A good training feat is making a horse better than somebody else could have made it,' he says. 'A bad training feat's not getting the best out of it. You could only make a true judgement on that if a particular horse changed trainers. As I said to you earlier, this job is not rocket science. It's not particularly clever to be a good racehorse trainer. But at other times I remind myself that it's blatantly obvious some are more successful than others. We are one of the best set-ups, and that has proved that it's not all from having the best opportunities. Because we *didn't* have the best opportunities. You can't start any lower than we did.' From that novice hurdle at Towcester, the ascent to his present habitat amid the elite of his profession among men such as Aidan O'Brien and Sir Michael Stoute has been strewn with the falling rocks of discouragement. Johnston has tossed them aside.

The early Classics are now the priority. Central to his plans is a typical Johnston specimen: a colt who has achieved nothing more than victory in a Listed race at Pontefract, albeit by four lengths, at the back end of the 2005 season. Johnston, however, believes he is laden with latent ability.

CHAPTER TEN

I haven't ever had an owner sell a horse for big money and regret it,
regardless of what the horse goes on to do afterwards.
I've had plenty not sell and regret it.

It takes much to stir Mark Johnston's sense of expectancy for he has witnessed too many disappointments and setbacks over the years, but there is a growl of anticipation when he broaches his principal 2,000 Guineas hope for 2006.

'Nakheel has to be the big hope at the moment, the one we're most excited about,' says Johnston of Sheikh Hamdan's colt, even if on paper his qualifications are like comparing a pupil with an A level with a graduate holding a degree. Yet Johnston's grand servant Bandari, in the same ownership, had won the same race at Pontefract, by nine lengths, in 2001 before lifting the following season's Derby Trial at Lingfield, the Gordon Stakes at Goodwood and the Great Voltigeur at York. Indeed, the old boy (in Flat racing terms, seven is regarded as approaching the slippers and cocoa stage), who epitomises the kind of stayer with whom Johnston is so often associated, punctured the £500,000 prize money barrier with his triumph in last season's Royal Ascot's Hardwicke Stakes (run at York). It had provoked Johnston to reflect, 'This is a race I have a love affair with (it was the trainer's fourth victory in the race in seven years), but I also have a love affair with this horse.' Whether Nakheel, with his four white socks, white blaze and ostentatious good looks – if he was a car, you imagine he'd have a rear spoiler and be driven by a wealthy boy racer – would turn out to be predominantly a miler or a stayer, like Bandari, remains to be seen. Breeding can reveal much, but sometimes the genes are betrayed by performances.

Nakheel (Arabic for 'palm') is entered for the 2,000 Guineas together with Black Charmer, the yard's top-rated three-year-old who finished half-a-length third to Sir Percy in the Goodwood Vintage Stakes, and Atlantic Waves, who will probably require further than the mile of the 2,000 Guineas. It is planned that Prince Of Light, a Group 3 winner, will go for a trial race first. And Johnston believes that Nakheel, a son of Sadler's Wells, whose dam Matiya finished second to Bosra Sham in the fillies' equivalent a decade earlier, has been endowed with sufficient stamina, as well as speed, to persuade him to enter the horse for the Derby, along with Atlantic Waves, Prince Of Light and In Full Cry (the late Maktoum Al Maktoum's horse). On the distaff side, Johnston has no 1,000 Guineas entries. Desert D'Argent has fractured a pedal-bone and is likely to be out until mid-season.

Johnston has often prayed at the unorthodox church altar of training strategy, and again he is planning what would once have been regarded as a risky route for his principal representative. Nakheel will go for the 2,000 Guineas without a preparatory race. He will just have a racecourse gallop during the Craven meeting, as Mister Baileys and Attraction had done before winning the 1994 2,000 Guineas and 2004 1,000 Guineas respectively. Johnston emphasises, however, that at this stage Nakheel cannot be compared with his two Guineas winners. 'We had little doubt that Mister Baileys had class,' he says. 'It was which Group 1 we were going to run him in. The same applied to Attraction. There may have been some discussion about trip, and so on, but if she was fit, she was fit to run in the Guineas. The same also applied to Bijou D'Inde, who finished third. I was also very keen to run Lend A Hand, too, in the Guineas. He'd won a Group 1 as a two-year-old. Those horses which had won a Group 1 or 2 already had nowhere else to go. This year is very different. Of our four contenders, the only one that has won a Group race is Prince Of Light. In some ways it's a strange thing to be saying that these are Guineas horses, but my gut feeling is that Nakheel is our best chance, though I haven't proved it yet. In the days of Mister Baileys, he stood out from a relatively small string. Nakheel stands out from a very big string.'

That home enthusiasm would soon be translated into money supporting him, despite the mixed messages in the trainer's observations, reported in the *Racing Post*: 'He looks fantastic at the moment and probably won't have a prep run before the Guineas.

Getting horses fit for the Guineas has never been a problem for us. He's bred for further than a mile, so there is an issue over the suitability of the trip, and he's in the Derby, but he does show us a lot of speed.'

'Though the horse has wintered really well,' Johnston says, 'he hasn't really had a serious gallop yet because of the weather. He has to have one in the next week or so. He'll probably have a half-speed this week, and then a more serious one next week, with the aim of taking him down to the Craven meeting and giving him a spin on the track. Let Richard (Hills, retained jockey to Hamdan Al Maktoum) have a sit on him.'

It intrigues many people why Johnston eschews a preparatory run for his Guineas contenders. Initially it was borne out of a question of practicality rather than being some piece of elaborate equine science. 'The year Mister Baileys won the Guineas it was an atrocious winter, horrendous,' Johnston recalls. 'The reason we got into racecourse gallops was because Middleham gallops weren't fit to use. We tried him on the turf at home. He just wasn't handling the soft ground at all. Then we gave him one bit of work on the all-weather which in those days was woodchip, and not all that good. And then we thought, "Stuff this for a lark. We'd better take him to a racecourse." So we did. Michael Dickinson (the top National Hunt trainer now based in the US) has never believed me to this day that he only had four gallops. He had four gallops, and two of them were disasters. Attraction didn't have any more than that; she probably had less. She only had one racecourse gallop, at Ripon. But horses like that ... well, all we're doing is training them down to a weight. We aim to have them at their two-year-old racing weight, ready for the race. The daddy of them all was Double Trigger. He won all his races within a two-kilo weight band. The most common thing for people to say is, oh, he's ten kilos over or he's twenty kilos over, but he's grown. He'll be all right. The vast majority don't want to get any heavier.'

I suggest that it's similar to a boxer preparing for a bout, except in reverse. Johnston accepts the analogy. 'Even with Nakheel, although he hasn't galloped yet, we're very conscious of his weight at the moment. We know how much has got to come off. And it's not a huge amount. We're pretty sure we can get that weight off on the gallops. He'll be racing at the same kind of weight as he was last year.'

It could still be argued that a preparatory race has certain advantages. An exceptional run could persuade some of the trainers of Nakheel's rivals to seek alternative targets; an indifferent run could mean Johnston considering more viable alternatives for his colt. Also, it would provide important clues to the horse's stamina. But Johnston claims there is a dearth of suitable races anyway. 'Generally, in their early careers, I like horses to go through a progression of racing,' he explains. 'I don't like them to win a Group 2 and then come back and win a Group 3. I usually don't like them to win a Group 2 and come back and run in another. Sometimes they'll jump a stage. But I don't like them going backwards. With my other Guineas-winning horses there was nowhere else to go than Group 1. That's not the case with Nakheel. You could say that he should go next for a lesser Group race than the Guineas. That'll probably be the case for any of those others there (on the list) who run.' There *are* possible opportunities for Nakheel, though? 'Maybe a Guineas trial in Ireland, or you could say the Feilden Stakes (at Newmarket), but that's going up to one mile one furlong and it's only Listed and he's already won one. Otherwise the trials are seven furlongs. His minimum trip's got to be a mile.'

Clearly, there remains some ambivalence over that question.

'My feeling,' Johnston continues, 'is that he's a wee bit like Mister Baileys. I think, and so do Sheikh Hamdan, Angus Gold (the Sheikh's racing manager) and maybe even Richard (Hills, his jockey), that this horse is more likely to be a Derby horse. So do the bookies. They've got him at a shorter price for the Derby. He's bred for further, in that he's by Sadler's Wells. But his mother won the Irish Guineas. So, I say to myself, why can't he win a Guineas? People often say the Guineas is the best Derby trial anyway, so I say, let's run him in the Guineas. To some extent that was what we were doing with Mister Baileys when he won.'

Certainly, those who have been backing Nakheel for the first colts' Classic have no doubts about his potential to dominate over a mile. Johnston professes himself bewildered by the confidence in Nakheel beyond the stable. Weight of money has forced his price for the Guineas down to 11–1, with the Coral spokesman Dave Stevens saying, 'We have been happy all winter to take on George Washington (the Aidan O'Brien-trained favourite) and we are getting some positive vibes about

Nakheel.' Stevens added, mysteriously, that the support was 'good money, from sources we respect'. Mysterious because, as Johnston would tell Geoff Lester in the newly launched newspaper the *Sportsman* at the end of March, 'There is no logical reason why Nakheel's odds have tumbled. It was only this morning that he did his first fast piece of work upsides.'

Just one other concern. Is it conceivable that the exertions of the Guineas could take too much out of him for the Derby? 'In hindsight, with Mister Baileys, we certainly thought that trying to do a Guineas–Dante–Derby was a mistake,' Johnston offers in qualified agreement. 'But I think Guineas–Derby is all right. I'm never happy with fourth place, but you could say, well, fourth in the Guineas with Nakheel, we'd be quite happy with that, and we'd probably be quite looking forward to the Derby, particularly if he was a running on third or fourth. Let's hope we go there looking for a running on third or fourth, and he runs on to be first!' That's about as prophetic as Johnston gets. But there's a month for that little devil named Sod to cause those plans to be abandoned. 'Back in Mister Baileys' time we probably hadn't had enough knocks and we took everything for granted,' Johnston adds. 'We started planning in November what would run in the Guineas. Most owners would like to do that. But I hate planning ahead now, because so many things go wrong.'

Presumably, greater care and attention is afforded to such a horse within the yard? 'We try to carry on pretty much as normal, as though he's just another horse, but you can't help but … well, if something did happen to Nakheel, we'd all go running to see what's going on. You can't help but be more conscious of it. We may be slightly extra-cautious. But we don't actually treat him differently. He doesn't do different work. Physically, there's no different treatment.' And there's a queue of work-riders determined to partner him? Johnston smiles. 'They *all* want to ride him, of course. In fact, Nakheel's a very quiet ride. I don't stipulate that he needs a *good* rider. If you go back to the days of Mister Baileys, the head lad always rode him. He was the biggest, strongest horse, and he always went at the front of the string. But generally, if you've got something worth seven figures, you keep him at the front of the string, because he's less likely to get kicked! Yes, it's true that you make a little bit of an allowance. Something like Nakheel, or Mister Baileys or Double Trigger, it makes a difference ... the fact they're so flashy. His four white socks and a big white face. You always see where he is in the string. Everyone's conscious of where Nakheel is all the time. But he doesn't go up the front. Or rarely.'

Andrew Bottomley partners Nakheel most days because Nakheel is included in the yard he manages, so he has first pick. 'Deirdre has ridden Nakheel, but she rides our two-year-olds mostly at this time of year,' says Johnston. 'Deirdre doesn't ride them because we're extra-cautious, but she has been associated with quite a lot of the good horses we have, those who stay longer. She also rides ones who've had problems, and makes sure they are sound.'

It appears to be an auspicious time for the yard, despite the fact that Austrian (already owned by Sheikh Mohammed), Stepping Up and Winged Cupid, regarded as serious contenders, have departed to Godolphin, just as Shamardal did the previous season when eight days after his Dewhurst Stakes triumph the Johnston-trained son of Giant's Causeway was transferred to Saeed Bin Suroor. The latter hadn't been exactly a bolt from the blue, so to speak, but it had still been a critical loss. Instead of being readied for the 2,000 Guineas at Middleham – for which race he was at one stage the 3–1 favourite – that colt wintered in the United Arab Emirates, in preparation for the UAE Derby at Nad Al Sheba, a stopover before the onward flight to the ultimate destination: Bluegrass country and a tilt at the Kentucky Derby. In the event, the latter never occurred because the Frankie Dettori-partnered Shamardal took a pummelling from the opposition at Nad Al Sheba, causing plans to be reviewed. However, Shamardal went on to claim the Poule d'Essai des Poulains (the French 2,000 Guineas), the Prix du Jockey Club and the St James's Palace Stakes before being retired to perform his stallion duties in Australia. Johnston is far from being the only trainer to have potential glory seized from his grasp, and he is stoical about such moments. Unfortunately, that's the price of training them just too well. 'Nobody wants to lose such a grand horse, but we all know that's the name of the game,' he says. Here and now, in late March, he is just grateful for large mercies that he still has a horse of the stature of Nakheel among his armoury as he moves on to a war footing.

I raise again the subject of his former top horses who are sold out of the stable to Godolphin. Presumably there is a certain ambivalence about a horse like Winged Cupid, who will probably now be in opposition to his in the Classics? 'Bids often come in for our good horses,' Johnston says. 'I negotiate them. Winged Cupid's a really good horse who's really progressive. He started off small and unimpressive-looking. Of course I want to win the Derby with Nakheel or Atlantic Waves, but Winged Cupid would be the horse I regret losing more than anything this season. He's my Derby favourite at the moment. It's a great loss to lose something like that. On the other hand, you have to advise the owners to sell.' Such decisions can be finely balanced. 'Mister Baileys was nearly sold for £250,000 at the end of his two-year-old career,' says Johnston. 'Thank goodness he wasn't. Double Trigger was nearly sold at one stage. But for every one like that, there's two that could have been sold for far more than they're worth now. As soon as the offer gets to the stage of what it's going to be worth after it wins its next race, if they're giving you its potential value, then you have to take it.

'People have fanciful ideas about what stallions are worth. We've all read about that $10 million yearling (purchased by Sheikh Mohammed) walking out at Newmarket. There are plenty of horses worth those sorts of figures. There are stallions sold for £5–10 million. Take Motivator (the 2005 Derby victor) – £7 million he was sold for, wasn't he? Yet, there are plenty sold for a million, or even less, that go on to be commercial sires. Once you get over a million, you're into stallion value. That's what the horse is going to be worth at the end of his career; so if you get those sorts of figures for any horse during its racing career, you've got to sell.

'You've got to say to your owner of a good horse, "What's your dream? To win the Guineas or the Derby?" But even if he does that it won't be worth any more than it is now. And if it doesn't, it'll be worth a tenth of what it's worth now. We're going back a few years now, but Mister Baileys was eventually sold for £1.4 million. Bijou D'Inde, our Guineas third and St James's Palace Stakes winner, was going to be sold for a million. But the deal fell through, and he was later sold for less after a brief career at stud. If you've got something like (the two-year-old) Denbera Dancer, who I've got out there, who's a full brother to Rumplestiltskin, by Danehill, and the grand-dam is Miesque, the dam a sister to Kingmambo, now if *he* wins the

Guineas, you'd want $10 million for him – and you'd probably get it. But if you've bought a horse for ten grand and won the Guineas with him, you'd probably be lucky to get a million. So, if you can get a million for him when he's won his maiden and a Listed or a Group race, then for God's sake take it. The danger is, if you don't, he's going to be worth twenty grand again one day.'

It's a fascinating debate, and one that became particularly topical in that 2006 season. After Pam Sly, who trains no more than 25 horses at Peterborough, watched her Speciosa win the Nell Gwyn Stakes, the fillies' Classic trial, she revealed that her owners had turned down some 'obscene offers'. It transpired that there had been two bids of $1 million lodged. 'I told the owners to take the money, but they wanted to live the dream,' she said. They did. The filly won the 1,000 Guineas, before being placed fourth in the Oaks.

Selling is a necessity of horseracing in Britain, where the rewards for winning races, for all but the most prestigious contests, are still relatively meagre compared with the costs involved. Indeed, Johnston encourages his owners not to be seduced by romantic possibilities of what may be around the corner. 'I've given up being irritated by it,' he says of losing horses. 'Shamardal moved within the same ownership – he wasn't sold – and went on to win four Group 1s. He's the most successful horse that's ever left here. A great example was Celtic Silence. A lot of people were trying to wind me up and get me to criticise (owner) Peter Savill for selling that horse. They were saying, "Peter Savill doesn't need the money. He shouldn't sell the horse. He should leave it with you." But he was right to sell it.' Johnston believes that the best analogy is a small football club under pressure to sell its star player. 'We are only "the managers",' he says. 'Better to sell that one superstar and upgrade the other ten. That gives them a better chance of continuing to compete at the highest level. No matter how. People who think there are lots of owners around who don't need these huge figures, or can afford to lose them, are silly. It's actually very sensible to sell those kinds of horses. Racing's not sensible in Britain any other way. Some people are so rich they can afford to take multi-million-pound racehorses and race them for five-figure prize money. But most people can't, and shouldn't, be doing that. If a horse acquires a seven-figure value, for the owner to say I'm going to keep it and race it for five-figure prize money is just plain stupid. You must sell it to someone who can really afford to do it. That keeps you in horseracing.

'British owners are not racing for prize money. British owners are racing for re-sell value. It's naive to think that you will get super re-sell value when their racing career is over. That's the worst time to sell. Plenty make the mistake of saying, "Oh, we'll keep it," or, "We don't need the money." I hear that all the time. Or, "The money won't change my life." I'm sure that when they say that it's true, but the loss of the money changes their future attitude to racing. I haven't ever had an owner sell a horse for big money and regret it, regardless of what the horse goes on to do afterwards. I've had plenty not sell and regret it. I'd say 90 per cent are now not worth what they were sold for. People who have paid us anything in excess of £100,000 for a horse … it's hard to think of a horse that's now worth more. Celtic Silence was one; it just faded away. There are loads of them. There was Love You Always, a horse of Mick Doyle's, which won unbelievably impressively at Hamilton. Sheikh Mohammed bought it after one run. That's been disappointing since.' Johnston recalls that last season Godolphin's first three Group victories were achieved by ex-Kingsley House horses, Shamardal and Fight Your Corner. He adds, 'They also won the Queen's Vase with a horse that left here. But inevitably they've had their failures too. Sheikh Mohammed knows when he buys a horse that has run, it is like buying yearlings – there are no guarantees.'

There are no certainties, either, when it comes to how Johnston's battalions will perform in 2006. Which leads us to predictions for the forthcoming season. Johnston is rarely anything but sanguine. '2003 was our best ever season in terms of winners,' says the trainer. 'There's no reason why 2006 can't beat it. This is where it begins to get exciting. The pressure will build, but I resist getting excited now because there's too much water to flow under the bridge.'

And so it would prove. It arrived in a torrent of misfortune.

CHAPTER ELEVEN

I got accused at times of playing God. It's a fine line, but I think it's part of the vet's job to take responsibility away from the owner ... Like every farmer and commercial animal keeper, you have to understand that where there's life, there's death. If you hide yourself from it, you're not going to be good at keeping animals.

Early April 2006, and those mighty twin peaks of the jump season, the Gold Cup and Champion Hurdle, have been conquered by War of Attrition and Brave Inca respectively. If Mark Johnston had timorously accepted the initial offer of a 'jumps only' licence from that panel all those years ago, who knows, he might have been present himself, amid the tumult. The thought does enter your mind. But only for an instant. He'd have got his hands on that Flat licence somehow.

Johnston has cast only a cursory glance at the National Hunt showpiece events. He has other priorities. Though it scarcely appears possible, the first two Classics already lie waiting to pounce, just around the corner – that moment when trainers discover whether their two-year-olds have matured as expected and are ready to assert themselves in two early examinations. We have already heard the first grumbles about their timing. Even though the two events have been established from time immemorial to take place in early May, some trainers are still barely prepared for them. Like the first call of the cuckoo heralding spring, you know you will hear the plea for the calendar to be adjusted; it's just a matter of when, and by whom.

This year it is Mick Channon, who enforces his point in inimical style, protesting, 'I've got polar bears on the gallops.' He adds, 'The programme book is telling me that I should be ready in early May, but my horses are telling me that it is too early. We should put the Guineas back by at least a fortnight.' Johnston disputes the West Ilsley trainer's contention. 'Not with all-weather gallops,' he contends. 'You can work them through the winter now. It's not relevant. I don't agree with Mick. It's not got anything to do with weather. The decision on when the Guineas should take place is based on the maturity of the horses, presumably, not the condition of their coats and the weather on the gallops. The pattern (the European format of high-class races) has evolved to encourage the breeding of precocious, mature, speedy racehorses. The reason the Classics have evolved is because they give a progression for the horse and test it in all sorts of manners and means. The aim of the Guineas is to find out which is the most precocious, speedy three-year-old. So, it's going to go to stud not just on its ability to win a Group 1 race but on its ability to win a Group 1 race *early*.

'That's why a Guineas winner is probably worth more than a St James's Palace Stakes (run at Royal Ascot in late June) winner as a stallion, given the same pedigree, despite the fact that you'd say that the St James's Palace is the perfect race. I used to think that the Guineas was the spectators' race and the St James's Palace was the professionals' race, because it was a true judge of horses once they were more mature. But the reality is that stallion owners and breeders want to know which was ready early, which was most mature. In terms of breeding stock, a Guineas winner is worth more than a Derby winner, which is worth more than a St Leger winner. It's the same for the mares.'

The new Flat season, normally greeted with a drum roll and pyrotechnics of hype, has begun insipidly, with barely a whimper. True, the Lincoln meeting had to be relocated from Doncaster, which is undergoing renovation. It was run instead, inexplicably, at Redcar. Stalls problems at the Cleveland course merely added to the inexplicability of that decision. Still, at least the runners there competed on turf. Elsewhere, the turf Flat season has begun on sand.

'What a damp squib! Whose idea was it to start the season at Lingfield, Southwell and Redcar?' asks Johnston. 'Well, we know whose idea it was. Arena Leisure, who own two of the three tracks. So, we start on the all-weather at Lingfield, then go to Southwell and run in a field. Then we go to Redcar. The Lincoln should never have been run at Redcar. It's true that places like York and Haydock wouldn't want it because they'd be saying it was too soft. Newcastle, well, it's probably only one step up from running it at Redcar. It's difficult, but I'd have probably said move it to Newmarket. They've got a straight mile and it's a better track than Redcar. I think it was run there once before?' His views are shared by many. As one correspondent to the *Racing Post*, one P. Robinson, opined, claiming that the real start of the Flat was the Craven meeting in mid-April, 'The phoney starts at Lingfield, Redcar, Kempton et al have been a shambles that does not reflect well on the sport's authorities.'

Johnston's Royal Island contested the Lincoln and finished a game if frustrating second, defeated only three-quarters of a length by Blythe Knight. Far worse was to follow, however. A couple of weeks later, Johnston and Royal Island's owner Markus Graff suffered one of the many reverses that would befall the yard during this season. As the *Racing Post* informed us on 4 April:

> Mark Johnston suffered a blow yesterday morning when Classic-placed colt Shalapour collapsed and died on the gallops.
>
> The four-year-old, third in the Irish Derby last year when trained by John Oxx, had only recently made his debut for his new yard, having been bought by owner Markus Graff.
>
> 'He just cantered up, walked off the gallops, went 50 or 100 yards, started to stagger and keeled over,' Johnston said. 'It was one of those things, no drama, and it could have happened at any time. Kevin Dalgleish was on him – Keith's brother. He jumped off before the horse went down. We haven't had the result of the post-mortem yet, but it's most likely a heart problem or a ruptured aorta. It's very sad for Markus. He has done so well buying that kind of horse in the past.'
>
> Shalapour, beaten at 1–6 on his first run for Johnston at Southwell twelve days ago, won two of his six races for the Aga Khan in Ireland and finished just four and a half lengths adrift of Hurricane Run at The Curragh last June.

Death. It is a perennial peril for the racehorse. Not just on the National Hunt fields of conflict – and, by heavens, Cheltenham provoked a fusillade of condemnation from the anti-animal cruelty lobby when nine horses died at this year's festival – but on the Flat racecourse too, frequently on the gallops. The power of a half-ton thoroughbred is transmitted through limbs that are rendered remarkably frail if they encounter a hazard. Sometimes the heart simply fails them, as it probably did in the case of Shalapour. Even for a veterinarian and experienced trainer who has witnessed such moments before, it can be a devastating experience. One of Johnston's worst memories is the death of Eldorado at Leopardstown in August 1997. He wrote in his *Horse & Hound* column at the time:

> I remember the delight of winning my first Group 1 race in Ireland and my first Group 1 ever with a two-year-old when Princely Heir landed the Heinz 57 Phoenix Stakes. And I will remember the horror of losing Eldorado, my only Classic hope for this year.
>
> Eldorado had completely ruptured his superficial flexor tendon and the suspensory apparatus (the system of tendons and ligaments which allows the limb to bear weight) was collapsing. The decision was made almost immediately. We all agreed that to keep him alive would be inhumane. Repair is impossible and the degree of pain and suffering involved could not be justified. Eldorado was put down very soon after the race.
>
> Thankfully such injuries are extremely rare. So rare in Flat racehorses that I have never seen one and I hope I never will. The vast majority of injuries that we see are minor, and fatalities are few and far between. Injuries will always occur in this sport where highly tuned equine athletes compete with an inherent desire to run that human athletes could never emulate. Despite what some people say, racehorses are still getting faster and racing is getting more competitive, so the risk of injury will increase to some extent. Luckily, however, advances in veterinary medicine are more than keeping pace with this.

Most racehorses still have an easier death than most humans, I suggest. Even when they are dispatched with a bullet. And, for all the tears that understandably flowed at Best Mate's death in November 2005, there was no prolonged agony for the three-time Gold Cup victor when he collapsed at Exeter. The light was extinguished quickly.

'I was there when Persian Punch died,' says Johnston. 'People will always wonder: if he hadn't had that one last race, would he have died? But it would have died in some other way, some other time, perhaps in more pain. My father died, aged 65. Snap. Just like that. You think at times, "What a waste, what an age to go at, what a way to go." My mother phoned me one morning out of the blue and said, "Your dad's dead." My mother, on the other hand, was in hospital, dying for maybe two or three weeks, mostly unconscious with a morphine pump. You think, "Rather his unexpected death." The same applies to racehorses. They drop dead, doing their job. That's fine, isn't it?

'I shot one of the kids' ponies recently. I'd heard them talking about how it was ill, and had this and that. Deirdre and I debated what we were going to do with it. We were going to get the knacker-man. But I said, "I'll deal with it." I drove up the road and I could see it from about 200 yards away, and there it was, grazing. Standing there eating grass, looking as happy as Larry. I thought, "What am I doing, coming to kill this wee boy?" But then I went towards it, and he had a big bowed tendon. It had Cushing's Disease, big hairy legs; it had hair falling out on its face. I had no problem with it. None whatsoever. Like all the others, I just thought, "Best thing." I didn't miss a moment's sleep over it.

'Most of the time I'm still quite practical and straightforward about it. I use a gun. There are still people, including the vets we use, who would rather see them put down with drugs. Some people don't like guns, particularly if you've had a bad experience with one. We had a case where a horse had to be put down. The guy from the knackers' did it with a captive bolt gun, like that principally used for cattle, not a free bullet, which causes much more damage and is therefore much more instantaneous. I didn't like it. Following that, I instructed Debbie that I didn't want the knackers coming any more, because if I'm not here I don't know what they're using. For the moment, I shoot them myself.'

The difficult part, then, must be relaying the news to owners. 'We've got generally professional, knowledgeable owners,' Johnston replies, 'and they accept that it's the downside of racing. When I look back at my career, when I was in vet practice I had a different attitude to it. I got a jokey reputation among friends of being a bit trigger-happy, of always putting things down. I would say, quite truthfully, that I've got more gifts for putting animals down than I ever got for curing them. That's definitely illogical.' You're the demon executioner of Middleham? 'I got accused at times of playing God. It's a fine line, but I think it's part of the vet's job to take responsibility away from the owner. You find owners of pet animals in particular, including semi-pet horses, who, when the animal is suffering because it's got a long-term problem – for instance, a pony with laminitis (inflammation of layers of tissue inside the hoof), so it's not going to recover – they will talk about how they've "given it its best chance". So long as the vet keeps telling them there's a chance, even if it's only 25 per cent, 40, 50 per cent, that owner continues to feel obliged to give that animal that chance. What is not weighed up against it is the pain it will have to go through. The owner suffers along with their animal, and there is such relief when someone comes along and says, "The best thing you can do for your animal is put it out of its misery." And, "Please don't watch. Go outside and I'll do it for you." I think that's a good vet. It takes the burden off the owner. That was my policy.'

However, Johnston also insists that economic reasoning should come into play. 'For me, horses are commercial animals. They're not pet animals. I see them in a commercial sense, in the same way that a farmer sees a calf. If it is going to cost £50 to fix a problem and it's only worth £40, he wouldn't fix it. He'd put it down. That's how it's going to end up anyhow. If your dog is going to cost £2,000 to fix and it's only worth £400, that's irrelevant. You still pay the money. Horses are sometimes on the borderline. In the days when I was in practice, you could have horses suffering from colic and the chances of recovery, if they went for surgery, were very slim. It's different nowadays. Rightly or wrongly, I would guide the owners along economic lines. Say surgery would cost £1,500 but there is only a 20 per cent chance of survival. The owner, if they spent that and the animal died, would not be able to replace that child's pony. Better to say, "Put it down and spend that fifteen hundred quid on a new pony." That's the way I'd guide owners. That's how I got a reputation for being trigger-happy. But I've probably changed. These days I probably wouldn't be so brutal about it. I do find it harder.'

Johnston directs my gaze towards one of his paintings. 'That's one of my quarter-horses, 22 years old, and he's got a dicky leg. My yard managers were riding him, leading yearlings, and he was getting lamer and lamer. I'll put him out in the field for winter and see if it gets better. I've had him for ten or so years. I'll probably give him to somebody who'd like him as a hack, who'd ride him very steadily. I'm slightly troubled whether that's the right thing to do, or whether I should put him down. A few years ago that's what I would have done. I'd have said, "He's worth £500 to the knacker, so take him away."'

Such beliefs were formed almost in response to his parents' attitudes, it becomes clear. 'It goes back to when I was seven or eight,' Johnston says. 'My parents weren't like that. My father definitely wasn't like that. He was desperately emotional about his animals, to a fault. He was very much one of these people that, as a vet, I certainly didn't like working with: people who would keep animals through thick and thin, trying to keep them alive, thinking they were doing them some wonderful service. I don't approve of that. If an animal died, he'd go off on a bender and literally drink for two or three days because he was so upset. I was maybe so influenced by that that I reacted against it. Like every farmer and commercial animal keeper, you have to understand that where there's life, there's death. If you hide yourself from it, you're not going to be good at keeping animals.'

Once on the subject of animal welfare, there's no holding Johnston back. Though quite how the discussion takes the tone and direction it does remains one of the great mysteries of my time with him. It's like being on a train journey. Just when you have been clack-clack-clacketing along on a slow line, enjoying the scenery, the driver of the conversation suddenly crosses on to the fast track in the direction of Controversy Central. Johnston has always questioned existing practices and perceived wisdom when it comes to the care of racehorses. I just happen to mention that there are still many ideas regarded as anachronistic. He seizes the moment.

'At a dinner the other day I sat with Harvey Smith and his son Robert,' he responds. 'I could agree with a lot that Robert (one of the country's leading showjumpers) had to say about training and keeping horses. Harvey Smith and I have almost no ideas in common. Harvey was talking about putting black sulphur on horses' legs to cure this, that and the next thing. There's a condition called rain rash, caused when a horse turned out in a period of wet weather gets this scabby condition called dermatophilus. "What do you think it is?" Harvey asked me. "Fungus," I replied. "No, it's protein coming out of them," insisted Harvey. Well, it's not, and I don't care what Harvey thinks it is.' Johnston pauses before continuing. 'There is some *rubbish* talked.

I broached the practice of firing and blistering horses. Firing is carried out on horses with tendon injuries. It involves placing an electrically heated metal plate on the outside of the leg to burn the skin (or, in the case of 'pin-firing', inserting red-hot needles through the skin to burn the tendons). The theory is that it creates scar tissue which tightens the skin around the tendon and gives support to it. Blistering is a similar procedure, except that chemicals are used. Are these practices barbaric, as some deem them? 'Possibly,' Johnston replies. 'But I'm not as dogmatic about that as I was twenty years ago, when I would have said that was a load of crap as well. There are some very good horsemen and even some good vets who still believe in blistering and firing. I don't really believe in it, but if all else fails, we send the odd horse away for firing. But it's very rare. We don't do any firing. It was banned at one time, but I'd use the same argument as I would in the fox-hunting debate: you shouldn't ban it unless you understand it. I wouldn't support a ban of firing and blistering, although we generally don't do it here. I'm not 100 per cent convinced that I understand it. I'm not 100 per cent convinced that it's wrong, or that it doesn't work.'

And that was it – the fire had been stoked.

'In the fox-hunting issue, we have allowed an ignorant minority to dictate to an educated majority. I am fiercely pro-hunting, and I don't even go. It doesn't really interest me. Deirdre and Charlie do go. I'm in favour of it because I believe fox-hunting is good for foxes. The fox is becoming a feral dog. It's becoming a dirty, scabby thing that lives in towns and scavenges out of dustbins, rather than what we know as a fox: a cunning, intelligent hunter that lives in the countryside, has a large patch of territory and is rarely seen in daylight.

'To me, one of the most misguided people in public life who talks about animal welfare is Paul McCartney. I mean, can you believe he sings songs about wanting to see sheep in the field?' Rather than carved, on his plate. I assume Johnston is alluding to the song 'Heart of the

Country', which contains the lyrics 'Want a horse, I want a sheep, / I wanna get me a good night's sleep, / Livin' in a home in the heart of the country'. 'Now *where* the hell does he think they're going to come from, and *what* does he think we're going to do with them, and *who* does he think's going to keep them in a field? As pets?' The incredulity rises. 'I've discussed this with Angus – that's ten-year-old Angus – who's obviously torn between what I say and some of the things he learns at school about animal welfare and thinks it's maybe not nice to kill animals for their meat. I say to him, "Do you not think it's nice to have cows in the field?" He says, "Yes." I say, "What are you going to do with them then?" Angus says, "Have them for milk." "What are you going to do with the male ones, then?" "Oh, keep them to breed." But I say: "You only need one male for every 50 females, so why are you going to keep them to breed? What are you going to do, marry them off and give them a semi-detached house together?" The same applies to horses. What are we going to do? Give every colt a filly?' Johnston is at top speed now, ignoring all red signals.

'There are so many cruelty and animal welfare issues that could be looked at, but governments pick and choose the ones they concentrate on, depending on the numbers and the power and influence of the people they impact upon. Some people may say, for instance, that the production of Kosher meat and the ritual slaughter that is involved is a far more important cruelty issue than fox-hunting. I don't know. I've never seen it – when I was a vet student, I missed that lecture at the abattoir – but no government would have the balls to say, or do, anything about it, anyway.'

And it's not just animals. 'Circumcision? Should people be allowed to do that to their kids in the name of religion? Or when I see a six-year-old with his or her ears pierced, I wonder whether those parents and the guy who carries it out should be allowed to do that to a small child. Is that not assault, as much as us gelding a colt or chasing a fox? If they get their backside smacked at school, the teacher'll get prosecuted for it. Yet they can put a hole in their ears.

'I sometimes have my doubts about man's association with animals. I like animals that are kept for work. That's always been the case. I like racing horses. I like racing dogs. I am appalled at the idea of people going to watch a dog fight, yet I keep a pet Staffordshire bull terrier, and I like bull terriers. The appearance of the animal appeals to me, despite the fact that I'm appalled at the job it was bred for. I like the fact that it's a bit of an athlete, albeit a bit of a fighter. I like working collies too. Working animals are usually well cared for. I don't like the idea of retired animals. I've got no problem with people having pets. They're doing a job. A cat or dog is being a companion for its owner, and it's usually well looked after too. But I cannot go along with the Paul McCartney school of thought which teaches about having sheep or cows in a field but not for a purpose. My feeling is that cruelty mostly exists wherever you have animals kept without any purpose. Cruelty in Britain is 99.9 per cent ignorance or lack of money. I don't like to see animals kept by people who are ignorant of their needs or who can't afford them.

'I have no problem with gelding horses. As I said, I don't have a lot of problem with shooting horses. But like everything, it's probably a natural progression in life. You start off communist, you end up conservative. You start off quite happy to kill things, you end up quite horrified to kill things. As I get older, I find killing things more difficult. You kill them for a reason, but I used not to think about the reason. I didn't need to think about it. Just Bang! Bang! Bang! Still, if you've got an animal suffering, you get a fantastic sense of relief from ending it. The faster you can do it the better. A thing with a leg hanging off or something – it's such a relief to hear the bang.'

We return finally to more topical themes. I suggest there could be potential among his unraced three-year-olds. 'It's not likely,' Johnston retorts. 'Most good three-year-olds have shown good two-year-old form.' Nevertheless, he is unrelenting in his search for that elusive surprise Classic package. 'I pencilled in a horse named Magic Moth to be entered for the Derby the other day,' Johnston tells me, matter-of-factly. (He swiftly adds that he would not have told me if I had been writing a newspaper article. 'The handicapper tends to pick up on these things, you see.') The horse had won on the all-weather first time out at Wolverhampton, by a length. 'But then Debbie told me, "You *can't* do that. He's only rated 72. He'll be put up to 92 (an increase of 20lb in the handicap) if he wins another race." I said, "You're right. We'll just go handicapping with it, and won't bother entering it for the Derby."'

But why even *consider* entering such a horse for the Derby? The question had to be asked.

'Because I think he may be that good.'

Why were you persuaded not to then?

'Because he probably *isn't* that good,' explains Johnston patiently, if a little perversely. 'If he *is* that good, OK, he'll win the Arc (the Prix de L'Arc de Triomphe, run at Longchamp in October). But he will have won five handicaps en route and had a shot at the Arc free, instead of gambling away a daft entry fee to put him in the Derby. It would be very expensive (requiring a £20,000 supplementary fee). It's crazy.' It's one of Johnston's bugbears that major races have too early closing dates. To miss them means stumping up a hefty supplement.

In an attempt to turn to more positive matters, I recall the conversation we had about his two-year-olds. Yet, here again, already his best-laid plans have gone awry. 'I think they're a lovely bunch, but we've already come unstuck with this number one group (the potential early runners). We thought we'd sorted out two or three, but none of them is fit to run for various reasons. One banged his head and his nose bled, otherwise he might have run at Redcar. Another we had made entries for is lame, so that's scuppered that.' It clearly irks the master of Kingsley House to admit it, but he says candidly, 'We're struggling to get our first runner. When you think we've nearly a hundred two-year-olds, we *shouldn't* be struggling to get our first runner. So we're not as far ahead as we thought we were. I still think it's a nice bunch. There are lots we like, but nothing we think is so sharp that it's time to get it out now.'

Not that his name has ever been synonymous with precocious two-year-olds, I remind him. He concurs, readily. 'I remember Mark Tompkins (the Newmarket trainer) standing next to me at Redcar for the Brocklesby, and he said, "I *can't* buy another two-year-old. I may be sent one or two, but I *cannot* bring myself to buy a little fat runt that isn't going to grow." Well, neither can I. I want big, imposing horses. If you go out there (in the yard), they're all big. Or the vast majority of them are.'

It is true. Almost without exception, they have magnitude and, just as importantly, scope. As one television pundit expressed it excellently, 'You always feel as though the Johnston horses have been standing in Gro-Bags.'

'The Jack Berry early type has never been my style,' Johnston adds, 'not even when I had one grand to spend on a horse'. So, how does that policy satisfy impatient owners, ones who demand swift success? 'There are those kinds of owners around, but they're not here.'

CHAPTER TWELVE

It's been a terrible three weeks. I think we're down to a strike rate
of 5 per cent, or maybe even 3 per cent in the last two weeks.
It's as bad as it's ever been. It's one winner from 33 runners over
a two-week period. That's pretty horrendous.

Sometimes, the best-laid preparations can rebound on you. The belief that sustains a racehorse trainer through the winter can disintegrate, cruelly and without warning. Then you can understand why they envelop their hopes and dreams in the cotton wool of circumspection.

The 2,000 Guineas is looming ever closer, and Nakheel is not working like a fancied contender. In truth, he's not so much working as suffering. As Mark Johnston tells the *Racing Post* for its 18 April issue, 'Nakheel worked disappointingly on Friday and was feeling pretty sorry for himself afterwards and was off his food. It would be wrong to say that a Guineas bid is on hold, but it is still a worry with the Classic less than three weeks away, and there is no point in galloping him at Newmarket or anywhere else until he perks up. I will talk to Angus Gold (Sheikh Hamdan's racing manager) when he returns from Australia this week and we will review the situation.'

Johnston arrives at Newmarket on the Thursday of the Craven meeting, where we have arranged to meet, having spent the morning at Newsells Park Stud in Royston, Hertfordshire, looking at the foals. It is a welcome distraction and brightens his mood on arrival at the track. He has trained for the owners of the stud, Klaus and Renata Jacobs, for two seasons. Their horses include Soapy Danger and Linas Selection. The former had prevailed in a one-mile-four-furlong handicap the previous day at Beverley, prompting the following in the Form Book notebook: 'There should be plenty more where this came from.' 'Mr Jacobs likes me to go and have a look at the foals and yearlings with him,' Johnston explains. 'I hope it's useful for him. It's certainly interesting for me.'

He is further cheered when Atlantic Waves thrusts no more than two flared nostrils in front of his four nearest rivals at the business end of the Feilden Stakes. It is a gutsy performance by the colt, owned by the Dubai-based Jaber Abdullah, a friend of the Maktoum family. Atlantic Waves had looked beaten, but under jockey Joe Fanning's galvanising drive he just prevailed in this Listed event, which is a traditional Classic trial.

We turn to Nakheel. Johnston's silent prayer is that the colt has only suffered a muscle injury. However, he is to undergo a precautionary bone scan in Newmarket. 'He's already had an ultrasound scan and X-rays taken of his hind limbs, and nothing was found, but this is to make doubly sure,' says Johnston. 'Ninety-nine times out of a hundred when someone says a horse has pulled a muscle, it hasn't. Because I know that, I never say they've got a muscle injury. But that was the hope. He was sore all over, hind end and front, and he was off his food, looking like a horse who had really hurt himself galloping. If the scan shows up nothing, and that's all it was, we'll be back in business in a week. If not, and it's something more serious, well, it's heartbreaking at this time of year, and frustrating.' He could conceivably be back in time for Epsom. 'I'm not sure,' Johnston responds. 'He's a sharper horse than this fellow (Atlantic Waves). He's more of a Guineas horse than Atlantic Waves ever was. I wouldn't want to miss the Guineas with Nakheel. But the cut-off point will come next week.'

Curiously, doubts over Nakheel haven't inhibited the sustained nibbling at him by investors in the 2,000 Guineas market. He is as short as 10–1. Atlantic Waves had been backed for the Derby, although today's performance hasn't caused those odds to be trimmed. 'It still doesn't make sense to me that Nakheel has been a market mover, because nothing has changed since his run at Pontefract (the previous October),' says Johnston. 'You know, it reminds me of a horse called Beware Of Agents that we had in the early nineties,' he adds wryly. 'At one stage he was the gambled-on horse in the Lincoln. At the time, do you know where he was? He was out in the field. It was just ridiculous. The bookmakers would deny it, but I remember thinking that they were sitting there thinking, "We've got to drum up some business. How are we going to do it?" It was almost like a marketing exercise. They pick on something, bring it down in the odds, and the rest of the money follows. I'm not sure if any of that goes on, but there was certainly no logic about those horses tumbling in the betting at this stage. Clearly, after today, there is logic that Atlantic Waves will now go to the Derby. But it wasn't certain two weeks ago.'

But will Atlantic Waves travel with stable optimism? 'It's a long way from a Listed race to the Derby, but we learnt a lot, that was the important thing. We were open-minded whether he was to run in the Derby or the Guineas. I think that probably put it to bed. You'd just have to think the Guineas would be too sharp for him.' And forcing the pace is the best tactic? 'I hate building characteristics into horses that have had just three runs and two wins. I'm sure the majority of other trainers would have watched that and said, "I'm sure the horse could have been doing with a lead and a stronger pace." So I'm not going to say that he must bowl along *in front*. But he does need to bowl along; he doesn't need to be held up for a sprint. He takes longer than others to engage top gear. He did get headed, but he came back. I did think he was going best at the finish.'

Atlantic Waves is one of the few stable stars glittering on an increasingly cloudy night. By now it has also been revealed that Black Charmer will be denied a tilt at the Guineas, having cracked a cannon bone and suffered an abscess. Johnston has a high opinion of the colt he describes as 'too often the bridesmaid, but actually ultra-consistent in Group races'. And the previous afternoon Baan had performed disappointingly in the Free Handicap. 'I'm not despondent; it was just too short for him,' says the trainer. 'He's been working very well at home. He ran his usual, very game, solid race. I knew I was taking liberties, because he needs another three furlongs minimum. But it looked a moderate Free Handicap.' He shrugs, as if to say, when the fates conspire against you, it can be unrelenting. 'I also had a filly, Happy Love, here yesterday who chipped a knee and went lame at the end,' he adds.

Despite the excuse of injury for all those representatives, overall Johnston is decidedly discontented with the first act of this season's production by the Kingsley House players. Results have been indifferent, runners far too few. As we sit outside the weighing room at

Newmarket taking stock of recent developments, I sense that if he was Andrew Lloyd Webber he'd bring the curtain down, claim it was only a dress rehearsal, and start again.

Back at home, the hills of Middleham are far from alive with the sound of stirring triumphalism. Johnston's not quite become the professional pessimist portrayed by his compatriot John Laurie as Private 'We're doomed' Frazer in *Dad's Army*. This is not yet a moment for mental wrist-slitting, but he is definitely subdued. 'It's been a terrible three weeks,' he says. 'I think we're down to a strike rate of 5 per cent, or maybe even 3 per cent in the last two weeks. It's as bad as it's ever been. It's one winner from 33 runners over a two-week period. That's pretty horrendous.' As always, statistics rate as more significant than impressions. 'Our overall percentage is very good, because we had a staggeringly good January and February. We had something like 50 per cent winners and 75 per cent places, which is incredible. But in the last month we've been down to under 25 per cent of our horses being placed, which is terrible.'

I tentatively raise the vexed issue of 'the virus'. Along with 'the cough', it is an expression no owner wants to hear. It has become a catch-all excuse for their horses being confined to quarters. Johnston is just short of contemptuous at the word. 'People talk about the virus and stuff, but I've always thought that's the biggest load of crap.' (Yes, he is rather fond of the Ratner word.) 'While there might be, at times, elements of an infection that make the horses perform below their best, it tends to be what I call a "poor performance syndrome". You can't have as many horses as we've got and they're all off colour. It can't affect the whole lot.' He smiles, and adds ruefully, 'Not unless its bubonic plague.'

I look for encouraging signs anywhere within the yard, but find none. I wonder out loud if in such circumstances all you can do is plod on until your fortunes turn. 'You do,' Johnston agrees, 'though the first reaction of most people – and I see it all around me in the yard from my staff – is not to have runners. I'm sure it's the case with other trainers. In really bad cases they shut down for a month, or whatever.' Indeed, Godolphin, suffering from a similar run of form, would proceed to do just that. At the end of May, a *Racing Post* headline would reveal that

'Godolphin shut stable in bid to find cause of wretched form' after just one winner from twelve runners. And there would be a certain irony in the fact that Godolphin's only intended Derby runner, the ex-Johnston-trained Winged Cupid, would be withdrawn. 'Nothing has come to light, but something is affecting them,' Godolphin's racing manager Simon Crisford would comment.

But Johnston is not a supporter of such a policy. 'My reaction is that my horses won't win if I don't run them,' he says. 'They won't lose if I don't run them either, but to me that's a defeatist attitude, simply to hide them away.' He tells how, towards the end of the season, when he is away at the sales, he has often discovered that some of his horses have gone home to their owners. 'My staff go racing with them, they run moderately, and the easiest thing to say is that they've had enough for the season. It's very easy *not* to run them.' Despite the obvious value of having both sophisticated veterinary technology on site, and the vets to employ it, Johnston actually suggests that that will reduce a yard's success rate. 'They don't actually produce more winners,' he says. 'Increase the vets you have and I will guarantee that will reduce the number of winners because it decreases the number of runners. Vets don't tell you that horses *should* be running. They are more likely to say, "You can't run that." However, what I will say is that we have almost certainly reduced our catastrophic accidents because we're spotting things earlier.'

It's a bit like kicking a man when he's down, but what the hell. I broach the subject of two of his horses, both odds-on shots, one of them at 1–6, that were turned over recently at Southwell. 'Mmm,' Johnston says. 'Well, it wasn't raceable that day. Anyway, one of them's dead, and the other was second next time out. That wasn't about unwell horses that day – although the dead one may have been unwell, obviously.' The gallows humour referred to the aforementioned Shalapour, Markus Graff's colt, who had collapsed at the end of a subsequent canter.

His death reminded Johnston of a discussion we had had about racing regulations. He has particular antipathy for the rule which states that trainers should offer an explanation for a bad run. According to the Form Book, the official explanation given after the race by Johnston was this: 'the trainer was unable to offer any explanation for poor form shown'. 'Slightly tongue in cheek,' says Johnston mischievously. 'After Shalapour died we did phone the Jockey Club and told them, "We were asked if there was anything to explain its poor performance when it got beat at Southwell when it was 6–1 on. Well, there is. It's dead." The fellow who answered told me drily, "We don't need to know that."' You actually phoned to tell them that? There is an expression of mock outrage. 'You're supposed to, if something comes to light, at the time or afterwards, that might explain the bad run. It's for integrity reasons, to ensure that nothing happened untoward on the day.'

Away from the racecourse, Johnston has donned his political hat again. The 48-hour declaration issue has rumbled on; it appears certain to come into effect. It is not a matter likely to exercise racegoers or punters, except that bringing forward the declaration time so drastically is likely to mean that there will be more non-runners – as, indeed, has been proved since its implementation. There is more time for going conditions to change and for injuries to horses to occur. The move had been sought by the racecourses, allied to the satellite broadcasters At The Races and Racing UK. Their claim was that it would help market British racing abroad. A figure of £3 million was mooted. The National Trainers' Federation (NTF), of which Johnston is a past president, was vehemently opposed.

Johnston helped to man the barricades by representing the NTF – instead of chief executive Rupert Arnold, who was on holiday – in a meeting with the British Horseracing Board, when the implementation of an earlier declaration time was discussed. There had been suggestions that the training fraternity preferred Johnston to put their point of view across because he was a stronger advocate. However, he claimed, 'It's not my intention to give them a hard time. We just want them to see the trainers' point of view.' But even a vociferous appeal from the Scot failed to open closed minds. 'I went to the board meeting and said my piece, but probably not well enough,' he says. 'I feel more effort could have been made to sell British racing to the US on the basis of 24-hour declarations. Even those in favour admit there is not a US market; some say there's no Australian market. We all know, at the moment, there's no Asian market, so why are we doing it?'

Essentially, Johnston believes that trainers are being asked to make radical changes in their race-planning processes without any guarantee of income from abroad. 'Before you address foreign markets,' he asks, 'what about Britain? How is it going to improve things here? Are we going to improve British betting turnover by dumbing it down all the time (with an increase in all-weather racing)? My attitude is, cure the bloody disease before you start getting into another market. I went to Kempton the other day. I found it quite depressing really. In the early days of all-weather I was certainly in favour of it, but the beginning of this season has been such a damp squib. It's made me think, "What are we doing?" It's all very well going for all-weather racing like America, and 48-hour declarations like South Africa and Dubai, but if we start going for common denominators, the biggest weakness in Britain is that we don't have the prize money that these countries have. Why should anyone race at Kempton when they can race at Maryland or some other state in the US for twice the prize money?'

Johnston comes to a halt, rather reluctantly. The trainer recognises when he is over-egging the political pudding. After all, he has made a genuine attempt to remove himself from that particular overheated kitchen – although it's a topic he can't resist revisiting from time to time, as we will see. 'I was president of the National Trainers' Federation last year,' he says. 'Now I'm past president, which makes me a wee bit more than a council member. I'd had enough, and was trying to take more of a back seat.' He laughs at how ridiculous that sounds. 'Don't know whether I can or not.' Almost certainly not – that is quite evident. Johnston is like a pugilist, constantly in search of a corner from which to trade blows.

'I still feel slightly frustrated that I achieved more through my *Racing Post* column than through the proper channels, through the NTF,' he continues. 'Issues like 48-hour declarations and narrow-band handicaps I really fought hard on, and, more recently, the installation of the new (Steriline) starting stalls.' Johnston elaborates on the latter issue, in the process providing an insight into just how forensically he will examine a subject in order to prosecute his case. There had been incidents of horses being hurt and jockeys and stall-handlers being injured using those Australian-manufactured stalls. 'Now, I was not affected by this myself,' he stresses. 'None of my horses were injured in the stalls, but I was dragged along to a meeting with the Jockey Club. I was just going to take a back seat. It was nothing really to do with me.

'Typically for the Jockey Club, they were trying to blame problems with the stalls on trainers not having their horses schooled properly. They told us that incidents under rule 8 (trainers having to have a stalls test) "gradually deteriorated" from 1 in 196 to 1 in 144 in 2005 (when they last reviewed the penalties for trainers). Although using two different types of stalls, the number of incidents were evenly spread. This showed "categorically" that problems were down to the trainers, not the stalls. But their data man was there. In response to my questions, he revealed that in 2003, the figures were 1 in 191, and in 2004, 1 in 198. It hadn't got "gradually" worse, it had got suddenly worse in 2005, when there was the introduction of the new stalls. I questioned him on the number of runners going through each kind of stalls. What were the chances of having an incident in the old stalls against one in the new stalls? He said that the chances in the old stalls were 21 per cent, and in the new stalls 32 per cent. You might say those are tiny figures, yet it means that you were one and a half times more likely to have a problem in the new stalls.

'The Jockey Club had presented the facts as though it was the trainers' fault. They were trying to hide from the fact that they made an error with the new stalls, and were trying to cover it up. I had turned up prepared to just watch, but I cannot help but argue the toss. I just can't help myself. I enjoy it.'

But back to more immediate matters. Three days later, the wait for the specialists' verdict on Nakheel is over. Johnston's worst fears are confirmed. It has required a nuclear bone scan to determine that Nakheel is suffering from a stress fracture of the pelvis. The *Racing Post* of 23 April carries the following:

Nakheel has been ruled out of the 2,000 Guineas and looks extremely doubtful for the Derby after a bone scan revealed a problem with the Mark Johnston-trained colt.

The son of Sadler's Wells, a 12–1 shot for the Stan James-sponsored Classic, had been well backed for the Guineas during the spring, and his absence is the latest blow to ante-post punters following Greek Well's defection from the Derby and a string of high-profile casualties during the jumps season.

Nakheel was due to gallop at Newmarket on Thursday, but that plan had to be abandoned after he returned stiff and sore and failed to eat up after working at Middleham over a week ago.

He was sent to the Animal Health Trust in Newmarket for tests and Johnston said yesterday, 'The bone scan was positive and revealed a hot spot on the pelvis. Nakheel is undergoing further investigation in Newmarket and we hope to have a bit more news next week, but he has been ruled out of the 2,000 Guineas and will have a campaign in the second half of the season.'

On 2,000 Guineas day itself, Johnston is only a spectator watching George Washington cut down the field, allaying concerns that the Ballydoyle colt may have been deficient in stamina. The previous year's champion two-year-old inflicts a brutal execution of his rivals with Classic pretensions. George Washington is adjudged by the stopwatch and form wizards to be the most impressive victor in ten years. Certainly we are to hear considerably more of the runner-up, Sir Percy. As we know, Johnston is highly sceptical about the comparison of generations, but there is no doubt that Aidan O'Brien's colt has made a presidential impression.

One suspects that Nakheel, even fully fit, would have struggled to repel that turn of foot in the last couple of furlongs, but Johnston is reluctant to speculate, except to say, 'Over the winter we were definitely quite bullish. He was the best of our two-year-olds. But based on what we have seen from Nakheel earlier this spring, no, he wouldn't have won the Guineas. But that was because he was almost certainly carrying an injury.' Johnston also reveals that Atlantic Waves worked better than Nakheel in three pieces of work together earlier in the season. 'In that first gallop, Nakheel was travelling so well and then just downed tools. I just thought he was tired. By the end of the last piece of work, he walked off lame, and I just wonder whether that pelvis problem was troubling him even then. Of course, we also had no idea whether he could make the leap from Listed race to Group 1. As I've said, that is not a common thing for us to do. It was always going to be the big unknown.'

And it would remain so, at least for the time being, as Johnston prepared for the next colts' Classic. That most evocative name in British Flat racing, the Derby, beckoned.

CHAPTER THIRTEEN

"We do fall out occasionally. Sometimes it gets a bit heated. But it seems to work. I think he likes someone to take him on." – Debbie Albion, administrative manager at Kingsley House.

Tuesday morning, four days before the Derby, around 6.30 a.m. in the kitchen-cum-control centre of Kingsley House. This is the day of the weekly yard managers meeting, but first Mark Johnston confirms the following days' runners with Debbie Albion. And not merely the following day's entries but those who may contest Royal Ascot, like Winged D'Argent, who returned to form the previous evening at Sandown with a game second place in the Henry II Stakes, and is bound for the Gold Cup. 'If that had been Royal Rebel (the Peter Savill-owned two-time winner of the Royal Ascot centrepiece) you'd say he was going to *win* the Gold Cup,' growls Johnston defiantly of a race he regards almost proprietorily.

The cleaner tidies around the trainer as he scans a computer print-out of statistics with the intensity of a laboratory scientist. The family dogs seek their master's attention but get absolutely none for their troubles. Fudge, an Irish terrier, notionally belongs to Deirdre, I'm told; Gnasher (named after Dennis the Menace's dog), a ferocious-looking but thoroughly amiable Staffordshire bull terrier, is Johnston's. Gnasher has an ugly row of stitches in his features. Kicked by a horse recently, I am told; fractured his cheekbone; a natural hazard in a racing yard. There is not a great deal of sympathy. He's learnt a harsh lesson.

The Johnstons' youngest son Angus enters, complaining about a lack of clean socks in his drawer. As his father peruses entries worth potentially many thousands of pounds in prize money, and even more in stud and paddock values, it's possibly not the best timing. Johnston is unmoved by his son's plight. Meanwhile, his elder son, Charlie, avidly scans the *Racing Post* and attempts to place the yard's recent indifferent run into perspective by declaring that Mick Channon hasn't had a rewarding time of it recently either. It isn't much consolation for anyone. Both trainers have had 232 runners. Johnston has amassed 31 winners, a 13 per cent strike rate; Channon's tally is only 25 victories at 11 per cent.

In fact, take a snapshot of statistics on Monday, 29 May 2006 and scrutinise the whole list, and you discover many illustrious names, including Classic-winning trainers, where you don't really expect to find them. Among them Paul Cole, with 12 from 80; John Dunlop on 11 winners from 104 runners, at 11 per cent; Luca Cumani, only 43 runners, but 12 victories. Henry Cecil, who later in the year would celebrate the 3,000th winner of his distinguished career, is not even in sight at this stage on the *Racing Post*'s stats page. Last season he had a total of only ten winners, and this a character who once instilled fear in the opposition whenever he introduced an unraced two-year-old and whose Classic victories stand at 23 domestic and eleven in Ireland and France. All those trainers can offer explanations. Often it is the departure of an important and influential owner. Yet, in this harsh, ever-changing landscape of Flat horseracing, Johnston is one of the few constants. Those figures, though, are a constant reminder of the precarious nature of the business.

Coffee and tea are taken, but there is no sign of breakfast. 'At the yard managers meeting,' I'm told tersely. 'Get your own. Let's go.' Johnston gathers sheaves of paper into his arms. He puts me in mind of a general preparing to address his chiefs of staff.

We decamp over the road, to Riders, the staff café. You don't see too much evidence of the healthy option. Sausage butties, hand-sculpted caringly by each member of staff, are consumed with relish, and tea is swilled as the yard managers, the vets and Deirdre assemble. One of the vets is James Tate, the son of trainer Tom and nephew of Michael Dickinson. He is also married to trainer Len Lungo's younger daughter Lucinda. Oh, and he also rides as an amateur. Seemingly, he is handcuffed to horseracing whichever way he turns, though he appears a willing enough prisoner. James usually travels with the trainer on his sales expeditions. 'He'll make a good trainer one day,' mutters Johnston.

The previous night, Johnston had outlined how the yard managers, the equivalent of seven department heads in an office environment, came into being. The structure was introduced around the turn of the millennium. Godolphin has a similar hierarchy, though their top staff are referred to as 'barn managers'. 'When we first came to Middleham, the structure was me, Deirdre, a head lad, who was Declan Condell, and an assistant head lad,' he says. 'Everybody was answerable to the person above him. Then we went to head lad, two assistant head lads, and two enormous teams of people beneath them. At one time we had a vet-cum-assistant trainer, who was James Given, a head lad, and two assistant head lads. But in reality it was just an opportunity for folk to pass the buck. Anything that was wrong was always somebody else's fault. It took me a while to realise it just didn't work.

'I was at the sales one day with John Warren, quite a demanding manager who manages for Lord Hartington and the Duke of Roxburghe. John kept asking me questions, like "How did they gallop last week?" I had to phone somebody to check that out. "What weight was he today?" I had to phone somebody else to check that out. There were three or four different questions and I had to phone three or four different people. I realised that was wrong. One person should know the answer to all those questions, and not one person who's got 150 horses under him. It should be one person who's got 30 horses.

'The vet/assistant trainer was done away with once James Given left. The danger was that the vet wouldn't want to do any vet work. Although ours are based here, they operate like an outside vet. Each yard manager is responsible for everything in his or her yard. There's no way the yard manager can say, "Oh, the groom did that; I didn't know about it." The yard manager cannot say, "The vet's dealing with that." He's responsible for whether it's been wormed or vaccinated. He *cannot* pass the buck. If the vet is called because a horse is injured and he diagnoses it and treats it, it is still the yard manager's job to know what he did, what he gave it and what he's got to do with it.'

Initially, Johnston split the operation into four yards and created a new staff bonus system. Flaws in that scheme soon became apparent. 'Originally, all staff were on a straightforward tenner a winner. Now we said that the winner bonus wouldn't be £10, but £40, except it would only apply to winners from the yard responsible for that horse. We realised by the end of the first year that it was not right. The people in charge of two-year-olds are usually the best people, but they were getting fewer winners because two-year-olds don't win as many races as older horses, just as fillies don't win as many races as colts. And there was another problem. Brendan Holland had been head lad prior to the change-around. He effectively got a demotion. He was suddenly one of four yard managers. So, say he had an empty box in his yard. He would see that a particular yard manager across the road had an entry in three weeks' time, and he fancied the horse could win. Well, he'd go and nick it from him. Move it to his yard. And his team got that winner's bonus. People would go on holiday and half their best horses would be missing because Brendan had swapped them with ones in his yard! So we changed back to ten quid, and it applied to all the yards on the principle that we all have to work together for a winner. At the moment, winners' bonuses range from a fiver to £20.'

Johnston admits it has all been a continual process of trial and error and changing systems. His principal aim has always been to increase everyone's degree of responsibility. 'I want to improve the business by pushing that responsibility further down the line. That's the hardest thing to do.'

Back to the business of today, and there is a scraping of chairs in a side room of the establishment as seats are occupied, but not much chat. The tone is subdued, the atmosphere reminiscent of a hushed courtroom before the judge arrives to pronounce sentence. His Honour strides in, grim-featured, armed with the evidence – or statistics, at least – and a head buzzing like a wasps' nest with irritation. Or so you suspect.

The yard managers have varied backgrounds. Before the meeting I glanced at their profiles produced in the yard's monthly house magazine the *Kingsley Klarion* (no prizes for guessing its columnist). These are Johnston's yard managers, with edited Q & A's from the Klarion at the time of writing.

Andrew Bottomley (born 3 May 1968, Malton, North Yorkshire), the son of a trainer, was employed directly by Johnston. 'He was out of racing before he came here,' says Johnston. 'He was working in a factory. We think of him as the "ideas" man, always coming up with something new. A lot of man-management stuff he got from working in the factory.'

What attracted you to the racing industry, and how did you first get involved with horses?

My dad has worked in racing since he was twelve years old, first as stable lad and then progressing through head lad to the position of trainer. As far back as I can remember the topic of conversation in our house was always racing. So I think from an early age my fate was sealed.

Who is your racing hero/heroine, and why?

Without a doubt, Steve Cauthen. I regard him as the best judge of a horse ever to get a leg up. And also my old boss Keith Stone, who was brave/stupid enough to let me loose on a racetrack for the first time ... and to expect me to negotiate eight flights of hurdles on the way round!

What was your best day in racing?

Newmarket, 28 August 1989. My dad trained his first winner that day. It was a £25k Nursery live on Channel 4. The whole yard was on at 33–1 in the morning! The race was run in a torrential downpour, so when we returned to unsaddle the July Course was deserted except for us poor devils drenched through to the skin, singing and dancing in the winner's enclosure. Priceless!

And your worst?

Riding an odds-on shot for my dad in a three-runner race at Leicester, and getting beat. I'm not saying he took it badly, but I remember it was a long, lonely walk home up the A1 that night.

If you were given the power to change one thing about the racing industry as a whole or your job in particular, what would you change?

I would love to see stewards accept that racing never has been and never will be a non-contact sport.

Andy Larnach (born 12 May 1971, County Durham) is a former jump jockey who rode for the late Arthur Stephenson.

What attracted you to racing?
It was my father – his hobby and interest.
Biggest achievement in racing to date?

To have ridden on every jump track in the country.
Best day in racing?
Riding my first winner on one of my father's horses.
Worst day?
The day W. A. Stephenson passed away (my old boss).
Racing hero?
John Francome – great judge, fantastic horseman.

Chandrapal Singh (born 1 March 1979, Bankli, India) comes from a famous racing family in India. 'I was born into a family which has produced four trainers,' he says. 'At a very young age I got involved with horses, so young that I don't remember when or how. I suppose I'm just following in the family footsteps. I lost one of my brothers on the racetrack due to a fall.'

Who is your racing hero/heroine?
It has to be my grandfather. He won every Indian Classic three times (1,000 Guineas, 2,000 Guineas, Oaks, Derby and St Leger) with fillies.

Carrie Sanderson (born 19 March 1981, Glasgow). 'Became a yard manager on 1 February, when Gail Alderson left,' says Johnston. 'She's been here since sixteen and applied for the job last time when it was available, but didn't get it because somebody else had more experience. Carrie had a race ride for us, and went to the British Racing School. She looked after both Yavana's Pace and Attraction.'

What attracted you to the racing industry, and how did you first get involved with horses?
When I was young I always watched racing on television, unless I was helping out at the local stables. When I turned sixteen I went to the British Racing School in Newmarket and was lucky enough to get a job with MJR.
Who is your racing hero/heroine, and why?
John Francome. He was a great jockey and I think he talks a lot of sense.
What is the best thing about your job?

I think the best part is working with the yearlings when they first arrive at the stables, watching them develop and eventually seeing them run on the racecourse.

Penny Skilton (born 21 May 1969, Leicester). 'She's in charge of the out-of-training horses,' says Johnston. 'Anything that's sick, injured, in a field, anything like that. She's degree-educated and came from a riding school teacher background. Originally came as a yard foreman, the non-horse work, in charge of the mucking-out teams during the day when the strings are out, and involved with ordering of feed, fodder and so on.'

What attracted you to the racing industry, and how did you first get involved with horses?
I was a horse-mad child and learnt to ride at the age of eleven. After completing my A levels I trained for my riding instructor's certificate (BHSAI). It was the job description, the location and the very positive reputation of MJR that attracted me to Kingsley House rather than the racing industry itself.

Who is your racing hero/heroine, and why?
I don't have one. My childhood heroes were eventers and showjumpers like Lucinda Green and Eddie Macken, both of whom were supreme stylists at their respective sports.

What do you consider your biggest achievement in racing to date?
It would have to be getting this job. I've never done anything else in racing prior to this!

What was your best day in racing?
Attraction winning the 1,000 Guineas at Newmarket (in 2004). The atmosphere on the yard that evening was great!

Jane Hedley (born 22 April 1977, Edinburgh) came to the yard from Hamdan Al Maktoum's breeding empire Shadwell Estate, in Newmarket, where she was involved in marketing and nominating. Other yards she has worked at include Henrietta Knight's stables in East Hendred.

What attracted you to racing?
I grew up on a farm and we always had horses around. I do

remember idolising Desert Orchid aged eleven or twelve to the point that I couldn't bear to watch him run. I was a very boring teenager, preferring to stay in on Saturday nights watching re-runs of the day's racing while my schoolmates were out discovering pubs.

Racing hero/heroine?

The Henrietta Knight/Terry Biddlecombe combination. They knew with an absolute, unwavering certainty from the first day they set eyes on Best Mate that he was a Gold Cup winner in the making, and planned his entire career accordingly. To achieve that goal and bring him to his peak on one day in March for three successive years was a magnificent achievement and I sincerely believe that it wouldn't have happened had the horse been in any other hands.

Biggest achievement in racing to date?

I have been involved with some of the leading horses in recent years. I have sat on the likes of Best Mate (triple Gold Cup Winner), Rooster Booster (Champion Hurdler), Edredon Bleu (Champion Chaser), Chorist (multiple Group winner), Saluter (six times Virginia Gold Cup Winner) and Les Arcs (July Cup Winner). I'd love to add a Classic winner to the CV.

Hobbies outside racing?

This job gives you a healthy appetite, and I love my food. I'm a keen cook. But I miss my hunting these days. I used to go around twenty days per season, but unfortunately it doesn't really fit around racing hours.

Best thing about your job?

Fresh air, exercise, stunning surroundings and quality horses.

Worst thing?

I find injuries, both to horses and humans, pretty hard to deal with. I suppose they are part and parcel of the game, but at the same time I don't like to see people cutting corners and taking chances.

Best day in racing?

I don't think anyone forgets riding their first ever winner. Mine was in a modest point-to-point at Friars Haugh, but the yard I was riding for had a treble on the day and a serious amount of champagne was consumed that night.

Worst day?

I had a broken collarbone point-to-pointing and had to watch my good horse being ridden by someone else. He broke down very badly and in the end had to be shot. I'll never forget him resting his head on my good arm while the vets tried to patch him up. It was absolutely heart-breaking. I was inconsolable for weeks.

If you were given the power to change one thing about the racing industry as a whole or your job in particular, what would you change?

The hours. In this particular job, they are very good, probably the best in the country, but the way hours are structured in the industry as a whole means that it is virtually impossible to have a life outside work. We get a good block of time off in the afternoon, but unfortunately the rest of the world is at work. Looking at the same old faces thirteen days out of every fourteen can get pretty wearing and can make for a fairly lonely existence. I sincerely believe that if some way could be found to make the hours more sociable many of the problems relating to staff morale and retention would be instantly solved.

David MacLeod (born 29 October 1956, Perth) trained at Lauder, in the Scottish Borders, before joining the yard this season.

What attracted you to racing?

The owner of the estate where we lived had horses and ponies and asked me when I was nine if I would like to help out in the yard. She taught me to ride and gave me a pony of my own, which I hunted and took to shows.

Racing hero/heroine?

Pat Eddery – a true professional.

Hobbies outside racing?

Bit of golf, fly fishing, Scottish history.

Biggest achievement in racing to date?

Getting a horse called Billy Two Rivers to win a race. He was a chronic windsucker, and had ulcers and colic. In the end he lived in a field and was only ever fed pony nuts.

Best day in racing?

Getting my first ride over hurdles.

Worst day?

Whenever a horse you are close to has a fatal accident. I have had a few worst days.

Brian 'Jock' Bennett, Johnston's assistant, was born on 8 December 1956 in Edinburgh. 'He came here as deputy head lad, having been (travelling) head lad for Bill Watts,' says Johnston. 'He had been at Hurgill Lodge since he was an apprentice jockey. When Bill Watts packed in, Jock moved here.' Although Johnston believes that the best staff training is the one they receive at Kingsley House, he made an exception with Bennett, who learnt his skills under a trainer he hugely respected.

Bennett had only two rides in public. 'I knew I was never going to be the greatest jockey in the world,' he says, 'but in those days competition was fierce. At Bill Watts's yard I was just one of eight apprentices looking for rides, and as one or two of the other lads had already been among the winners I was always going to struggle for rides.'

What is the best thing about your job in racing?

It's a great feeling seeing any of our top horses achieve at the highest of levels. Obviously Attraction last year was the prime example of that. I also enjoy seeing the younger members of staff learn and develop. I enjoy seeing how the whole team thing works, and watching the kids get on.

What was your best day in racing?

I enjoyed many happy years with Bill Watts, and my time there was capped by Teleprompter's win in the Arlington Million. A great day.

And your worst?

I suppose any day when you head off to the races full of hope and have to come back without a horse. It's hard to take and never gets any easier to accept.

If you were given the power to change one thing about the racing industry as a whole or your job in particular, what would you change?

I'd like to see more experienced racing professionals engaged in stewarding and racing administration. There is a vast pool of experience to draw upon.

Debbie Albion is also a vital component in the operation. She originally worked for Captain Ryan Price, who was five times the National Hunt champion trainer between 1954 and 1967 before turning to the Flat.

With Pepe, on holiday at Arisaig
in the West Highlands of Scotland.

Mark takes a view on the world. Taking a break from
his studies as a Glasgow veterinary student at the top
of the Eiffel Tower.

Proud day. Mark graduates from Glasgow
Veterinary College.

Another cause for celebration. Deirdre's
graduation day.

Above left: *Aboard the love boat on Loch Achray. Mark and Deirdre on their wedding day.*

Above right: *Charlie Johnston gets a ride from jockey Jason Weaver.*

Right: *Mark with the Scallywag colt he bred. He kept it on a client's farm when he was in vet practice in Essex. It would later be named Rapscallion and would be one of the horses he trained at his first stables in Lincolnshire.*

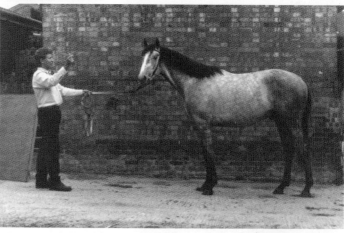

Right: *Up a telegraph pole, watching his horses. It provided a useful vantage point when he trained at Bank End Stables in Lincolnshire.*

Top: *Mark's first winner. Hinari Video, at Carlisle, on July 1, 1987. On the left is owner and then business partner, Brian Palmer.*

Middle: *What a feeling. Mark (punching the air) celebrates his first classic winner, Mister Baileys' 2,000 Guineas triumph at Newmarket in 1994.*

Bottom: *Deirdre celebrates with owner Paul Venner (of Baileys Horse Feeds) after Mister Baileys wins the 2,000 Guineas.*

Right: *In perfect harmony. Attraction on the Middleham gallops, ridden by Deirdre.*

Middle: *Attraction strikes for home to maintain her unbeaten record in the Irish 1,000 Guineas at The Curragh in May 2004.*

Bottom left: *The centre of Attraction. Deirdre with sons, Charlie and Angus. On the right is the horse's groom, Carrie Sanderson. She is now a yard manager at Kingsley House.*

Bottom right: *A great day out for the Johnstons. Mark, Angus, Charlie and Deirdre on Irish 1,000 Guineas day.*

Left: *The fashion stakes. Deirdre prepares to saddle a runner at Royal Ascot in 2004.*

Above: *The dream team. Mark and Deirdre with Attraction at Newmarket.*

Below: *Mark at Royal Ascot at York, in 2005, preparing to saddle a runner.*

Mark and Deirdre in the Royal Procession at Royal Ascot in 1998.

Left: *Mark enjoying that winning sensation, at Royal Ascot, 2003.*

Above: *Sunshine days in Dubai, March 2002.*

Above: *Mark gets the verdict from Deirdre. She has just put Murgham through his paces at Sha Tin, in December 2000.*

Left: *In the four-wheel drive, out and about at Middleham.*

Below: *Scenic splendour, but there's work to be done. One of Mark's strings in the beautiful setting of Middleham.*

Above: *Keeping a close eye. Mark checks one of his string on the High Moor at Middleham.*

Right: *Attention to detail. Mark checks his work list.*

Bottom: *Planning department. Mark in his office, preparing declarations.*

When he retired, she stayed on with Price's former assistant Con Horgan at his new base near Wokingham, Berkshire, as head lad.

She had a licence to ride on the Flat, but a bad fall on the gallops meant she gave up riding. 'I went to work for Boots, and was supervisor in a healthcare department at two large stores in Reading,' she says. 'I still had my friends in racing, and thought I'd like to get back into racing and work on the admin side. I'd had a bit of an insight from working in the office at Con's. I wanted to move back north too. I just wrote to Mark on the off-chance, in 1993. He caught my eye, because it was the year that they won the Ebor with Quick Ransom. I thought it looked an up-and-coming yard. At the time he had 65 horses. Then there was just one secretary, Polly, plus Deirdre in a supervisory position. Now we have five in the office.'

Declarations are a crucial responsibility of hers. Potentially, many thousands of pounds of prize money can go begging if deadlines are missed. 'I come over to the kitchen and go through them meticulously with Mark, Deirdre and Jock,' Debbie says. 'One of the girls in the office declares them while I start ringing the owners and telling them their horses are running, or why they're not. It's my job to make sure Mark's got all the information in order to make his decisions. We have systems in place, and they have improved as the yard has grown. Each manager is now responsible for coming to tell us about his 30 horses. We keep a coloured chart, so we can tell an owner what their horse has been doing in the last six weeks.' Debbie adds that, despite the scale of the operation, she believes the owners received as much attention as they would in a smaller yard.

What about the MJR branded fleeces, with the staff members' names printed on them – does everyone like them? 'It separates us from the other yards in the village,' she replies. 'It's like kids going to school just wearing a T-shirt and a pair of jeans. If they're in casual clothes, they're in a casual frame of mind. If you go with a uniform on, it puts you more in mind for the job you're doing, doesn't it?'

Debbie did have a break from Middleham. 'After about two and a half years I went to work for a construction company up in Kendal. I was there for five months. At the time I didn't like Middleham. I'd been living down south for fourteen years; I was only half an hour's train journey from the middle of London. I came up here and … well, nothing. But I came back. I'd kept in touch with Mark and Deirdre, and I came and rode out at weekends. To be honest, I missed the racing. I'd been working for Gary Middlebrook, a big racing man, a Jockey Club steward, and when I came back I brought him, as a new owner, with five horses!'

Later in the year, during another visit to the yard, Johnston and I are interrupted by Debbie Albion and Nicky Shepherd, the yard's personnel manager.

'One of the yard managers (Debbie gives his name) had an incident this morning with one of his staff, and I think he's taken it a bit too far,' Debbie tells Johnston. 'He bollocked her because the horse was getting into a muck sweat, and she gave him some lip. He thinks she should be shown the door.'

It turns out that a girl work-rider on one of the horses that was a bit fresh had been 'pulling it about'.

'He (the yard manager) says it was gross misconduct,' Debbie continues. 'And he's written it all down.' She proffers a piece of paper. 'I told him he had to manage the situation.'

Johnston listens impassively. A few years ago he would, no doubt, have intervened. Now he says very quietly, 'Have her in, give her a warning, go through the warning procedure. She'll be disciplined, and he'll learn.'

Debbie agrees with him, and says that was what she and Nicky had intended to do. 'But we just wanted to check.'

Johnston readily accepts that delegation can have its problems. 'One time,' he recalls, 'when we were first here, Deirdre and I came home to this horror of horrors: the longest-serving member of staff, Stephen Rabjohn, had been sacked by our then head lad Declan Condell after some kind of incident – breaking a window, I think. There was nothing we could do. You can't undermine the guy who's in charge. So, we waited until Declan Condell left, and then re-employed him.'

I ask Debbie how good the boss is at delegating. She laughs. 'He says this all the time: "You shouldn't have to come to me and ask me that. You should make your own decisions. You should make up your own mind." But if we do that, he'll turn round and say, "That's the wrong decision." We generally think it's preferable to go and get a bollocking here than wait to get a bollocking later.'

Still, from what I've observed, Debbie tends to be more blunt with Johnston than most. In fact, at times she actually gets stroppy with him. 'I suppose that's right,' she agrees. 'We do fall out a lot. Sometimes it gets a bit heated. But it seems to work. I think he likes someone to take him on. I don't do it just for the sake of arguing. It's because there's a point to be made. I think he likes you to be honest and straightforward. I've absolutely no idea at all why he takes any notice of me, but I think we get on extremely well. He can be difficult, but I'm sure he thinks that about me as well. He'll come and shout and bawl at me about something that's absolutely nothing to do with me, rather than go and shout at the person who's actually involved with it. People are amazed at the insults that fly between us. And that's on a good day. Clare Balding (the TV presenter) heard us once, and she suggested that the BBC should do a fly-on-the-wall documentary in here at breakfast time. I suppose, really, that he's just not a "people" person. I don't think he's very good at dealing with individuals.'

The yard managers meeting in Riders begins. Johnston told me beforehand that he had decided the yard managers should chair meetings in rotation, not him. He doesn't want to dominate proceedings. *They* should take responsibility. Hmm. I just wonder ... Andy Larnach is notionally in the chair for this particular session, though essentially Johnston takes control, constantly pushing business along.

There is a discussion about the skills matrix. The idea is that all members of staff should learn one new skill every month. There are no fewer than 45 of them, divided into seven categories – Basic Skills; Stable & Yard; Riding; Racing; Driving; Veterinary; and Senior Skills – and they range from 'muck out', 'swim (assist)' and 'plait' to 'rasp teeth', 'riding work' and 'box driver'. Penny Skilton claims that some of her staff have reached the extent of their capabilities, but Johnston refuses to accept that observation. He lists some tasks he would expect any competent member of staff to be able to perform. 'It's not rocket science, is it?' he asks. One of his favourite expressions.

Then horses' and jockeys' performances are analysed. No rider escapes criticism, not even the Classic-winning Kevin Darley, who next year will celebrate 30 years in the saddle. He was champion in 2000. No punches are pulled. Shots are straight to the body. Or at least they would be if he was present. Perhaps fortunately, he is not. Both Johnston and Deirdre have told me they are concerned that, on two occasions, Darley has dropped his hands too quickly if a horse doesn't appear to be running for him. Now, that observation should be placed in context. As a rule, and as the trainer will emphasise at a later stage, Johnston is a profound admirer of Darley's riding prowess. These are worrying times, though, and everyone comes under more scrutiny.

Johnston is distinctly displeased. Most of the time, he is an apparently inert volcano, but occasionally he can erupt without warning. He refers, in the meeting, to the two excellent performances, from Winged D'Argent, runner-up the previous evening in Sandown's Henry II Stakes, partnered by Joe Fanning, and Call Me George who won under Royston Ffrench the same afternoon. Both had required invigorating rides from their jockeys. 'Ridden over 4f out, kept on under pressure to take second near finish' was the *Racing Post* 'comment in running' about Fanning's mount. Both horses had disappointed in their previous runs, under Darley. 'I hope Kevin Darley is ashamed of those performances on them last time out,' declares Johnston.

Not all the yard's ills can be attributed to riding deficiencies. There is concern about the condition and weight of the yard's runners. That remains the biggest issue. Feed is discussed. Johnston says, at one point, that he is 'ashamed' (it's a word that crops up persistently during this period) that when he surveys his horses in racecourse parade rings there is insufficient muscle on them. 'It's the age-old story,' he reminds the assembly. 'Looks well, runs well.'

He also considers his yard managers' targets, a substantial element of Johnston's management ethos and a subject we will discuss further after the meeting. Some have achieved their targets in terms of winners, though none has hit the forecast number of runners. Overall, both winners and runners are down on what they should be. The trainer demands that the yard managers search ever more diligently for runners capable of improving the yard's winner ratio. 'The strike-rate is abysmal,' Johnston says, although he then offers a note of encouragement: 'The last few days have been better; not brilliant, but better.'

Things go off at a somewhat comical tangent when the issue of work-riders' caps and distinguishing colours is discussed. That policy was brought in because it helps in the identification of horses on the gallops – particularly important if one is thought to be lame. A scheme was introduced for riders to choose their own colours, only for individuals to start wearing similar ones and arguing over who had first choice. 'You sort it out among yourselves' are the departing words of a slightly aggravated Johnston as we depart for the Low Moor, where Atlantic Waves is due to work.

CHAPTER FOURTEEN

Too often at meetings, all the staff would do was complain about people not pulling their weight, or wages, or the standard of food in the café. I gave them a lecture and said, 'This is not what it's about. It's about winning races.'

According to the calendar, it is nearly 'Flaming June' No one has told the sun though, and it makes only a somewhat reluctant and insipid appearance. It is still raw up on the moor. Despite grumbling about the cold, Mark Johnston enjoys being in the habitat he loves best. It is the equivalent of football or rugby coaches being out training with 'the lads'. Though other yards use the gallops, his team dominates the landscape.

This is where trainers plot and plan and are occasionally perplexed by a horse's performance. They are alone with their thoughts … only today, alongside the author in attendance there's also a cameraman and reporter from Tyne Tees TV and a *Racing Post* photographer to distract him. All eyes and lenses are focused on Atlantic Waves, for whom, next week, Epsom will be a step into the unknown, in terms of distance and racing environment.

We tramp over to the gallops, where Johnston gets on his mobile and issues specific instructions to the string leaders. He has already handed out a list of that day's activities for his horses. Those that are due to work are divided into five lots; others are scheduled to swim in the equine pool or are placed on horse-walkers. There are approaching 200 names in all. All his charges are at school today apart from those who have a note for teacher, because they are sick.

Here, on the gallops, is where Johnston's vast repository of experience and knowledge comes into play. He listens intently, as well as watches. This is where he identifies not just potential winners but possible deficiencies in his charges, particularly wind problems. He once revealed in a *Horse & Hound* article, 'I have to admit that, back in those days (early in his career), even when examining horses for purchase, I found many wind abnormalities such as slight "whistles" – very difficult to hear. It is not a skill that is easily taught and it has only come to me after many years of listening to my own string cantering past me on the gallops. Now they jump out at me as clearly as if the horse could speak and was shouting "I can't breathe properly!" with every stride. It is, just about, the last sound I want to hear. It is always bad news, and, although some wind problems might be temporarily caused or exacerbated by infection or level of fitness, once you realise that your horse isn't getting enough air into its lungs to allow it to perform to its best, there are no easy answers.'

En route, we discussed the managers meeting. I wanted to know how easy it had been to persuade 'horse people' to operate within a system more suited to an office or a department store. 'Usually Deirdre and I come out of the meeting and we're frustrated with them all or annoyed with them, or we say, "That was really good,"' says Johnston. 'It changes from week to week. It can be a bit of a shambles sometimes, when they get diverted off the agenda. But generally I come away thinking how far they've all come. They take so much more responsibility for things now compared with a couple of years ago. You once asked me "How big can this get?" I just think our set-up now is more efficient than it's ever been. I can take a step back and it'll run like clockwork without me. That's always been the dream. The ultimate aim is that standards will not slip an inch if I leave it for two weeks. Of course the worry is on my mind constantly that anything could go wrong at any time; if someone does something stupid, the buck stops with me where the owners are concerned. There were times when I couldn't go for five minutes without worrying about it. Some of that was me. Some of that was that the people weren't as good.'

He then offered an example of a slippage in standards. It was a subject that had actually been discussed at the yard managers meeting. 'Up on the gallops, if you leave everyone to their own devices, inexperienced riders will all gravitate together and chat together. In a string of racehorses, you'll end up with the weakest, most inexperienced riders out the back. If you allow that to happen there'll be accidents. All you need to decrease the injury rate is to shift wee Jimmy, who's sixteen and has just arrived from the racing school, up to the middle, in between more experienced ones. The difficulty is getting those experienced riders to take those responsibilities. But just move those young lads and lasses up there, and subconsciously they'll look after them. The inexperienced boy or girl will watch and copy people around them. Things like that can still slip a little bit when I go away. I remember coming back from holiday the year before last and going up to the gallops, and it looked like *The Multi-Coloured Swap Shop*. One's got a Manchester United shirt on. I couldn't believe nobody had done anything about it. Yard managers should not have allowed someone to ride out without the proper gear on.

'I got a bit depressed about how bad they were at the time. But then at times I forget just how standards have improved overall. People we had as head lads in the early nineties, even when we won the Guineas, who we thought were very good ... well, we're just in a different league now. I heard that Andrew Bottomley said to one of his colleagues, "If you left this place and worked somewhere else, you'd really be the dog's bollocks because we're made to do everything in such detail." I think that's a fantastic compliment.'

If you were to list Johnston's aims, the first would be to create a team ethic for everyone, from the youngest lad or lass who mucks out to the most experienced yard manager. They must all feel they have contributed to producing a winner. His systems are designed to encourage staff to identify runners capable of winning a race. They can be senior people, right down to the yard man. Johnston tells a story of Winged Cupid during the 2005 season to demonstrate his point.

'Winged Cupid was a very backward yearling, very small, and by In The Wings, who is known to be a backward sire,' he says. 'I could easily have left him a lot longer, could easily have run him less times. But his yard manager kept saying at meetings under "Horses Fit to Run", "Winged Cupid." And I kept thinking, "I can't run that thing." And she'd say, "Winged Cupid. You've got to run Winged Cupid." As a result he ran in races he wouldn't have run in otherwise. He was second in a Group 1 (behind Palace Episode in the Racing Post Trophy), and then sold to Godolphin for a huge amount of money. I might not have spotted that if I hadn't got feedback from the yard manager saying, "This horse is bouncing out of his skin." All I could see was that he was small, he was backward and his pedigree screamed at me, "Don't run him!"'

Johnston also tells me about an elderly yard man whose job was mucking out. 'While Attraction was here, because of all her leg problems the first thing that happened with her in the morning was that he'd put her on the walker for an hour. He didn't look after her, didn't groom her or anything, but because he was mucking out her box he would put her on the walker. Once a month, this guy might come to me and say, "Attraction was a bit stiff this morning when she walked out," or, "I wasn't 100 per cent happy with her," or, "She's not eating her food." One time we had an annual review meeting for all the staff. I said to them that if everybody treated every horse like he had Attraction then we'd win more races. *Far* more races.'

These days, as has been mentioned, all the yard managers have yearly and monthly targets which they set themselves, 'although Deirdre and I query them if they're not right for some reason'. 'The target this season is 160 winners,' he says. 'Last year (2005) it was 150 winners, and we had 144. Last year was the first that the yard managers set the target. When they came up with 150, I thought that was daft. It was too many; it would have been an all-time record for us. I also wasn't totally convinced that we should be going that route; that we should try to win better quality races, not more of them. This year, when setting the targets, I already knew I had all those early three-year-old horses ready to run in January and February. I gave them the target to set, and said to Deirdre, "If they come back with anything less than 150, or, for that matter, anything ridiculously high, I'll tell them to go away and think again." They didn't dare suggest a target lower than they had set last year, so they came back with 160. I said, "That's fine."

'Then I said to them, "How many Group races are you going to win?" Last year we won only five Group races, and that wasn't good enough. I already had it in my mind that I wanted to win sixteen, which is 10 per cent. Sure enough, they came back and said they'd win sixteen. That was exactly what I was looking for them to say. Then I said, "How are you going to get the Group winners?" Five of them were going to get eight between them; the other guy was going to get eight on his own. I said to him, "You've set your target for the year as 32 winners, but you've said that eight are going to be Group winners. That's one in every four." I've already told you our best strike-rate over ten years is 10 per cent Group-race winners; he was aiming for 25 per cent. He said, "Yeah." I said, "How?" He reeled off a list of eight names, including Atlantic Waves, Madaares and Prince Of Light, who he expected to win a Group race each. How could you argue with that? He was spot-on in his thinking.'

However, even as he tells me this, Johnston is forced to admit, 'I think we're lacking stars. That's the worry. Because Winged Cupid's gone, Stepping Up, Austrian … it is getting more difficult to realise your dreams when you don't have a big battalion of stars. If you lose half your best horses, it gets harder and harder to set those Group-race targets. That target worries me a wee bit. It's the main thing we want, but the most difficult to achieve. Apart from that, the gut feeling is that we'll get our 160. And we might end up higher than that. I will be going for a record number of winners in 2006. Might even be a record for anybody! The number of winners has got nothing to do with what you buy and what you're given. It's down to placing them properly and maximising their abilities. You can win more races with a 70-rated horse than a 100-rated horse.'

Johnston returns to what he expects from his yard managers, 'I told them, "Now go away, break it down and say how many each of you is going to win overall each month if we are to get to our target of 160." Somebody came in with two winners for February. I told him, "Our figures over the last ten years say you'd need fourteen runners to do that, on average. Where are you going to get fourteen runners? You've only got two horses fit to run." His target was unrealistic. He actually got one in February, from what turned out to be three runners. It's to make them focus. Clearly, if you have fourteen runners and one winner, your horses are running well below form. If you have one winner and four runners, you're actually running better than form, but not running enough. What it's doing is involving the yard managers much more deeply in the business.'

The most heinous crime, in Johnston's eyes, is a horse that could be winning a race standing in his stall. In any other business it would be called productivity. 'Now you're getting grooms asking, "Why are you not running that?" Most of the time, of course, there is a reason. So far, that's been the case every time. But I know that through the season there will be examples when some bright spark says, "Why are you not running that?" and he'll be right. There's no reason at all. A lot of owners think I'm the only person who can spot potential winners. In reality, there have always been six, seven or eight. But if we can have over a hundred people who are looking for horses to win a race with, we'll find more. We will definitely find ones we would have missed.

'What I'm saying to the yard managers is, don't just set a target and hope. If the target's five winners for that month, they need 35 horses to run. Obviously you cannot get 35 runners if horses have ringworm, or haven't been taught to jump out of the starting stalls, or if they forget to get them shod at the right time. What I'm saying is, if you generate 35 runs, I'll generate five winners out of it.'

At one time, there was a prize for the best team of the quarter: they all got a night out. 'But they abused it, so at the moment it's stopped,' Johnston says. 'The first two went ahead without me knowing about it. One of our owners said he'd give them a box at Sunderland greyhound track. They'd supply the food, and we'd pay for the drink. That was great. They booked it, went ahead, and didn't even tell me. If I could have found time to go, I would probably have gone. But worse than that, on the last occasion, the first I heard about it was when a load of people left early from evening stables to go to the dogs, and those people were nothing to do with the winning team.' Johnston looks slightly miffed when I suggest that it's perhaps understandable if they don't want the boss around. 'Well, maybe, and that's what you hear, but I obviously need to be there if they abuse it by taking along people not on the winning team. It's an incentive for winning. You don't take the losers with you. Anyway, at the moment it's cancelled.'

I return to the problem with the yard manager whose staff turnover had concerned him back in December. Had that been resolved? 'Not yet,' Johnston tells me. 'That yard manager is still a yard manager, and he's still got a staff turnover problem. It's not got any better. But it is something that will be discussed at one of our strategic planning meetings. As far as the individual is concerned, it's our job to teach him to run his team better.'

Yard managers, in conjunction with Jock Bennett and Nicky Shepherd, are responsible for recruiting new staff. Johnston doesn't normally vet them. That even includes salaries, though there is a wage scale. And here we enter highly contentious terrain, of course, because, as we know, in 2003 Johnston quit as a columnist of the *Racing Post* over that newspaper's campaign to highlight what they perceived as the inadequacies of wages and conditions in racing stables. 'The reason I was so upset with the *Racing Post* was because they cooked the figures,' Johnston says. 'They tried to present the worst-case scenario. It clearly wasn't true. There may be some people who think the wages aren't very good. But if you're looking at it from another perspective – say, someone teaching, or working in a nursery – you may say, "How can a stable hand or groom or rider earn as *much* as that?"'

One area that provokes no dispute is his quest for staff to develop more skills, though he concedes it is a perennial problem. 'There's very little formal training off the job available in the horseracing industry. If you ask one of our staff to design a training programme they'd like, they always come back and say first, "I'd like to learn about veterinary stuff." That's always number one on the list. You ask them, "How?" They say, "Bring in a vet and we'll have a wee lecture." I say, "It took me five years. How do you think you're going to do it in one hour?" If, say, we ran a course next Sunday, on their time off, on cuts and bruises, we'd get twenty people turn up. They'll be very enthusiastic and love every minute, but in two weeks' time they'll have forgotten everything.

'What I am forever saying to yard managers is that the biggest thing they can do to train the staff and make their job easier is to talk to them, to teach them as they go along doing the job. Don't wander into the stable, look at the horses' legs and wander back out again. They've got 35 horses to get round and 90 minutes to do it, and other things to do in that time; at best it's three minutes a horse. If a horse needs bandaging or some treatment, that takes five minutes. Ideally, that yard manager should want to be able to walk into a box and say to the groom, "How's the horse?" He'd either say it was fine or it wasn't. And you'd be able to rely on the fact that he knows because you've trained him properly. You train them by talking to them every night, by involving them. But I've felt that I'm beating my head against a brick wall trying to get the yard managers to do that.'

Johnston's utopia would be 110-plus staff with the same intuitive feel as himself for discerning a horse's condition. It will never happen, of course, but you can't blame him for trying. 'I cannot walk into a stable and not take in the surroundings,' he says. 'And this is not unique to me; it applies to any decent horse trainer and horseman. Someone like Mark Prescott would have it down to a fine art. Without thinking about it, I will look in the manger, look in the drinker, look at the bed.'

Earlier in the season, Johnston was also frustrated by the fact that too often there was no feedback from yard managers to their staff. They were supposed to have monthly meetings of their own, with five points on the agenda: (1) matters arising from the last meeting; (2) targets and results; (3) horses fit to run/win; (4) skills matrix; (5) review of the vet diary. 'That's the report I get from all the yard managers on things that are wrong with the horse,' Johnston says. 'Now I insist that they discuss it with their staff. If Jimmy's horse, Dobbin, has cracked heels, tell him what we're doing about it. But most importantly, they have to understand that the target for their team this month is five winners and they've only got two so far. How are we going to get the next three? It's a quantum leap, but what we want is the guy sweeping the yard and mucking out to realise that it's also his job to be concerned with winning races and meeting the target. It will make a huge difference when that guy walks into a box and he's thinking, "This horse is going to win a race," and suddenly he notices something that's going to stop him from doing that. Too often at meetings, all the staff would do was complain about people not pulling their weight, or wages, or the standard of food in the café. I gave them a lecture and said, "This is not what it's about. It's about winning races."'

It all made fantastic sense to this observer. Yet there was one aspect that troubled me. Wasn't it a trifle unfair to insist on targets when those concerned didn't have full responsibility for running them? They didn't choose their races, didn't ride them. Johnston takes on that slightly exasperated tone. 'Of course it's not unfair,' he retorts. 'If they want the whole responsibility, they'll have to go off and train horses. They're part of the team. The centre-forward hasn't got the whole bloody responsibility to win football matches. Somebody has to pass him the ball. The whole point of being a team is that everybody affects the result. We need to show them that.'

The most common beef among stable staff, apart from having to work at weekends, is people not being able to go racing with their own horses. 'It's the oldest complaint I get, dating right back to the first day I started training,' says Johnston. 'Having said that, they complain when it suits them. They don't want to go racing with their own horse when it's running at Wolverhampton on a Saturday night; they *do* want to go when it's running at Royal Ascot, or Goodwood, or Epsom.' Johnston recalls how, at one of the first staff meetings, Justin, the groom who then looked after Bandari, had said he'd like to accompany the horse to races. The trainer did not have any great sympathy. 'Our number one priority is winning the race. He's a horse that gets lashing with sweat, gets led round in a lip chain, that wears ear plugs that are removed at the start. So, our number one priority is matching the best possible person to lead this horse up, to maximise its chances of winning the race. If Justin's mind was focussed on Bandari winning; not on having a day out at Epsom, he wouldn't even ask the question. Instead he would be thinking, just like me, and just like Jock (Bennett), who does the race planning, who's the best person to lead up Bandari to win the race? At the moment, there's too many who don't think about that at all. And our yard managers don't think about it enough. And I would say that people in 50 per cent of yards don't think about it all, either!'

It's another area in which Johnston believes there should be an education process, for the public, the media and others. 'There's people writing in the *Racing Post* who think the race starts when the stalls open. There's people who crowd into the saddling boxes who know nothing about horses and racecourses like Catterick and Pontefract, who make us saddle in crap facilities. There's the Jockey Club, who say the public need to see the horses saddled. They all forget that the race starts with its training, and it starts in earnest the day it steps into the horsebox and travels to the races. The journey counts, the night in the stables counts, the saddling counts, the leading-up around the parade ring counts a huge amount. If it fights and wrestles for twenty minutes around the parade ring against the person leading it up, it's not going to run its best race. It's wasted a huge amount of energy. There's no way in the world you'd let the public into the Manchester United dressing room, or watch boxers prepare before they step into the ring. The staff need to understand that too. They need to realise that their job is not mucking out, it's not leading up at the races, it's not riding up the canter … their job is *winning races*. And the better they do it the more races they'll win. You can't totally dismiss the desire to be there, the job satisfaction, the perk. But the person who wants to lead it round the parade ring has to realise that by far the biggest perk of all is being involved in the result – genuinely believing that they have contributed to the result. At the moment they don't know that they have contributed to it.'

He then relates an astonishing story. 'We had someone here from that Investors in People thing. There was a woman here for a couple of days; she spoke to a lot of people. At the end there was a summary meeting with me and a few yard managers, and she said something which had us all breaking up in laughter. She was talking about communication – obviously an important part of any business. She said, in all seriousness, "I've had a number of complaints. They say you tell them when the horse is entered, you tell them when it's going to run, but you don't tell them the result." We couldn't believe that the staff didn't watch the races. We provide them with TVs. They're everywhere. You assume they go and watch the races. They expect us to put the result up. We expect them to know the result. We expect them to be *desperate* to watch the race. I just couldn't believe that we had people who look after a horse, it goes to the races, it comes home, and they don't know whether it's won or not.' He lowers his voice. 'Hopefully, it's not too many of them.'

After that we return to current business. At least Johnston can be pretty certain that everyone will be aware that the yard has a potent candidate for the 2006 Derby.

CHAPTER FIFTEEN

As they turn into the straight, all I can hear is John Keaney
screaming for his horse, and Deirdre, shouting even louder,
standing in front of him, yelling for Fruits Of Love to win.
I thought, 'What is the guy going to think of this?'

How the bunting would be unfurled and Middleham would rejoice at the triumphant return of a Derby victor if the prize, for once, was wrested away from Newmarket or Ireland. You suspect that even Johnston's local rivals, who to an extent exist in the shadows of Kingsley House, would relish a feat last achieved by Matt Peacock with Dante. And that was in 1945. I recall Johnston's sentiments a few years ago, recorded in the *Sporting Life*: 'I have always said there is no race I would rather win, and running fourth with Mister Baileys in 1994 strengthened my resolve,' he declared. 'For the moment it is still my number one goal, although races like the Dubai World Cup do make me wonder. Which is more important, the prestige of the Derby or four million dollars? The answer is only easy if you don't give it too much thought.'

Confidence, though, is not absolutely pulsing through his being. Whether it is just the general recession – hopefully a temporary one – within his stables, or a concern that Atlantic Waves will not be capable of a significant leap in class, is difficult to say. Probably something of both. Strict formlines yield some encouragement. Olympian Odyssey, runner-up to Atlantic Waves at Newmarket, finished third behind George Washington in the 2,000 Guineas. But the idiosyncrasies of the Derby make it foolish to prophesy anything. Stamina, speed, class, ability to handle the course, temperament – all will come into play on the Downs on Saturday. There is certainly stamina aplenty in the family. Atlantic Waves' dam Highest Accolade, by Shirley Heights, is out of a half-sister to the top-class twelve-furlong filly Awaasif. 'When I look back at what they'd achieved in their Classic races, I always thought that Mister Baileys and Attraction *should* win,' Johnston says. 'I can't say that about Atlantic Waves.'

The colt looks poised, alert, prepared. He is still, though, an innocent abroad. This will be only his fourth race. That partly explains why the previous week his trainer gave him a sighter of those famous contours, as the *Racing Post* reported:

Leading Vodafone Derby hope Atlantic Waves yesterday did what Motivator had done one year earlier by getting an early look at the Classic course in an exercise that left trainer Mark Johnston 'delighted'.

On a day when Marcus Tregoning gave his most positive bulletin yet about Sir Percy and Sir Michael Stoute revealed he wants Chester Vase victor Papal Bull to be supplemented, Johnston sent Feilden Stakes winner Atlantic Waves for a ten-furlong workout during Epsom's Breakfast with the Stars morning.

Motivator and Walk In The Park, first and second in last season's Derby, both took part in spins around Epsom in the build-up to the contest, and Atlantic Waves yesterday followed their lead, working with stablemate Boquilobo.

Ridden by his Derby jockey Joe Fanning, Atlantic Waves – as short as 11–1 with Stan James after beating likely Derby rival Olympian Odyssey in the Feilden – moved steadily on what Fanning called 'heavy ground' before increasing speed up the home straight.

'I'm delighted we brought him,' said Johnston, whose best finish in the Derby came when Mister Baileys ran fourth in 1994. 'It was a new experience for him, and I'm glad we've done it. You only find out on the day if they handle Epsom. Twenty per cent get a great advantage from running here because they cope with it so well, 20 per cent don't cope with it at all, and the rest are all in the same boat. We've just got to hope we cope with it, and having seen him come down the hill today, I don't see any reason why he won't.

'He's not a ridiculous no-hoper that someone's put in the Derby just to have a runner. He's a live contender, but he's an inexperienced live contender. He's not really tried and tested in Group company and we're going to find out next Saturday how good he is. He's a very inexperienced horse – that's the big gamble.'

As we return to the house, I mention a quote I had come across from Johnston's arch-rival Richard Hannon, suggesting that he'd rather see Mick Channon as 'top of the tree, winner-wise, than anyone else.' 'Money-wise.' he said 'It will always be hard for us to beat the likes of Sir Michael Stoute and Mark Johnston, who usually get the better horses sent to them.' Johnston shakes his head, both bemused and amused. He repeats his previous observation that the yard would not necessarily expect to receive the prime contenders of Sheikh Mohammed's or other Maktoum horses. Much of Johnston's satisfaction stems from the fact that most of his major horses are home-purchased. 'I put my neck on the line at the sales,' he says. 'Last year, I stuck my head out and bought Denbera Dancer. I stood that horse, as a yearling, with 170,000 guineas of my own money. There have been times when I've been 500,000 down on purchases, and have to find buyers.'

We are back in the kitchen now. On the wall are photographs of many of Kingsley House's major players over the years. They serve to remind you that Johnston has achieved what he has without expensive acquisitions. There are: Quick Ransom (cost 6,000 guineas); Spirit Of Love (1,000 guineas); Bijou D'Inde (20,000 guineas); Double Trigger (7,000 guineas); and of course Mister Baileys. The photographs are a reminder that the yard is capable of scaling remarkable heights, and not with a multi-thousand or even million purchases.

One comes to mind immediately. It was 1994 – the year of Mister Baileys' Guineas triumph, a season in which the yard amassed over £1 million in prize money and over 100 winners for the first time – when Bijou D'Inde arrived as a yearling. 'In hindsight I was very proud of buying him,' says Johnston. 'His pedigree had no black type in the first dam, and she'd had several foals. Yet I did my research and I discovered that three or more of these foals were rated over 100 and *deserved* to have black type. Two or three were the best sons of their sire. The mare had produced the best son of Electric and Norwick. She'd been to moderate sires, and here she was going to Cadeaux Genereux. At first, when Deirdre kept telling me one of his brothers had just won again over hurdles, I thought, "What have I bought here?" But from the first time he galloped I knew he was the business. He was a great horse, for Stuart Morrison, who'd had Quick Ransom. We call Stuart "Judge Morrison", although he's actually a senior partner in a big law firm in Glasgow.'

Bijou D'Inde was beaten in his first two outings, in maidens at Newcastle and Goodwood, 'but we had undying faith in him' recalls Johnston. He then went to the Acomb Stakes at York and won it, followed by victory at The Curragh. Like Mister Baileys, he went straight to the Guineas, and having gone for home three furlongs out, again like Mister Baileys, was caught but rallied to finish third in a freeze-frame of nodding heads, behind Mark Of Esteem. 'A lot of the time we don't know how good they actually are before they've won, but he and Mister Baileys … we were pretty sure they were decent horses.' The trainer then saw his miler finish fourth in the Irish Guineas, after losing a shoe. Victory in the St James's Palace Stakes at Royal Ascot was handsome consolation, followed by second place in the Eclipse.

Bijou D'Inde never won again, but he saw the world in the hands of his travel agents Kingsley House Globetrotters, travelling to Dubai, Longchamp and Sha Tin. He was brought down in the 1997 Dubai World Cup. 'It was right at the bottom bend, and Bijou D'Inde got up, he was OK, although he had clattered over a Japanese horse which had to be put down,' recalls Johnston. 'We were more concerned about his jockey Jason Weaver. I caught the horse and Deirdre went down in the blacksmith's car, and went with Jason to hospital. He was actually fine, but it was a worrying moment.

'It wasn't the worst accident we've had,' Johnston adds. 'It was nothing like the day Mister Monet was killed in the 2004 Champion Stakes.' The son of Peintre Celebre had already won in Group company at Deauville and Haydock. 'I went to the race thinking, "I'm going to win this." I had second and third favourites. One broke his leg and the other, Lucky Story, finished nearly last.' It severely tempered what would have been a day for riotous celebrations. The brilliant Shamardal had been installed as Guineas favourite after contemptuously dismissing his Dewhurst Stakes opponents, while Johnston's Contact Dancer won the Cesarewitch.

By 1996, Johnston's spending had increased significantly. With a burgeoning reputation to sustain him, he was prepared to outlay the most he'd ever spent at the sales when he successfully bid 75,000 Irish guineas for a horse that caught his eye at Goffs. 'I had no idea who I was buying him for, says Johnston. It was "on spec". I simply didn't buy horses for 75 grand then. When he walked into the ring, I thought, "I can't afford this. I can't buy this." But then I decided to have a go. I'm not sure what was in my head, but I was so taken by it I would have probably gone to 100,000. It was way, way beyond what I'd ever dreamt of spending on a horse. The sire was Hansel and I didn't know that he was something of a breeding no-no at the time. I just knew him as a multiple Group 1 winner. The dam's side was fantastic. It was a Secretariat mare. And the yearling was magnificent-looking as well. I drooled over him.

'At Goffs, I usually stand in this little pit at one end, and there were two or three of my owners around. I would normally have gone up to 50,000 maximum. Most of the time, my owners around me would know what I was doing, how much I was prepared to go to. They were all a bit shocked when I kept going. Eventually he was knocked down to me. Almost immediately, Mick Doyle tapped me on the shoulder, as I was signing the ticket, and said, "Who's that for?" I said, "I don't know." He pointed at himself and said, "Me."' Doyle, owner of a super trawler and fish-processing plant based in County Donegal, named the yearling Fruits Of Love. The long-standing owner had fished deep financially and netted an outstanding specimen. 'It's hard to say between him and Lucky Story the best horse I've had that didn't win a Group 1 race,' says Johnston. 'I mean, Lucky Story was the champion three-year-old miler, without winning a Group 1 race. But Fruits Of Love is right up there. He is proving a very respectable stallion.'

In the living room at Kingsley House, the largest trophy on display is that presented for Fruit Of Love's Dubai Turf Classic triumph, when partnered by Kieren Fallon. 'Yes,' says Johnston with a rueful smile. 'The only thing is, it was worth $600,000 in total prize money when he won it, the very next year it was worth $2 million, and now it's worth $4 million.'

It was the return home from that success on 1 April 1999 that resulted in a mobile call to Johnston that no trainer wants to receive. It came from Robynne Watton, his travelling head lass, when the horsebox conveying Fruits Of Love had just turned off the M25 on to the M1 northbound, en route from Dubai to Middleham. The horse, evidently spooked by something, was attempting to climb over the partition in the box. He succeeded too, despite the valiant efforts of Watton and Fruit Of Love's own lass Gail Alderson, and ended up lying upside down in the groom's passageway in front of the stalls. The driver had pulled on to the hard shoulder, but what was to be done to extricate the horse without him damaging himself?

Seven years on, the emotions of that night remain infused in Johnston's mind. 'I was on the motorway ahead when I was called to be told he had jumped the partition in his stall and had his front legs in the air thrashing around. Now, as a rule, I don't panic when I have a problem with horses. I'm a vet, after all. I'm used to them having legs hanging off. I might not do much practice, but I do some. So what went through my head was just wanting to be there, needing to take control of the situation – not being at the other end of the phone. That was driving me mad. I was on the phone to Robynne, who was in the cab, and I could hear the horse bashing about in the back there, upside down.

'My first thought, as a vet, was, "What drugs do we have in the lorry to sedate the horse?" Most people would assume that the first people you need are the fire brigade and the police, but I'm thinking, "What can *they* do any more than the vet from the local dog and cat practice up the road?" And I'm thinking, "Where is the nearest experienced equine vet who can get there?" By now, the box driver had called the fire brigade, and it was one of their lads who said, "We're only one junction away from the Royal Veterinary College at Potters Bar. We'll drive it there."

'Once at the college, a vet named Sarah Freeman, assisted by three colleagues, had to risk flying hooves to sit between Fruits Of Love's front legs and put a catheter in his jugular to give him a fluid anaesthetic. Then the fire brigade cut out the interior of the horsebox and winched him out.' He was moved to an operating theatre because there were concerns that the patient might have broken a bone in his pelvis or back, but he was unscathed apart from requiring a few stitches for cuts. 'I phoned Robynne at the veterinary college and asked what they were doing,' Johnston continues, 'and she said they were giving him fluids, but wasn't sure what they were giving him. And then I suddenly realised, "I'm getting in the way here." I said, "Just phone me back when it's over." She called me back later to say he was OK.'

It was a remarkable escape. Johnston told the *Racing Post* at the time, 'My thought was that there was little chance of him surviving. Even if he did, there were few chances of him having a stud career as the race in Dubai had no Group status. It never entered my head that he would race again. It also occurred to me that he was desperately under-insured. His owner Mick Doyle had just won the biggest race of his life, and his horse was upside down in his box. Today, Johnston reflects; 'The whole thing was unbelievable. But looking back, the only disappointing thing was that nobody filmed it. It would have made great TV.'

However, he prefers not to think too deeply about the potential consequences. 'The luckiest part was that there was none of the usual paraphernalia lying there in the groom's compartment – buckets, spades and forks – which could have done a lot of damage to him. We actually learnt a big lesson from the incident. It taught us a lot about managing horses. The attitude at the veterinary college was to give him an anaesthetic, knock him out, so that then you've got an unconscious horse and you can do with it what you have to do. So now, here, if there's an accident with a horse in the starting stalls or on the walker our first reaction is just to give them a sedative so that they're manageable.'

Astonishingly, Fruits Of Love was racing again by the beginning of June. By the end of that year he had won the Hardwicke Stakes at Royal Ascot. A year later he repeated the feat. Between those victories he sustained a suspensory ligament injury in the Japan Cup, and again recovered. Deirdre Johnston told the *Racing Post* after that second Ascot triumph, 'We've nursed, cuddled and looked after this horse and he couldn't deserve it more. I ride him out every day and rode him on the course this morning.' Johnston reflects, 'He lived a charmed life, because he also fractured his pelvis at two.'

When Fruits Of Love went off to stud in October 2001, having by then also finished third behind Daylami in the King George and second in the Grade 1 Canadian International, Johnston reminisced in his *Racing Post* column, 'My purchase was a half-brother to the young, up-and-coming sire Mujadil. Later in the bar we joked with Maurice Burns of Rathasker Stud and told him that he could start building another stallion box. I was convinced that I had bought a horse with the looks and pedigree to be a stallion, but I couldn't really have imagined that my prophecy would be quite so accurate. Fruits Of Love will be leaving my yard next week to join the now highly successful Mujadil at Rathasker.' In that same column, Johnston referred to his current stock of two-year-olds, stating, 'They are clearly good, but I am not sure that they have surpassed the class of '97 when Fruits Of Love used to cruise up the High Moor with the likes of Lend A Hand, Princely Heir and Land Of Dreams. That trio netted two Group 1 races and a Group 2 as two-year-olds, but Fruits Of Love was my favourite.'

A pleasing postscript to the whole drama is that Sarah Freeman, who was later made lecturer in equine surgery at the Royal Veterinary College, had her efforts recognised by being named Lanson Lady of the Year for 1999 for her contribution to the racing industry. The panel of judges included Clare Balding and John Francome.

If that image remains indelibly fixed in Johnston's brain, the second of Fruits Of Love's Hardwicke Stakes victories at Royal Ascot, in 2000, when the stable's enigmatic Yavana's Pace was only a length and a half behind in second, doesn't lag too far behind. The trainer relatively often runs two, or more, of his horses in the same race. 'Owners can get upset if they are beaten by another horse in the yard,' he says, 'but it's not really logical. If Michael Stoute trained the horse, it would still beat theirs. Generally, if horse A's best chance is at Beverley and horse B's best chance is at Pontefract I'll try to keep them apart, because I want to win two races. But if for both of them their best chance is in the Hardwicke, you'd be unfair to one owner not to run theirs. That's definitely what I was doing when I declared Fruits Of Love and Yavana's Pace to run in the 2000 Hardwicke Stakes.'

However, it proved to be a curiously excruciating spectacle for the trainer, despite the result. 'Yavana's Pace was not normally considered anything like a front-running horse, yet Darryll Holland went off in front on him,' recalls Johnston. 'I couldn't believe it. Fruits Of Love was known for coming from off the pace. So I'm watching this race and cringing. What's the owner going to be thinking? Probably that we're using Yavana's Pace as a pacemaker! Anyway, as they turn into the straight, all I can hear is John Keaney (owner of Yavana's Pace) screaming for his horse, and Deirdre, shouting even louder, standing in front of him, yelling for Fruits Of Love to win. I thought, "What is the guy going to think of this?"' Fruits Of Love eventually established the lead a furlong out, and maintained that advantage, with Yavana's Pace just behind. 'When I turned round, John was hugging Deirdre. His reaction to coming second was one of the great things, for me, about that race.' Indeed, Keaney, a house builder, was so magnanimous in defeat that he went out and commissioned for the Johnstons a painting of the finish of that Hardwicke Stakes. It has pride of place in their living room. They bought the copyright and used it for that year's Christmas cards.

Ironically, of the two horses, Yavana's Pace turned out to be the Group 1 winner. Johnston remembers the horse being 'very difficult to train, very temperamental. He wouldn't go on the gallops; he'd whip round and dump his jockey. He was also very temperamental on the racecourse until the stalls opened. He had to go down early. God knows how many jockeys fell off him on the way. Olivier Peslier, Darryll Holland and Michael Hills were definitely unshipped by the horse. John Carroll famously parted company from him on the occasion when Yavana's Pace cantered loose for a mile and a half, then turned round and won a Listed race. John Keaney would tell jockeys to go for a canter before the race on him, and if necessary go the whole way round the track. We were always terrified that something was going to happen to him. He was a horse full of quirks, but we had some fantastic days with him.'

They had begun when Johnston received a phone call from Keaney in early 1998. The Irishman told him he wanted to send the yard two geldings by Accordion, a four-year-old and a six-year-old. The trainer thanked him for the call but told him politely, 'I don't train jump horses.' Still, Johnston sought counsel from the Irish trainer Michael Cunningham, who vouched for Keaney and advised him to go ahead and train the horses, the elder of whom turned out to be Yavana's Pace. The horse had already won four races in Ireland. Johnston had also received a message from John Keaney's father, Terence, who explained that the objective was to obtain 'black type'. As Johnston recalls, 'I concluded that the whole Keaney family must be stone mad.' Nevertheless, he went ahead and accepted the pair.

'In his second race for me, Yavava's Pace won, and then we ran him in that Hong Kong Jockey Club Trophy at Sandown – a valuable handicap. His jockey was W. M. "Eddie" Lai, a tiny Hong Kong apprentice who had been sent over by the Hong Kong Jockey Club to gain experience. That was his one ride of the day. To give him this ride was the biggest thing he could have had.' Yavana's Pace was one of the outsiders of the 20-runner field, at 20–1. 'The instructions were to "bury yourself in the pack, and then go for it at the last minute, when you can see the winning post".' Johnston can barely stop laughing at the memory. 'I don't think Eddie could understand what I was saying. He didn't speak much English.

'Anyway, he was stuck in against the rail, and was getting bounced around. I don't know how he even stayed on it. It was such a difficult ride. There was a hot favourite in the race, ridden by Walter Swinburn. He was sitting pretty. But the turn into the straight, and a false rail, gave Eddie the space he needed and he just went straight up the inside, headed for home, stick in the air, and won. After that Yavana's Pace just went from strength to strength, through the handicap ranks all the way up to Group 1, when he won (the Credit Suisse Private Banking Pokal) under Keith Dalgleish at Cologne on a very emotional day. Finally, the ten-year-old, after a career spanning eight racing seasons and 74 starts in eight countries, he had vindicated that early faith of Terence Keaney, who had died before he got to see the horse run for us. Many locals told me that they had never seen a foreign winner given such a warm reception in Germany. There were aspects to the character of the old horse that most people could identify with. No horse has given me so much pleasure and so little pain as Yavana's Pace.' His jockeys, though, might qualify that statement ever so slightly.

There were attempts to dislodge Yavana's Pace from his pedestal in the aftermath. The *Racing Post*'s John Randall, referring to the horse becoming 'the oldest horse to win a Group 1 race in Europe', contended that 'in terms of absolute merit, his performance on Sunday was probably no better than when this supremely tough and genuine gelding carried 9st 10lb to victory in the November Handicap in 1998'. A wounded Johnston brought out his heavy weaponry in his veteran's defence in his column in the same paper, but in truth, it was unnecessary. The triumph had stirred the soul, and the calculator of the form-fixated could not detract from the sheer poignancy of the moment.

Yavana's Pace had earlier been second in two other German Group 1s, and had been runner-up in the Irish St Leger. Another Johnston horse that should have collected air miles, he had also contested the Melbourne Cup in 1999. It was Johnston's third tilt at the race they say 'brings Australia to a halt', and another disappointment, following Quick Ransom, who had started a well-fancied 7–1 chance in 1994, and Double Trigger, who had been the 7–2 favourite a year later. Between them they had beaten only three horses home at Flemington, outcomes their trainer described as 'absolutely disastrous'. Before the 1999 race, Johnston, a little put out at Yavana's Pace's 30–1 price, conceded, 'I have certainly learnt that I got it wrong (in the past). I think I have learnt not to be too hard on the horses when they are here. In the past we tried to do similar work to what we would have been doing at home. I remember having Double Trigger doing something like fifteen laps around the Sandown track. This time we have been much easier on Yavana's Pace, which I think is the way to do it.' The attempt was in vain, once more. Yavana's Pace was in contention in the straight, but despite jockey Richard Hughes's urgings he finished twelfth of the 24 runners, beaten seven lengths.

Rather like his countryman Dr David Livingstone, foreign travel has always appealed to Johnston, although he is less a missionary and more a visionary. 'I first started sending horses over to Ireland when we were in Lincolnshire,' he says. 'I've no idea what triggered it, but I got a real taste for it. I even had a pacemaker in that first one. I ran our two-year-olds, Hinari Televideo and Hinari Disk Deck. Hinari Televideo came third.' Lifewatch Vision was also sent to Ireland in Johnston's first year at Middleham, 1989, though the trainer still bridles at a decision by the Curragh stewards to relegate the two-year-old colt to fifth after he had finished third, beaten only half a length, in a Group 3 race.

'We travelled far more in those days than we do now,' Johnston says. 'All we were interested in was prize money. We went where the prize money was best; we didn't care where it was. I'm ashamed to say in some ways that is not always the case now. Winning black-type races have become a bigger priority than the prize money. It's a shame. It's one of the things that's wrong with British racing. We race for prestige more than we race for prize money. We have to, otherwise we wouldn't be in business.'

What kind of reception had he received abroad, that of a welcome guest or merely a man come to pillage the money on offer, often against weak local opposition? 'I don't take the crazy Australian attitude where they only welcome you if you get beat,' replies Johnston, a firm advocate of international racing against the forces of self-protectionism. 'As soon as a foreigner wins the Melbourne Cup, (trainer) Bart Cummins and people start moaning about it. But, generally, we are treated fantastically from one end of the scale – being lavishly hosted in Dubai and Hong Kong and Japan – to the other: the embarrassment of going to Switzerland. They're so nice to you when you're taking their prize money. And really you're not putting anything back.' He reconsiders his answer. 'That's not quite true. In places like Germany and Italy our presence does attract more interest, and does drag up the standard of their racing. But they do get a huge thrill out of beating us – even coming second to us.

'It does bother me a little bit that I've become a bit less ambitious in that respect,' he adds. 'But prize money has got better here. If it starts heading down again, we'll start going abroad more often. If we've got to declare them 48 hours in advance in Britain, we may as well declare them in Ireland. The problem is that, because of the time it takes to ship the horses over there, we have to make our declarations in Ireland 48 hours in advance. Aidan O'Brien and the other trainers in Ireland only have to make declarations 24 hours ahead, so they have an advantage. We're on the boat before they've declared, so they know what we're running before they make their decision. But if 48-hour declarations come in here (soon after Johnston says this, it becomes official), I'll run more horses in Ireland, because the prize money is so much better. If I have to make a decision on Thursday that I'm running at Sandown on the Saturday, I could virtually as easily make a decision to run at The Curragh in a similar race for three times as much money – and it's not that much more difficult to get there. We're treated extremely well there. The Curragh's probably one of the nicest racetracks to visit. They treat visitors better than they do their own owners!'

He nods. 'Yes, we're really going to have to get stuck into the Irish racing calendar. Of course, we won a Group 1 there last year (2005), with Attraction, but there was one year when we raced in seventeen countries in one year. Another year, in the mid-nineties, when Gothenburg was around, and he was a big money-earner abroad, we had 100 winners in Britain who earned just over a million and ten winners abroad who brought in half a million in prize money. We used to run a lot more, and were right up there at the top of the international table every year.'

Gothenberg, whose two-year-old victories included the Listed Woodcote Stakes at Epsom, never had a Group 1 success, but the bay, who cost only 5,700 guineas as a yearling, did claim three Group 2 prizes abroad: the International Stakes at The Curragh, the Premio Emilio Turati at San Siro, and the Berlin-Brandenberg Trophy at Hoppegarten. The top-class sprinter-miler Lend A Hand also won at San Siro, the Group 1 Gran Criterium. It was one of eight victories in a twenty-race career for the son of Great Commotion before he followed what was becoming an adopted route for top Johnston horses: moving straight on to the Guineas. In the Newmarket Classic, Darryll Holland made a bold bid for victory two furlongs out, but he was caught by King Of Kings and finished second. Lend A Hand was later moved to Godolphin. Another Johnston raider, Princely Heir, won the 1997 Heinz 57 Phoenix Stakes at Leopardstown.

The Peter Savill-owned stayer Royal Rebel won twice at Leopardstown and was third in the Prix du Cadran at Longchamp on 'Arc' day 2000, but reserved his best performances for home matches. Twice winner of the Ascot Gold Cup, overcoming the lionised Persian Punch on one of those occasions, and once triumphant in the Goodwood equivalent, he was, according to his trainer, 'the great unsung hero'. 'People talk about the best stayers of the last ten years and they don't mention Royal Rebel,' Johnston says. 'I was probably as guilty as anybody, because when he won his first Gold Cup all people wanted to talk about was comparisons with Double Trigger, and I said he didn't compare. But that wasn't fair. Definitely not. He won two Gold Cups. He was a really great horse.'

Such memories merely exacerbate the present plight. But that could all change if Atlantic Waves, Johnston's Derby hope for 2006, discovers the necessary progression. One day he may be remembered with similar affection. Amid the unease, there have been occasional injections of optimism. Against The Grain, the three-year-old owned by Sir Alex Ferguson's Right Angle Club, annihilated the opposition on his debut. Peppertree Lane, owned by Peter Savill, became the yard's 1,700th success of all time when he was victorious at York in May. But these are only rare emergences from the shadows. It says it all about the current state of affairs when Greg Fairley, the yard's apprentice, enjoys a 440–1 double – though not for his guv'nor but for Johnston's Ayr-based compatriot Linda Perratt.

The 2006 Derby epitomises the turf season thus far for the yard. Atlantic Waves looks the part on the way to post, and, with that bravado so typical of the stable's runners, leads the field for a mile, down to Tattenham Corner, under Joe Fanning, entrusted with his first Derby ride. But the distress flares are soon fired, and he finishes around seventeen lengths behind Marcus Tregoning's Sir Percy, who squeezes home ahead of Dragon Dancer, Dylan Thomas and Hala Bek in a real mêlée at the line. It is a popular triumph. Sir Percy was cheaply purchased and, though nudged out of second favouritism by Coolmore's Horatio Nelson, well backed. The Irish challenger breaks down, and has to be destroyed.

Atlantic Waves is also found to be injured afterwards. Nowhere near as seriously, but it explains a distinctly moderate performance. The diagnosis is a bad quarter crack (a hoof injury). 'He had a patch on it for the Derby and it seemed perfectly sound,' says Johnston a few weeks later. 'But he came home lame. His foot was a bit of a mess afterwards. That's why he hasn't run since. That wasn't his running. I'd have expected him to be closer than that. Time will tell how good he is. But his owner is patient. He just wants us to get the horse right.' It is the response you would expect from Jaber Abdullah, and indeed any of his Dubai-based counterparts who have become such familiar faces on British racetracks.

Today, the Boys in Blue of Godolphin are exceedingly popular with British racegoers, and not merely because they employ the country's most celebrated jockey, Frankie Dettori. Their contest with Coolmore, both in the sales ring – where it turned into something of a cold war in 2005 when the Maktoums boycotted their rivals' yearlings at the most prestigious sales – and on the racecourse, makes for a compulsive spectacle. Some of us are old enough to recall when there was opposition to the Maktoum family's increasing influence in British racing. They were said to be discouraging British owners by stripping the prize-money tree of too much of its best fruit simply because they had the purchasing power and breeding operations to do so. The only beneficiary, it was claimed, was an exclusive, highly fortunate elite of trainers who ran a cosy cartel, vacuuming up Arab patronage. Fortunately, there is now a more enlightened approach to the Maktoums, that large extended group of family and friends, including Jaber Abdullah.

Johnston regards any antipathy towards them as 'stupidity'. Of course, he does declare an interest as one of their trainers, but adds, 'It's pathetic. It's the insular attitude of a backward racing nation, and we shouldn't be like that. That's for Scandinavia and Germany and second-rate nations, who will remain second rate if they want to restrict the opposition so only the locals can win. It's so short-sighted. To some extent, you can understand the Germans and Scandinavians, or a tiny racing country like Switzerland. Let's say German racecourses are putting up £10 million prize money. The local owners put in £20 million into training and running costs, and somebody comes along from outside, makes no contribution to the country, and takes £7 million of the prize money. You're going to be pretty upset. That happens to these little countries all the time. We've not spent any money and we've taken a big chunk of their prize money. But here we don't need to be like that, although you still find certain aspects of protectionism in Britain. I don't approve of things like the EBF (European Breeders' Fund) races (in which horses competing have to be "EBF eligible"). I don't like restrictive racing at all. If you want to be the best racing nation in the world, you need to have open competition that welcomes the best horses, no matter who owns them, where they came from or where they're bred.

'But to get back to the Maktoums, for every £1 prize money the Maktoums win, they put in £4 into running their horses. That's not a benefit to them, it's a benefit to us. So long as owners are net losers in this country, you want to welcome everyone you can get, wherever he comes from. They're not taking it away, not taking a penny out of this country. They're only putting it in. A win for a Godolphin horse is a win for a British-based trainer. That money is re-invested in Britain, and much more is added to it. They're British owners, with horses cared for, on the whole, by British staff. Of course, there is an element of Dubai training, but they're a lot more British than anyone coming in from outside.'

Johnston has been a frequent visitor to Dubai. It would be foolish not to. 'We send horses there because it's fantastic prize money,' he admits. 'They also pay all your transport costs if you run twice. And they give you $2,000 a time just for running. The thing that astonishes me is that, though the horse operation is huge there and obviously the Sheikh has been part of the whole project at Nad Al Sheba, from how the track was constructed to the prize money, we horsey people tend to forget that horseracing's just a tiny drop of sand in the desert. He's got so many other projects going on, and some of them so much bigger than horseracing. Somebody once said that 50 per cent of all the cranes in the world are in Dubai. He has huge involvement in other things, right down to the decor of the Burj Al Arab Hotel (the sail-shaped building that thrusts 321 metres into the sky above the Arabian Gulf). That, to me, is staggering. It's fascinating the way he runs the whole country.

'I'm sure people looked at the horseracing side in Dubai and said, "You can't throw that much money at it, it's crazy." Or, "You can't build a hotel that costs as much as the Al Arab because it can't repay its costs. How much would you have to charge for a room for a night?" But he's seen beyond that, obviously. Who knows what the finances of the Al Arab are, and whether it can ever make money? But it's become a symbol of Dubai. It's put Dubai on every holiday programme in every country in the world. I'm sure he sees every venture as part of a bigger picture. It doesn't have to pay in the short term, so long as it has a knock-on effect for the country. Horseracing is a prime example. Look at the Dubai World Cup. If you look at the bank balance of the Emirates

Racing Association, it has to be negative, but the Sheikh looks at what visitors contribute to the bank balance of Dubai. He's not just throwing money senselessly at it.' Johnston pauses, then adds pointedly, 'In a way, it's a bit like us coming to Middleham and everyone thinking we're mad, and waiting for us to fail. And then, after a while, realising we're not going to fail.'

One suspects that Sheikh Mohammed would have greatly admired what Johnston has achieved when he visited the yard with his wife, Princess Haya of Jordan, in 2004. Johnston smiles at one recollection of the royal visit. 'The only embarrassing moment was some local came storming in, shouting and swearing about us apparently not waving to acknowledge him when he stopped to let us pass in a narrow bit of the lane up the road. That was a bit of a dampener! It wasn't the best introduction to Yorkshire for Sheikh Mohammed. But it was very informal. We looked round the horses, then went up to the High Moor and watched all his horses cantering. By some miracle that day, all his horses were fit and well, and sound. We were able to canter his whole string for him, every single one; managed to put them out in one lot and cantered them all. We came back to the yard and he asked questions about all sorts of things. He's very interested in the hay, and the feed, and so on. The Sheikh doesn't talk a lot. He asks more questions than expresses his opinions. It's one of the best things about training for the Maktoum family: they just judge us on results. They don't come in and try to tell us how to train the horses, or where they should run.

'It takes about an hour for horses to come back from the High Moor. I asked whether he wanted to see them back in their boxes. He said no; the only horse he wanted to see was Attraction. He wanted to see her, and take a look at those famous legs.

'It can be a bit intimidating, but they're not beyond cracking a joke. The more you can relax with them, the better it is. I remember Princess Haya was asking about the uniforms our staff wear. I said we did it on a points system: they had to earn their uniforms and get their points on the jacket. She said, "I don't think I could be bothered with that. I think I'd just buy one." And (racing manager) John Ferguson, who was with them, said, "It's all right for you, you're a princess."'

Johnston believes the Maktoums' crucial legacy is that they have maintained British racing's position among the world's elite during an era when otherwise it would have fallen dramatically. 'Not only have they invested in racing stables, studs, staff, every aspect of British racing, but they have also brought the best American blood, and European as well. They win the top races with it, and they stand it here in stud. So, the next generation become British. Obviously they may have a dream that some may become UAE-British, but really they've allowed us, despite poor prize money and funding, to stay up there, competing with Japan and the US.'

There has, though, been concern in some quarters that they have over-dominated major races with their runners, I point out. 'The wonderful thing about horseracing is that's never the case,' Johnston counters. 'Of course, if money, or the best breeding, could guarantee success, then very few people would be in it.' It's a sound point, especially during a year in which the 1,000 Guineas is won by Pam Sly's Speciosa, who cost only 30 times that. And Derby winner Sir Percy was bought for 16,000 guineas. 'The wonderful thing is that every horse has a chance,' says Johnston. 'We started with very cheap horses, and climbed a long way up.' A fact to which that photographic evidence on the wall of the kitchen of Kingsley House so amply bears witness.

CHAPTER SIXTEEN

There are two distinct branches of Clan Johnston, those from Caskieben in
Aberdeenshire and the border reivers of Annandale in Dumfries and
Galloway. I, personally, have not traced my ancestry beyond early twentieth-
century Glasgow, but I must assume that I am descended from the latter
group: the desire to raid and plunder in England has never left me.
MARK JOHNSTON'S COLUMN IN *The Times* (2000)

Only the Druids, gathering at Stonehenge, await the summer solstice with more expectancy than Mark Johnston. Those five days in June, together with the Goodwood Festival and the Classics, are what stimulate Johnston, what has him planning his regime many weeks, months, a year even, ahead.

'By far the greatest race meeting in the world' was his description after the 1997 Royal Ascot meeting, as reported in the *Sporting Life*. 'I love it. I can't stand the pressure in the preceding days, but once we are up and running, I love it.' Over the last decade, Johnston's success has been as predictable as the royal procession. A total of 23 victories between 1995 and 2005 puts him fifth in the list of the trainers (who still hold a licence) with most winners at the meeting. His record in the five years prior to the 2006 meeting, sixteen winners from 98 runners, is peerless. 'Ascot has always been very special,' he says. 'We've had a long love affair with that course since our first win at the Royal meeting when Double Trigger won the Gold Cup for us in 1995.' His runners, had you cared to back every one of them, would have yielded a profit of £54.10 to a £1 stake. Johnston has had at least one winner at every Royal Ascot since 1995, apart from in 1998, although he had to wait until the 23rd race of the 2005 meeting (staged at York) before Melrose Avenue produced a victory for the yard.

For most of us, the Royal meeting represents a delicious combination of cultures which co-exist admirably: those who perceive themselves as connoisseurs of the equine elite, and those who arrive to make a fashion statement, more intent on promenading in chic and outlandish fashion on the turf catwalk. Whether you are invited into the Royal Enclosure or arrive by charabanc in the Silver Ring, for the ladies it's about donning and being seen in your finery, topped off by some magnificent millinery. Or at least it was. Finery, these days, is a relatively loose term. Royal Ascot offers all manner of spectacles. 'We can't stop fashion,' an Ascot official observed drily during the 2004 meeting. 'As long as the girls look smart, it's OK. We are not even checking for bare legs any more.' Bare legs are the least of it; bare navels are more likely these days. What would Mrs Schilling have made of it?

This is an occasion when the Johnston tartan is proudly produced from the trainer's wardrobe. A sartorial flying of the Saltire by this proud Scot, confronted by the old enemy? He relishes the week of competition. You suspect that every victory is another thrust from the loyalist's blade. He dons tartan waistcoat and tie. No kilt, although he does possess one. 'My father would have never worn a kilt, but I think I probably had one when I was five years old' he says. 'I never wore one again until I got married. In fact, I've still got the jacket and waistcoat.' He laughs. 'It would probably fit Charlie now. In fact, Deirdre and I were joking the other day that we'd get him a kilt when the time comes for his wedding.'

This discussion leads us on to the whole issue of nationalism. One day, when Johnston alludes to his eventual retirement, I bring up the subject of a possible conflict of allegiances. 'Perhaps that's when you'll get the knighthood,' I suggest, only half-joking.

'I won't get a knighthood,' he retorts. 'I'm a Jacobite.'

One has to assume that he isn't a strict adherent of the political movement dedicated to the restoration of the Stuart kings to the thrones of England and Scotland; simply that, despite his years down south, he remains a staunch advocate of Scottish nationalism.

'Quite,' Johnston responds. 'Well, very, I suppose. But I can't always equate that to my other beliefs. I hate nationalism when I think of Nazi Germany; I also hate nationalism when I look at the Middle East. I think it's not worth dying for. Yet I was brought up talking about nationalism, as though it *was* worth dying for. But it's not. That's for sure. Second to religion, there's terrible things done in the name of nationalism. I'm not a believer in it in that sense. But I suppose, like so many Scots, there's still a bitterness bred into us, taught into us at school even, through Scottish history. We're taught that for 800 years we've been persecuted by the English, and we rebel against it – as do the Irish.'

Is that an explanation for why Scots frequently appear more driven, more ambitious than their English counterparts?

'You can say that's just a chip on Scottish shoulders. On the other hand, there's an immense pride, confidence and arrogance about Scots. We all think we're better than the English. I was brought up with that as well. That the best brains in Britain come from Scotland; that our biggest export is people; that we invented anything that has been worth inventing; that we fought all the battles. We were brought up not to feel inferior, but to feel downtrodden, and therefore rebellious. That may be stupid in modern-day terms. I become quite embarrassed when I'm arguing the toss at the National Trainers' Federation, or something, and I realise that, almost invariably, I'm the most argumentative in the room. You think about the unions and the government, and basically any political forum there is, and it's always the Scots that are the ones up front doing the arguing. They come at all levels, and on both sides of parliament. Considering how few Tory Scots there are, there's been a significant number of them who have reached office, including a prime minister, Alec Douglas-Home. For some reason, it's in our nature.

'From quite a young age, my father used to tell me, "One of your great advantages is your Scottish accent. Never lose it. You will be able to move in all circles." Because in Scotland, a Scottish accent is perceived as being working class. The upper classes, the landed classes, were Anglo-Scots educated in England or in Scottish public schools in the Highlands or in Edinburgh, and they emerged with an English accent. In England, a Scottish accent is classless to most Englishmen. It's not like having a Liverpool or Geordie accent.'

I put it to him that despite today's cosmopolitan society, history still forms our attitudes. 'Of course,' he says. 'I take the mickey out of Deirdre because she's got a great-grandfather who was an English soldier. I never let her forget that. I will maintain that my father is pure Scottish. I don't actually *know*, not beyond two generations – my parents and their parents. I joke about that. I also joke to the boys that I'm sending them off to university in Scotland, and they're not to come back until they find themselves a wife!' And he adds, with rather more gravitas, 'There is no country in the world I would rather see Scotland beat at anything than England. If England play Wales or Ireland, I'd definitely support those two. I'd definitely support Italy, France, Samoa, anyone you like. Yet recently, for the first time in my life I found myself wanting England to beat Australia, particularly at cricket, but at rugby as well. It probably goes back to the Scottish thing of always supporting the underdog, and the Australians are so arrogant. I was particularly pleased about the cricket (the Ashes win in 2005).'

He spreads his arms – a plea of guilt. 'It's prejudiced and it's wrong, but it's built into me. It's probably a very good thing if my boys grow up less prejudiced than I am. Charlie's got an England rugby shirt which my mother bought him before she died. Both boys have got some Manchester United shirts. But any shirts they've been bought by me or Deirdre are those of Scotland or Scottish teams. Yet they were born in Northallerton and they speak with English accents.' Hmm. To my ears there's definitely a Scottish burr developing.

'I will always maintain I'm Scottish, never British,' Johnston continues. 'Even, say, in Dubai, where it may be more difficult for people to understand where I come from. Country of domicile? I say UK, never GB. I don't like the expression Great Britain, even though presumably it's nothing to do with being great as in fantastic. Or has it? No, it's probably great as in size.'

He pauses for a moment, as though he has said too much.

'Everything I say I believe. Yet if it was written down, I'd be ashamed!'

'Too late for that, I'm afraid.'

'In that case, we probably shouldn't get started on the religious thing.'

But he does, regardless. 'In Scotland, one thing worse than being English is being Protestant or Catholic, depending on what side you're talking from. There's probably more bigotry in that area than there is against the English. I was brought up as a Scottish Protestant, and a Rangers supporter. Yet I wouldn't buy my kids a Rangers shirt, that's for sure. Charlie's got a Celtic shirt. I brought them up as Celtic supporters because I'm so ashamed of that bigotry. Now, there's just as much bigotry on the Catholic side, but because I was brought up as a Rangers supporter I buy my kids Celtic shirts, just to show that I've got away from that. I hate that. I also hate the fact that I see Rangers as not being Scottish. When I was working in Northern Ireland, I saw all these people wearing Rangers shirts, going to watch Rangers play every weekend and waving union flags. I thought "you should stay in bloody Ireland and keep out of Scotland, because you've got nothing to do with Scotland". I became so ashamed that I decided never to encourage my sons to support Glasgow Rangers in the the way that my father had when I was a boy – although he later became ashamed of it, and disassociated himself. He'd been brought up that way. After his father died, his mother married a Dutchman. He'd take me to see Rangers play. Lovely guy, but they're as bigoted as the Scots when it comes to religious divides.

'We used to joke that the real working class in Scotland are very bigoted, and they would know whether someone was Catholic or Protestant from their name. Move up the class ladder just a little to the middle class and they would deny that they were bigoted, but would be very conscious of not wanting their son or daughter to marry someone from the other religion. They'd still support Rangers or Celtic, but wouldn't wear a scarf and shout about it. Most families of the generation before ours were quite divided in Scotland.

'Funnily enough, at times I think of joining the Secular Society, or the Humanists. I'm a bit anti-religion. The only time I've been to church was at school, when I was dragged along, and I've attended some funerals. I got married in a church, of course – Deirdre insisted – though I always thought it was wrong. But the kids aren't christened. I wouldn't have it.'

Johnston's sister Sharon says that her brother's attitudes were forged predominantly by their upbringing. 'You don't grow up in a house like ours without having nationalistic tendencies,' she says. 'I'm sure if he could have done in Scotland what he has done in England, he wouldn't have left. As he's said, North Yorkshire's as close as he can get to Scotland and still be in a top training area. If he was offered a knighthood, or any other honour, I would hope that he would turn it down. I'm sure he would. But I don't think he would ever be offered such a thing anyway. One thing about him, if Mark disagrees with someone, or doesn't care for them, he'll not hold back, whether it means a backward slide for him or not. It hasn't always done him a favour. I am proud of him for that.'

In 1998, Johnston was invited once to ride in the royal procession at Ascot, preceded by lunch with the Queen. And did he accept? 'Of course,' he says, as though any other response was unthinkable. 'Deirdre did – I didn't get any choice in the matter! Whichever monarch it was, here, Dubai or wherever, I'd be delighted to do it. We had lunch at Windsor Castle, and I had what they call the "hot seat", between the Queen and the Queen Mother. Of course we talked mainly about horses. Deirdre was next to the Duke of Edinburgh. Then we rode in the royal procession, down the course, and spent the afternoon in the royal box. It was very interesting. I'd do it again.'

But back to June 2006, and the nation is sweltering under a heatwave. Those south of the border are sweating with World Cup fever as well, as England torture them with some mediocre exhibitions in Germany. There is a kind of drought seriously affecting Johnston's yard. Midway through the month he has been rewarded with just three victories from 44 runners. The timing could scarcely be worse. With only a few days remaining before the Royal meeting returns to Ascot after its temporary removal to York, this bulletin from the *Racing Post* says it all:

Mark Johnston yesterday expressed concerns about the well-being of his string and said that he would struggle 'to count ten contenders' he might have for Royal Ascot, a meeting at which he has enjoyed huge success. Johnston, who has not saddled a winner from 20 runners since McEldowney scored at Catterick on 2 June, said, 'I am concerned about my horses. At the moment, the priority is getting them right, and if this doesn't happen before Ascot, then it doesn't happen. With less than two weeks to go, normally I would have about 20 to 35 candidates, who would then be narrowed down to 15 to 20. This year I would struggle to count ten.'

Johnston has been unable to put his finger on the problem.

'I have no theories as to what is wrong. A number of them still have their winter coats and they have not been thriving. Everything that we can do so far has been done and there is no simple explanation.'

There was a small ray of hope yesterday when his only runner, Adaptation, 'ran very well', according to the trainer, when runner-up at Hamilton.

Admittedly, this year some of his horses are performing decently enough without winning. Nevertheless, these are not statistics a trainer wants to contemplate when finalising his Royal Ascot preparations. In particular, some of his juveniles haven't quite performed as expected. Johnston believes it is less an indifferent crop and more a case of berries being picked before they are fully ripe. 'I was talking to Sir Alex Ferguson once, and he asked me how things were going,' says Johnston. 'I quoted what he'd said to me after his team were beaten in the FA Cup final in 2005 by Arsenal. That they were playing really well, just not finishing. That's the same with us. We're getting plenty of horses placed, but we're not getting the goals. I need to turn that around.'

Winners at Thirsk and Ripon are beginning to materialise, representing further buds of recovery, when Johnston and Deirdre arrive at Ascot. The Berkshire racecourse has been radically altered since we were last here. There are many fine innovations, but the most important, a new grandstand, enjoys a decidedly mixed reception. It is aesthetically splendid as a piece of contemporary architecture – if you are expecting to see Heathrow's Terminal Five. As a structure for viewing horseracing, on the occasions when over 40,000 are in attendance, it is, in many eyes, a serious misjudgement. Today, however, Johnston's only concern is what takes place on that newly nurtured sward, laid during the hiatus when the meeting was transferred to the Knavesmire at York. 'I'm just praying that it hasn't changed the character of the track,' he says of this land which was once a forest clearing until Queen Anne chanced upon it while out riding from Windsor one day and decided it would make an excellent location for some sport.

Normally, Royal Ascot witnesses an all-out assault by Johnston. All troops are placed on alert, prepared for action. Anything with any chance of being involved is pencilled in. As he says, 'That's what's different about this meeting. At any other, there's no way I'd declare so many of my horses to run against each other. We throw everything at this meeting.' Roll up, roll up! Like a fairground coconut shy, the more balls you throw, the more chance you have of dislodging that hairy oval. 'It must make sense,' Johnston declares. 'You're giving yourself a far greater chance.' He has been known to declare as many as five in some handicaps. The policy is easily justified. 'It's huge prize money and every owner wants to win it.'

Marina Park was Johnston's first Ascot victor, back in July 1992, but it would not be until 1995 and Double Trigger's Gold Cup triumph that he would effect a breakthrough and claim that special badge of honour, a Royal winner. 'In between I made many attempts at breaking my Royal duck, and I had Deirdre convinced that it was some crazy obsession which led me to take our best horses to the same meeting every year to get beaten,' Johnston once said. 'It has been well reported that by Wednesday of the 1995 meeting we were close to requiring some marriage guidance after Gothenberg, Argyle Cavalier, Star Rage, Unconditional Love and Sweet Robin had been beaten. Double Eclipse's second in the Queen's Vase was the only ray of hope and I was losing our long-standing argument by five goals to one, and that was only by virtue of a place. The next day, however, I made a miraculous recovery and settled the score once and for all. Not just a winner, not just a Group 1 winner, but a double (completed by Diaghilef, in the King George V Handicap) for good measure. Now we were both hooked.'

It's a meeting that prompts many reminiscences. 'Far and away our best Ascot year was 2003,' Johnston says, luxuriating in the memory. 'If you'd spoken to me then, I'd have said it was between Attraction and Pearl Of Love as to what was the best Ascot chance. Attraction was going there with one thing in mind; second wouldn't do. We really thought we were going to win the Queen Mary. We had the best two-year-old filly in Britain. And we were right in the end. We also thought Pearl Of Love would win the Chesham. It was just a question of getting them there in one piece.

'I get much more of a buzz of anticipation thinking about Ascot and Goodwood,' he adds. 'They're the only meetings I think about.

Otherwise I only think about individual races. It's the only thing I plan for years in advance. When a horse like Melrose Avenue wins, as he did the Queen's Vase last year, I start thinking "Gold Cup", although he's gone now to Godolphin. If I think a two-year-old is going to be a high-class handicapper, and may even be a Group horse, and looks like being a mile-and-a-half horse, I think "King George V Handicap". I think, "What can we win at Ascot and Goodwood with them?" Even when they're two-year-olds.

'As we get nearer and nearer the day, it's like approaching exam time. I start looking out the statistics, and see what the chance is of me winning anything. I look back to how many runners I had last year, and think, "The team's not big enough." I do it every year. I start thinking, "How many runners did we have last year? How many did I think had a chance last year?" It never seems like this year's good enough. And I find it harder to get excited about an individual horse. It's much better to think about the whole team event.'

Sometimes, though, there are moments when one player just can't avoid being fêted as the main attraction.

CHAPTER SEVENTEEN

We thought that Mister Baileys had been underestimated after the Guineas,
but I will never forgive them for Double Trigger not being champion stayer.
Nothing could be more hideous than Double Trigger not being named
champion stayer in 1995. There was not a horse even close to him.

Ron Huggins' weekend interests had always been playing rugby
and sailing. He was a fly-half and had played at Loughborough
University and at county level, and later founded a small rugby club in
Kent, called Linton. When he turned 40, Huggins who, until this year,
worked for Kimberly-Clark (the company, from which, you will recall,
Johnston was to derive some of his management systems) gave up both
rugby and sailing, and devoted his energies to a sport that was far more
liable to bring despair than euphoria.

His interest in horses up to that point had been limited. He had
ridden a little as a child, and had followed eventing – his sister and her
husband Sam Barr had event horses – but he had only followed
horseracing as an occasional racegoer. But one Christmas he'd watched
a film about Desert Orchid, and how he was bred. 'I said to my wife,
"I'd be interested in trying to breed a Desert Orchid,"' Huggins recalls.
'So I went off and bought a broodmare. Then I realised it was going to
be quite a long process, getting her progeny to the track. So I thought I'd
better get something to run in the meantime.'

He sought out a trainer. 'I looked at both experienced ones and up-
and-coming ones who had a good ratio of wins to horses. I considered
Jon Scargill, Bill Elsey and Mark. When I drove into the yard at
Middleham we just got on very well. I just thought that this was the
place to be. That was 1991. I was one of his early owners. At the time he
had 31 horses. I bought a horse out of a field, which was Better Be Bold,
and split it between four of us. She ran a few times, and was absolutely
useless.' To be precise, the filly ran three times and finished tenth, last

and last. Not the most auspicious liaison, perhaps, but the new owner was unperturbed. 'Our second horse was Double Blue, and he won his first four races in 23 days.' That was in April 1992. The Town and Country sprinter, bred by the Queen, would go on to win twelve of his 68 races. 'That's what got it going for us, and what got the "Double" thing going as well.'

Huggins and his fellow owners decided to invest some of the winnings. 'I went to Goffs in Ireland with Mark. I had learnt a huge amount from him. I selected the horses I wanted to look at, and I earmarked Ela-Mana-Mou as a top-class stallion, even though he was unfashionable and his progeny were going a lot cheaper. But they were something I could afford. The horse that we came to name Double Trigger was the one I really liked. Mark actually bid, and we got him for 7,200 Irish guineas. Incredible really.'

That impression changed when the chestnut with the distinctive white blaze went into training at Middleham. 'I owned half, and two friends, Dick Moules and Julian Clopet, owned 25 per cent each,' Huggins continues. 'We all went up to see Trigger on the gallops, not long before his first race was planned. He came plodding up like an old jumper. I can still hear him today: p-dum, p-dum, p-dum. Not galloping at all, just cantering, really. After the gallop, Mark asked Bobby Elliott (then chief work-rider) what he thought. He said, "He'd make a good circus horse."

'We adjourned to the pub in Middleham, the Black Swan, to decide what we should do. There were options. Should we have him gelded? Should we send him eventing? Should we sell him without racing him? Should we run him? After we'd had a couple of pints, we said, "Oh, let's run him."'

It was an epoch-making decision, for the owners and for Johnston, who now concedes wryly, 'I think Ron was a bit annoyed with my attitude; that I had just written him off and kept saying, "Oh, he shows nothing."'

Why geld him? the uninitiated may ask. Put crudely, in order to ensure that a colt concentrates solely on racing and doesn't become distracted by fillies, particularly if the horse is unlikely to have any future stallion value. But Johnston is not one to rush in and make the unkindest cut of all. 'People do say some need gelding because of their behaviour as two-year-olds, but I like to run them first,' he says. 'It's amazing how a race changes their attitude. It's not all that uncommon for us to have a horse who doesn't concentrate on its work. Our attitude is to race it, and that will wake him up. Trigger was one of those.'

Even now, the trainer can't quite believe how badly the horse performed at home. 'He spent more time on two legs than four,' the trainer recalls. 'He was just full of himself, always clowning around. In all the time we had him, he never did a good gallop. Ron would probably say that he did a great gallop with Mister Baileys in the spring of the next year. But it wasn't that *he* did a great gallop but that Mister Baileys did an atrocious gallop in muddy, heavy conditions. Other than that, you can say that Double Trigger never won a proper gallop – and he used to work with some of the worst horses in the yard, some of the real runts. Actually, he did "win" a gallop, but only when he worked over a mile and a half, only when the thing in front started to tire. He just didn't raise his game at all. Never.'

Johnston remembers how Trigger used to work with a horse called Milngavie, who was rated about 60 (very moderate). Double Trigger was rated 119. In theory, that meant the latter would need around four stone extra on his back for them to finish together. 'They used to gallop together, and Double Trigger wouldn't catch him until the last furlong over a mile and a half. Some of that was just laziness. Yet he was actually capable of doing a phenomenal amount of work. You could give him a five-furlong canter on the Low Moor, a seven-furlong canter on the High Moor, then turn him around and do a mile-and-a-half canter, and he'd still be bucking and kicking all the way home. He had incredible stamina.' And something of a temperament? 'He was a colt,' says Johnston. 'He could take a chunk out of you at times. He wasn't the easiest horse in the world.'

The date of Trigger's first race, 25 September 1993, began as one of enormous promise for the yard. Not, it should be said, because of the son of Ela-Mana-Mou, who had been dispatched to Redcar to run in the EBF Reg Boyle Bookmakers Maiden Stakes, a Class D one-mile-one-furlong event. It was because Mister Baileys was entered for the Royal Lodge Stakes that day at Ascot. Quick Ransom and Marina Park were the other runners at the Royal track. 'We went off to Ascot; he went off to Redcar, with Jason Weaver, the apprentice who had just lost his claim and had turned up at the door one day saying he would ride for us,' recalls Johnston. 'He got the odd ride, including this horse. As I recall, Ron didn't want to go to Redcar that day. He was a bit depressed about Double Trigger, that he was such a disappointment.' As Huggins lived not too far from Ascot, Trigger's owner was persuaded to meet up with Johnston there to watch the stable's runners in the big races and follow Trigger's race on the TV.

Johnston was understandably preoccupied with his Ascot runners. Mister Baileys had just fulfilled his initial promise with victory in the Royal Lodge when Huggins went off to view Double Trigger's debut on a TV screen with Richard Huckerby. 'He was actually out the back at the start,' he recalls. 'About a third of the way into the race, Jason started to ease him forward. Suddenly, he took off. It was the first time he'd ever galloped in his life. He beat the field by ten lengths and broke the track record. Jason had time to ease him down 100 yards from the line, put his stick away and give the horse a big pat, so he hardly knew he'd been in a race and loved every minute of it. I was absolutely amazed. While this was happening, Mister Baileys had won, and Mark had gone off to have a glass of champagne. He came back out about two minutes after Trigger had won. I said, "You won't believe this, but Trigger's just won by twenty lengths."'

Johnston didn't believe it. 'I came into the bar and Ron Huggins and Richard Huckerby were standing there with a bottle of champagne and glasses. They told me he'd won by twenty lengths. At first I thought they were making a joke of it, with the champagne. I refused to believe it and went out to look for the results. Yes, he had won. He didn't actually win by twenty lengths, he won by ten lengths. But I had absolutely no idea he was a good horse. The remarkable thing was, that day we won the Krug with Quick Ransom and Marina Park was third in her race. So no fewer than three of the top twenty horses we've ever had were running that same day. We could not have believed that by the end of the day there'd be a fourth – probably the horse for which I'm best known.'

Huggins admits he still frequently relives that moment. 'The Cup wins were obviously high points later on, but that first race still stands out for me. I can remember it as though it was yesterday. That sounds crazy because it was a small race, but when your expectations are zero, to win by ten lengths and break the track record is incredible.'

The Zetland Stakes at Newmarket, that real stamina examination for two-year-olds, was next, but before that Huggins and Johnston were back at the sales to purchase Trigger's full brother, to be named Double Eclipse. They could not have foreseen that two years later racegoers would experience the ultimate in equine sibling rivalry as the pair slugged it out to the line in the 1995 Goodwood Cup. Trigger would prevail by a neck, but there was no family honour lost by the kid brother. 'I took huge pride in Trigger,' says Johnston. 'It was fantastic to have a horse that will go down in history. The fact that we had his brother as well made it all the more pleasurable. The 1995 race was one of the most thrilling I have ever been involved in.'

Before he was retired to stud in 1998, Trigger won seven Cup races, and the devotion of the racing public. Those flying sprinters, milers and middle-distance horses have their disciples, but for many of us there is no finer spectacle than a scrap between those doughty warriors of the staying game. Trigger's record of achievement – his 29 starts resulted in fourteen victories, two seconds and one third; total winning prize money £431,209 – is worthy of repetition:

September 1993, Redcar, EBF Maiden Stakes, 1m 1f, £4,127
October 1993, Newmarket, Zetland Stakes, 1m 2f, £8,140
November 1994, Turin, St Leger Italiano (Gr3), 1m 6f, £30,497
May 1995, Ascot, Sagaro Stakes (Gr3), 2m, £25,480
May 1995, Sandown, Henry II Stakes (Gr3), 2m, £25,500
June 1995, Ascot, Gold Cup (Gr1), 2m 4f, £111,750
July 1995, Goodwood, Goodwood Cup (Gr2), 2m, £36,080
Sept 1995, Doncaster, Doncaster Cup (Gr3), 2m 2f, £21,019
May 1996, Ascot, Sagaro Stakes (Gr3), 2m, £25,000
May 1996, Sandown, Henry II Stakes (Gr3), 2m, £25,120
Sep 1996, Doncaster, Doncaster Cup (Gr3), 2m 2f, £19,072
July 1997, Goodwood, Goodwood Cup (Gr2), 2m, £38,724
July 1998, Goodwood, Goodwood Cup (Gr2), 2m, £40,000
Sep 1998, Doncaster, Doncaster Cup (Gr3), 2m 2f, £20,700

So, where does Trigger stand in the pantheon of staying greats? 'I never, ever allow anyone to belittle anything that Double Trigger did,' says Johnston. 'I don't deny the fact that people are entitled to their opinions. The trainer of Kayf Tara and Classic Cliché (Godolphin's Saeed Bin Suroor) could make a strong case for saying those horses were better Gold Cup winners. I could argue that Trigger was better on his day. There's also a sound case to say that some St Leger winners who went on to win Cups were better. But certainly in 1995 there wasn't one of them who could beat Double Trigger. In that year he won five races, all over two miles and above: the Sagaro, Henry II, Gold Cup, Goodwood Cup, Doncaster Cup. He was also fourth in the Prix du Cadran (at Longchamp), when boxed in. Then he went to the Melbourne Cup, where he was beaten, as he had been in the Yorkshire Cup earlier in the season. He won five out of seven starts that year. It got to the stage where he was *expected* to do it. Frankly, in 1995 he was in a league of his own.'

Maybe in Double Trigger Johnston sees something of himself ... this horse who could always be relied upon to fight back if apparently losing an argument. Certainly he is a fierce protector of Trigger's reputation, as he is with all his horses. Sure the chestnut had chinks in his armour, but that should not be an opportunity for some to inflict grievous wounds. 'We thought that Mister Baileys had been underestimated after the Guineas,' he says, 'but I will never forgive them for Double Trigger not being champion stayer. Nothing could be more hideous than Double Trigger not being named champion stayer in 1995. There was not a horse even close to him. Yet Strategic Choice (trained by Paul Cole) was champion stayer, based on winning the Irish Leger and finishing third in the King George (and Queen Elizabeth Diamond Stakes at Ascot). Nonsensical.'

Johnston regards Trigger's penultimate race in the Goodwood Cup and valedictory performance in the Doncaster Cup as his most treasured moments. 'The days of Trigger being favourite and there being huge pressure were probably gone by then,' he explains. 'It was probably one of the reasons why those wins were all the more pleasurable, because he was probably past his best. To do that was fantastic really. You couldn't have planned it better.'

In five years, there were more gradients of emotion than the downlands of Goodwood, where Trigger won three Cups and was undefeated. Some would reflect that he wasn't always putting in 100 per cent. The *Racing Post's 100 Greatest Racehorses* publication, in which Trigger is 27th, refers euphemistically to his 'quirks' and being 'invariably very much in control of his own destiny'. Johnston contests the point. 'Most days he did put everything in,' he insists. 'The owners and the public have to accept that these horses that have long careers can't be expected to win every time. They're much easier to train when you're not constantly trying to find an excuse and a reason for defeats. Everybody gets more out of it when losing isn't the end of the world. He was a great, great horse. Of course he had his defeats, but then we kept him going for so many years.'

During that time he was partnered by five different jockeys. Jason Weaver rode him nineteen times, Michael Roberts four, Darryll Holland three, Frankie Dettori twice and Thierry Jarnet once. 'The strange thing about Trigger was that though he had this front-running style, each jockey would give him a new lease of life,' says Johnston. 'He'd get in a rut, and maybe the jockey would lose confidence in him, and you'd change the jockey, and away you'd go again. They were so different in the way that they rode him. Michael Roberts, for example, would be pushing and shoving at him all the way. During that period we always believed that Double Trigger had to lead in his races, that once he was headed he downed tools. Then Darryll Holland got him and rewrote the rules, rode him completely differently and just as successfully. Michael was an extremely stylish jockey, but on Trigger he resorted to bullying the horse into going. He used the stick on him more than most others did, and pushed him harder. Yet Darryll Holland, often a very strong jockey with the stick in a finish, managed to conjure runs out of the horse, almost on a loose rein, from a different position in the race.'

So what does that tell you about Trigger's character? Johnston is extremely wary of anthropomorphism – endowing animals with human characteristics. 'It tells me that people try to build characteristics into horses far too much,' he says. 'We're all guilty, though hopefully me less than most other people. With something like Double Trigger, you get to know him, and think you know exactly how he should be ridden. Punters start saying a horse needs soft ground because it's won on soft ground. Or it doesn't like firm, because it got beaten once on firm ground. Or it has to be ridden a certain way. And from that comes this idea that jockeys should be given strict instructions on how to ride their race. Double Trigger is a very good example of what nonsense that is. His last Goodwood Cup was probably the most spectacular, when he led, fell away into midfield, met the rising ground, then came back again. If you analyse it, you'd probably actually find that the leaders slowed down, and he stayed on again.'

Johnston insists that his words are not meant to diminish Trigger's prowess in any way. However, he adds, 'People talk about fighting spirit, and character, and fighting back against another horse, when the reality, sadly, is that the other horse is probably simply slowing down. It's not fighting spirit, it's just stamina. I believe there's leaders and followers. Horses learn how to win, and how to lose. If you put them all out in a field and let them run around, some are faster, some are braver. Some are bullies. Generally, those tough leaders are going to lead the pack and push the others around. But it's not just a matter of being the strongest horse. Because they're flight animals, speed counts for a lot. They've got all those natural instincts, but life is not a race for them. Having said that, if you put two horses side by side on the gallops, they'll go faster than on their own. They will race with each other, and you can teach them to win. Similarly, I believe that if you deliberately get them beat, you'll teach them to lose. They become followers not leaders.'

It had immediately become evident during that first race at Redcar that Trigger was in the latter group. The initial prognosis of Trigger as more of a circus performer, one who would provide laughs more than thrills, has made the reality even more pleasurable for his owner. 'The Gold Cup was incredibly special, as were all the Goodwood Cups, and particularly the one against Double Eclipse,' says Huggins. 'It was amazing how the crowd really took to him. His third Goodwood Cup victory was an incredibly emotional experience. Even some of the journalists were in tears.' Despite Johnston's words, *he* is in no doubt of his horse's courage. 'The horse was incredibly brave,' he says. 'When he came back in that third Goodwood Cup, Jim McGrath's commentary was actually that Trigger was dropping back. Within a couple of seconds he had picked up the bit and charged on again. He never knew when he was beaten. It's very tough, running a lot of those races from the front. The Ascot Gold Cup he led pillar to post, on good to firm ground. Running a lot of those distances – and a lot were on firm going, as it happened – is incredibly tough on horses. Everyone has their off day, and he had a couple of those. But if he was on song, he just didn't want to be beaten.

'Mark was an absolutely brilliant trainer to handle him. We had very clear race plans, although with stayers it's a lot easier. The programme almost picks itself. It was tremendous fun working closely with Mark on all those plans, and with Eclipse afterwards. Although Eclipse was in Trigger's shadow, he did in fact break the track record at Longchamp.'

Trigger bowed out in 1998, with a GNER railway engine named after him and a plethora of plaudits. The *Racing Post*'s Alastair Down, one of the country's more perceptive and original observers, opined at the time:

Dry old statisticians with minds like adding machines and hearts of granite will tell you that Double Trigger wasn't anything special. With meticulously prepared arguments, rooted in fact and figure, taking into consideration weight, age, going, the exchange rate with the dollar, the direction in which the grass was cut and the price of crude on the Rotterdam spot market, they will gently let you down with the fact that Trigger was not among the all-time great stayers; that while he was admirable he was not exceptional.

They are right of course, but not as right as they are wrong. The point is that you cannot reduce a horse like Double Trigger to mere numbers – ratings … are not the only means by which greatness is measured.

He was one of those horses who had something to say about what racing is all about. Most races are interesting, but the overwhelming majority are only interesting to a very limited degree – but it is the very banality of humdrum events which throws the remarkable ones into such stark relief.

I have seen few Flat races which engendered so much pleasure as this summer's Goodwood Cup. Just under two furlongs out, victory for Double Trigger seemed out of the question, yet a furlong and a half later he had won. Ten minutes later, the course was still buzzing, and for those who took the time to fix details of it in their mind, the moment will always be fresh.

In Trigger's case, the fact that he was a character made him all the easier to identify with. He was no saint, and you never heard Mark Johnston trot out the old nonsense that 'a child of three could sit on him'. A child of three could indeed sit on him, but not if you entertained any hopes of the child seeing four. And there was a wonderful sense of his sheer bloody-mindedness. Sure, there were times when he wasn't having a going day, but that merely added to the allure because it made him fallible, just like the rest of us. But on those wind-behind, God-is-in-his-heaven afternoons when Trigger was in full cry, he could play a tune on the disparate souls who make up a race crowd like few other horses in recent years.

Double Trigger was a star and one who, for season after season, bullied his way into your affections in much the same way as he bullied his rivals out of it on the run to the line.

The curious thing, of course, was that Trigger, who in a career which took him to Italy, France, Australia and Hong Kong as well as England's most prestigious racecourses had more adventures than Enid Blyton's Famous Five, overshadowed the stable's Royal Rebel. That Robellino gelding, owned by then BHB chairman Peter Savill, not only lifted the Ascot Gold Cup in successive years but was involved in two heart-pounding finishes when out-pointing another mightily popular chestnut, Persian Punch, and Vinnie Roe, in 2001 and 2002 respectively. That is less a reflection on Royal Rebel and more a measure of Trigger's persona.

Trigger, a senior citizen in equine terms – he is fifteen at the time of writing – is now at stud at East Burrow Farm near Crediton, Devon. 'He's basically going to be a National Hunt sire, although I've got a couple of two-year-olds of his,' says Huggins. 'But as we all know, producing jumpers is a hell of a long haul. I still see a lot of Trigger. He's got this huge personality. A real character. It's true of a lot of the good horses. When you see a lot of these Group 1 horses strutting around, they actually know they're good. They know they're special. Even today, John Haydon, who owns and manages the stud where he is, will turn him out and he'll wander off down the paddock. Then he'll charge back at him, and swerve out of the way at the last minute. It's all a big joke to him. That's how he is. He can nip people and hold on to you, but he never actually bites. It's just a game with him.'

It is evident that when Huggins came along it was a case of right owner at the right time for Johnston. They were kindred spirits. 'I've always been very ambitious with the horses I've had so we had a natural affinity,' says Huggins. 'I wasn't really interested in handicaps. Looking back, we were trying to buy quality horses at ridiculously cheap prices. I didn't really think that at the time, though.' Johnston's drive was always there, right back in the early nineties? 'Absolutely. He was always amazingly ambitious, and very open about it. He was quite determined to get the top owners in the country into the yard. He's always reaching for the stars. And, as I say, if you do that, you won't come up with a handful of dirt.'

I was also intrigued to know if Huggins, who has had nine horses at Middleham over the last decade or so, thinks Johnston's veterinary knowledge is a crucial element of his success. 'To be honest, I think his background as a vet is useful, as opposed to being the key,' he replies. 'The absolute key is that he's a hugely intelligent guy who studies everything to do with his business and horses, and then plans everything meticulously in the way that's going to do the best for him. Things like his feeding regime – feeding them four times a day including during the night because he says it's maximising the digestion processes. There are very few trainers who do that. Everything like that is incredibly well planned. That is his forte. He has strong philosophies too, like, if things aren't going well and there's a minor bug, whatever, he will train through that and come out the other end, whereas lots of people shut up shop, as Godolphin did this year. He's an incredibly focused and determined guy, but at the same time great fun. At the sales, he doesn't regard you as an inconvenience. He'll spend time with you, enjoy jokes. He's a very rounded guy.'

Johnston's name has become synonymous with stayers, and there is a pragmatic explanation for that. He concedes that stamina races are generally easier to win than sprints. 'Probably, you can win a mile-and-a-half race with a miler, but not a mile race with a mile-and-a-half horse. The best horse to make an Ascot Gold Cup winner, though, is a St Leger horse, but most have been retired and don't get there. If I had an open cheque book to buy next year's Ascot Gold Cup winner, I'd be off buying this year's St Leger winner.'

It concerns many of us whether there remains a future for staying races. Owners and breeders invariably seek out bloodlines that will confer fleetness of hoof. Yet the author was among many who supported a campaign which helped save the longest Flat race on the calendar, Royal Ascot's Queen Alexandra Stakes – run over the marathon distance of two and three-quarter miles (it started off as *three* miles in 1864, incidentally) – when it was under threat of removal from the meeting a few years ago. Was that evidence, if any were needed, that the stayers will always enjoy the public's affection? 'There's a future for them, as long as these guys who are currently driving racing in a different direction wake up,' snorts Johnston.

'Attraction won five Group 1 races,' he adds, 'and was far and away the biggest achiever we've had. And Shamardal, admittedly mostly after he left us, was arguably the best horse I've ever trained. Yet if you go out in the street and ask the casual punter to name a Mark Johnston horse, the first one they'll think of will be Double Trigger. He's still the horse I'm most associated with; more than Mister Baileys, more than Shamardal, more than Attraction. Not because he's the best, but because he ran in staying races, and the public love it. To do away with those races would be horrendous.'

Fortunately, the possibility of that receded greatly in 2006, when the Ascot Gold Cup is won by Yeats, who exudes class. The Ballydoyle colt has Sergeant Cecil and Distinction behind him in the centuries-old race – 2007 will be its 200th year – and also well adrift is Johnston's Winged D'Argent. After three days, this is only his second runner at this year's royal meeting (McEldowney having finished fifth in the Ascot Stakes), and things look ominous.

Johnston is not the only major stable suffering. By the end of the Royal meeting, the two-year-old races will have been contested by only one Ballydoyle representative and none from Godolphin. Admittedly, Sheikh Mohammed's operation has had its troubles and Aidan O'Brien's juveniles have made a tardy start. But there is also a definite dearth of runners from other major trainers. So, could it be, as a *Racing Post* article suggests, that two-year-old racing is losing its prestige?

There is no evidence of improvement later on the Thursday for Johnston. He has three runners in the Britannia Stakes, Crime Scene, Peppertree Lane and Desert Realm; they finish 15th, 24th and 29th respectively (although Johnston subsequently maintains they were all badly drawn). On the Friday, Baan is seventh in the King Edward VII Stakes. Then, that same day, at a little after 4.30, something strange happens. Those remaining of Royal Ascot's best-ever crowd of 71,000 look on as Joe Fanning, in typically relentless, hell-for-leather style, is never headed on Johnston's I'm So Lucky in the Listed Wolferton Handicap. It is Fanning's first ever Royal Ascot winner. The yard's Crosspeace finishes third. Then another for the stable as Soapy Danger, under Kevin Darley, claims the Queen's Vase. Finally, Linas Selection, also ridden by Darley, asserts his authority in the King George V Stakes. Chaff has suddenly turned to corn. From nowhere, Johnston is the 2006 meeting's leading trainer. His Royal Ascot winners total has increased to 26. All is well with the world once again. Can this truly be the transformation in fortunes so desperately sought during the past few weeks? Certainly, the previous day had been propitious, with four winners at minor meetings.

I was absent at this time, covering the World Cup in Germany, but the Press Association wires told all under the heading 'Dream Treble for Johnston':

Mark Johnston's yard is back in business after a remarkable 466-1 treble in the last three races of the day at Royal Ascot. The Middleham handler has made no secret of the fact his string have not been firing on all cylinders this term, but he has clearly turned the corner judging by this outstanding three-timer.

'I was looking at the betting at the beginning of the week and

I saw I was 33–1 (to win the trainers' title),' smiled Johnston. 'Deirdre (Johnston, the trainer's wife) saw I was 33–1 and she suggested that I should get some fifties!

'It's been bad, and there's no getting away from it, and I still wouldn't say all the horses were well. We never thought about shutting up shop and have had to be very choosy. I can't honestly say that I'm So Lucky was one of the well ones either because he lives in the section of the yard which has been most affected. But he's run a superb race.'

That leading trainer accolade actually eludes him, narrowly. Not that it troubles him. That trio of victories are a booming volley of cannon fire, warning that he is back, and the powder, lots of it, is dry.

On the Monday after Royal Ascot, James Willoughby, the *Racing Post*'s chief correspondent, includes in a piece entitled '10 Lessons We Learned During Five Days of the Royal Meeting' the following verdict on Johnston's season:

Until his terrific treble on Friday, it just seemed as though the Middleham trainer had no naturally gifted horses and was merely ticking along a little below his self-imposed high standards. Then I'm So Lucky, Soapy Danger and Linas Selection provided a sudden reminder of the power and resolution that his horses exude when they are firing.

You wonder what type of ambitions Johnston harbours for the remainder of his career. He has constantly proved himself capable of producing a stream of black-type runners from limited resources. Klaus Jacobs, the owner of the last two legs of the treble, is a powerful, relatively new source of talent for the trainer to draw upon, but, strange as it sounds at this stage, he has long deserved more spending power at the sales and better raw material.

To which concluding note Johnston himself would no doubt say, 'Amen.'

CHAPTER EIGHTEEN

Her legs obviously hurt her at times. But she was the sort of horse
that coped with it … It's the main difference between a good and
a bad racehorse, and the same with human athletes, probably.
They don't stop when they're tired; don't stop when it hurts.

August, 2006, and it's approaching a year since Attraction departed Kingsley House for a liaison with Ouija Board's sire, Cape Cross, but just utter the name of the mare to Deirdre Johnston and she'll admit, unashamedly, 'I want to cry, just thinking about her. She's so special.'

That horse was indeed an extraordinary phenomenon, both in what she achieved on the racetrack, given her relatively humble birth and her physical impediments, and because of what she represented in Mark Johnston's career. If Master Baileys was the drum-roll in 1994, and Double Trigger the fanfare in the mid- to late nineties, then the filly who as a yearling had not even been dispatched to the sales by her breeder, the Duke of Roxburghe, because there was no likelihood of anyone buying her was the official proclamation and five-gun salute that her trainer was ready to consort with the kings of the turf.

Not that by the new millennium Johnston required any further witness to his prowess as one of the nation's leading trainers. By the time Attraction entered his life, the adjective 'powerful' would automatically preface any mention of his yard, as his horse numbers increased annually and he rolled out centuries like Brian Lara at the wicket. It was not just that he was the fortuitous recipient of a filly blessed with such awesome raw speed but who could also stay a mile; it was that the Middleham trainer achieved so much with her despite the fact that had she been human she would have qualified for a disability allowance. At the time of writing she is enjoying life as an expectant mother in the pastures of the Duke of Roxburghe's stud at Kelso in the Scottish Borders. It completes the perfect circle, and, in a sport that can be unforgiving and cynical at times, it is one of racing's truly romantic tales. But those involving damsels in distress and ancient castles usually are, aren't they?

Attraction was bred by the Duke at his Floors Castle Stud. He had sent his Pursuit Of Love mare Flirtation to Efisio because, as he explained at the time, 'we were looking for an inexpensive sire to get the mare started'. That mating cost around £6,000. Attraction ended up winning more than £800,000, and far, far more in terms of what it meant to his owner-breeder. As the Duke observed, 'She was fairly commonly bred, but turned out to be one of the best fillies of the century.'

So, who is the Duke of Roxburghe, whose name often appears in racecards as owner, breeder or both? According to the *Sunday Times* Rich List, 'Guy', to his friends, is one of Scotland's wealthiest landowners. The 10th Duke of Roxburghe inherited his title and Floors Castle, the largest residence in Scotland, in 1974. It has been home to the Duke and Duchess and their predecessors since the house was built by William Adam for the 1st Duke in 1721. The Duke is said to be a confidant of the royal family; it was at Floors Castle that Prince Andrew proposed to Sarah Ferguson. Apart from the stud farm, he also owns a golf course, 65,600 acres of land, and Kelso racecourse.

The facts surrounding Attraction have been embroidered at times, but the Duke has memories of his filly's early days. 'When she was a yearling, she was pretty incorrect in front,' he says. 'One knee, probably both knees, were off-set. So as a sales prospect she was not a runner at all. I never considered taking her to the sales. Well, actually, I did show her to one of the sales agencies, and they said, "Don't even think of selling her. She'll make nothing." It came to the end of the sales season and I thought, "What are we going to do with her?" At the time I had leased two fillies to trainer John Hills and he had agreed to try to find people to take them. One of them was still up at my stud. I rang him and said, "I've got this filly coming down to you next week. Oh, and I've got this other filly. Would you mind taking her?" He said, "Yes, stick her on the horsebox and I'll see what I can do." When John and I spoke again he said he'd found someone to lease one of the fillies, but he hadn't got anyone for the second. There was also the third one, which was Attraction, but he said, "I really can't have three horses, and two without owners." I thanked him, and sent the one who would be named Attraction to Mark.'

Johnston had trained for the Duke for around a decade by this time. The Duke had originally had his horses only in the south, with the late Alec Stewart and Roger Charlton, but he decided that if he had a trainer in the north there would be more likelihood of him getting to see his horses run. Johnston was just coming to the fore then, and having made initial contact, the trainer appeared at his door one day. It was the beginning of a rewarding relationship.

'The filly – she was still unnamed then – went up to Mark, having been broken at John Hills' (Lambourn yard),' the Duke continues. 'She was probably there for six weeks, and went to him in the first week in January (2003). I told Mark, "Look, I'm sending you this filly. She's pretty crooked. See if you can win a race with her – but I'm not sure she'll stand training."'

Deirdre Johnston takes up the story. 'She had sore shins before she first ran. She also got a wee bit strong while cantering. So Mark said, "You ride her and tell me whether she's OK." The minute I sat on her, I thought, "Wow." I told him, "Find a race for that horse." The feeling she gave me was just incredible. That was it, the start of a fantastic rollercoaster ride. It was clear from very early on that she had an engine.'

Johnston phoned the Duke in March and said, '"You'd better name this horse because she's going quite well." He hadn't expected that. He'd sent her here with a target – win a race. He thought that was maybe quite a tall target in itself.'

Attraction, as she was now known, was declared to run at Nottingham, in the lowest class of five-furlong maiden. 'Roger Charlton had the favourite in the race and asked if mine could win,' Johnston recalls. 'I said she *could* do, but I was not expecting her to.' The Duke's filly led over one furlong out, and won by five lengths. After another victory, at Thirsk, her owner and trainer believed she was capable of acquiring some black type, and she headed for Beverley and the Hilary Needler Trophy (for juvenile fillies).

'The first time she ran, I don't think I had any particular expectations,' recalls the Duke. 'Mark just told me, "She's going quite nicely, she's got a bit of ability. I haven't done an enormous amount with her. I don't want to stress her because of her legs. Although she won that first race very easily, it was a pretty crap event. I didn't get too excited. Her breeding didn't suggest anything special. The dam was a non-winning mare (Flirtation had been unplaced in her only start at three), and although Efisio was a successful stallion, he was not one that was particularly well known.' He did, however, start to allow himself more fanciful notions after the Hilary Needler. 'It's a Listed race, and she absolutely hacked up. It's normally regarded as a good Queen Mary trial. That was the first point when we knew we had something quite special.

'I had never had a Royal Ascot winner at that point,' the Duke adds. 'In fact, I'd barely had an Ascot runner.' Johnston could not envisage her getting beaten that day at the Royal meeting, I tell him. The Duke laughs. 'I don't think I was so certain. She started favourite, although there were some well-bred and expensive fillies in opposition. She won by three lengths, and five lengths, so it was a pretty impressive performance. She then won the Cherry Hinton (stepping up to six furlongs in the process). It was remarkable that a horse should run three times in just over a month, in a Listed and two Group races, and win them all.'

Through it all she had been kept sound, but such fortune couldn't last. Attraction went lame. 'The vets inspected her X-rays, compared them to earlier in the season, and found marked changes,' the Duke recalls. 'The advice was that she shouldn't run again, that we should retire her. I actually got as far as starting to draft a press release to that effect. But Mark was brilliant. He said, "Hang on a minute. Why don't we try to get her sound again and run her in the Cheveley Park (Stakes, the Group 1 race at Newmarket in September)?" The idea was to coax her there by swimming her and keeping the stress off her legs. But then she had an unrelated problem: she fractured her pedal-bone (the area where the foot joins the limb) behind, which, with the wonderful benefit of hindsight, was probably the best thing that could have happened to her. She came back here and had eight weeks' box rest. Mark said she should be fed as normal right through that period, so she was quite a handful by the end of that eight weeks.'

In all, Attraction had been off the track for nine months when she flew from the stalls at Newmarket on 2 May 2004 to lead the field of sixteen in the 1,000 Guineas. It was an audacious strategy by her trainer. Again, one of his Guineas contenders had had no preparatory race. On those dodgy front legs, she was also attempting a mile, two furlongs further than she'd attempted as a two-year-old. This time the examination was sustained, but she prevailed, by half a length, from runner-up Sundrop. The sum of searing speed and a powerful gallop equalled a sixth straight win. Three weeks later Attraction completed a unique double on an even more exacting track than Newmarket, defeating Alexander Goldrun in the Irish equivalent at The Curragh. Kevin Darley, who partnered Attraction in twelve of her fifteen races, reflected after that race, 'I am almost speechless. She is such an incredible filly. Mark has the hard job, keeping her sound and right at home. My job is easy.'

For Deirdre Johnston, the 2004 English Guineas will always remain a gloriously colourful page in her mental scrapbook. 'Although she'd not run after July, the previous year, Attraction had finished her two-year-old season on such a high,' she says. 'There was all the worry about her knees through the winter. Then she fractured her pedal-bone. Was she going to run again, or wasn't she? We went through all that and just took her straight to the Guineas. Then it was, "Is the ground going to be OK? Was it going to be fast enough for her? Was she going to be the horse she was before? Would she train on? Would she stay a mile, or should she stay at six furlongs? It was all exciting. There were so many ifs and buts. In fact, all through the season we kept thinking, "Shall we take her back to sprinting?" Mark, Charlie and I were walking the course on the morning of the race, and picking the ground for her, and Charlie was saying, "This is where she's going to win." All those things I look back on and think, "That's what makes it really special." It was complete elation. The Irish Guineas was fantastic too, but the pressure was off because she'd already won the English one. We hoped we'd have runners in both the Guineas that year so we booked a hotel and stayed over from one day to the next. We'd never done that before. It was the first year we'd gone as a family. For us all to be there was fantastic.'

Her husband had never had anything but utter faith in the filly. 'The Queen Mary was by far the biggest pressure,' Johnston recalls. 'I put it on myself. I really went there thinking, "I'll be devastated if she gets beat." But after that it was plain sailing. At the Guineas I went there believing that if she stays, she wins. Mister Baileys had started at 16–1 for his Guineas; Attraction started at a very generous 11–2, but it was a very simple form race to assess. You just looked down the racecard and this horse had five 1s next to its name, the last one being in the Cherry Hinton. And there's no question: if she stays a mile, she wins. There was nothing in the race with the class to beat her.'

The same was true of the Coronation Stakes at Royal Ascot, an eighth successive triumph, a scintillating performance which had the Duke of Roxburghe reflecting, 'She is the best filly I can remember. Of course, there were Bosra Sham, Oh So Sharp and all those great horses, but I can't recall one doing what she has achieved – winning eight from eight, and three Group 1s on the trot.' Even rival trainers eulogised over her achievements. Mick Channon, trainer of Majestic Desert, who finished runner-up, placed Attraction's achievements in context with the words, 'You probably won't see another horse like her in your lifetime. Horses like that don't come along very often.' Johnston could only concur. 'She wins her races by having an incredible cruising speed. She is really a very relaxed filly and I am not actually certain you can fire her up.'

The trainer was considering the Breeders' Cup, at Lone Star Park, Texas, in October as a possible target for his filly when two defeats by Soviet Song, between which she finished last of ten at Deauville, caused a rethink of those plans. But Attraction had supreme 'bouncebackability', as one of our football managers once said, and before her three-year-old season was out she had secured the Sun Chariot Stakes at Newmarket.

The Lockinge at Newbury might have been many trainers' option for the filly's first run as a four-year-old, but why should Johnston start to obey convention now? He harboured the notion that the Champions Mile at Sha Tin should be her destination, not least because second place there was worth as much as victory in the Newbury race. Attraction's remarkable story preceded her. She had been deemed a 'freak' by the local media in Hong Kong, and the confrontation with champion sprinter Silent Witness was hugely anticipated. In the event, in hot and humid conditions, Johnston's filly never struck a blow and finished eleventh. Silent Witness was narrowly defeated as well.

The omens were hardly portentous when the filly disappointed again in the Group 3 Hungerford Stakes at Newbury. One concert too many for the diva of the turf? With almost a sense of mischief her response was victory in what would transpire to be her final performance, in the Matron Stakes at Leopardstown. The tenth of September 2005, and she had made her final bow. Injury confirmed there would be no encore. This time, the press communiqué from the Duke of Roxburghe went ahead. As the US-based *Thoroughbred Times* put it:

> Standout filly Attraction, champion two-year-old filly in Europe in 2003, has been retired after her connections detected a small problem as she was training for the Sun Chariot Stakes on Saturday at Newmarket.
>
> 'I'm afraid she's not going to run on Saturday and that's going to be it,' the Duke of Roxburghe, Attraction's owner, said. 'That is the end of her career, I'm afraid. Obviously it's very sad, but maybe in some ways I'm rather relieved.'
>
> Trainer Mark Johnston was preparing Attraction for the Sun Chariot Stakes, but once the Duke of Roxburghe was informed that she was not at 100% the decision became easy. 'It's a niggly little problem, but we had not really been able to get to the bottom of it and to find out what it is and why,' the Duke told the *Racing Post*. 'She had been very marginally lame, but you can't be going into a Group 1 race with any sort of problems. We have taken a decision that the logical thing is to say we are not going to run and therefore retire her. It's nothing to do with her much-fabled action in front. She's just marginally lame behind.'
>
> Attraction concludes her career with ten wins, including five Group 1 victories, from fifteen starts and lifetime earnings of $1,583,910. Even in real money, that's a pretty hefty haul.

For the majority of us, those three years would have been a life-transforming period. Whether they meant quite the same to a man who inhabits a Scottish pile ... the Duke swiftly abuses you of such a notion. 'I think it probably was a life-changing event for me too. Not too many people have a horse that is champion two-year-old filly in Europe, and then to go out and win three Group 1s on the trot, including two Classics. Also she was the only filly to do the English–Irish Guineas double. Don't forget, it has been an era of fantastic fillies, too: Ouija Board, Alexander Goldrun, Soviet Song. Those three fillies and Attraction have won 21 Group 1s between them. Three of them are from the same generation.'

Could anyone but Johnston have achieved it, given the circumstances? Not just because of his veterinary expertise, but his perseverance. 'I'm not sure the veterinary factor was anything to do with it,' the Duke replies. 'But I think, without any shadow of doubt, that what she achieved in her first season and latterly achieved in her second season was, in huge measure, down to him. He has a very cavalier – perhaps that's a bit too strong a word, but you understand what I mean – attitude to training. He gets his horses very fit. Once they're fit, he wants them at the racecourse as often as they can. There are very few other trainers in the country who would have produced that filly to run five times and win five times, and in the process win a Listed and a Group 3 and Group 2. It's enormously to his credit. I think it's his ability as a trainer rather than his veterinary experience. I think the fact that he was a vet probably was quite useful when it came to the dramas we had with her between two and three. He was able to take a more sanguine attitude than maybe another trainer, who would possibly have taken the straightforward view of the vets and accepted it. To win the Guineas after nine months off was quite fantastic. That was the most exciting day of my life. It's a great testament to him and his staff.'

Johnston analyses it all in purely rational terms. 'When you get one with questionable front legs, your job as a trainer is just to keep her sound,' he says. 'But it did surprise us all that she stayed sound so long. She had plenty of problems with them. Her legs obviously hurt her at times. But she was the sort of horse that coped with it. We had many excuses not to run her, on many occasions, like just before the Coronation Stakes. She could be lame on the Thursday and run on Saturday. If you wanted to get a vet's certificate, you could have got one any day of her racing life, because there was no way her legs were normal. It's the main difference between a good and a bad racehorse, and the same with human athletes, probably. They don't stop when they're tired; don't stop when it hurts. There was an element of throwing caution to the wind in those early days. But then we learnt that she could cope with it. In many ways, she was an incredibly easy horse to train.'

Deirdre Johnston takes pride in her own contribution. 'I often rode her in work, and saddled her at the races. Each time she won, I loved thinking I'd actually done something to help that horse achieve it. I rode her at two. I rode her before she ever ran, and saddled her for her first race. I rode her, on and off, through all her career, although I was actually relieved not to be riding her out all through her Group 1 wins, because there's quite a lot of pressure on you when you're riding a horse like that. But I would often sit on her when they thought she had a problem. I often do that when somebody's not happy with them, when they can't make them trot or they're worried whether they're sound or lame, or whatever. And we had that a few times with Attraction. Of course she always moved a little bit funny. There were only maybe four different people that rode her who knew how she moved and knew if she was different from normal.

'She was a real character. She wouldn't let anyone catch her in the box. She had her own mind and she knew exactly what she liked and what she didn't like. Yet she was brilliant when she went to the races. She was so laid back. You never had to worry about her in parades or anything. Before the race she'd just have a good snooze, then she'd get up and go. Anyone could get near her when you were saddling her. The kids would come in and pat her and she'd just stand there. The only time to watch her, though, was when you put the jockey up. Then she might kick you. But that's great – I like attitude like that!'

It has to be said that trainers are rarely blessed with such owners. Black type and the prospect of mega-money, in prizes and later in parenthood, have been known to turn the most undemanding character into a monster. The Duke accepted triumph with appreciation and defeat with stoicism. 'I think the Duke would have sold her just before Beverley,' says Johnston. 'Someone was trying to buy her. The Duke is a commercial breeder from generations of commercial breeders. That's his business, after all. But this chap wanted to get her vetted the day before the race. He said, "That's ridiculous. You can't vet the horse and run her the next day. If you don't buy it, forget it, and we'll discuss it after the race." We were all slightly surprised that there was never a serious attempt to buy Attraction, apart from that one – but that's probably because after she won the Queen Mary she was never for sale. As the Duke says, it's every breeder's dream to have a Queen Mary winner. To have a proper mare who can win at Royal Ascot, and has got speed. After that, everything was just a bonus. We wanted to win a Group 2, then to win a Group 1. But as the Duke was always saying, "Everything she's done is so far beyond expectations that it doesn't really matter. She owes us nothing."

'The way the Duke handled that horse was absolutely wonderful, from the successes to the defeats like the Prix Jacques Le Marois (at Deauville) and seconds to Soviet Song, and the fascinating one in 2005 when we went to Newbury and finished fourth in a Group 3, which was such a comedown for Attraction after always finishing first or second in Group 1s. It was great for him to come out afterwards and say philosophically, "That was good enough. That was all we wanted to see. If she's sound tomorrow, that's fine. She's come back from the horrors of Hong Kong and the injury and shown that she's still got the speed there. That's OK." It was OK as well, because she won a Group 1 on her next start. Virtually every race, including the Guineas, he'd say, "It's just another race. Let's not worry about it. This is everything we've dreamt of. This would be a bonus." He took any defeat on the chin and just got on with it.'

'Every race we won with Attraction we celebrated with the Duke,' Deirdre adds. 'Even when she went to Deauville and was last, we all cheered ourselves up afterwards, and we all had a lovely day. But then I like the celebrating, and being with the owners. I like the socialising. I'm a people person. The Duke was a really good owner; he made everything really good fun. He's got a huge scrapbook of every cutting and made a DVD of her career. It included the letter from the vet saying she wouldn't race again between two and three. He loved to plan everything, and walk the track, at the Guineas, and in Ireland. He liked to have every detail covered before the race. Then he'd say, "Right, nothing more we can do. There's no pressure." It was a fantastic attitude to have with such a good horse.'

There were mixed emotions when Attraction left the yard for good. 'She lived across from our bedroom window,' says Deirdre. 'First thing in the morning and last thing at night when I went to bed I could see her. I remember one day when I went to close the curtains. I saw her box empty and I nearly fainted. Then I thought, "Thank God, no, she's gone to Ireland." Having her there all the time ... If someone said, "Oh, she's not moving very well this morning," I'd be running down the hill to look at her. But I have to say, when she went to stud, fit and well, without having an injury, there was great relief. She had done all that racing yet she was in great condition. I was both sad and happy. We didn't really want a big send-off because we would have found it very hard. We just wanted her to go quietly; almost not know she was going.'

Not that that day was the last Deirdre saw of Attraction. 'I was desperately keen to compete at the Duke's horse trials, at Floors Castle,' she says. 'When I went up she'd just come back from stud, where she'd been covered by Cape Cross, and there she was, galloping around the field. It was just fantastic to see her looking so well, ready to have her first foal next year. I bet she'll be a great mum. She'd let down so quickly, just really looked like a broodmare.'

Following her retirement, there would be thorns among the bouquets of flowers. It wasn't the first occasion that the reputation of one of Johnston's outstanding horses was diminished in some quarters. The *Racing Post*'s Flat Horses of 2005 suggested that 'even in her Classic season she did not hit the heights sometimes claimed for her. Hers was not a vintage generation of fillies.' Johnston has long grown weary of comparisons between horses of different generations. 'As I've said before, trying to compare horses of different eras, and running over different trips, is a nonsense really,' he insists. 'But what she achieved was more than we could have imagined for any horse, let alone one with dodgy legs. But in terms of how far they are ahead of their peers, probably Shamardal is the best horse I've ever trained, though Attraction actually achieved more. It was fantastic that he came along while Attraction was still here. To have two horses like that at the same time, both free-running and front-running, was remarkable. Both had the speed to be sprinters – in fact Attraction did win. Shamardal could probably have won five-furlong races as well. He had so much early speed and could get the rest of the field quickly off the bridle.

'Between 1994 and 1997 we had five Group 1 winners; Attraction did that by herself. She did what all those horses did rolled into one. It's incredible to think she won an English Guineas, an Irish Guineas and a Coronation Stakes in the space of three months. There was every reason for saying she wasn't sound and shouldn't run a race, but she won five Group 1s and five others, and went off to stud happy as Larry.' And left behind a trainer's wife who's seen thousands of horses come and go through the gates of Kingsley House but who can still become moist-eyed at mention of 'the special one'.

CHAPTER NINETEEN

You know you'll lose horses. We did lose horses, two or three that I would
directly blame on the fact that we were out of form. We had one new owner
took their horse away before it had even run.

A virtual desert had not suddenly become a fertile valley overnight, but the Friday of Royal Ascot 2006 was sufficient to indicate a welcome climate change. Winners had begun to flow once more.

When we speak again at Kingsley House, just before Glorious Goodwood, Mark Johnston's demeanour has been enlivened by the sequence of events. 'The real turning point was I'm So Lucky, who bounced back from oblivion,' he says. 'And we were still waiting for our two bankers. It was said our three winners on the Friday was a *huge* surprise. It wasn't actually a huge surprise. We ran fifteen and normally we try to run twenty, so we were a bit down in numbers, but if you had asked me at the beginning of the week which two had the best chance of winning, I'd have said Linas Selection and Soapy Danger. They were both in-form horses. The only other big hope which didn't materialise was Always Fruitful (who finished seventh in the Chesham Stakes on the Saturday). We were being cheered all the time by what was happening at other tracks. Things *were* better. We just had to do it at Ascot. I remember saying on the Thursday (of Ascot), "Well, that's great, but I don't want to be top trainer at Ripon."'

But the revival was underway. Ascot confirmed it. 'From there the thing snowballed,' Johnston says. Renewed confidence began to seep back into the pores of Johnston and his staff. 'We had a crap percentage,' he concedes. 'I looked every morning and the winners, at one stage, hit 5 per cent and the placed horses were 20 per cent. It was just horrendous. But we turned around throughout July, when the winners reached 21 per cent. Both the three-year-olds and two-year-olds are now running well. It was fantastic how we recovered. It was as bad a dip as I can remember, ever. Yet,' he adds defiantly, 'even during that period, which I agree by our standards was awful, we never dropped out of the top ten trainers in the country.'

It's not merely his pride that's at stake. He goes on to reveal that not everyone has responded to such an indifferent period rationally and patiently. 'You know you'll lose horses,' says Johnston. 'We *did* lose horses, two or three that I would directly blame on the fact that we were out of form. We had one new owner took their horse away before it had even run. You know that if that happens right the way through to the end of the season, you'll lose a significant number, or you won't get the numbers you have planned for.' I tell him I find that almost unbelievable. He shrugs. It won't be the first time owners' knees have jerked, and it probably won't be the last.

To some extent, that goes with the status Johnston has acquired. 'We certainly get to go a week without a winner before people start saying we're having a bad time,' Johnston says. 'But at that time the horses were running atrociously.' I remember Johnston being very concerned about their appearance. He actually said he was 'ashamed'. 'It was very poor. I was very worried about how they looked, and very concerned about how we could turn that around. I've always been a firm believer that you have to train them down in weight until you reach their optimum weight. You can't *put* weight on a horse and get it fit at the same time. I had this huge dilemma in June. It was getting to the stage where I was thinking it was insurmountable; of the horses being underweight so they shouldn't go racing. But then it just came right without trying, really.'

An analysis has revealed little. 'We changed a few things, like the hay, but it's almost identical on analysis – made by the same man using the same grasses. We made minor changes to try to get the calorific value of the feed up as high as possible. But it's so high in the first place. We experimented with other feeds prepared by Baileys. We wouldn't normally experiment in the middle of the season, but we were desperate. We gave them multi-vitamins. We hit them with everything. We don't know what, if any of those things, changed the position. I suppose that's why I've always been a bit paranoid about keeping my foot on the pedal, because of the way we did spiral upwards. You fear that the same could happen in reverse.

'The main thing that went through my mind was that you start worrying that there's no skill in this job. If it's all down to skill, when something's wrong you should just apply your skills and find you've fixed it. Yet here I found myself incapable of dealing with the problem, or putting my finger on something that could solve it. So you start thinking, "Maybe it's just luck." You just wait for fortunes to turn. And to a certain extent that was the case.

'There's a couple of things stick in my mind. There's that saying "Horses are like flowers: leave them alone and they'll bloom in their own time". I'm not sure who first said it, but I often think of that when things are wrong. You must just leave them alone and let them emerge. I tried to keep that in my mind. I also remember, just from two or three years ago, John Warren speaking to me. It was at a time when I felt we were going through a bad patch, and every time I spoke to an owner I was apologising for it and saying we were trying to do something about it. John said, "You're not doing anything different from what you usually do, so it'll come. Leave it alone and it'll come right."

'When things do go wrong, the main things I do is just to check everything, make sure we aren't doing anything different that has caused a problem. I always say, "these horses can't all be sick at the same time." It's an impossibility. When it happens I have to get out of here, and get in amongst them. That's why it's important Charlie ... if he doesn't go to vet school, he's still got to realise that so much of this job is knowing about horses. When things are going badly, the only solution is to get out there and look for those that are well.

'Possibly one of the things that does set me apart from some other trainers, when things are going wrong, is that I never shut down completely. On the one hand there's the principle that you must leave them alone and let them come right in their own time; yet, equally, you've got to remember that your horses won't win races standing in boxes. '

Though the winners are free-flowing once more, there is still one vexed issue: the lack of Group-race victories. 'I've always said that the places are a more reliable guide than wins, simply because there are more of them, so it's more accurate,' Johnston says. 'Look at our Group race places and we're on around 50 per cent. That's absolutely fantastic.

But we've only won two, which is very frustrating. Overall, when running at 50 per cent places, we usually get 20 per cent winners. If we had that with Group races, then our position in the trainers' table would be different. We'd be up there, possibly even competing with Sir Michael Stoute. The gap between us and Michael is not insurmountable. At the moment, it's £700,000 (in prizemoney). Now, two good horses can win that. We've missed those opportunities to win those big lumps of money.' I suggest that, invariably, Stoute tends to be more powerful than anyone in the quality of his older horses. 'The best prizemoney is for races contested by three-year olds, and older, and quite simply, Michael's got more than we have,' agrees Johnston. 'The chances are that he's going to win more of those kind of races. 'But even then, normally, I'd expect our prizemoney to be boosted by the two-year-olds. We've got a lot of them who've been running well, but haven't yet won Group races. Hopefully their time will come.'

If I was a trainer, I'd be desperately conscious that a slump like he had experienced had meant that numerous valuable races were just passing me by. 'Definitely,' Johnston agrees, 'and particularly with the two-year-olds; they will never come again. We're already thinking about next year for some of them.'

Conversely, though, a poor run does have a curious sort of advantage: it helps bring handicappers' ratings down. 'That's exactly what it means. That's what I'm thinking every time a horse doesn't run well. That we've gained something out of it. It's got another day. But that's as the trainer, not the owner, who may take a different view.'

Johnston appreciates the irony of the situation. 'There's so many trainers out there supposedly having to go to such great effort to get their horses down the handicap. All you actually have to do is get them beat. They get beat often enough by themselves, without you making any effort to do it. John Francome (of *Channel 4 Racing*) has said many times how, more than other trainers, our horses seem to come bouncing back from a bad run to win in a matter of days. One of the reasons is that I don't look for excuses. Once you start doing what the Jockey Club encourages us to do, and say, "This horse ran below form because it's coughing, or because it's got some mucus on its trachea, or because the ground is unsuitable," then you're stuck with not running it again –

until those reasons no longer apply. If you say, "Well, I don't really *know*, I can't see any reason why it finished tenth and not first," then you just run it again. We should do that more often. In fact, I do it less now than I used to.'

I broach the subject of his jockeys, all of whom have also benefited from the upturn in fortunes. I return to that time just before the Derby when both Johnston and Deirdre criticised Kevin Darley for his riding. I put it to Johnston that perhaps the lack of belief in the yard's horses had permeated its way through to the riders. If a stable is going through a bad spell, do jockeys subconsciously stop trying far more quickly? That is, when horses *appear* to be beaten, their riders accept more readily that they *are* beaten. 'Definitely. I think that comes into it, although they won't admit it.' He pauses, then adds, 'But I hate seeing jockeys drop their hands.

I ask if he had spoken to Darley about his concerns? He shakes his head. Then he concedes: 'Probably I don't say enough.' However, it is clearly a very sensitive area, the relationship between trainer and jockey. The trainer adds: 'Kevin's been complaining about not getting enough rides. I haven't really thought he was justified. One of the horses he complained about (not getting the ride) was Joseph Henry. I told him: "Well, you gave him a bad ride at Epsom. I put Joe Fanning on it, and he won the next time." On that occasion, Kevin asked me: "How did I give it a bad ride?" I told him: "We were stepping him up in trip (going up from six furlongs to a mile), he needed covering him up, and what did you do? You hit the front three furlongs out?" 'Kevin said: 'Well, why didn't you say something to me afterwards?" And he's right; it was not really fair; not to tell him. I just switched to Joe (Fanning), and told him! In hindsight I probably should have told Kevin, kept him on the horse, and he would probably have got the same result as Joe.' It is a candid admission from a man who stresses throughout his admiration for Darley's talent. However, you can understand Johnston's reasoning. 'A lot of time with jockeys, I don't like to bombard them with criticism of how they ride because I think confidence is everything. I like them to be instinctive, and I like them to be confident.' He makes a further observation. 'Another thing I hate is jockeys running wide. But I don't like telling them, or if I do, I want to tell them when they're not actually riding for me. I don't want them to go out there thinking about it.'

We talk about the pecking order of his jockeys. None is on a retainer. They are named, on a board, in order of priority in the office for Debbie and her colleagues to consult. And their position can change. I happen to mention Jean-Pierre Guillambert. He rode well the previous day on Bailey's Encore, at Redcar. A poor race, but not the easiest of rides. 'Yes,' Johnston agrees with a laugh. 'I think they were all trying to lose. A very capable lad. I rate him highly.'

But apart from the list, how does he assign them? 'A lot of it is association with different horses, or owners who particularly prefer having a certain jockey,' Johnston answers. 'Obviously with Richard Hills, Sheikh Hamdan retains him.

It's a thankless task, which the girls in the office have to deal with. They get the rough end of it because jockeys are never happy. It has been a big issue this year, over Kevin, because he did start as our number one. And he was always complaining about what he got. I still feel that whatever Joe Fanning gets, Kevin feels he should be given something better. He complained a couple of times about it, and then he asked to see me. We sat down at Sandown and discussed it. I basically told him that he should do his own thing a bit. "Just tell us where you're going," I said, or something like that. "But if you want to do it that way, you can't be number one."

'Number one is not only the guy who rides most winners for us, but the one who gives us the most loyalty in return,' Johnston adds. 'He's the guy who will go to Lingfield to ride one – as Joe did two days ago, when he rode one not very good horse. He will rush off from Ripon to Carlisle. He will go to wherever we ask him to go, without complaint. Joe's agent complains, but Joe never complains. That's why Joe's number one. Then Kevin at two, Greg (Fairley) or Royston three and four, Stanley Chin five, J-P Guillambert six and Richard Hills seven. The main thing that shifts them down is not being available. Or getting off one of our horses and riding someone else's. The main thing that raises them up the table is riding winners. What's made it more awkward is that Kevin has taken a retainer now from one of our owners, Valentine Feerick. They have six horses. They may have one runner at a meeting, and he'll have to go there, but it's not necessarily the meeting where we've got other runners.'

You assume that Darley would be Johnston's first-choice jockey, though. He's been riding at the top level for so many years. Champion in 2000 with 155 winners, during a year when Kieren Fallon was injured, Staffordshire-born Darley is, like many leading riders, a former apprentice of that great mentor Reg Hollinshead. A French Derby triumph on Peter Savill's Celtic Swing in 1995 and his association with Johnston's dual 1,000 Guineas winner Attraction are the badges of distinction that place him at the pinnacle of his profession. 'Kevin would say that he's coming from a different level from Joe,' says Johnston. 'Kevin's been there, done it and got the T-shirt. Joe's trying to aspire to that. Yet, as it stands at the moment, Joe's higher in the jockeys' table (in terms of winners). Their percentages are very similar. It's all personal opinion. I think they have different strengths. Joe is better out of the stalls and getting into a position in the race, while Kevin rides a tighter, probably a better finish than Joe, who's more likely to drift around the track. Kevin's much tidier, not necessarily stronger. But really there's not a lot in it.'

A few weeks later we discuss the running of Princess Taise, runner-up to Barry Hills' English Ballet in the Sweet Solera Stakes at Newmarket. Johnston regards her as one of his best fillies. 'Joe rode two bad races at Newmarket on Saturday (on Princess Taise and Crime Scene in the opening handicap) probably because the ground was soft, and he lacked the confidence to ride his horses the way he would have done on firmer ground. He thought probably that the horses wouldn't get home, so he held them up. But it's not our style to be holding a horse up when it's a slow pace.' Even if it's a commonly-held belief that that's the best strategy? 'They don't get home any better if you do that,' insists Johnston. 'Everybody can see it's a false pace, but nobody has the confidence to go on. As I always joke, "They say jockeys have clocks in their heads when most haven't even got clocks in their bedrooms." Maybe I can't judge the pace, but sometimes it's frighteningly obvious. You look at the time and you say to yourself, "Why did he sit there?" I was disappointed, but I didn't think that was Princess Taise's running. She sat second and stayed second. I would have been reasonably confident that if he'd upped it two miles an hour she'd have maintained it anyway. That would have been the difference between second and winning. The commentators love to say, "It's Fanning from the front." But Fanning in second stays second!'

He hadn't said anything to Darley about his riding earlier in the season. Had he spoken to Fanning now? 'I haven't done, but I should have done,' says Johnston. 'I really don't do that enough. I don't think many people do. We don't sit there with jockeys and criticise their races. Maybe we would be better if we did. If you do it once in a blue moon, you dent their confidence and they ride badly for the next week. Ideally you'd do it every day, win or lose. I've always believed that if I wanted to give up training horses and instead train jockeys, I could create a champion jockey. And I could make the champion jockey out of any of the top ten. I think there's a desperate lack of lifestyle coaching and management where jockeys are concerned.'

I ask him about Greg Fairley, the yard's talented apprentice. One of the racing channel pundits had recently suggested that he did not appear to have 'trained on' quite as anticipated this season. 'He had a double at Redcar recently, and a second,' Johnston says. 'He needed that really badly. He's had a really poor run. Obviously when our horses weren't going well that started the trend. It's not a good time for an apprentice. When they're not running well, you don't want to leave anything to chance. So you give your apprentice fewer rides. But I didn't think he was riding that well anyway. I'd started to reduce his number of rides. I thought he gave a couple of horses particularly poor rides.' The trainer recalls an apprentice race at Goodwood when Fairley was riding Joseph Henry (yes, that horse again). 'I don't often give strict instructions. But here I did, strict instructions, three times, and I repeated them as I walked alongside him before he went out on to the track. The instructions were "to tuck him in, keep him behind, and you don't move until the leader hits the rising ground. Then you go." In the event, he pulled him out just coming round the bend three furlongs out,' says Johnston. The partnership finished fourth.

Johnston explains: 'Basically, this is a sprinter, but Joe Fanning had won on him when upped to a mile. This race was one mile one furlong, and I wanted the horse buried in the pack until the final furlong.' And words were said later?' 'Afterwards I said to Greg: "When we get home, we're going to have to sit down and look at this race", but we never did.' Johnston adds: 'It's probably a lack of confidence on Chris's part. Still, in the last week he's picked up – and he's still third on our list.' So, how does someone like Greg improve, then? 'Exactly. He doesn't. That's my fault. I'm too busy doing other things.'

Much of Johnston's analysis may appear harsh. Yet it must be remembered that the labours of many staff back at the yard, which can often go unnoticed, and on the gallops can be undone by a piece of injudicious riding. Lack of concentration or poor jockeyship can cost the yard a winner, and the owner thousands of pounds. And Johnston's attitude can be uncompromising when it comes to dealing with his riders. There was an incident in August 1999 when Johnston accused his then stable jockey Darryll Holland of an 'unprofessional act which let down the whole team' after the rider failed to turn up in time to ride the trainer's Gaelic Storm at Jagersro racecourse in Sweden. Holland also failed an alcohol test and was banned from riding in the Swedish Derby. The following day, Johnston replaced him on three horses he might have been expected to ride, at Ayr. Holland had formerly been employed as stable jockey by Johnston in 1995, but that relationship was severed when the rider left to go to Hong Kong. Holland had then returned to win the Goodwood and Doncaster Cups on Double Trigger for Johnston in 1998, and had also ridden stable companion Lend A Hand into second in that year's 2,000 Guineas.

The question that was asked in August 1999 was, is another split imminent? 'Sunday was the first time Darryll has missed a ride for me, but not the first time we have been waiting around for him,' Johnston reportedly remarked before adding ominously, 'I'm not very happy and I'll be considering how much he is going to ride for us in the future.' The answer was that Holland did continue to ride for the yard, but increasingly there were more opportunities for other jockeys, particularly Joe Fanning.

Johnston attempts to marry a particular riding technique to a horse that will benefit from it. 'Everybody has a different style. Bruce Raymond (racing manager of Gainsborough Stud), for instance, loves Joe Fanning's style because he's usually the last jockey to go for his stick.

That's extremely good practice, because the first jockey to throw everything at the horse, and it comes off the bridle, is probably going to get beat.'

This new strand of the discussion prompts one of those bar-room-style debates: do today's jockeys measure up to the supposed golden era of Piggott, Eddery, Carson and Mercer? 'You're showing your age,' chides Johnston, who may be considered a more authoritative voice than most. 'It's back to that old argument: were the Nijinskys and Mill Reefs better than the horses of today? I'm afraid my head rules my heart. I don't think they were. The same with jockeys. Frankie Dettori is certainly the biggest star since Lester Piggott, and you could argue that he is bigger, which is not to take anything from Lester because he's an absolute legend. But so will Frankie be. Frankie's got a different personality, but he's right up there. Of course, Pat Eddery and Willie Carson were household names, but is not Kieren Fallon a household name? You could say for some wrong reasons, but also for some right reasons as well. Lester sums it up. Confidence is so important a quality in race-riding, and Lester had any amount of confidence. Remember his fantastic ride on Royal Academy (in the 1990 Breeders' Cup Mile)? Frankie has it too. Fallon has it, in abundance. He's like McCoy over jumps; he's winning races he shouldn't win. He *believes* he can win from anywhere virtually.'

We then dwell for a while on the contentious subject of whip use, and abuse. I suggest that although Johnston's horses are often ridden vigorously, the whip is used sparingly by his jockeys. Was that his wish? 'They are professional jockeys,' Johnston replies. 'It's not for me to give them instructions. What I will say is that if jockeys go out and abuse horses, they won't stay riding for us for very long. The vast majority of owners and trainers would say the same. It doesn't need the Jockey Club or RSPCA or anybody else to tell us that. You can be Dean McKeown and hit Quick Ransom seventeen times and win the Ebor, and I don't consider that abuse. And you can be Jason Weaver and hit Bijou D'Inde however many times it was when he was head to head against Mark Of Esteem and Even Top in a head-to-head battle for the Guineas, and all three jockeys get banned, and I don't believe any one of them should have got banned. I don't think there was any question of abuse there either. None of the horses was hurt. And yet, you can hit a horse at home, once, maliciously, and that's once too many for me.' Johnston says that in seventeen years there have been two incidents of staff being fired for striking a horse on the gallops. 'On the racecourse the only time I was not happy with a jockey in that respect was when I reported a jockey for hitting a horse after the line, when pulling up. A TV cameraman told me, and I reported it to the stewards, that he had whacked in a fit of madness.'

The subject has long been debated, and one character who can be guaranteed to ensure that it remains in the public's consciousness is *Channel 4 Racing*'s John McCririck.

'You can't hit your cat, your dog, you can't even hit your wife,' he said in an interview with Brian Viner of the *Independent*. 'So why can you hit a racehorse? They say The Minstrel wouldn't have won the Derby without the whip, and I say, "So what?" It is a disgusting situation where, to prove he's trying, a jockey hits a horse. There will be a court case, and it will be stopped. The whip will be banned. I would keep it for steerage purposes, but that's all. Because beating animals in the name of sport is totally unacceptable. I agree that it helps the horse to go faster, but I can think of another way: put electrodes on his private parts. Would anyone accept that?

'We have made progress. It was terrible at Cheltenham 25 years ago, those Irish jockeys thrashing their horses up the hill. But there is still a long way to go. The problem is that you can thrash a horse and still win the race; the penalties come later. One way to change that would be instant disqualification. After all, if you get a chap out with a no-ball in cricket, it doesn't count. In football, if you score a goal and it's offside, it doesn't count. If you whip a racehorse twenty times and win the race it should not count. Then it would stop. And jockeys could show us what horsemen they are.'

I can still recall the public outrage against the perceived 'carpet-beating' treatment of horses by those jockeys at Cheltenham. In recent years the whip has been 'softened', and regulations have been introduced regarding the number of times jockeys are allowed to hit horses, and in what manner. But Johnston disagrees, not for the first time, with the human loud-hailer. 'It's not about winning a race, it's about believing that whips are right,' he says. 'I think that whips are essential for riding horses. You cannot ride them properly without them. It's an essential tool for riding the horse, for making it go places you want it to go, for steering it, for making it behave itself, for preventing it from savaging another horse. I liken it to a second in a boxing corner. He's slapping the fighter in the face, shouting and swearing at him, telling him to wake up, keep his wits about him. He's saying, "Keep your chin in and look after yourself. If you don't you'll get your head knocked off." He's being aggressive to his man. He's getting the adrenalin flowing. It's the same with a jockey with the whip. We get an endorphin and adrenalin response which is conditioned into the horse both genetically and from the first time it runs; you get this response to the sting of the whip. It keeps it alert and on the ball on that run to the line so that it doesn't lose its action, doesn't let its head drop. You could well argue that a horse under the drive of a whip is far safer in terms of long-term injury to itself than a drive which is mostly hands and forward weight.

'They're essential round the yard too, big long ones. I'm not talking about eighteen inches of whip. I can't agree with Monty Roberts (the so-called Horse Whisperer who 'talks to horses') who won't have them in the yard. We have a lungeing whip out here that's fifteen feet long. It's far preferable to hit a horse with that once when it refuses to go in a horsebox than to drag it about with ropes, trying to entice it with a bucket full of grass, pushing and shoving, and risk it falling over on the ramp and injuring itself. Not only are you putting it on the horsebox safely and efficiently today, but it will do so every other time in the future. It gives it confidence because it hasn't been *asked* to go on, it's been *told* to go on.' Although Johnston admires Roberts, he maintains that much of what the Whisperer says is nothing new. 'I can remember catching horses by pushing them away until they "asked" to come back when I was only about ten years old,' he says. 'I discovered that system by myself, just as Monty did. I have never allowed horses in my yard to be caught using a bucket or a titbit. I have always insisted that the horse which doesn't want to be caught should be pushed away until he wants to come back. Monty didn't invent the idea. It is one of the simplest principles of animal behaviour.'

The whip debate really does frustrate Johnston. 'Those who argue against use of the whip aren't actually interested in the horse's welfare,' he maintains. 'They are only interested in the public's perception. They are more concerned about how it appears to be than how it actually is. Why is the whip such a big issue for the RSPCA? Why are racehorses such a big issue? Why, for that matter, are homes for ex-racehorses? One reason: because racehorses get an awful lot more coverage than laminitic ponies out in a field who can't walk. Racehorses belong to rich people, and they stir emotions, and consequently they fill tin cans. Laminitic ponies and donkeys with curled feet are not very good at it. But laminitic ponies are a much bigger animal welfare issue in Britain than racehorses ever will be. So are neglected donkeys. We have far too much political correctness and nonsense on issues like that. We shouldn't be pandering to what the public at large want if they have no knowledge of the subject. We should be educating them.'

CHAPTER TWENTY

The price dropped further during the programme, and McCririck
came back to him and said 'It's now 6–4', or whatever it was. 'Do you still
advise punters to back it?' Charlie said, 'Back it at any price.'

It's as if Old Faithful has suddenly started gushing again for visitors to Yellowstone National Park after a period of dormancy. In Middleham, normality has returned to the Johnston yard. The winners, and placed horses, are emerging once more, and Mark Johnston can peruse his statistics with satisfaction rather than incomprehension. One of his Royal Ascot winners, Soapy Danger – a horse which five months earlier was defeated in a maiden at Wolverhampton – has displayed admirable resilience at Newmarket, under a splendidly judged ride by Kevin Darley, to secure the Group 2 Princess of Wales's Stakes. 'I've always said he was a decent horse,' says Johnston. 'I always thought he might just have it because he never got left behind on the gallops. He was just never impressive, no matter what we worked him with. There was never daylight between him and the other horses.'

The performance underlines Soapy Danger as a serious St Leger contender. That's if the colt isn't directed first towards a considerably more ambitious test, the King George VI and Queen Elizabeth Diamond Stakes at Ascot. It would be an audacious strategy for the son of Danzig, who would be the only three-year-old representative. Andre Fabre's Hurricane Run, the 2005 Irish Derby and 'Arc' victor, Saeed Bin Suroor's Electrocutionist and the Japan raider Heart's Cry are such ominous-looking opposition most trainers of possible rivals are making their excuses and finding something better to do that weekend. It looks like being one of the smallest fields for years. Yet with nearly £426,000 in prize money to the winner and even £10,000 to sixth place, it appears too good an opportunity to miss. It would be a mission of discovery.

Failure to lift one of the season's top prizes, or even to finish in the places, would scarcely diminish him. In the words of Henry Wadsworth Longfellow, 'If you would hit the mark, you must aim a little above it. Every arrow that flies feels the attraction of earth.' Whatever the decision, the fact that he is even being considered for the mile-and-a-half event, which has been won by such leviathans of the turf as Dancing Brave, Nashwan and Lammtarra, and produced such epic duels as Grundy and Bustino in 1975, is testament to Johnston's policy of bringing his horses through quietly, stepping them up gradually, and always leaving something to work on.

Another Royal Ascot winner, Linas Selection, who has developed through handicap company, is another case in point. Johnston's elder son, Charlie, appeared on Channel 4's *The Morning Line* to advise anyone who cared to be listening that, in his opinion, Linas Selection was the better of the pair. Both that Selkirk colt and Soapy Danger were in the same ownership – the Jacobses, who own the Newsells Park Stud. Whether it was Charlie's advice or merely that after his Ascot triumph he still looks a handicap good thing despite rising nearly a stone in the weights, punters' money forces Linas Selection into odds-on for the Listed one-mile-six-furlong handicap at York on John Smith's Day. In the event Linas Selection leads with three furlongs to run, and though there is an ominous challenge by Balkan Knight, the Johnston horse stays on resolutely. John Francome is far from the first pundit this season to reflect, 'Like the majority of Mark Johnston's horses, they don't like horses going past them.' As Linas Selection returns to the winner's enclosure, the Channel 4 director cuts not to Johnston or Deirdre, but to Charlie. The sorcerer's apprentice? Dressed in a smart suit, wearing stylish shades, carrying binoculars and studying his racecard, Charlie belies his fifteen years. Cast your mind ahead fifteen years, and you can imagine him here in his own right one day. Would it be Charlie Johnston and the Winner Factory?

Not every parent would necessarily want their teenage son exposed to such TV scrutiny, but Charlie's father has no such anxieties. 'I'm often asked to be on *The Morning Line* and Sky's *The Winning Post*,' Johnston says, 'but I'm asked to talk about every race. I'm no good at that. Deirdre is an awful lot better. Charlie would do the "prep" work for us. I said for ages that he'd be better on *Morning Line* than I would. The day before John

Smith's Day, (Channel 4's) Jim McGrath rang and asked me about appearing on the following day's *Morning Line*. I was at Newmarket and I just wanted to get home. I said no. Then I had a thought, rang back and said, "What about Charlie?" They thought that was a good idea. He did it, and it was fantastic. He was far better than I'll ever be. Although I'm not sure about his tipping of Linas Selection to win at York. Understandably, John McCririck immediately latched on to that, claiming that the bookies stood to lose millions. The price dropped further during the programme, and McCririck came back to him and said "It's now 6–4", or whatever it was. "Do you still advise punters to back it?" Charlie said, "Back it at any price."' They do, down to 11–8 on. Afterwards the bookmakers Blue Square claim it is their worst result of the season.

Meanwhile, Linas Selection and Soapy Danger are installed as joint second favourites, at 6–1, for the final Classic. The decision has finally been taken to sidestep the King George with the latter and head for the Great Voltigeur at York's Ebor meeting instead, with the St Leger a longer-term target. It means that, as the *Racing Post* reports, the field will be only six strong – the smallest for 36 years:

> The big three – Hurricane Run, Electrocutionist and Heart's Cry – will be joined by Electrocutionist's pacemaker Cherry Mix, Maraahel and Enforcer in the £750,000 spectacular. The Ascot purse and the prestige of the event were not enough to persuade the connections of Soapy Danger to run the Queen's Vase and Princess of Wales's Stakes winner at Ascot, leaving the Ladbrokes St Leger as the Mark Johnston-trained colt's major objective.
>
> Explaining the reasons for Soapy Danger's defection, owner Renata Jacobs' racing manager Gary Coffey said, 'We had a debate and the main reason for not running was that we felt it was too big a question to ask of him at this stage.'

Before a vast crowd, when the inadequacies of the new Ascot were again apparent, Hurricane Run asserts himself in the final furlong from his two market rivals in a thrilling renewal of the King George. What would 'Soapy' have made of it? Would he have got himself in a lather? The likelihood is that he would have finished fourth, at least.

By the following day, the heat haze has diminished at the Royal course, crowds are down, and there is room to breathe once again. Charlie Johnston has brought out his crystal ball and turned Gypsy Rose Lee once more, advising *At the Races* viewers that Road To Love will win the one-mile-two-furlong handicap. Actually, his information is based on particularly close scrutiny: he rode the horse in work the previous week. Again he is proved correct. The son of Johnston's old friend Fruits Of Love is an impressive seven lengths too good for the remainder of the field. His stablemate, London Express, finishes second.

'Charlie appeared again on TV after the race, and by Goodwood all the media had latched on to this,' Johnston tells me a couple of weeks later. 'I felt I had to put a bit of a halt to it. Newspapers wanted to interview him, but I said no by that time. It has got a little bit out of hand. I want him to keep his feet on the ground. He's got to go back to school and concentrate on his exams.' He adds, with mock exasperation, 'It's got to the stage where *At the Races* were ringing up for *him*. Charlie was in France at the time, so they couldn't have had him anyway. So, as an afterthought, they asked me!' I remind him that he did say how important it was to get yourself on TV when starting out. Johnston insists that in Charlie's case that day is some way off.

'I still worry about him,' he says. 'It's inevitable that Charlie will take a different route into racing to me. He will walk in near the top whereas I went in as near to the bottom as you can get. But possibly even at his age I knew more about horses than him. For me, the form, the racing and the betting weren't important. I was focused on knowing about *horses*.' Johnston is adamant that he won't hand over his business to either of his sons unless they are suitably prepared. 'Our strong feeling is that Charlie should only take over the yard if we consider that he's qualified for it. As soon as he says "I don't need the education", he'll need a big kick up the backside to make him realise that this place will not come that easy. Charlie does very well at school, but when we went to see the career teacher she suggested he study equine science.' Johnston grimaces at the words, as if they are something nasty stuck to his boot. 'I know it's rather insulting to those who are doing that course, but I just think that, by comparison (with becoming a vet), it's a Mickey Mouse degree.'

The fact that Charlie would probably study that course at what Johnston regards as a former poly adds to his dissatisfaction. 'I do feel that the government has devalued education at all the universities,' he says. 'I think of universities as being Glasgow, Edinburgh, Durham, Liverpool, Oxford, Cambridge – those that have always been universities, not those which have been created out of colleges and polytechnics. When Charlie suggests a degree which you get at a polytechnic, I throw up my hands in horror and say, "What a waste!"' I suggest he's being a touch elitist. 'It's true. I am a believer in education for education's sake. I suppose I'm a bit of an education snob. I'd much rather see him go and study stuffy law, mathematics, physics, French or chemistry at an old established university than I would see him go and study animal science at Worcester.'

It will have become evident by now that Johnston's expectations of his staff, and that includes his elder son and heir, are exceedingly high. It all begs the question, just how does *anyone* get to become a yard manager or even assistant trainer at Mark Johnston Racing? Not easily, it turns out.

'I get applications from these people with degrees like those (animal science) once a month at least and they don't get the job because they haven't got the practical experience that makes them of value to me,' he states firmly. 'They don't want to come and work as stable hands; and neither would Charlie. They don't have the experience to come and do Andrew Bottomley's job or Debbie's job or Jock's.' Johnston then emphasises what qualifications he does value. 'Someone like James Tate, who's two years out of veterinary college, is different. He can come and be my senior vet and be my highest-paid employee, because his degree and his skills far outweigh all that experience my other staff have got. That's what I keep trying to get across to Charlie: there's a huge gap between a vet degree and these other qualifications. It's why I wanted to do work in veterinary medicine, although there were other reasons as well. If I hadn't worked with horses I would have definitely worked with some other animals – cows, sheep, something else.

'There are other trainers' sons out there with a huge knowledge of the sport, but there are big gaps in Charlie's knowledge, particularly on the animal husbandry side. He knows how to ride them; he knows how form works; he's got a hundred opinions on racehorses; he can go on television and do an interview. Half the industry knows him. Half the industry already thinks he's got capabilities beyond his years. He's way, way ahead of where I was in many ways at his age. He's a far, far better rider than I was at fifteen and he rides out with the staff and mixes with them. Unfortunately, he thinks that's training horses. It's not. He hasn't even scratched the surface in terms of knowing how to handle them and care for them. I know when they look well. Now, looking well doesn't always win the race, but over the whole season it's important. A trainer's horses that always look well will beat the trainer's horses that never look well. If Charlie Johnston gets this business in ten years' time, it's because he'll have been trained for it, and will be ready for it. If he isn't, he doesn't get it.'

I remind Johnston that many sons do go off to become 'pupil assistants' for other trainers. Couldn't he organise for Charlie to do the same? 'I could, but I don't know that it would satisfy me that he was good enough to run this business.' You're very demanding, I say. 'Damn right I am,' he replies. 'But it's a very demanding business to run.' He is not that enamoured with the concept of pupil assistants anyway. 'They're the parasites of the racing industry,' Johnston says. 'They come, stay a year, steal the phone book, and go. Having said that, we do take a few pupils, for just a month, from the Darley Flying Start scheme.' Under that project, instigated by Sheikh Mohammed, 'graduates' complete two years of study in Ireland, America, Australia, Dubai and the UK. The programme is a combination of formal courses with lectures from leading industry figures and practical experience in areas including stud work, racing, veterinary and bloodstock. 'Generally, though,' Johnston adds, 'if we have a trainee, he or she must be training for a job that exists within our structure. There's no point having them if it's guaranteed they're going to leave. We're great believers in training and education, but we don't like training for training's sake.'

Those who benefited from Kingsley House tutoring enjoyed contrasting success once they moved on. 'The first head lad we had when we came here was Declan Condell,' says Johnston. 'He went on to train very briefly. Andrew Murphy took over from him. James Given was also here, and Brendan Holland. At the time we trained for a guy called Chris Buckley. He wanted his son Mark to come as assistant. Brian Palmer, who was then our partner here, and I hatched a plan. We decided that we would go into business with Mark Buckley, and we would own half his yard. Mark would hold the training licence, but we would bring to it many of the things we had learnt from running this business, particularly the systems, accounting, liasing with owners, and control of money. As I've said before, one of the hardest things when you start up is getting the cash in. It was like a mini-franchise. We said he had to come for a minimum of six months, to understand how it all worked. We also said that we had other people here who had similar experience and who had already been here for a length of time, so we had to offer them the same deal. So we offered the same terms to James Given, Andrew Murphy and Brendan Holland. James said he'd no interest in training. Andrew said that he didn't think he wanted to train at that moment, but would do something in the future. Brendan said he wanted to go back to Ireland at some point, but probably not to train.

'After around three or four months, Mark Buckley handed in his notice, as did Andrew Murphy. And Polly, our secretary. They were going off to train on Polly's father's farm, down in Devon. I think the idea was that Mark would hold the licence. Later on, Mark and Andrew split and both trained separately.' Buckley now holds a dual licence at Castle Bytham, Lincolnshire. Andrew Murphy works with Aidan O'Brien. James Given, who was vet/assistant trainer under Johnston, was granted a licence in 1998 and now trains over 100 horses in Gainsborough, Lincolnshire. His big-race victories include the Cambridgeshire, Ebor and Chester Cup. 'The only one who stuck by what he said was Brendan Holland, who we're still in touch with,' says Johnston. Then he makes the aside, without any prompting, 'Frankly, they all thought they could do it better than I could. Mark Buckley actually said so. Obviously they all thought, "We don't need him any more, or his expertise."

I suggest they had probably stolen his ideas by then. He looks me in the eye and mutters, in a dismissive tone, 'Clearly not. Since then, Andy Oliver, another vet, has left and set up training in the north of Ireland (in Caledon, Co. Tyrone). That was very much with our blessing. We have even sent him a few owners. Another of our vets, Anthony Cosgrave, has set up in Australia. We were very sorry to lose him. He was a fantastic vet, and was with us for four years. He started with two horses this year and has had a winner at 50–1 and a second. He's now got six horses. He sent an email saying he's had to double his staff. In other words, he's employed somebody. I only wish he hadn't had any winners, because I'd have liked him to come back.'

We return to the subject of Charlie's future. I question whether it is right for a man of his principles to be handing down a business like this to his son. 'You're absolutely right to ask that,' Johnston says. 'As I've said, there's no way I'm just going to *hand* it to him. But I have to stress, nor do I think that would be morally wrong. As I say on many issues, I didn't write the rules. I'm not in a position to do something for everybody else. So, for my own kids I am, one, trying to get them the best education they can get – although that doesn't mean I'm paying to send them to private school. And two, yes, I want to give them both opportunities and advantages. Maybe if I was to start with a blank sheet of paper I'd say that the state takes everything and we all start from scratch, that we all get the same education and the same chances in life, which everybody doesn't get. If he took my route, went to vet school and had a couple of years in practice, I would probably believe, with what he knows now about this business, that he was capable of coming back here as trainer. But he'd need an awful lot of back-up to start with 150-plus horses instead of the fifteen he should start with. If he goes off and studies something else, he's going to have an awful lot of proving still to do to demonstrate that he's capable of coming in here as trainer.'

Such is Johnston's conviction in this respect that he then makes a statement that slightly takes me aback. 'When I was discussing our "exit strategy" with one of our accountants, and adviser, Ian Harland, one of the things I said was that if anything happens to Deirdre and me, if we both die at the same time, the business must close. That's written in our wills.' Detecting some astonishment on my part, he elaborates. 'The boys are not old enough to decide for themselves what to do with it. So the business must close. That's the decision I've made. Because I know how fast this business can lose money. People would be staggered by how fast it can lose money. If it drops down below 150 horses, it's losing money.' Staff, Johnston explains, are 42 per cent of turnover. 'If you look at October 2005 onwards, staff grew to around 54 per cent because we'd sold a lot of horses and hadn't replaced them with yearlings. We were *losing* money. Of course, the horses came in the end. They came in their droves.'

Uncertainty over horse numbers is a topic we have visited before. Until a few years ago, yearlings from the major owners would arrive late the previous year. Generally speaking, those horses wouldn't be evaluated until the end of the season. That has now all changed. 'Over the last two years particularly, and there's no sign of it changing, we've been having to say that staff holidays must be taken principally between October and December, and to a lesser extent between July and October,' Johnston says. 'We don't want them to go away between January and June. A lot of that is because of the Maktoum horses. They are saying, "Let's find out how good they are, and if they are not good enough to aspire to our aims of winning Group races, let's sell them." So we have much bigger drafts of horses going to the July and then the October sales.'

We return to the long-term future of Kingsley House in the event of Johnston and Deirdre both dying. 'What often happens to people in my position is that someone like Jock would take over the licence. No disrespect to him, but if that happened it would be like pouring it down the drain. All you'd need to do would be to lose 50 horses – and you can lose 50 horses overnight. Then, wham! Unless they could understand how to get it back on track and cut the overheads, it would lose fortunes. At the time, Ian insisted that it wasn't necessarily what he would do. I said, "What would you do? Put Brendan Holland in as trainer?" – or whoever was head lad at the time we were discussing it. Ian replied, "No, I'd probably look at the trainers' table, look around the country, see who was the best person for the job and head-hunt them." But our industry doesn't work like that, does it?'

Johnston pauses.

'You know, there's a side to me which thinks in ten years' time I should look for the best successor, not Charlie Johnston. But racing stables, as they are structured at the moment, under the rules of racing, don't lend themselves to that. Yet if this was a shoe manufacturer, that is exactly what we should be doing. It's an interesting thought, but I'd still be concerned that if a young up-and-coming trainer came in it would be exactly the same as the Jock Bennett situation. If he lost 50 horses there'd be money problems. At least if you bring in Charlie Johnston you can maybe have a seamless transition, because it's the same name above the door.'

That is where racing differs from other industries. But isn't the trainer's name a significant marketing device? Johnston believes there is no reason why training businesses shouldn't have a corporate identity rather than a personal one. 'Staff would get more of a kick out of it,' he says. 'They'd feel more a part of a team. Also, the business would have some value, and you'd be able to pass it on. It wouldn't just be bricks and mortar.' It's an anachronism of horseracing that, though yards are run as businesses, they all *have* to be called by the name of a trainer. But, Johnston insists, 'It's not always the case. The public think of Godolphin; they don't say, "Oh, Saeed Bin Suroor's just trained that winner." We could be called Kingsley House. If Kingsley House had a winner, not Mark Johnston, wouldn't it be better for the person who travels with the horse, or works with it here? I believe that the whole staff would feel it was their moment of glory if we had a team name instead of an individual. From a staff perspective it would be much better working for Kingsley House Ltd than Mark Johnston Racing.

'Most trainers wouldn't do it, of course. It would take them years to make them realise the worth of it. If Richard Hannon stayed as Richard Hannon and I became Kingsley House, and we had roughly equal results, and he wanted to pass the business to his son (Richard Junior), and I wanted to pass this on to mine, the chances of my business taking a dip would be a lot less. All we would be doing is changing managing director, as it were; the company would remain the same. My business would be easier to pass on. But most important of all, my business would acquire some value. At the moment it has no value; only the bricks and concrete. It has goodwill, but the minute I leave all the goodwill leaves with it. I can't sell my company as a going concern – unless I go with it. If we could give racing stables their own identity, they would acquire some value.'

But, I submit, some names have a cachet about them. Yours? John Dunlop's? Barry Hills'? The name becomes a byword for quality and success, and if it is handed down, it creates a dynasty. Marks and Spencer didn't do too badly in that respect. Essentially, Johnston just wants a say in the matter. 'If they changed that rule, then maybe John Dunlop would feel that he wanted to keep the name John Dunlop. But I might feel that I wanted to change to something completely different. Either way you've still got to brand the business; you've still got to sell it; you've still got to build a reputation for quality around it. You can do that with a person's name *or* a company name.' Anyway, I suggest, most trainers would have too much ego to sacrifice their name. 'I would definitely be willing to do that though. I'd still have to be Mark Johnston, the trainer, but I have thought about dropping the Mark from the business name and just calling it Johnston Racing. Then any member of the family – or, indeed, another trainer completely – could step into the breach without us changing the name of the company. I'd like to see the rule changed so that limited companies could hold a trainer's licence.'

With the first week of August fast approaching, we return to more immediate matters. A few days amid the splendour of the Sussex Downs are promised. And on the racetrack there is much lost time to be made if the Johnston name is to register highly in the end-of-season trainers' table.

CHAPTER TWENTY-ONE

What made me so angry about the Racing Post *campaign was that people from outside the industry should think it was their place to dictate to us how we organised our workforce and how we organised payment to our workforce when they haven't got a bloody clue.*

Before Glorious Goodwood, there are the implications of a defeat for Johnston to digest. Not on the racecourse, though. This is a political reverse. He has been closely involved in the rearguard action, but it is 1 August 2006 and 48-hour declarations have come into force. It will have ramifications for every trainer in the country.

It is the day after Road To Love has scorched home at Ascot, an exhilarating moment which has the BBC's pundit Willie Carson eulogising about 'Mr Johnston's horses' and alluding mysteriously to the way he works them 'up on the moors' as though those contours might contain some mystic power, distilled by a wizard. But the following morning some newspapers prefer to project not Johnston's mastery as a trainer, but his alter ego. 'Johnston Hits Out at the New Racing Format' is the headline in that day's London *Evening Standard*. The trainer immediately offers an example of how the new system will affect him: he declares both Linas Selection and Luberon for that week's BGC Gordon Stakes when he would have preferred to run just one. 'But with the 48-hour decs I was terrified that something might go wrong and I'd be left with nothing in the race,' he says.

In the glasshouse of horseracing politics, it is not exactly exotica. The issue is not liable to impact upon the racing public unduly. Not for the moment, anyway. Not until the graph of non-runners takes a spectacularly upward turn. But in Middleham, as in all other racing centres, it has made race-planning for trainers a whole lot more complex. Not that that troubles the *Racing Post*'s Howard Wright, who earlier in the year reflected that 'the Luddites seem to have been beaten off at the door marked "International Progress"'. Johnston views the move with incomprehension and resentment, and regrets that he no longer had a platform in Wright's newspaper in which he could have engaged in battle more effectively. But who was to blame for that?

Let us rewind a little over three years to the time when Johnston did possess that opportunity. For a man who in two decades has become horseracing's voice of dissent, of reason, and frequently of devil's advocacy, it was inevitable that Johnston would be coveted by the print media. They don't come any more trenchant than the Scot. On the mainstream newspapers, opinion-makers are a prized breed, and the same applies today to the racing trade press, which has evolved significantly from the days when the *Sporting Life* was the high-street bookmakers' wallpaper and was principally a chronicle of record. The épée of discontent has been replaced by the scimitar of excoriation. Can anyone forget the edition of the *Racing Post* which damned Peter Savill for having the temerity to run his Lady Herries-trained Celtic Swing in the French Prix Du Jockey Club rather than the English Derby? 'Sad. Mad. Bad.' was the headline – on the front page. That was back in 1995. Today, the *Racing Post* is a many-tentacled beast, grasping its readership from many sources. Still, primarily, they will be punters and professionals seeking education on the day's runners, but it is also consulted widely within the industry by many who regard it as a valuable debating chamber. Much has altered since the days of the *Sporting Life*, with which it initially sparred as a newcomer before, to the regret of many of us, consuming it. This author regarded it a privilege to work there, albeit briefly.

When the *Post* hired Johnston in 2000, they appeared to be natural bedfellows. He was offered space to deliver his views, and his column made essential reading in a newspaper that was also blessed with the writing of Paul Haigh and Alastair Down. Granted such freedom of expression, Johnston was as happy as the proverbial porker in a field of clover. They lived in harmony for three years. Johnston spoke about his runners but also aired grievances, in the process raising temperatures and hackles. Consider this extract, taken from a column just before Fruits Of Love was due to contest the Breeders' Cup Turf at Churchill Downs in November 2000:

I have never been too self-righteous about the use of medication in racing. Frankly I'm not at all sure that we, the British, are right and the Americans are wrong. Those who shout loudest on the subject are probably doing so from a position of relative ignorance.

Fruits Of Love will be on medication tonight in the Breeders' Cup Turf. I have never made any secret of the fact and I don't feel any need to offer excuses. I admit that, to some extent and particularly in the case of Lasix, we are giving him drugs to level the playing field with the other competitors. But I am pleased to be able to give the horse some Bute and/or other anti-inflammatory drugs. I feel that the use of Bute will help Fruits Of Love come through this race with fewer aches, pains and other stresses than he may otherwise be expected to encounter in a tough international race.

It was a provocative stance. It would be anathema to many of his counterparts and readers generally; yet, as in all of Johnston's views, there is a rationale about his argument.

Another contentious issue is the entry system for the Derby, which Johnston has long believed prevents the best horses from running in the premier Classic. He claims that the entries should be made later and should cost less. 'Then the best horses would run in it. How are owners meant to know what trip or ground their horses are going to need as yearlings?' he asks. He has also been vociferous in his opposition to Instructions H14 and H19. Under the first, trainers must report anything that might have adversely affected the performance of any horse they train in a race. Under the second, trainers are asked, in certain circumstances, to give explanations for improved performances.

The man who would become president of the National Trainers' Federation inspired support and provoked controversy in equal measure – until that fateful day in May 2003 when the *Post* announced its A Fair Deal for Stable Staff campaign. So much for bedfellows after that. Johnston hurled his breakfast tray on the floor.

The campaign, which was spearheaded by writer David Ashforth, attempted to identify the reasons why racing suffered a persistent shortage of suitably qualified staff, and how the situation could be resolved. Ashforth wrote, 'They are issues to do with pay, including overtime pay; with hours, particularly a lack of time off; with facilities and treatment at racecourses; and with a common perception that they and their skills are not sufficiently respected or considered.' The *Post*'s front page claimed that a survey 'has revealed many stories of low pay and ridiculously long hours. Racing is lucky to be able to rely on such a skilled workforce. The *Racing Post* believes that, as a matter of urgency, stable staff must be promoted from the bottom to the top of racing's priorities.'

There was an inevitable polarisation of positions. Stable staff reportedly backed the campaign, and the *Post* reported that its 'hotline' received many callers with tales of long hours and poor wages, which were duly published. Some trainers took exception. Charlie Mann accused the *Post* of 'stirring things up', but proceeded to rather abet the paper's case by adding that if staff 'don't like the job, they can get out of it'. Johnston's response was rather more considered. He enforced his opposition in his final column on 6 June 2003, describing what had appeared in the *Post* as 'drivel'. He added, 'This "campaign" is very bad for racing. It is bad for all of us: trainers, owners, stable staff and, maybe, ultimately, racing journalists. What message is it sending to potential investors? How many sponsors will be looking to get involved with a training yard this week if they have believed even half of what David Ashforth has written? How many less recruits will we have now, thanks to this "campaign", to help us with the seemingly ever-expanding fixture list?' He conceded: 'There are issues that need to be addressed and many of us are trying to address them, but this ill-conceived, poorly researched and thoroughly biased "campaign" has not helped one iota and, frankly, I don't think it will.'

Johnston spoke of his staff training initiatives, and wages, which he said were in excess of the national minimum, and which he regarded as only a 'safety net'. He also addressed the problem of unsociable working hours. However, his main issue with the newspaper was a lack of 'any constructive or sensible ideas in these areas; only pointless and unhelpful criticism'. He also objected to anonymous complaints, particularly from people no longer working within the industry, such as the 'former groom' whose reported observations led to this story which appeared in the *Post*:

> A trainer in Berkshire has 'sacked' more than 60 members of staff
> inside a year in a display of the feudal system that persists in
> British racing, a former stable worker claimed yesterday. The
> groom, who left to work in the manufacturing trade, highlighted
> the plight of staff with the extraordinary tale of a current trainer,
> and wondered why the authorities were not taking action.
> Wishing not to give his name, he said, 'I left the industry twenty
> years ago due to the poor returns highlighted this week and
> nothing has improved. The *Racing Post* is doing the right job to
> highlight this but somebody along the line is not helping – the
> abuse of stable staff is still going on. They are treated to
> ignorance, ill manners and being shouted at. There is one trainer,
> in Berkshire, who has handed out 63 sackings in the past six to
> eight months. He is having to import staff from abroad as no-one
> here will work for him. He is mostly ill-mannered, ignorant, and
> someone at the Jockey Club ought to be keeping an eye out for
> such troubles.

To this day, Johnston remains highly sceptical about such anonymous
'testimony'. At the time, Ashforth responded to criticism from Johnston
and others by stating, 'Trainers have complained that our spotlight on
bad practices and poor treatment of staff, rather than on the fact that the
majority of trainers pay well above the minimum rates and treat their
staff well, will make recruitment even more difficult. The problem is not
the *Racing Post*'s exposure of abuses; the problem is the abuses. While
we have devoted a fortnight so far to stable staff, there are trainers,
hopefully a small minority, who have been damaging the industry for
years by alienating staff and harming racing's public image.'

This, to an outsider, appeared to be the crux of the matter. Do you
sully the name of a whole industry for the perceived sins of a few?
Nevertheless, the campaign had an effect. The following month, the
Post claimed a victory when the British Horseracing Board set up an
independent commission under former government minister Lord
Donoughue to investigate problems for stable and stud staff. Johnston

was equable to the proposal. 'Obviously there was a bit of concern when we first got wind of the fact that this was going to be done – that this would add fuel or give some credence to what I believe to be a thoroughly wrong and ill-conceived campaign,' he said. 'But that being said, I cannot see that this inquiry can do any harm whatsoever, and no doubt we will be looking to make sure it is a positive and thorough look at the industry.'

When the commission reported, it concluded that 'a significant number of staff express their dissatisfaction with pay, long hours, working weekends and the lack of respect shown to them in the workplace. Without improvements to attract, train and retain more staff it will be difficult to service the growing demand from an expanded fixture list.' The commission made many recommendations, referring to 'antiquated overtime arrangements', lack of proper pension cover, recruitment strategy, accommodation for staff, the 'wasteful exodus' of graduates who had attended the racing schools, on-the-job training, and better facilities for stable staff at racecourses. It also called for a change in the culture of racing 'to eliminate bullying and harassment and create a modern work environment'. It advocated training for trainers and stud managers to help them deal with staff issues and said that a 'kitemark' system should be introduced to acknowledge and reward the many trainers and stud owners who treat their staff well and are good employers.

Three years on, Johnston remains unconvinced by the campaign and what it actually achieved. 'What makes me so bitter against the *Racing Post* is that, like any industry, you've got no choice but to move with the times and progress. Like all labour-intensive manual industries, we had staffing problems here. We had recruitment problems and retention problems. We had problems which the *Racing Post* maybe highlighted. But these were things that I'd been looking to do something about for as long as I'd been a trainer. Wages and conditions, retention, recruitment of staff, conditions they live in, how they get treated at the races, whether they call trainers "guvnor", whether some trainers shout and swear at them … it's the same in every industry in the land. They're all things that were accepted once upon a time, but are not acceptable now. But what did the *Racing Post* contribute? Absolutely zero. They didn't give us any new ideas. All they gave us was negative PR about horseracing. It basically said to people, "If you want to work with horses, don't work in racing." They were basically saying, "Low wages, bad hours, come and get treated like shit." How dare they? It was so far from the truth it was abysmal. If the *Horse & Hound* or *Eventing* magazine had said this about racing, we'd have taken them to court. But it was the *Racing Post*, which effectively said, "You're better off working in showjumping or eventing, or in a riding school." And that's just damn lies.'

He insists there remains a basic lack of understanding about how racing stables function. 'I see things every day, some of the little changes that have come probably as a direct result of that campaign. Like you go to the races and in the racecard it says "J. Dobbin, groom" next to the horse. There may even be a wee picture of him. They're supposed to want us to modernise this industry, but don't they understand? It's not just about the groom; there's a team out there. There's a guy who sweeps the yard, and he's as entitled to get credit when Soapy Danger wins at Royal Ascot as the guy leading him around the paddock is. And so is the vet, and so is Debbie in the office who is as white as a sheet because she never sees the light of day. But the people at the *Racing Post* are too blind to see that. They are as far in the dark ages as the trainers who were doing things they shouldn't.'

We revisit the topic of wages. It is evident in his yard – and it is almost certainly true elsewhere – that bonuses and overtime account for a large share of total salaries. And that means all staff, not just those responsible on a day-to-day basis for horses. When we spoke about this earlier in the year, the yard was about to replace a tractor driver. Johnston's personnel manager, Nicky Shepherd, asked him how much the new person should be paid. Johnston told her, 'The same as the last man.' Nicky told him that was £14,220. 'So I asked her what he actually got paid in the past year. It turned out he received £18,106 in total pay, including overtime. Then he also got £1,440 compensation for the loss of Shamardal (from Sheikh Mohammed), £1,300 pool money, £720 in owners' bonuses, £1,430 in winners' bonuses, £400 pension and £418 clothing allowance, totalling £23,814.'

I tell him I find it surprising that a tractor driver should receive some of those bonuses. 'It may sound strange,' Johnston says. 'There's obviously a lot of difference between driving a tractor and riding a horse. But it's been a gradual thing over the years. In one sense it's crazy; yet they're all part of the team. It's very difficult to say where you should draw the line. If you draw the line above tractor driver, what about the guy who mucks out the yard but doesn't actually touch the horses? I like there to be productivity bonuses, and loyalty bonuses. That's good. It's all about the package. So they get wages, pool money, a percentage of prize money, winners' bonuses and owners' presents dished out at the end of each year. There can also be a tip. The Maktoums, for example, give a certain amount for a winner, and more for Group 3, Group 2 and Group 1 wins. It's very significant. But there is the problem that our industry's too reliant on it. You've got almost a tipping culture. When we get more winners, we all earn more. That's great. But you can't take that to the extreme of saying if you don't win any races, you don't get paid.' Bonuses are never guaranteed, are they? Not in any industry. 'That's what Nicky said to me. Some of those bonuses, like £10 a winner (some people are on £16), no, they're not guaranteed; but the worst we've had in ten years is 106 winners.'

The big question is, is Johnston happy with what he pays his staff? 'I have to look at it from both sides,' he says. 'There are times we worry we don't pay enough, normally when you suddenly hear that another yard is apparently paying more. But then when you take into account all our productivity bonuses you realise that our overall package is actually better. Exactly the same thing applies to the training fees, in reverse. You lump all these extras, like veterinary expenses, into the training fees, which the owners say they like. But then they keep hitting you with the fact that you're 20 per cent dearer than the next trainer.'

Johnston explains the advantages of having a strategic planning board, which can take a more detached view of the business than he can. 'We've brought in two advisers, one of whom is an accountant, and he looks at areas like how our wages stand as a percentage of turnover. If I just up wages by 10 per cent, I have to up training fees by 10 per cent. There comes a point where I can't do that any more. It's not entirely me who says what the wages are; it's what the market will stand. If we are successful enough that our customers will accept a higher price, then we can pay a higher wage. The business has to generate X amount of profit. I used to think that didn't matter, of course. I used to think that we could not have profit. We could take what we wanted, staff could have what *they* wanted, and the end figure should then be zero. I now realise that was very naive of me. If I want to buy Park Farm, if I want to make improvements, if I want to borrow money, the bank has to see that the business makes sufficient profit for the amount of money invested in it. If it doesn't, I'm in trouble. I won't be able to survive. After that, the wage scale can go up and down, dependent on how far we can push the prices in percentage terms. So it's not down to me to be *happy* with what I can pay, it's down to me to pay as much as I can pay, and charge as much as I can charge.'

Johnston says that over recent years, his wages have risen by a minimum of 5 percent and an average of 10 per cent; owners have seen a training fee rise of 6 to 7 per cent to cover that. This year they have attempted to keep fee increases as low as possible 'because we felt we'd reached a pressure point. We just didn't know whether we'd have the horses. Probably we could have got away with a higher rise. But at one stage we thought we might be 50 horses down, and if we pushed the price any higher we could start to spiral downwards and have fewer horses. Fewer horses means less profit, and the whole thing's going the wrong way. There is no way we can allow that to happen.' He anticipates the obvious question. 'It's all very well saying, "Oh, there's people out there who can afford to pay millions for a horse so they can afford to pay 10 per cent more on training fees. It won't make any difference to them." But not everybody pays millions. It's what the *Racing Post* were trying to advocate, that the whole industry should put its prices up. The whole industry must pay more to its staff. But, one, the figures they were quoting weren't correct; and, two, it was unrealistic. If I push my prices up 10 per cent, I'll lose horses to somebody else who hasn't. We're trying to set the prices as high as we can without losing the customer.

'There's a formula. Wages, in this business, Mark Johnston Racing, are 42 per cent of turnover. If they become 46 per cent of turnover, we've got a problem. If they become 36 per cent of turnover, those guys out there aren't getting paid enough. It's a key performance indicator. We look at it regularly to see if it's out of kilter. September, October, November last year (2005) it was way out because we were overstaffed. We were up to 50 per cent. And the accountant was saying, "Something's wrong. You're paying too much, or you've got too many staff. This is getting out of hand. You'll either have to cut the number of your staff or cut what you pay." Actually, he was probably wrong. It was just fluctuations with the number of horses. But it illustrates the point.'

A significant problem, the trainer claims, is 'racing expenses', the cost of actually getting horses to the track, which 'have gone through the roof'. 'Things were driven by a stable staff agreement, which absurdly places the emphasis on the people going racing. It's an overtime payment effectively, and it's gone sky-high. Somebody has to drive the box, and he gets the same wage as the guy leading the horse up. We were finding it difficult to budget. The *Racing Post*, and others, naively think all this is passed on to the owner, but of course it's not. The most ridiculous idea was that staff who went racing should be given a one-off £50 payment every time. We've got nearly 120 staff, fifteen of whom go racing. I've got 100 guys at home. Why should they not be paid? They did as much to get the horse to the races. What made me so angry about the *Racing Post* campaign was that people from outside the industry should think it was their place to dictate to us how we organised our workforce and how we organised payment to our workforce when they haven't got a bloody clue.'

Neither did he accept some criticism from *within* racing. The role of owners is an interesting one. Back in 2003, Chris Deuters, president of the Racehorse Owners' Association, had entered the stable staff debate and claimed that 'the minimum rates are appalling', before adding obliquely, 'I know that a lot of trainers pay £7.50 or £8 an hour, but the *Racing Post* has unearthed some curious practices.' Johnston suspects that 'the owners quickly realised that it wasn't their place to get involved'. 'You don't go into a restaurant and decide whether you think the price for the product is fair or not, or dictate how many staff they should employ, or how much to pay them. Actually, that's not quite fair. In an ideal world you would. You may choose not to buy clothes from a particular place if they are using slave labour. But you see the point?

What annoyed me most of all was politicians getting involved, saying that racing's minimum wage was inadequate when they had set a minimum wage for the rest of the country that was lower. How *dare* they sit in a bloody glasshouse and throw stones at us.'

It is evident that Johnston still has much to say on this and other matters. Why, then, quit as a columnist? A case of an impetuous piece of nasal surgery just to taunt his face? Couldn't he have argued more effectively from inside? 'Definitely,' he concurs. But afterwards I realised just how much time I was putting into it. It was actually a relief not to be involved any more. I've also left the council of the National Trainers' Federation (he represented Flat trainers). I decided to go back to the back benches, basically. It's nothing to do with the NTF or what it may have done or failed to do, but there was a desperate frustration at my own failures.

'I had those three years of influence on the NTF, as vice-president, president and past president. I said, when I was first involved, that every president should have an aim, something he wanted to achieve in those three years. The first thing I wanted to do was to get rid of 48-hour decs. I thought it had been achieved. There was a trial of the system, and it failed. In 2004, when all Heritage Handicaps and Group 2 and 3 races had 48-hour decs, Ladbrokes' figures for those races dropped by 6 per cent. OK, it was a tiny sample and only one bookmaker, but there must be a risk that all British turf races will drop by 6 per cent. If that happens, we lose £480 million turnover to gain what they say will be a £100 million turnover (from selling TV rights abroad). Why dare risk that the rest of us lose £480 million so that people like Racing UK, At the Races and Arena (owner of several racecourses) can gain £100 million? It's absolute madness. British bookmakers think it's wrong, and for once they and I are on the same side.'

He can barely contain his irritation. 'These 48-hour declarations – it's worse than I could ever have imagined.' The number of non-runners is said to have increased by 84 per cent since the system started. Vindication for the trainers, I ask him, or just you chaps dragging your heels and trying to make your point? 'Where do the media and the racecourses get the idea that it's an advantage to me to have a non-runner?' Johnston counters. 'I had three non-runners at Newcastle last week. That's £50 to plate them each, and £50 to get a vet's certificate – that's £100 a horse. Absolute minimum. Then entry fees and so on. Probably £400 a non-runner; and if you take it to the races, not much change out of £1,000. It's chaos. We don't want non-runners any more than they do. We make 900 declarations a year, from 5,000 options. Richard Fahey took five horses to Haydock and none of them ran (because of the going). Twenty-five of his owners turned up. And they think he's pleased about that? It's not just about administrative problems for trainers, or the going, it's about what British racing is losing. All these non-runners, and what have we got to show for it? What have Racing UK or At the Races given us since 48-hour decs came in? Nothing.'

His other target for his presidency of the NTF was to get a seat for the organisation on the BHB (British Horseracing Board). 'We only managed to get a non-voting seat, but I thought at least we had a meaningful voice. Then, in one fell swoop, the 48-hour decs went ahead, and through that I realised that effectively we didn't have a significant voice at all. I had failed.' Is he suggesting that he'll retire gracefully from the battleground of racing politics? 'Yes,' Johnston replies. 'No. I'll never retire entirely because I'll always have something to say.'

He shrugs. 'It's a sad thing, isn't it? In industry, in politics, in every walk of life, people start off as radicals and end up as conservatives. So, all that energy I put into the NTF … and I've always said, I'm not arguing for me because I'm doing fine. I'm arguing for people that aren't doing fine, and arguing for British racing because I passionately believe it's not doing fine, or at least not getting what it should get. Frankly, I just got fed up. I thought, "Never mind what everyone else does; let's just look after number one." I may as well put all that energy into my own business. If people want to cock up the system … Now I just let off steam, if I want to, in my own newsletter, the *Kingsley Klarion*.'

He pauses. Something is still troubling him.

'Maybe I could have swung those issues if I'd still been writing in the *Racing Post*.'

CHAPTER TWENTY-TWO

It's madness to be continually fighting this battle to catch people
cheating the system when the system itself lends itself to cheating.
So, why not remove that potential instead of spending millions a year
on little detectives in raincoats running around trying to catch people?
Why not try to correct that flaw in the system?

Glorious Goodwood. It is no alliterative hyperbole dreamt up by a marketing man. Traditionally the culmination of 'The Season', it is England at its most idiosyncratic – and, it might be said, its most anachronistic. A week of Panamas, picnics and Pimms; of linen suits and elegant frocks.

For Mark Johnston, it is a week that is invariably glorious, both for his ego and the yard's seasonal prize-money tally. Though it is true that traditionally he farms the five-day festival of racing like a harvester cutting a swathe through those adjacent golden fields of whispering, waving sheaves of corn, there will always be those who over-decorate him with accolades. Take Peter Oborne in the London *Evening Standard*, who advises his readers in 2006 that 'horses sent down by Yorkshire trainer Mark Johnston can pretty well be backed blind, especially in the Goodwood Cup'. But you'd have to go back a few years, to when Double Trigger was in his prime, to argue that. Plunge on Johnston's Goodwood Cup horses this year and you'll probably end up in penury. This year, Golden Quest is contesting Thursday's feature, but it is his first race since his second in the event the previous year. Winged D'Argent is the other Johnston contender entered for that searching test of stamina. On the day, Yeats, Ballydoyle's newly transformed Cup horse, succeeds in becoming the first Ascot Gold Cup winner since Double Trigger to follow up with Goodwood's showpiece staying event in the same season. The feat evokes some sentimental memories.

Nevertheless, there is no doubt that some of Johnston's finest days of his training career have been spent here on the Downs. Before the 2006 meeting he has been leading trainer at this meeting five times in the last eight years. His booty has included five Goodwood Cups and the Vintage Stakes. And certainly this year the momentum from Royal Ascot has continued, and he has his eye on three winners from the week's competition. He duly exceeds that target, with four: a meeting double with Crosspeace, Road To Love and Prince Of Light. Linas Selection, one of his probable St Leger pair, is third, behind Jeremy Noseda's Sixties Icon, in the BGC (formerly the Gordon) Stakes – a trial for the final Classic. But he will relish the extra distance of the St Leger. The two-year-olds are not quite meeting expectations. Kirklees and Silent Waves are third and fourth respectively in the Vintage Stakes. However, by the conclusion of the week the prize-money pot will be around £125,000 healthier, and Johnston will have ascended from fourth to second place in the trainers' table. He is still adrift of Sir Michael Stoute, who looks unassailable, but has hurdled Richard Hannon and Aidan O'Brien. It may be true that O'Brien secures most of his rewards on his home Irish soil, but nevertheless this is a significant moment for the yard.

When Johnston's Crosspeace defies top weight to secure the opening handicap by a neck, after Royston Ffrench had produced him with an unerring run, it takes the yard's total prize money for the year over the million mark. It transpires that the horse may run again on the Friday in the Glorious Stakes, and many would merely proceed to extol the horse's virtues. But this is no time for platitudes. Johnston seizes his opportunity to air a grievance that has long troubled him. 'It's been a long time since this horse has won,' he says of the 12–1 shot. 'You would have said he was all that was wrong with the handicap system, with a rating of 108, and not having won a race since November, and having run a lot of races without winning. He's what used to be called a "twilight" horse, who, with different owners, would have been sold to Hong Kong, or the United States, where he could earn big money. He's hardly run a bad race but never comes down the handicap. Putting horses into narrow-handicap bands and rewarding them according to ability was supposed to change all this, but it hasn't happened. Second division horses, just below the Group horses, often earn less money than fourth division horses. That's sad, because what happens is these horses get exported to where they can race for better prize-money levels.' You suspect that some rather more Machiavellian types would have contrived that the four-year-old would have slid down the handicap, before connections went for the proverbial "touch".

This is a heritage (top-class) handicap, and Crosspeace wins his owners, a syndicate named Favourites Racing, £31,160. Decent prize money by British standards. But it will pay for his training, keep and other expenses for just over a year. There is some justice because the ultra-game Crosspeace completes a festival double in the Listed Coutts Glorious Stakes. Challenges have come from the four-year-old's opponents, but the son of Cape Cross shrugs them aside. 'These Johnston horses are *so* tough,' exclaims the BBC's Clare Balding. 'Not just in terms of the number of races they run, but they're tough in their races, too.' Her associate, Willie Carson, adds, 'Everybody says that once the Johnston horses get in front, nobody can pass.'

Well, not strictly accurate, although on occasion they do give that impression. Certainly Johnston likes to see his horses dictate the pace and stretch the opposition from the front. In one interview at Goodwood, the trainer gives the impression that he doesn't even mind seeing his horses come off the bridle quite early to achieve that – normally a sign that a horse is beginning to labour. A few days later I ask him about the truth of that. 'No, I don't like to see them really off the bridle, as such,' he says, 'but it's preferable to them being restrained, and expecting any acceleration when you let them go, because you won't get it. I like to see them bowling along and getting into a rhythm at a constant speed – of course, it's never going to be constant because they are actually slowing down – and maintaining it as long as possible. I think that's maybe why Goodwood suits a lot of our horses.'

We talk about the ability of horses to accelerate away from their rivals. The spectacle of a top horse cutting down his rivals with sheer velocity or emerging out of a pack is what captivates racegoers, isn't it? I refer to Holy Roman Emperor, who had done just that in the Phoenix Stakes at The Curragh. As the Form Book tells us, he 'quickened clear'. Johnston doesn't share my enthusiasm. 'It doesn't matter how good they are, they don't accelerate at the end of races,' he says bluntly. 'It's the other horses slowing down. It would be interesting to know whether that O'Brien horse really accelerated or whether it just looked like it did when the others were decelerating. Anyway, I don't think a horse has to come whizzing through from the back. People always talk about Dancing Brave, and how he did that. But was that more impressive than the way Shergar did it? I don't know that it is. It's like comparing the old days of Grand Prix racing and today. In the days of Jim Clark, he and others would overtake, and it was considered very exciting, because it was much more down to the skill of the driver. Now, Schumacher or Fernando Alonso, or whoever, gets to the front, and, barring engine failure, stays there. Nobody says, "Oh, he's not as good as Jim Clark." The fans just accept that things have moved on.'

Scrutiny of perceived wrong-doers in racing has also moved on, apace. One can only imagine the skulduggery that took place before the all-seeing camera eye detected transgressions of the rules of racing. Today, it seems, nobody is above suspicion. As the champagne is swigged, there is an unpalatable aftertaste when it is revealed that the country's leading trainer, Sir Michael Stoute, the eight-times champion whose patrons include the Queen, has had his appeal against the non-trying rule not only rejected by the Horseracing Regulatory Authority (the mouthful that replaced the Jockey Club's justice-dispensing function); to his chagrin, he has been punished *more* harshly. He had already received a record fine of £6,500 after his horse, the Khalid Abdullah-owned Florimund, finished eleventh in a Windsor maiden the previous month. Now he is looking at two grand more. One would not have liked to be the stable cat that night.

It was not so much the fine that irked Stoute, of course. Effectively, he has been tarnished as a cheat and a liar. According to the appeal panel, 'The video recordings show it (Florimund) was being ridden in a manner that appeared designed to achieve a highly advantageous handicap mark.' Now, there are certain trainers who would receive such a penalty and the dishonour that accompanies it, and you'd simply nod knowingly and turn your attention to something more useful. But Stoute? A horse owned by Khalid Abdullah? 'Angry ... that would be right,' was about all he was prepared to say, although the pursed-lipped expression spoke volumes. Mr Angry, the nom de plume of the former

BBC commentator Julian Wilson, writing in the *Racing Post*, lived up to his name: 'The outcome of the Florimund affair is so shocking that Mr Angry is simply seething.'

To précis the issue, one of Stoute's riders, Stephen Davies, had been asked to ride what is acknowledged as a difficult horse in his races because Florimund was considered a possible danger to a jockey who did not know him (he would normally have been partnered by Khalid Abdullah's retained jockey Richard Hughes). The drawback was that Davies, although work-riding fit, was not race-riding fit. In the event, having put Florimund into the race in the straight at Windsor and picked up his whip, the jockey tired before the horse did. The implication of the stewards and appeals panel was that Stoute was giving the horse an 'easy', though as Mr Angry wrote, 'Abdullah does not include winning a 0-60 handicap at Yarmouth among his racing priorities; nor would Stoute feel that winning such a race was a significant step towards his ninth championship.' Still, the warning was explicit for all trainers: if Stoute could have his considerable reputation assaulted, it could happen to anyone.

Johnston has not seen the race, but tells of a colt he trains. 'It is very difficult,' he says. 'It's lazy, reluctant and rears, it doesn't go on the gallops and generally gives us bother at home. Very few people in the yard are even willing to sit on it. On the gallops, he won't go past anything. Won't do a tap. When it runs, we'll put blinkers on it straight away. I could imagine that Stoute's horse may be similar. The guy who rides it at home takes his licence out to ride it on the track again. It runs on the track and halfway round the jockey says he's exhausted. But the appeals panel can't accept that the jockey's exhausted. Perhaps they should try to ride it themselves. You see plenty of jockeys who are exhausted. I remember when Wayne Hogg (who works for Johnston and rides in amateur races) had the first ride of his life on Mana D'Argent at Haydock. Afterwards the box driver had to lift him off the horse, and then we had to untack it for him and carry the saddle into the weighing room.' The manner in which Hogg lifted the Amateur Derby at Epsom on Bank Holiday Monday, partnering the stable's Nero's Return, confirms that Hogg's fitness levels have improved since then. But to return to the Stoute case. Johnston declares, 'I think that argument's quite feasible, and also quite acceptable. Have they protected anybody by throwing the rule book at Michael Stoute?'

It should be stressed that Johnston placed his position firmly on the line back in 1997 in his *Horse & Hound* column, and has not swerved from it since:

> So the Jockey Club are going to get tough on non-triers. I can't say that it's the most important issue in the world to me, but I will find it very interesting to see how they go about it and how successful they are.
>
> Frankly, I don't really feel that these rules are aimed at people like me and so I won't be losing any sleep over it. Most people know that, as far as I am concerned, every single one of my horses is trying to win on every occasion that it runs and if there is ever any suggestion that one of mine was 'stopped' then I'll be on the side of the prosecution.
>
> The majority will agree that horseracing in general would benefit from any action which aims to ensure that all horses run on their merits, but there is an argument that the intrigue and rumour add to the excitement of the sport.
>
> Many punters actually believe that trainers can manipulate the results of races, and the betting industry encourages those beliefs.
>
> I have for a long time argued against the many rules in racing which are based on the wholly unacceptable principle of 'guilty until proven innocent', and there is an element of this in every Rule 151 inquiry.
>
> A system which encourages and rewards cheats must be wrong, and if they are ever going to stamp out non-triers they will have to change their own attitude to them and do away with the system that leads to them.

He refers, of course, to the whole ethos behind handicapping. 'I just think handicap racing is wrong,' he says. 'Which is not to say I don't think that the handicappers do a great job. If you're looking for something untoward in a race, that the result's not true, who would be better judges, a panel of stewards or a panel of handicappers? No doubt the latter. Probably if you had a panel of bookmakers they'd be ahead of the stewards as well. Together with the new veterinary department, under Peter Webbon, they're the most knowledgeable people in the HRA. They understand much more about our jobs than the stewards or anyone else. They can see whether horses are doing their best or not.

'But.' And one senses it's a mighty big but. 'It's madness to be continually fighting this battle to catch people cheating the system when the system itself lends itself to cheating. So, why not remove that potential instead of spending millions a year on little detectives in raincoats running around trying to catch people? Why not try to correct that flaw in the system? The reality is that bad horses should run against bad horses for very little money. Good horses should run against good horses for lots of money. You shouldn't have good horses running against bad horses and giving the good horses two stone extra to carry. Where's the sense in that?

'We should have stages. Put simply, you race in class F; if you win, you can race in class E. Right up to class A. That's what (Peter) Savill (the former chief of the British Horseracing Board, and an owner of Johnston's) was trying to do. Under him, the BHB went a long way with its modernisation of British racing, with narrow-band handicaps and so on. That was a great step in the right direction, but they all rubbished him. Bookmakers and people like McCririck who want big-field handicaps rubbished it. It doesn't matter to them whether they're good for racing or good for punters, as long as they're good for bookmakers. Which they are, because they're very difficult and you get a bigger margin. They want big, wide-range handicaps, with the weight in the saddle determining the result rather than the ability of the horses. And the racecourses rubbished it, principally because they're paranoid about small fields. Lastly, some trainers rubbished it, because they believed they had the chance of winning the Ayr Gold Cup or Ebor off 7st 10lb.'

He pauses.

'Fat chance. The reality is those trainers who objected to narrow-band handicaps aren't going to win as many wide-band handicaps as I am. It's why I was in favour of the banding system and the creation of narrow-handicap bands. OK, you can still get your horse down to four classes lower than it should have been. That's between you and the bookmakers. But you can't do that *and* walk away with top prize money as well. That's a disincentive to cheat. Ten years ago you could get your horse down to a rating 65–70, which was just above selling plate class, and then run your horse in the Ebor, which was worth £100,000. At least they've taken that away. At the moment, we're still telling people that there's an advantage to being low in the handicap. We should be saying, "Sorry, there's a great *disadvantage* to being low in the handicap." We should reward the best horses, keep them in Britain. I've been saying this ever since Henry Cecil was talking about "twilight horses" and having to sell them to America.'

Johnston offers an analogy with the boxing world. 'You want to fight for a big title, you've got to come up through the ranks. You can't just hide in the amateur ranks and then suddenly say, "I'm going to fight in a world title boxing match next week and everyone can have a big gamble." So why do they allow it in horseracing? People claim I say that because I've got a yard full of good horses. That's not true. I was saying that when I had very poor horses.'

So, to return to where we began this discussion, does Johnston believe that instances of non-triers are commonplace?

'Of course it goes on, although maybe not quite as much as people think it does. Deirdre watches other people's horses more than I do, and she sees it. And people are openly talking about it. And I don't just mean jockeys and trainers. I mean stewards, Jockey Club members, people in the press who own horses, who you hear talking about having three quiet runs to get a horse handicapped. They think this is the normal, accepted way of training a handicapper. It's accepted throughout the industry, from the stable staff right up to the Jockey Club.'

Johnston boasts a clean record when it comes to the non-triers rule. No doubt there would be some guffaws from amongst those who envy him his success if that wasn't the case. It would ill behove a man whose branding is 'Always Trying' to be hauled before the beaks, wouldn't it? He did once fall foul of the local stewards, at Newcastle in July 2000, but won his case on appeal. It involved a horse named Champfis, ridden by Darryll Holland, which finished fourth of eight in a one-mile maiden event. The *Racing Post* comment on its running was 'steadied start, never near to challenge'. Johnston was not at the meeting and Bobby Elliott was called in as his representative. In his absence, Johnston was found to be in breach of Rule 158 of the Rules of Racing and was fined £750.

'Basically, Bobby was stitched up,' says Johnston. 'It's probably changed a bit now, but the way they run these things is wrong. It's like a little kangaroo court. They have before them our representative, who, with the best will in the world, is unlikely to have a law degree. But they're not really trying to get to the bottom of it. You've got somebody (the stewards' secretary, the professional involved) who fancies himself as a Perry Mason, setting out to catch people who may be out of their depth, and trying to wring a confession out of them. They *should* be trying to get to the truth. When I eventually saw the transcript there were things like this stewards' secretary asking Bobby Elliott what he thought of the way the horse ran, and it has Bobby saying, "I think Mark just wanted to give it a run." He would probably have continued "because it hadn't been out for a long time", or something, but they cut him off. The attitude was, "That'll do. There's something we can hang you by." Apart from anything else, there was no question of us not trying to win, and the jockey understood that. Darryll actually took the rap in the end (and received a seven-day suspension).'

Since then, Johnston has never been confronted by the rules that cover the point that 'every horse which runs in a race shall be run on its merits'. 'I have this feeling, whenever we're had in for anything remotely like that, it usually happens when I'm not on the racecourse,' he says. 'They know I'll give them a hard time. They have this situation at the moment where they ask whether you are satisfied with the riding by the jockey. If you say no, you condemn the jockey; if you say yes, then if he goes down, you must go down with him. If they ever ask me that question, I will say, "*You're* the stewards. *You* judge his performance. Don't ask me to judge him." The rules are totally cock-eyed.'

Coincidentally, during Glorious Goodwood the country's most talented rider, Kieren Fallon, went to the High Court but failed in his appeal to overturn a decision by the Horseracing Regulatory Authority to suspend him from all British racing. The ban was imposed when he was charged with conspiracy to defraud. Fallon has ridden for Johnston over the years, particularly in the late nineties, when their most famous association was Fruits Of Love's victory in the 1999 Dubai Turf Classic. Fallon is still awaiting trial at the time of writing. Johnston says, 'It's desperately sad. Innocent or guilty, racing loses.'

Where sport and gambling meet, suspicion will always abound. A generation of Dick Francis readers have been brought up with the belief that behind every victory, and, indeed, every high-profile defeat, there are nefarious minds at work. Yet, despite the charges brought against Fallon, and others, the cases in question are minute, even if proven, as a proportion of the number of races run annually under both codes.

Johnston has never been a gambling trainer. 'It doesn't really interest me,' he says. 'It doesn't give me much of a thrill. I have the occasional bet, mostly when I'm insulted by the odds offered against my horse. And the kids bet. They ask me to go to the bookie's for them. I've not got anything against it. Perhaps I should suggest to Charlie he becomes a bookie. He had an invitation to go and have a look at the odds-compiling department at William Hill. It's open 24/7. He should definitely take it up. Maybe it would change his view.

'One of the things I made a decision on at the beginning is this: I'm a trainer pure and simple; I'm not a horse-dealer, and that I've got no interest in betting. That's why I get so frustrated when people ask me about one of my horses, "Is it going to win?" If I knew that, if I really believed that I had that sort of edge, I'd take up betting, that's for sure. But I know I haven't, and that's why I don't bet.' Most people would agree, though, that racing is nothing without the betting element. 'It's not *nothing*,' Johnston retorts. 'I'll always dispute that. It's something that gets bandied about all the time. For a long time football depended on the pools and there is a huge amount of betting on it. The bookmakers are forever telling us how fast football betting is growing in relation to horserace betting. But take the betting away from football and football would still exist. Always has. Horseracing was around before betting and would still be around if there was no betting. It's a myth that you have to be interested in betting to be interested in horseracing.

'I'm not trying to minimise the importance of betting to horseracing, but it contributes no more than 24 per cent of our income. That's our owners' return through betting, sponsorship and racecourse gate money, indirectly. It's not the bookies, nor the punters, who employ me. That's why, when John McCririck and people at the Jockey Club are shouting the odds about (Instructions) H14 and H19, saying I *must* tell the punter everything about why my horse hasn't run well, my response is, "Why? I don't work for them. They don't pay my wages." The punter likes to think he pays my wages, but he doesn't. Three-quarters (76 per cent) of my wages come from my owners. *Their* return, on average in Britain, is 24 per cent, not counting the capital they've put into the horses. That's simply prize money against running costs. When I'm continually told by the media that I owe a debt to the punter, I don't go with that – and I won't until the punter contributes as much to horseracing here as he does in Japan, Australia, America. In those countries, trainers ultimately gain their living from the punter.'

Johnston is insistent that prize money should be increased. Should that come from punters? 'No, I don't think we should take more off them, he retorts. But I do think a greater percentage of the bookies' deduction should come to make sure the sport survives, as it does in most other major racing nation. Prize money has improved in recent years, but we're still languishing way down at the bottom of the scale.'

It's an age-old issue which ricochets around any discussion of horseracing like a pinball. Johnston may be correct in his assertion, but you can hardly visualise the storming of Number Ten by a concerned public on behalf of poor, impecunious racehorse owners. I happen to mention that I'd noticed a £7,000-added novice hurdle race at one of the minor jump courses, and suggest that is reasonable prize money for probably moderate horses. In recent years, the money has vastly improved, hasn't it? Johnston assesses the question with what I detect is a degree of derision. 'Say you've got twelve runners,' he says. 'The transport bill alone for them would be more than the added money. Just to get them to the races. The training bill for them for one month alone would be £18,000. That's £25,000 to get them to the races, and you're getting £7,000 back. You haven't yet put a jockey on them, or paid the Jockey Club and Weatherbys for entry fees. What other professional sport, where you're betting on them, doesn't pay the expenses of the participants? In golf, they're paying money a long way down the leaderboard. In essence, they're paying many just to turn up and play. In football, you don't refuse to pay the losers.'

There are answers to that, of course. Everyone involved *does* get paid, apart from owners who do not win prize money. But that is the chance you take with racehorse ownership. There are also less tangible rewards, like prestige, which are deemed to compensate. Frankly, sympathy will be limited for people who can afford to invest in even a leg of a horse. But Johnston is not convinced by the argument. 'In Japan, if you could get together the money to buy a racehorse, I'm sure you would because the return's 200 per cent. I would! In Britain, it's like owning a football club or a yacht. It's an indulgence and an extravagance. Not in Japan. Their racing's clearly going to grow faster than ours, so long as that's the case.'

'But while there's always.'

'Another mug?' he interrupts, with a smile.

'No, I say. No matter what the prize money, there will always be prospective owners.'

'Thankfully,' he adds.

'And many of them do so because they enjoy backing their horses.'

'They like the thrill, not necessarily just the betting side,' Johnston says. 'Quite honestly, the vast majority of my owners did not come into it because of the betting. Some did. If you look at someone like Alex Ferguson, he had an interest in betting before he had an interest in owning a racehorse. I do have a number of owners like that. But they're very much in the minority, and that's old money and new money. The Duke of Roxburghe (owner of Attraction) didn't come into it because he likes a bet. Sheikh Mohammed certainly didn't. Even a lot of owners who do like a bet came into it because they like racehorses and they like competition between racehorses. Brian Palmer (Johnston's former business partner) came into it and ended up buying half a racing stable, yet he hardly had a bet. He had no interest whatsoever in that. He had reached a peak in his own business where he didn't get the same kick or thrill out of it. That's what horseracing gave him.

'For people who have been very successful and can seemingly have everything they want, who can buy success, it gives them competition. They can buy success in certain areas but they can't buy it in horseracing. It gives them a new challenge. An uncertainty. They think they've got a lot of money and can spend a hundred grand on a horse, and then they find there's a guy out there who can spend £1.6 million, or in the case of Sheikh Mohammed $9.7 million. You get people like Stuart Morrison, who owned Quick Ransom and Bijou D'Inde, who do come into it because their first interest is betting. But they lose all that interest. It's inevitable when you're taking Bijou D'Inde to race for 250 grand in prize money, and 500 grand up or down in the value of the horse.

'It's one of the reasons we've been successful. If you find a trainer where the majority of the owners' principal objective is betting, then he's probably not been very successful. I wouldn't for a second suggest that there are a lot of gambling yards, because there aren't. But when I first came to Middleham there were all these stories in the pub about horses being "not off". And then, when it is "off", it gets beat. It's an absolute mug's game. There are a lot of myths about the amount of gambling there is behind the scenes among "insiders" in the racing industry, whether they be trainers, owners or stable staff. It goes right up to the level of J. P. McManus and Michael Tabor. Maybe they bet huge amounts, I don't know. But I don't really think they make their living at it. All I know is that there's still a lot more bookmakers driving Rolls-Royces than stablehands. And there always will be. Some ignorant punters think we know the result before the stalls open. Some owners, too. They wouldn't last very long now, though I have had them in the past. You hear them saying, "Oh, the trainer had one over on me. He said it wasn't going to win, and then it did. There'd been a big bet on and it must have been him." Somebody who's made his living out of bookmaking knows that we don't operate like that. I have come to realise now that some of my best owners to work with are bookmakers, like John Brown (the former chairman of William Hill). He's a fantastic owner because he doesn't expect me to know how his horse is going to run. John made a fortune out of the fact that trainers don't know how their horses are going to run. And neither do jockeys, and neither do punters.

'I remember there was once a front page on the *Racing Post* which had a long list of all the losing horses laid by this guy (on a betting exchange). I looked at it, and said to myself, "God, that's shocking.

Something needs to be done about this." It happened that John Brown was here that morning. He looked at it and said, "What's news about that? Anybody could do that. You don't need to have inside information, or be stopping them. Picking that number of losers isn't difficult. If you picked that number of winners, that would be a different story." Picking that number of losers is not telling you that the races were fixed, or that those horses were stopped.'

Johnston summed it up in a *Racing Post* article on 27 May 2000, when he quoted some lines from the Fleetwood Mac classic 'Tell Me Lies',

> a great song that I used to listen to a lot. But I didn't think until just the other day that the composer may have had horseracing, and in particular punters, in mind when he wrote those lines, rather than cheating lovers. It seems that some people just don't want to hear the truth no matter how many times you tell them, and this infliction seems to affect those that follow horseracing more than other sections of the population.
>
> But, what the hell, here goes again. I'll try once more to explain some of the realities of training and placing horses and to dispel the myth that every trainer, jockey and stable lad has millions in ill-gotten gambling gains stashed under the bed and simply chooses to work a minimum of twelve hours a day in all sorts of weather out of some form of mass masochism.
>
> I have said before, and I'll say again, that if you want to be a successful punter, you must study the form. The vast majority of reliable form is established on the racecourse, not on the gallops, and the information is there in the *Racing Post* for you all to see.

The form is definitely there for all to read at Glorious Goodwood in 2006. Soon afterwards Palo Verde is victorious at Thirsk. Jock Bennett, representing Johnston there, informs the media that it is the yard's 44th winner since 1 July. To borrow again from Fleetwood Mac, Johnston is again a man of the world.

CHAPTER TWENTY-THREE

Of course, there are those good horses that are aimed at long-term, high-class targets and need to be thoroughly tested at home to establish their ability and fitness. But if people think that we are pitting horses against each other in full-speed gallops or holding Godolphin-style trial races to establish what chance we have in a 0-70 handicap at Redcar, then they really are living in cloud cuckoo land.

The week before the St Leger. But in this season when Mark Johnston's Classic plans have been frustratingly punctuated by injuries to his leading horses, there is almost an inevitability to the fact that neither of his intended representatives will run in the final Classic.

Soapy Danger's St Leger 'prep' race was the Great Voltigeur Stakes at York, but there is no fourth successive victory. For a time there's a question of whether there's much future of any kind for the colt, in whom there'd been so much stable confidence. He leads into the straight, but finishes fifth to Mick Channon's Youmzain, and very lame. The X-rays reveal a fractured pastern. Johnston tells the *Racing Post*, 'My understanding is that the injury is not life-threatening, and that the prognosis for a return to racing is fairly good. But we are talking next year.' 'Soapy' undergoes surgery. By the end of the month, Linas Selection has joined his stablemate in rehabilitation. The *Racing Post*, becoming more a casualty register than a racing newspaper, reports, 'A St Leger seemingly losing leading contenders by the day lost another one yesterday when Linas Selection, Yorkshire's big hope for a home-trained victory, became the latest market fancy to be ruled out of the Classic on Saturday week. The Gordon Stakes third, whose stablemate Soapy Danger was forced out of the Leger through injury last week, has suffered a setback serious enough to stop him running at York, and almost certainly for the rest of the year.'

Johnston will be absent from the Leger meeting himself. When we meet, he is preparing to travel to the Keeneland September yearling sales. He will be far from the only British- or Irish-based trainer or representative present. Not for the first time there is a concerted battle between Sheikh Mohammed and Coolmore's John Magnier for the top lot. The former eventually emerges victor, the hammer going down at $11.7 million (£6.2 million) on a son of Kingmambo. Johnston's name features on the results sheet, but against sums of five figures. Before departing, he says, 'It's not a good St Leger (its status as a Classic has come under debate once again, particularly given the march towards precocity) because a bunch of good horses, like ours, are now injured. As James, our vet, says, the only way to ensure a good St Leger is to run it in July, but you can't do that because of the trip. Maybe they should turn the Guineas, Derby and Leger into a genuine triple crown, a bit like in the US, and increase its prestige.' But, he adds, 'I'm bitterly disappointed. I desperately wanted to win that race.' The closest he has come were with his grand servant Bandari, who finished third to Bollin Eric in 2002 after starting favourite, and Double Trigger, similarly placed behind Moonax in 1994. 'And you'd have said after Royal Ascot that the chances of us winning (with either Soapy Danger or Linas Selection) were very high.'

Overall, though, the galleon has steered clear of the doldrums. The sails are still billowing sufficiently to engage the enemy, and there is powder remaining in the Johnston cannons. Peppertree Lane secures the big handicap at Haydock in a 1–2–4 for the yard, while Crosspeace is a runner-up in a feature race at Kempton. Already, in mid-August, Johnston has become the first trainer this season to attain a century of winners. It is the thirteenth consecutive year that he has achieved such a feat. Can he overtake his personal best of 146, established in 2003? If he can, after that indifferent start to the turf season, it would be remarkable.

I mention to Johnston that I have just interviewed, for my newspaper, Ed Dunlop, trainer of Ouija Board. During my conversation with him he had described the Scot as 'a genius', adding, 'He's the man, isn't he? Forty individual two-year-old winners this season (actually it was a bit less, but not by much). He's amazing. Totally different style of training, though.' There is a mythology surrounding Johnston. We talk about this perception when I ask the trainer what lessons he has learnt in a career which by

February 2007 will have been flourishing for precisely twenty years.

'That you can't change the world – you can't make it flat,' he replies. 'I've changed little bits. I started thinking I would be completely different from every other traditional trainer, and it's probably evolved into something that's not much different from the vast majority of them.' The theory, I remind him, is that his horses do more work than at other stables. 'Marginally, compared with *some* other trainers, that may be true,' he says. 'There are probably little differences. But then I don't really know what all the other trainers do. I'm only going by what owners say and what I read in the papers. There's no dramatic difference. The methods are much the same, but you try not to cut any corners. For example, here (he looks at the *Racing Post*) it says that Ouija Board did a really good piece of work under Jamie Spencer (ahead of the Irish Champion Stakes). And I'm thinking, "Really?" I wouldn't think of galloping a horse on a Tuesday before it races on Saturday. He may sit on it, or have a canter, but nothing more. We have that kind of thing reported of our horses here, and it's nonsense here as well. If, say, Soapy Danger was said to have worked really well, it's only because he was pulling up at the end of a canter and his work companion pulled up more quickly! They weren't racing. A horse like Soapy Danger won't have galloped at home since November. There are a lot of things that are reported wrongly, and the punter believes it. What worries me is that some racing professionals seem to have the same thoughts. I do suspect, however, that I do less galloping with my horses than most trainers – or less trial galloping. It's the same with our two-year-olds. Yes, they do fast canters upsides other horses, but we're not trying to find out which one is best.'

One area where he may differ from other trainers is his feeding routine. Johnston's horses are fed at night. 'Because we've found we get more food into them,' he says, answering the query before it arrives. 'It's accepted horse husbandry to feed them little and often. The average people feed them is three times a day. Some people only feed them twice. We feed them four times a day. I discovered that their feed at night does them most good of all. So now we have two men on nights to do it. They feed the horses and also do the stable laundry.'

We talk about placing horses, particularly in handicaps, which, as he's already said, are anathema to him, but can hardly be avoided. 'I probably argue the toss with the handicappers more than any other trainer in the country,' he says. 'But my main grouse with them, and some will accept it, certainly more than the "amateur handicappers" you get, is that it's not maths or science. I'm sick of them suggesting that it is. It's nothing more than opinion. It's not clear-cut. It works out pretty well, overall, because they do a lot of it, but basically it's trying to put a figure to an opinion. For all level-weight sellers, claimers, condition races, Group races, we check the official handicap ratings and use *Timeform* to assess all the horses in a particular race. Those people do a pretty good job at it, so why think you can do it better?'

Johnston confesses that when he started out he was slightly overawed by what placing horses entailed. 'In the early days I was embarrassed by my own simplicity towards it. I thought, "These other guys must be so much cleverer than me. They have opinions about what handicap ratings should be, and they study the form." And then, over time, I realised that I'm right and they're wrong.

'There's a simple answer to handicaps. In the early days of training for Darley Stud, before Godolphin, Anthony Stroud used to say to me, "Our handicapper says we're better in at Pontefract, for example, than we are at Thirsk." But you can't be "better in" in a handicap; you're running off the same rating, unless it changed during the week. I could never understand that. However, that doesn't mean that some handicaps aren't easier to run in than others.'

He pauses before continuing, like a scientist about to reveal a secret new formula, although his method of placing horses in handicaps is actually a very straightforward process. Johnston explains how, on average, a slightly higher ratio of horses that have won last time proceed to win next time in handicaps (15.3 per cent), compared with those who were second in their last race (13.5 per cent). That difference increases even more when compared with those who were third last time out (11.5 per cent). However, all those percentages are significantly greater than that of horses that were unplaced last time out and go on to win next time (6.4 per cent).

'So, there's a routine we go through every morning, or the secretaries do. We do a count up, look at how many last-time-out winners, seconds and thirds we've got to run against in the possible races we could declare in; and we declare where there's least of them. Sometimes you change it because of the money that's on offer or the overall class of the race. Basically, if they're carrying 8st 5lb at one place and 9st 5lb somewhere else, you're more likely to win the latter. Deirdre and I will make that decision. At times, it can be just guesswork. If you've got, say, a horse rated 60, running over a mile there's so many opportunities. There are twenty possible races for it to run in, and 40 entries in every race.'

I had noticed that, even at the first declaration stage, published in the *Racing Post*, there was always a jockey assigned to Johnston's horses, though clearly many of those runners were not declared. Is that a declaration of intent? That he is going to attack that race? 'The jockeys don't like it, but I like everything jocked up,' Johnston responds. 'Debbie feels under pressure, because I'm always saying, "Why's that not jocked up?" I say "fill the page with ink", because it makes it look like we're going to have loads of runners. Amazingly, it works. Even if we've got six in the same race, all to be ridden by, say, Joe Fanning, it still makes people think. It can put people off (declaring their horses).'

We move on to consider Johnston's faults – or those he will admit to. 'I'm a bad loser,' he says. 'For someone who wants to win so much, it's very hard to accept losing. I don't think there's any virtue about being a good loser, is there, although everybody likes to say there is. I don't think you become very competitive if you're a good loser. I want to be a good winner. I sometimes realise, in managing the business and in general life, that I've looked for someone to blame for something that was my own fault. I'm then pretty disappointed with myself. It's one of my flaws. I'm sure I do it far too often. Maybe everybody has that? But as far as the horses are concerned, when they run I don't look for excuses. I don't like owners who do that, and a lot do. They want to blame the jockey, or someone, or something. They say, if he'd done that, or this, or the next thing, the result would have been different – he would have won. They're always blaming the preparation or the way the race was run.'

Johnston believes that the rules of racing make that situation even worse, with explanations being sought for poor performances. 'It's bad enough everyone making excuses for beaten horses instead of just saying, "The truth is that on the day the others ran better." Why do you have to have an explanation for something getting beat? It's ridiculous.

The only logical explanation is that it didn't run fast enough. You shouldn't spend your life looking for the reasons.'

As we talk, Deirdre is preparing for the short journey to Catterick, to saddle two horses. One turns out to be a winner, at 33–1. Her husband and I view that and his other four runners on TV. A two-year-old, Celtic Step, wins at 11–1. He is pleased for the owner, who sold Stepping Up to Godolphin at the end of last season. The owner invested in three more horses, and this is the first winner from among them. 'It's sod's law that the owners you'd desperately love to have a good horse don't have one,' says Johnston. 'While some of the miserable types who take success for granted get them all the time. One day, when I'm retired, I'll tell them. Can't really tell them now. Certainly not the ones still with us ...'

Deirdre is the Duracell bunny, the one with long-life batteries. She is constantly on the move. Few trainers' wives enjoy the lifestyle of footballers' wives, but Deirdre is about as distant from the image of England players' WAGs at the World Cup as you could ask for – apart from one thing. Her love of jewellery. But we'll return to that. Mostly, she loves horses. Her husband refers to her as an 'obsessive'. 'Deirdre has withdrawal symptoms if she goes away somewhere, even on holiday, and can't ride a horse,' says Johnston. 'Obviously at certain times of the year we're very busy. We need every hand on deck to ride all these horses. If she said, "I'm not riding out tomorrow," I'd say, "Why not?" But she's got herself into that position. I know that she'll ride four racehorses in the morning, and then goes and rides three hunters, eventers or ponies in the afternoon, purely for pleasure. She's driving me insane at the moment, now that she's got her own barn of horses at Park Farm. She rides horses for six or seven hours a day. And talks about them for another ten. Sends text messages backwards and forwards to all her pony friends about all her horses.'

Earlier, Deirdre showed me the photo of her eventing horse, Silver Kris. It is an ex-American racehorse which Johnston bought in the States. She has another former racehorse called Saint Clements. In the summer she goes eventing, and is involved in Pony Club activities as both her sons ride. In the winter she hunts with the Bedale, which covers the area of the country between Ripon and Scotch Corner in North Yorkshire. 'I've always wanted to be with horses,' she says. 'I love the social side, but I'm not one of those "oh, bring them all in and I'll cook for everybody" people. That's not me. I want to be with the horses, or at the racecourse.'

Deirdre's input is crucial to the success of the business. 'Mark and I have always discussed everything,' she says. 'No decision is made without consulting me about it. So, I'm involved all the time. And I have my own ideas. It's always worked well.' Can you be in too close proximity at times? 'It's not like that,' she replies. 'We're quite often apart. I'm not with him when I'm riding out. Take last Saturday. Mark was at Haydock and Ayr, while I was doing Newmarket. I hardly saw him until we went out for supper. We're not always in each other's pockets.'

I suggest that, as the rather more glamorous partner in the relationship, her engaging personality had enhanced the stable's profile in TV appearances. 'I don't need to be interviewed,' she says. 'I don't need the limelight. But because I'm always there, it just happens. Like Charlie is there too, and it's happening to him. It doesn't faze me. Remember, I'm used to standing up before a classroom of 30 children. Because I'm so passionate about the horses, and I'm with them every day, that's why it's easy for me to come across well. I genuinely love it. I love being out there. I just couldn't *not* ride out in the morning.'

I tell her that her husband says she's obsessed. She laughs, concurs, and tells me how one day she got up at 5.30 and drove her horsebox up to Tow Law. 'An hour and a half in the lorry. I got there and it's a freezing cold, windy, horrible day. I did a one-day event – dressage, showjumping and cross-country. I had to wait to get my prize. I drove home – another hour and a half. When I got back, I sat and had a cup of coffee, and Mikaelle (Lebretton, a multi-talented young Frenchwoman who initially arrived as an au pair eleven years ago after Angus was born and enjoyed it so much she has never left) said, "I'm going out riding." I said, "Oh? What time are you going?" This is at four thirty. I just went straight out there. I just love it. I just love to ride. I rode five yesterday, five the day before. I could ride all day.

'In the winter, when we've got loads of staff but not many horses in, I love to go hunting. Even then I'd probably ride out first lot. I can't do it once it gets really busy in February because I feel very guilty when I'm not here when they need me. If they need me to ride, I'll always put that first. When it gets really hectic and I have to ride my four lots, I'll do that and then run in here, have a sandwich, jump straight in the horsebox, meet up at the hunt at half past one and hunt until half past four, until it gets dark. So I've been on a horse from virtually seven in the morning until four thirty. I can't sit around, even on days when I try to have the afternoon off.'

She confides that Charlie has been bought a horse to go point-to-pointing. 'He doesn't know about it yet. He'll get it for his birthday on 4 October, if he does well in his exams.' He does. The twelve-year-old gelding, an ex-chaser that has won six races from 49 runs, is called Tacolino. Johnston admits he has a few qualms about his son riding over obstacles, 'but I've got no real problem with it. If I had a daughter, I'd definitely be worried. It's inevitable. Soon he'll be too heavy, I would imagine, so it's better that he starts now.' But better this than what Charlie did have in mind? Recently he told his parents that he harboured ambitions of becoming a National Hunt jockey. His father was incredulous. 'He's got size eleven feet, weighs ten and a half stone and he's only fifteen – and he wants to be a jump jockey!'

Charlie events and competes in the Pony Club Tetrathlon (running, swimming, shooting and cross country riding) and is an avid hunter. Johnston himself has no interest in any other equestrian sports. 'It's a shame,' he admits. 'Deirdre criticises me, quite rightly, for not going to watch the boys compete often enough, whether it's rugby, swimming or riding they're doing. It's terribly wrong that I don't, because they do very well. I can blame some of it on circumstances, but she's absolutely right. I should make the effort. She goes a lot. But then she's deeply involved in it all. Having said that, we have a regular argument. I say it's her hobby, and she would turn up anyway, even if the boys weren't competing. I did watch Charlie in the Yorkshire Show last year. Mostly it's Pony Club competitions and one-day events he goes to. But when I do go, I think that these are the most boring sports under the sun. You sit about all day to watch them go past for a hundred yards and jump a couple of fences. Maybe you run across the other side and watch them jump another couple of fences. And then they sit about for the rest of the day, waiting for the result. Sometimes they leave before they get the result. You've no idea who's winning, or what. I'm absolutely certain that if they rode in races, I'd go and watch them.'

Out of the saddle, Deirdre is renowned for her singing. She appeared recently for a local fundraising event in Leyburn, singing songs from *Les Miserables* and *Evita*. She's also, as I mentioned, interested in jewellery. 'Buying it, and wearing it, of course. But I'd really like to go on a gemmology course and learn more about it.'

Johnston lists his hobby in the *Directory of the Turf* as 'cycling (time permitting)'. The cynic might suggest 'gleaming yellow Porsche permitting', considering the vehicle that is parked outside the house. But it is true. He is a Lycra man too. It is a relaxation for him, although a dangerous one. He has suffered several breaks and bruises on the road.

He still likes to keep in touch with friends from his past. They include one of his fellow students from veterinary college, Gordon Watt. 'Although he lives in Australia, I met up with him at the Melbourne Cup three times running, and on one occasion we went for a few days' holiday together. He was over for Royal Ascot this year. He first practised in Middleham after he qualified, so he knows a few people round here.'

There is, as well, camaraderie among the trainers, despite the fierce competition. 'Yeah, I think I get on with most of them,' Johnston says, 'although I don't have time to socialise. I suppose I'm not one of those who particularly goes out of my way to get to know them. We had dinner not long ago with James and Sally Bethell (who are based at Clarendon House in Middleham; James Bethell is chairman of the Middleham Trainers' Association). But it was the first time we'd ever done it. I get on with William Haggas. He invites me round if I'm down at the sales. I get on very well with John Hills, and I know Michael Stoute quite well. I've stayed at his house. Deirdre gets on very well with Coral (Pritchard-Gordon, Stoute's partner). If we're abroad, they go shopping together, that kind of thing. Deirdre's always the more sociable one of us. I say hello to Aidan O'Brien. It would be nice if we both had time to spend some time talking. Maybe I should suggest it? And I know Saeed Bin Suroor quite well. I've been for lunch in the desert in Dubai with him, on a carpet in a wadi.'

There have been periods in his career when Johnston has enjoyed a magic carpet ride. Not this year, though. There have been no spectacular triumphs, despite that post-mid-summer flourish.

CHAPTER TWENTY-FOUR

You can't hide behind bad luck if you're not performing when you've got 200 horses. That's why I never say mine are a bad bunch. Similarly, I would never accept one yard manager saying that he would have 30 winners that season and another guy saying he'd have 40 'because I've got better horses'. I never cease trying to explain to people that better horses don't win more races. Not with the system we have in Britain.

Summer begins its farewell as the final Classic, the St Leger, staged this year at York, takes place. Sixties Icon wings home under Frankie Dettori. More a case of Noughties Nobility, really. He is a mightily impressive winner and looks bound for the Prix de l'Arc de Triomphe at Longchamp. Who knows what would have been the outcome if Soapy Danger or Linas Selection had been fit enough to take on Jeremy Noseda's colt. But then, who knows, too, what would have happened had Soapy Danger contested the King George.

It has been that kind of season for Mark Johnston's stable, though he remains sanguine about both of his charges for next year. But what of those horses denied their chance in the earlier Classics because of injury? Nakheel finally returns in the Group 3 extended mile which immediately follows the Leger. Coltish in the paddock, he is given a restrained ride by Richard Hills, and threatens briefly, but finishes fifth. In his next race, a Listed event at Goodwood, he finishes strongly, under Martin Dwyer. Again he is fifth, but beaten less than a length. Johnston is delighted. The colt could have gone on to contest the Champion Stakes, but developed an abscess in his foot and missed the race. He will return next year, if not this. Another one-time Johnston Guineas contender, Black Charmer, is back in action, too, but he has three times been disappointing. It may be that the needs faster ground. He's likely to be gelded and remain in training next year. And what will become of the yard's Derby entrant, Atlantic Waves? Further patience will be required by his owner. The colt has still not recovered from that 'quarter crack' injury and will not return until next year.

You only get one shot at the Classics. Even the Maktoums and associates can't pay to have another chance. There will be other exciting opportunities though. Towards the end of September, Empire Day, partnered by Daragh O'Donohoe, carries the colours of Sheikh Maktoum bin Mohammed Al Maktoum to victory in a mile maiden. He becomes the 40th individual two-year-old winner for the yard from 80 horses. Another rifle for next year's Classic shooting gallery? O'Donohoe rides because four of Johnston's riders are at The Curragh for one race. The Shelbourne Hotel Goffs Million for two-year-olds is worth virtually that in euros to the winner. The race is heavily influenced by the draw, but the yard's Drumfire, ridden by Joe Fanning, is third, claiming a tidy 133,000 euros for his owners, Kennet Valley Thoroughbreds.

So Johnston is optimistic, despite the absence of an obvious juvenile stable star. 'This is the best group of two-year-olds I've had in years,' he says. 'That's why it's frustrating they haven't won a Group race. Several have been placed. Armigerent was second in a Group 2, but has gone backwards since then. Dubai's Touch was third in a Group 2. He'll be unlucky not to win well at some stage. I'm keen on Kirklees, Silent Waves, Champery, Steady As A Rock, Drumfire and Lovelace. And some haven't run yet. I'd say Silent Waves is the best colt so far, and Princess Taise the best filly. Interestingly, both by Cozzene.' He nearly forgets Teslin, who wins the race in which Winged Cupid was successful last season at Sandown before going on to be runner-up in the Racing Post Trophy. And is there any among them who could eventually compare with Bandari? An era has come to an end. Johnston's doughty multiple Group winner, the famous earplug-wearer who won here at York the previous year in the Hardwicke Stakes (during the transferred Royal Ascot meeting) and in the 2002 Great Voltigeur, has been retired to stand at Peria Stud in Tallow, Co. Waterford. The seven-year-old, owned by Hamdan Al Maktoum, won eleven of his 33 races, including six at Group level, and finished third to Bollin Eric in the 2002 St Leger, amassing in the process £547,045 in win and place prize money.

Given that slough in form in May and early June, the fact that Johnston could still finish second in the trainers' table, behind Sir Michael Stoute, is remarkable. At the time of writing, in mid-October, his total is 130 winners from 872 runners – a commendable strike-rate of 15 per cent. His record with two-year-olds is outstanding: 52 victories from 276 runs, a percentage of just under 20 per cent. And what's more, there have been 42 individual winners. Just not sufficient Group race victories in all ages, though. Only three up to now in races in Great Britain.

It's all relative, of course. Back in the late eighties, Johnston would have relished the prospect of just entering a horse for a Group event. But today he is playing a much bigger, more rewarding but potentially much more precarious game. As Double Trigger's owner Ron Huggins says of the trainer, 'I certainly thought he could achieve what he has, even back then when Trigger first came along. Basically, it was a numbers game. Which Mark has always said, of course. And he's done that. But, obviously, Mark needs more Group 1 winners. That's the challenge that remains for him. He needs the better pedigree horses, the ones that tend to go to Michael Stoute, rather than the second division ones that he tends to get.'

'I've always said that I've never been content,' Johnston muses, 'never been someone who was satisfied to have his life mapped out and know where he was going, what his wages were going to be, what his pension was going to be. I've never been content with my lot. I always want more.' Given that, I ask him whether he ever takes stock and reflects on what he has actually achieved. 'No,' he replies. 'I never stand still, but I do switch off now, which I never used to do. I took up skiing six years ago, and until last year I would have stopped skiing, actually while I was on the ski-slopes, to answer the phone, and on a regular basis – maybe three or four times a day. I switch the phone off now. When we were in Switzerland last time, I went down to dinner and didn't take the phone. Two years ago I wouldn't have dreamt of doing that. I was available, on the phone, 24 hours a day. And, I can tell you, owners would phone me at the weirdest times. I would never, never be unavailable. Not now, though – although I did still check it afterwards to see if there'd been any calls … and I'm more relaxed, I've mellowed slightly. And just in the last year I've become far more successful at delegating.'

Johnston's sister Sharon feels that though he still has ambitions to fulfil, ones that can only be realised by running a major yard, his job satisfaction is not what it was. 'At one time he made every decision about every horse,' she says. 'He doesn't today, and I'd question whether he still gets the same amount out of it.' Deirdre adds, 'He's never lost that drive to succeed. The year we got more horses, it got really tough. He was just out there all hours, doing the list (of the following morning's work schedule). He never came to bed, hardly. We both felt we couldn't work any more hours, and we still felt we weren't doing things as well as we wanted to do them. Once we made the change in the system, we got all our drive and enthusiasm back. There was a little bit of breathing space.'

I want to know how Johnston reacted to that bad spell early in the season. 'Amazingly calmly,' Deirdre says. 'At times like that before, he used to get like a bear with a sore head. But we just kept having our meetings. He just kept saying to the staff, "More attention to detail. You've got to really know your horses and pick the right horses that we know we can win with." He just kept drumming that into them. He'd keep looking at the list. "Are we doing the right work with them?" he'd say. He just put the emphasis on running the horses that were well, and hopefully winning, so we could get through it until the other horses took off again. It's really tough when they aren't winning. I was riding five lots a morning. It was really hard work. There's a little bit of adrenalin you get when they're winning. Everything seems easier. You can be up late in the evening, and get up earlier. It's when they aren't winning, and you don't know why, that it seems really daunting.'

I ask her husband whether the 2006 season has finally convinced him that this business is more about luck than judgement. He prefers to turn the question on its head. 'You can't hide behind bad luck if you're not performing when you've got 200 horses,' he says. 'That's why I never say mine are a bad bunch. Similarly, I would never accept one yard manager saying that he would have 30 winners that season and another guy saying he'd have 40 "because I've got better horses". I never cease trying to explain to people that better horses don't win more races. Not with the system we have in Britain. It's completely wrong for trainers to say, "I don't have the horses." That's total bullshit. Neither is success just down to money or who your owners are. The fact is that throughout the nineties the average cost of our horses was very low. It's only since 2000 that we've bought more expensive ones.'

So, what advice would he offer a young trainer harbouring similar aspirations as he did, all those years ago? 'It doesn't matter how good your horses are; it's your job to win as many races with them as possible,' he says. 'If you have 20 horses, and you win 20 bad handicaps with them you'll get noticed, and the next season you'll get more horses.'

Johnston's own priorities are tomorrow's, next month's and next year's plans, for his own charges. We've spoken of many throughout the season: in particular, Atlantic Waves, Nakheel, Black Charmer, Linas Selection and Soapy Danger. In addition there was mention of Prince Of Light. He was successful at Glorious Goodwood and a Chester conditions race. The trainer also spoke of In Full Cry who was placed in two handicaps. The two-year-olds touched upon included Eradicate. 'He has had various minor problems and may have to wait until next year but nothing is written in stone,' says Johnston. 'Forty-eight hours is a long time in the life of a racehorse, never mind several weeks or months.' Princess Taise was disappointing after initially suggesting Classic potential. 'We are just hoping that the last two runs are not her form.' Tartan Tie was placed twice at Ayr, but like Atlantic Waves, 'also has a quarter crack in a foot'. And Schermuly 'has had various problems and has shown very little. We will try to run before the end of the year if he isn't sold in the sales'. Magic Moth, the horse Johnston had hoped may be a Derby prospect after his one early victory, didn't run again in 2006. It is expected he'll be back next season.

It all demonstrates just how capricious this sport this can be in bestowing its favours and what a speculative business, too; a point that is enforced in October, when Jalil, that $9.7 million colt purchased by Sheikh Mohammed makes his debut at Newmarket. The son of Storm Cat, the most expensive horse to race in Britain, finishes sixth.

A couple of days later, at San Siro, in Milan, Johnston belatedly records his first Group 1 victory of the season when Frankie Dettori coaxes the two-year-old Kirklees to the narrowest of victories. The owner: Sheikh Mohammed.

By now, Johnston is installing his team for next year, his 21st as a trainer. Throughout late summer and autumn he has been occupied at sales at Deauville, Goffs, Keeneland, Doncaster and Newmarket. He purchases 45 lots, for a total outlay of just under £1.75 million. The most expensive are a Giants Causeway filly and Hennessy colt, bought at Keeneland, both at $150,000. The majority of his buys are spoken for; though when we are last in touch, Johnston has 12 still for sale, at a total value of around £500,000. His own money. His own risk. 'It's the reason I am limited to relatively cheap horses,' Johnston explains. I ask if there are any amongst them he particularly likes. 'Owning them yourself, even for a short time, ensures that you need to like them all – a lot,' he says wryly.

As the New Year beckons, those purchases will be complemented by consignments from the Maktoum family's sources as Johnston's 'all-conquering juggernaut' – the words of his former jockey, now TV racing pundit, Jason Weaver – sets out again. This season, it suffered a blow-out en route, but this must still be regarded as a highly successful campaign. As he looks forward, he receives a letter which evokes the past. It advises Johnston that Hinari Video, his first winner, has been put down, at the age of 21. It is a poignant reminder of those early days and how far he has travelled since. What will 2007 bring?

All you can be certain is that his acute competitive edge will be honed once more as an atmosphere of rich expectancy permeates the moorland around Middleham; and at its centre a formidable, assertive Scot who continues to question conventional wisdom while challenging all limits placed on his ambition.

As Mark Johnston maintains: Always Trying. As he would be entitled to add: And Frequently Flying.

MARK JOHNSTON'S RACING CAREER

1989

DATE	COURSE	HORSE
14/06	BEVERLEY	HINARI DISK DECK
19/07	AYR	HINARI TELEVIDEO
24/08	BEVERLEY	JUST PRECIOUS
09/09	DONCASTER	JUST PRECIOUS
15/10	CATTERICK	CRAFT EXPRESS

1990

30/03	DONCASTER	CRAFT EXPRESS
05/05	HAMILTON	HINARI VIDEO
19/05	THIRSK	ADDISON'S BLADE
20/05	HAMILTON	HINARI SUNRISE
21/06	RIPON	LIFEWATCH VISION
24/06	ASCOT	HINARI TELEVIDEO
28/06	SALISBURY	HINARI SUNRISE
28/06	SALISBURY	LIFEWATCH VISION
08/07	HAYDOCK	LIFEWATCH VISION
18/07	LEICESTER	SOLOMON'S SONG
02/08	PONTEFRACT	STARSTREAK
21/08	DONCASTER	CRAFT EXPRESS
21/08	HAMILTON	SOLOMON'S SONG
01/11	MUSSELBURGH	GO BUY BAILEY'S
07/11	LEICESTER	STARSTREAK
06/01	SOUTHWELL (A.W)	HINARI VIDEO
23/01	LINGFIELD (A.W)	CRAIL HARBOUR
27/01	LINGFIELD (A.W)	SOLOMON'S SONG
27/01	LINGFIELD (A.W)	HINARI VIDEO
17/02	SOUTHWELL (A.W)	SOLOMON'S SONG
31/03	SOUTHWELL (A.W)	HOP THE TWIG
18/04	AYR	STARSTREAK
21/04	THIRSK	LIFEWATCH VISION
02/05	ASCOT	STARSTREAK
04/05	HAMILTON	CRAIL HARBOUR
07/05	DONCASTER	ALJANAN
10/05	CARLISLE	CRAIL HARBOUR
10/05	CARLISLE	KANDARA
08/06	HAYDOCK	SOLOMON'S SONG
27/06	SALISBURY	SOLOMON'S SONG
20/08	HAMILTON	HINARI VIDEO
25/08	NEWCASTLE	KANDARA
27/08	NEWCASTLE	HINARI TELEVIDEO
15/09	CHEPSTOW	QUATRE FEMME
19/09	AYR	HINARI VIDEO
24/09	HAMILTON	PAPER CRAFT
08/10	PONTEFRACT	KINGSLEY
24/10	MUSSELBURGH	SMALL DOUBLE
08/11	LINGFIELD (A.W)	SOUTH CROFTY

1991

12/01	LINGFIELD (A.W)	QUICK RANSOM
23/02	LINGFIELD (A.W)	HINARI VIDEO
20/03	SOUTHWELL (A.W)	HINARI VIDEO
17/04	AYR	QUICK RANSOM
20/04	LENNYMORE	SIMPLY PERFECT
22/04	BRIGHTON	LIFEWATCH VISION
10/05	BEVERLEY	KIVETON KOMET
13/05	MUSSELBURGH	ARMAITI
18/05	HAMILTON	PRETONIC
27/05	DONCASTER	ARMAITI
29/05	RIPON	LUKS AKURA
12/06	HAMILTON	PRETONIC
12/06	NEWBURY	LIFEWATCH VISION
11/07	HAMILTON	NO CANDLES TONIGHT
15/07	BEVERLEY	LIFEWATCH VISION
18/07	HAMILTON	NO CANDLES TONIGHT
26/07	CARLISLE	KIVETON KOMET
31/07	CATTERICK	KINGSLEY
05/08	NOTTINGHAM	KINGSLEY
12/08	LEICESTER	NO CANDLES TONIGHT
09/10	YORK	ISAIAH
09/10	YORK	HINARI TELEVIDEO
19/10	CATTERICK	BE VISIBLE
24/10	PONTEFRACT	ISAIAH
25/10	PONTEFRACT	FORBEARANCE
01/11	NEWMARKET	ISAIAH
07/11	MUSSELBURGH	BE VISIBLE

1992

09/01	LINGFIELD (A.W)	JUMBY BAY
26/02	SOUTHWELL (A.W)	AKURA
03/03	LINGFIELD (A.W)	HINARI VIDEO
21/03	LINGFIELD (A.W)	EDUCATED PET
30/03	NEWCASTLE	TAUFAN BLU
01/04	HAMILTON	DOUBLE BLUE
15/04	PONTEFRACT	DOUBLE BLUE
18/04	KEMPTON	DOUBLE BLUE
23/04	BEVERLEY	DOUBLE BLUE
04/05	HAYDOCK	QUICK RANSOM
07/05	CARLISLE	STRAW THATCH
12/05	YORK	MARINA PARK
21/05	CATTERICK	BOLD COUNTY
29/05	NEWCASTLE	TAUFAN BLU
30/05	WOLVERHAMPTON	EDUCATED PET
06/06	CARLISLE	LUKS AKURA
06/06	CARLISLE	BOY MARTIN
06/06	CARLISLE	EDUCATED PET
10/06	HAMILTON	EDUCATED PET
11/06	HAMILTON	LUKS AKURA
18/06	RIPON	AKURA
20/06	AYR	SWEET ROMEO
20/06	AYR	EDUCATED PET
20/06	ASCOT	TAUFAN BLU

29/06	HAMILTON	AKURA
29/06	HAMILTON	FIELD OF VISION
03/07	SANDOWN	MARINA PARK
07/07	PONTEFRACT	MILNGAVIE
10/07	YORK	QUICK RANSOM
18/07	NEWMARKET (JULY)	EDUCATED PET
22/07	REDCAR	ARCTIC GUEST
23/07	HAMILTON	BOLD COUNTY
25/07	ASCOT	MARINA PARK
30/07	HAMILTON	JUST BAILEYS
01/08	WINDSOR	BOLD COUNTY
08/08	AYR	FAIR FLYER
19/08	YORK	QUICK RANSOM
28/08	THIRSK	FAIR FLYER
05/09	THIRSK	DOUBLE BLUE
17/09	BEVERLEY	PINE RIDGE LAD
17/09	BEVERLEY	PRETONIC
26/09	ASCOT	QUICK RANSOM
01/10	LINGFIELD (A.W)	STARDUST EXPRESS
05/10	PONTEFRACT	BRANSTON ABBY
13/10	CHEPSTOW	BRANSTON ABBY
22/10	PONTEFRACT	BRANSTON ABBY
29/10	NOTTINGHAM	BRANSTON ABBY
03/11	HAMILTON	HINARI VIDEO
05/11	LINGFIELD (A.W)	BOY MARTIN
07/11	DONCASTER	BRANSTON ABBY
10/11	SOUTHWELL (A.W)	PRETONIC
17/11	SOUTHWELL (A.W)	PRETONIC
28/12	SOUTHWELL (A.W)	PRETONIC

1993

01/01	SOUTHWELL (A.W)	HINARI VIDEO
08/01	SOUTHWELL (A.W)	PRETONIC
19/01	LINGFIELD (A.W)	TAKE YOUR PARTNER
19/01	LINGFIELD (A.W)	PRETONIC
01/02	SOUTHWELL (A.W)	PINE RIDGE LAD
04/02	LINGFIELD (A.W)	ARCTIC GUEST
06/02	LINGFIELD (A.W)	TAKE YOUR PARTNER
08/02	SOUTHWELL (A.W)	ALWAYS BAILEYS
08/02	SOUTHWELL (A.W)	PINE RIDGE LAD
11/02	LINGFIELD (A.W)	STARDUST EXPRESS
13/02	LINGFIELD (A.W)	EWALD
15/02	SOUTHWELL (A.W)	PINE RIDGE LAD
25/02	LINGFIELD (A.W)	STARDUST EXPRESS
16/04	THIRSK	ASHGORE
17/04	THIRSK	EWALD
23/04	CARLISLE	BRANSTON ABBY
26/04	SOUTHWELL (A.W)	NORTH ARDAR
30/04	HAMILTON	MILNGAVIE
05/05	MUSSELBURGH	DON'T BE KOI
10/05	SOUTHWELL (A.W)	PENNY BANGER
11/05	YORK	BRANSTON ABBY
14/05	THIRSK	ENCORE UNE FOIS
15/05	LINGFIELD	FIELD OF VISION

15/05	LINGFIELD (A.W)	ARCTIC GUEST
17/05	MUSSELBURGH	MISS MAH-JONG
07/06	NOTTINGHAM	EWALD
07/06	PONTEFRACT	INDIAN CRYSTAL
09/06	HAMILTON	BRAILLE
09/06	YARMOUTH	ARCTIC GUEST
11/06	YORK	QUICK RANSOM
12/06	LINGFIELD	PENNY BANGER
18/06	REDCAR	FIELD OF VISION
22/06	YARMOUTH	KING RAT
25/06	NEWCASTLE	MISTER BAILEYS
28/06	HAMILTON	CASPIAN GOLD
28/06	RIPON	ROCHE ABBEY
01/07	NOTTINGHAM	SHIRLEY ROSE
01/07	CATTERICK	NORTH ARDAR
02/07	SANDOWN	FIELD OF VISION
05/07	MUSSELBURGH	SHIRLEY ROSE
07/07	REDCAR	CERTIFICATE-X
10/07	SOUTHWELL (A.W)	PENNY BANGER
13/07	FOLKESTONE	ARCTIC GUEST
14/07	SOUTHWELL (A.W)	SWEET ROMEO
16/07	THIRSK	POTSCLOSE
17/07	AYR	CUT THE RED TAPE
21/07	DONCASTER	SHIRLEY ROSE
26/07	NEWCASTLE	ASHGORE
27/07	BEVERLEY	MILNGAVIE
28/07	CATTERICK	NORTH ARDAR
29/07	GOODWOOD	MISTER BAILEYS
01/08	MUNICH	BRANSTON ABBY
02/08	RIPON	FAIR FLYER
16/08	WINDSOR	SHIRLEY ROSE
20/08	SANDOWN	EDUCATED PET
21/08	RIPON	JUBRAN
25/08	REDCAR	SHIRLEY ROSE
26/08	MUSSELBURGH	MISS MAH-JONG
28/08	WINDSOR	SHIRLEY ROSE
01/09	YORK	PEARL KITE
08/09	DONCASTER	MARINA PARK
20/09	MUSSELBURGH	MISS MAH-JONG
25/09	REDCAR	DOUBLE TRIGGER
25/09	ASCOT	MISTER BAILEYS
28/09	BRIGHTON	KING RAT
28/09	NEWCASTLE	CAN CAN CHARLIE
30/09	LINGFIELD	PENNY BANGER
01/10	NEWMARKET	BRANSTON ABBY
16/10	CATTERICK	CERTIFICATE-X
21/10	NEWBURY	BRANSTON ABBY
27/10	YARMOUTH	PENNY BANGER
30/10	NEWMARKET	DOUBLE TRIGGER
02/11	REDCAR	BRAILLE
06/11	DONCASTER	QUICK RANSOM
16/11	SOUTHWELL (A.W)	ASHGORE
22/11	SOUTHWELL (A.W)	ASHGORE
01/12	SOUTHWELL (A.W)	ARCTIC GUEST

16/12	SOUTHWELL (A.W)	MUZZ		06/06	PONTEFRACT	NORTH ARDAR
				08/06	HAMILTON	PERCY BRAITHWAITE
1994				09/06	HAMILTON	LOVEYOUMILLIONS
03/01	WOLVERHAMPTON (A.W)	MILNGAVIE		10/06	MUSSELBURGH	BENJARONG
08/01	WOLVERHAMPTON (A.W)	ASHGORE		14/06	THIRSK	ANOTHER BAILEYS
08/01	WOLVERHAMPTON (A.W)	MILNGAVIE		25/06	WOLVERHAMPTON (A.W)	INDIAN CRYSTAL
10/01	WOLVERHAMPTON (A.W)	CROFT IMPERIAL		25/06	NEWCASTLE	QUICK RANSOM
14/01	SOUTHWELL (A.W)	KING RAT		27/06	WINDSOR	SURPRISE GUEST
15/01	LINGFIELD (A.W)	TRUBEN		27/06	WOLVERHAMPTON (A.W)	RUBY ESTATE
18/01	LINGFIELD (A.W)	HINARI VIDEO		28/06	CHEPSTOW	ROSE CHIME
01/02	LINGFIELD (A.W)	CROFT IMPERIAL		29/06	WARWICK	STAR RAGE
14/02	WOLVERHAMPTON (A.W)	SURPRISE GUEST		29/06	CATTERICK	INDIAN WEDDING
15/02	LINGFIELD (A.W)	MILNGAVIE		07/07	REDCAR	NOOSA
15/02	LINGFIELD (A.W)	CAVERS YANGOUS		08/07	AYR	JUST BUY BAILEYS
19/02	WOLVERHAMPTON (A.W)	ASHGORE		09/07	WOLVERHAMPTON (A.W)	IT'S SO EASY
19/02	LINGFIELD (A.W)	SURPRISE GUEST		09/07	YORK	PERCY BRAITHWAITE
26/02	LINGFIELD (A.W)	EWALD		09/07	CURRAGH	MILLSTREAM
05/03	WOLVERHAMPTON (A.W)	KING RAT		11/07	LEICESTER	TILER
05/03	LINGFIELD (A.W)	SURPRISE GUEST		11/07	WOLVERHAMPTON (A.W)	MAGIC TIMES
07/03	WOLVERHAMPTON (A.W)	HINARI VIDEO		12/07	MUSSELBURGH	STAR RAGE
08/03	LINGFIELD (A.W)	EWALD		12/07	MUSSELBURGH	JUBRAN
17/03	LINGFIELD (A.W)	PRETONIC		12/07	MUSSELBURGH	ROBBIES RAINBOW
19/03	WOLVERHAMPTON (A.W)	MILNGAVIE		13/07	CATTERICK	WATER BEBE
21/03	LINGFIELD (A.W)	MUZZ		15/07	HAMILTON	RUSSIAN HEROINE
23/03	SOUTHWELL (A.W)	CAN CAN CHARLIE		15/07	THIRSK	INDIAN WEDDING
24/03	DONCASTER	SURPRISE GUEST		18/07	AYR	CAERPHILLY
31/03	LEICESTER	CAVERS YANGOUS		19/07	BEVERLEY	STAR RAGE
08/04	BEVERLEY	CAN CAN CHARLIE		19/07	BEVERLEY	KING RAT
14/04	RIPON	WILD ROSE OF YORK		21/07	HAMILTON	HAPPY HOSTAGE
14/04	RIPON	DOUBLE BLUE		23/07	NEWCASTLE	ARAK
16/04	WOLVERHAMPTON (A.W)	ARGYLE CAVALIER		23/07	AYR	JURAL
16/04	THIRSK	ARAK		04/08	PONTEFRACT	HAPPY HOSTAGE
22/04	CARLISLE	SURPRISE GUEST		05/08	REDCAR	NOOSA
23/04	LEICESTER	HERE COMES RISKY		06/08	NEWMARKET (JULY)	JURAL
29/04	HAMILTON	MUZZ		06/08	AYR	TILER
30/04	NEWMARKET	DOUBLE BLUE		06/08	AYR	IT'S SO EASY
30/04	NEWMARKET	MISTER BAILEYS		08/08	LEICESTER	POTSCLOSE
02/05	DONCASTER	ASHGORE		08/08	THIRSK	BAILEYS SUNSET
04/05	MUSSELBURGH	STAR RAGE		09/08	YARMOUTH	MISS RITZ
05/05	HAMILTON	RUSSIAN HEROINE		10/08	BEVERLEY	RUSSIAN HEROINE
05/05	HAMILTON	CAN CAN CHARLIE		10/08	BEVERLEY	STAR RAGE
06/05	BEVERLEY	STAR RAGE		15/08	HAMILTON	CAN SHE CAN CAN
07/05	LINGFIELD	BRANSTON ABBY		17/08	YARMOUTH	MISS RITZ
09/05	SOUTHWELL (A.W)	ARGYLE CAVALIER		25/08	MUSSELBURGH	ROSE CHIME
09/05	SOUTHWELL (A.W)	STAR RAGE		27/08	CURRAGH	LOVEYOUMILLIONS
10/05	YORK	MILLSTREAM		27/08	CURRAGH	JURAL
19/05	NEWCASTLE	MILLSTREAM		30/08	RIPON	ENCORE UNE FOIS
23/05	AYR	ASHGORE		30/08	RIPON	NOOSA
24/05	SOUTHWELL (A.W)	EUCHAN FALLS		30/08	RIPON	JUBRAN
25/05	RIPON	ARGYLE CAVALIER		17/09	WOLVERHAMPTON (A.W)	WILD ROSE OF YORK
25/05	HAMILTON	THREE ARCH BRIDGE		17/09	AYR	HERE COMES RISKY
28/05	WOLVERHAMPTON (A.W)	STAR RAGE		19/09	MUSSELBURGH	ROSE CHIME
30/05	REDCAR	ARGYLE CAVALIER		26/09	HAMILTON	DOUBLE BLUE
04/06	DONCASTER	STAR RAGE		27/09	NEWMARKET	CAERPHILLY

Date	Course	Horse
01/10	WOLVERHAMPTON (A.W)	KING RAT
03/10	PONTEFRACT	DOUBLE ECLIPSE
08/10	ASCOT	MILLSTREAM
11/10	CHEPSTOW	DOUBLE BLUE
17/10	NOTTINGHAM	DEANO'S BEENO
20/10	NEWBURY	BRANSTON ABBY
25/10	LEICESTER	HAPPY HOSTAGE
27/10	NOTTINGHAM	DOUBLE BLUE
28/10	NEWMARKET	DOUBLE QUICK
29/10	NEWMARKET	DOUBLE ECLIPSE
31/10	NEWCASTLE	LEVEL EDGE
04/11	TURIN	DOUBLE TRIGGER
05/11	DONCASTER	DOUBLE BLUE
09/11	LINGFIELD (A.W)	LEVEL EDGE
18/11	EVRY	BRANSTON ABBY
15/12	SOUTHWELL (A.W)	WASBLEST

1995

Date	Course	Horse
02/01	SOUTHWELL (A.W)	ARGYLE CAVALIER
03/01	LINGFIELD (A.W)	BAILEYS SUNSET
11/01	WOLVERHAMPTON (A.W)	ARGYLE CAVALIER
12/01	LINGFIELD (A.W)	BIYA
20/01	SOUTHWELL (A.W)	LEGAL FICTION
01/02	WOLVERHAMPTON (A.W)	LEGAL FICTION
08/02	WOLVERHAMPTON (A.W)	LEGAL FICTION
18/02	LINGFIELD (A.W)	PROFIT RELEASE
03/03	SOUTHWELL (A.W)	WARLUSKEE
08/04	BEVERLEY	UNCONDITIONAL LOVE
10/04	FOLKESTONE	BAILEYS SUNSET
11/04	SOUTHWELL (A.W)	THREE ARCH BRIDGE
29/04	SANDOWN	DOUBLE QUICK
29/04	RIPON	ARGYLE CAVALIER
03/05	ASCOT	UNCONDITIONAL LOVE
03/05	ASCOT	DOUBLE TRIGGER
04/05	WOLVERHAMPTON (A.W)	AFISIAK
08/05	NEWCASTLE	DIAGHILEF
11/05	HAMILTON	GOTHENBERG
12/05	CARLISLE	PROFIT RELEASE
13/05	BEVERLEY	PRINCE ASLIA
13/05	BEVERLEY	EQUERRY
20/05	HAMILTON	THORNTOUN JEWEL
20/05	THIRSK	DOUBLE QUICK
20/05	THIRSK	CELESTIAL KEY
20/05	THIRSK	SWEET ROBIN
22/05	MUSSELBURGH	MARY'S CASE
25/05	NEWCASTLE	GOTHENBERG
27/05	HAYDOCK	DESERT TIGER
29/05	SANDOWN	DOUBLE TRIGGER
01/06	AYR	DOUBLE OSCAR
03/06	CATTERICK	RUSSIAN HEROINE
05/06	LEOPARDSTOWN	MILLSTREAM
07/06	BEVERLEY	BOLDINA BAY
09/06	EPSOM	PRINCE ASLIA
10/06	WOLVERHAMPTON (A.W)	MISS OFFSET
10/06	HAYDOCK	CELESTIAL KEY
10/06	EPSOM	GOTHENBERG
11/06	EPSOM	DOUBLE QUICK
12/06	PONTEFRACT	CAVERS YANGOUS
15/06	CHEPSTOW	RUSSIAN HEROINE
15/06	YARMOUTH	MISS OFFSET
15/06	NEWBURY	CELESTIAL KEY
22/06	ASCOT	DIAGHILEF
22/06	ASCOT	DOUBLE TRIGGER
26/06	MUSSELBURGH	RUSSIAN HEROINE
26/06	MUSSELBURGH	EVERYONE CAN DREAM
28/06	CHESTER	RUSSIAN HEROINE
29/06	CARLISLE	NINIA
01/07	NEWCASTLE	BRANSTON ABBY
02/07	DONCASTER	SHONTAINE
03/07	WOLVERHAMPTON (A.W)	ITSINTHEPOST
06/07	CATTERICK	RUSSIAN HEROINE
07/07	HAMILTON	PROFIT RELEASE
07/07	HAMILTON	THREE ARCH BRIDGE
10/07	MUSSELBURGH	LEGAL FICTION
14/07	HAMILTON	DESERT TIGER
15/07	AYR	PURPLE MEMORIES
15/07	CHESTER	ADMIRAL JONES
16/07	AYR	BAILEYS SUNSET
19/07	CATTERICK	CROFT IMPERIAL
22/07	WOLVERHAMPTON (A.W)	EQUERRY
22/07	NEWCASTLE	NINIA
23/07	DUSSELDORF	BRANSTON ABBY
24/07	NEWCASTLE	SHONTAINE
27/07	GOODWOOD	ADMIRAL JONES
27/07	GOODWOOD	DOUBLE TRIGGER
29/07	HAMILTON	THREE ARCH BRIDGE
29/07	THIRSK	EQUERRY
31/07	BRIGHTON	BAILEYS SUNSET
02/08	NEWCASTLE	STAR RAGE
05/08	WOLVERHAMPTON (A.W)	DOUBLE DIAMOND
05/08	REDCAR	NINIA
06/08	GELSENKIRCHEN	BRANSTON ABBY
09/08	BEVERLEY	STAR RAGE
09/08	BEVERLEY	PLEASANT SURPRISE
11/08	WOLVERHAMPTON (A.W)	ASHGORE
12/08	RIPON	MR OSCAR
13/08	PONTEFRACT	CLINCHER CLUB
14/08	WINDSOR	BRANSTON JEWEL
15/08	YORK	DOUBLE ECLIPSE
15/08	YORK	TILER
15/08	YORK	BIJOU D'INDE
19/08	WOLVERHAMPTON (A.W)	BUMBLEFOOT
19/08	RIPON	DOUBLE BLUE
22/08	PONTEFRACT	DESERT TIGER
24/08	BEVERLEY	NINIA
25/08	NEWMARKET (JULY)	INDIAN RHAPSODY
28/08	NEWCASTLE	DOUBLE DIAMOND
28/08	NEWCASTLE	STAR RAGE

Date	Course	Horse
28/08	RIPON	CROFT IMPERIAL
30/08	YORK	BRANSTON ABBY
30/08	YORK	BRANSTON JEWEL
01/09	HAYDOCK	MICK'S LOVE
02/09	CURRAGH	BIJOU D'INDE
02/09	THIRSK	NINIA
05/09	LEICESTER	MR OSCAR
07/09	DONCASTER	BRANSTON ABBY
07/09	DONCASTER	DOUBLE TRIGGER
13/09	BEVERLEY	THREE ARCH BRIDGE
13/09	BEVERLEY	DOMOOR
15/09	NEWBURY	MICK'S LOVE
16/09	WOLVERHAMPTON (A.W)	NOSE NO BOUNDS
16/09	AYR	MARY'S CASE
24/09	HAMILTON	MARCOMIR
11/10	HAYDOCK	POLAR ECLIPSE
23/10	LINGFIELD	TADEO
28/10	NEWMARKET	CELESTIAL KEY
06/11	FOLKESTONE	MILNGAVIE
14/11	LINGFIELD (A.W)	ITSINTHEPOST
16/11	SOUTHWELL (A.W)	DOUBLE DIAMOND
25/11	LINGFIELD (A.W)	SOUTHERN DOMINION
25/11	LINGFIELD (A.W)	THORNTOUN ESTATE
27/11	WOLVERHAMPTON (A.W)	DOMOOR
30/11	LINGFIELD (A.W)	MASK FLOWER

1996

Date	Course	Horse
02/01	LINGFIELD (A.W)	MILNGAVIE
03/01	WOLVERHAMPTON (A.W)	ASHGORE
08/01	SOUTHWELL (A.W)	YOUGO
15/01	SOUTHWELL (A.W)	PANAMA JIVE
24/01	WOLVERHAMPTON (A.W)	FIELD OF VISION
25/01	LINGFIELD (A.W)	DOUBLE-O-SEVEN
30/01	LINGFIELD (A.W)	THORNTOUN ESTATE
31/01	WOLVERHAMPTON (A.W)	FIELD OF VISION
02/02	SOUTHWELL (A.W)	BALIOS
15/02	LINGFIELD (A.W)	DOMOOR
15/02	LINGFIELD (A.W)	MISTER ASPECTO
21/02	WOLVERHAMPTON (A.W)	CHAUVELIN
26/02	SOUTHWELL (A.W)	MISS OFFSET
01/03	SOUTHWELL (A.W)	DISC OF GOLD
02/03	LINGFIELD (A.W)	MISTER ASPECTO
16/03	WOLVERHAMPTON (A.W)	MISS OFFSET
23/03	DONCASTER	GREEN BARRIES
01/04	SOUTHWELL (A.W)	MISTER ASPECTO
03/04	HAMILTON	FIELD OF VISION
06/04	HAYDOCK	DOUBLE ECLIPSE
25/04	LONGCHAMP	DOUBLE ECLIPSE
26/04	CARLISLE	LALLANS
27/04	CURRAGH	GOTHENBERG
29/04	SOUTHWELL (A.W)	MISS OFFSET
29/04	SOUTHWELL (A.W)	MASK FLOWER
01/05	ASCOT	DOUBLE TRIGGER
02/05	WOLVERHAMPTON (A.W)	PEARL ANNIVERSARY
05/05	DIELSDORF	DOUBLE DIAMOND
09/05	HAMILTON	LYCIUS TOUCH
13/05	REDCAR	HULA PRINCE
18/05	HAMILTON	MATTAWAN
19/05	LONGCHAMP	DOUBLE ECLIPSE
20/05	MUSSELBURGH	LORD OF THE MANOR
23/05	NEWCASTLE	HULA PRINCE
27/05	SANDOWN	DOUBLE TRIGGER
29/05	RIPON	NINIA
30/05	CARLISLE	MAGIC CAROUSEL
31/05	WOLVERHAMPTON (A.W)	PEARL ANNIVERSARY
01/06	NEWMARKET	BRANSTON ABBY
03/06	HAMILTON	THREE ARCH BRIDGE
05/06	BEVERLEY	THREE ARCH BRIDGE
05/06	BEVERLEY	EQUERRY
07/06	HAYDOCK	DOUBLE AGENT
08/06	HAYDOCK	FUTURE PROSPECT
08/06	HAYDOCK	PLEASANT SURPRISE
10/06	NOTTINGHAM	DOUBLE AGENT
13/06	CARLISLE	ETTERBY PARK
13/06	CARLISLE	THREE ARCH BRIDGE
15/06	SANDOWN	DOUBLE QUICK
17/06	MUSSELBURGH	TOP OF THE FORM
18/06	ASCOT	BIJOU D'INDE
21/06	REDCAR	DESERT FROLIC
26/06	CHESTER	HALEAKALA
27/06	CARLISLE	DESERT FROLIC
28/06	NEWCASTLE	EQUERRY
30/06	CURRAGH	GOTHENBERG
03/07	CATTERICK	ETTERBY PARK
04/07	AYR	DESERT FROLIC
04/07	YARMOUTH	BRANSTON ABBY
05/07	HAMILTON	SHIRLEY SUE
05/07	SANDOWN	GREEN BARRIES
06/07	CARLISLE	DESERT FROLIC
06/07	WOLVERHAMPTON (A.W)	ETTERBY PARK
06/07	CARLISLE	CAN CAN LADY
10/07	NEWMARKET (JULY)	FREEDOM FLAME
11/07	WOLVERHAMPTON (A.W)	ETTERBY PARK
12/07	HAMILTON	PLAN FOR PROFIT
12/07	CHESTER	DESERT FROLIC
13/07	YORK	TOP OF THE FORM
16/07	BEVERLEY	GREEN BARRIES
16/07	BEVERLEY	CLINCHER CLUB
20/07	AYR	DOUBLE PARK
20/07	RIPON	PERCY BRAITHWAITE
22/07	SOUTHWELL (A.W)	SHIRLEY SUE
25/07	CATTERICK	OUR HOME LAND
25/07	CATTERICK	SHONTAINE
26/07	THIRSK	TILER
29/07	NEWCASTLE	EQUERRY
30/07	BEVERLEY	MISTER ASPECTO
02/08	GOODWOOD	GREEN BARRIES
03/08	GOODWOOD	DOUBLE PARK

04/08	MUNICH	BRANSTON ABBY
07/08	NEWCASTLE	SHIRLEY SUE
12/08	THIRSK	BALLADOOLE BAJAN
12/08	THIRSK	SHIRLEY SUE
14/08	HAMILTON	MISTER ASPECTO
17/08	RIPON	NINIA
29/08	LINGFIELD	SAD MAD BAD
31/08	SANDOWN	NINIA
07/09	WOLVERHAMPTON (A.W)	PERICLES
11/09	EPSOM	NINIA
12/09	DONCASTER	DOUBLE TRIGGER
16/09	NOTTINGHAM	HAPPY MINSTRAL
17/09	SANDOWN	GAELIC STORM
19/09	YARMOUTH	CAN CAN LADY
19/09	AYR	ETTERBY PARK
20/09	AYR	EQUERRY
21/09	AYR	DOUBLE FLIGHT
22/09	DIELSDORF	MATTAWAN
24/09	EPSOM	MAID FOR BAILEYS
24/09	EPSOM	BALLADOOLE BAJAN
24/09	EPSOM	ATLANTIC DESIRE
30/09	BATH	ELDORADO
05/10	HAYDOCK	TADEO
12/10	ASCOT	TADEO
13/10	MUNICH	BRANSTON ABBY
15/10	LEICESTER	OUR PEOPLE
18/10	CATTERICK	KADEENA
21/10	PONTEFRACT	DOUBLE ESPRESSO
27/10	COLOGNE	BRANSTON ABBY
29/10	REDCAR	MORNING STAR
31/10	NOTTINGHAM	RESTLESS SPIRIT
04/11	SOUTHWELL (A.W)	STAKIS CASINOS LAD
04/11	SOUTHWELL (A.W)	MISS OFFSET
09/11	DONCASTER	POLAR FLIGHT
11/11	WOLVERHAMPTON (A.W)	MIGHTY KEEN
15/11	LINGFIELD (A.W)	DOUBLE ESPRESSO
18/11	SOUTHWELL (A.W)	EROSION
19/11	LINGFIELD (A.W)	TISSUE OF LIES
22/11	SOUTHWELL (A.W)	COMPACT DISC
22/11	SOUTHWELL (A.W)	SHONTAINE
30/11	WOLVERHAMPTON (A.W)	PREMIER
07/12	WOLVERHAMPTON (A.W)	LIGHTNING BOLT
11/12	LINGFIELD (A.W)	CEE-N-K

1997

04/01	WOLVERHAMPTON (A.W)	GLOBETROTTER
06/01	SOUTHWELL (A.W)	ASPECTO LAD
14/01	LINGFIELD (A.W)	GLOBETROTTER
18/01	LINGFIELD (A.W)	GLOBETROTTER
21/01	LINGFIELD (A.W)	AS-IS
24/01	SOUTHWELL (A.W)	GLOBETROTTER
27/01	SOUTHWELL (A.W)	THREE ARCH BRIDGE
27/01	SOUTHWELL (A.W)	MIRROR FOUR SPORT
28/01	LINGFIELD (A.W)	LAWN LOTHARIO

03/02	SOUTHWELL (A.W)	LIVE PROJECT
08/02	LINGFIELD (A.W)	BELLE BIJOU
10/02	SOUTHWELL (A.W)	THREE ARCH BRIDGE
11/02	LINGFIELD (A.W)	AS-IS
13/02	LINGFIELD (A.W)	RAMIKE
15/02	LINGFIELD (A.W)	LAWN LOTHARIO
17/02	SOUTHWELL (A.W)	TOUCH'N'GO
24/02	SOUTHWELL (A.W)	LAWN LOTHARIO
24/02	SOUTHWELL (A.W)	LOVE ME DO
27/02	LINGFIELD (A.W)	AS-IS
01/03	WOLVERHAMPTON (A.W)	LAWN LOTHARIO
01/03	LINGFIELD (A.W)	TOUCH'N'GO
04/03	LINGFIELD (A.W)	LIVE PROJECT
05/03	WOLVERHAMPTON (A.W)	GLOBETROTTER
13/03	LINGFIELD (A.W)	SHONTAINE
14/03	SOUTHWELL (A.W)	MIRROR FOUR SPORT
20/03	DONCASTER	FLY TO THE STARS
31/03	NEWCASTLE	THREE ARCH BRIDGE
31/03	NOTTINGHAM	RAMIKE
12/04	WOLVERHAMPTON (A.W)	MIRROR FOUR SPORT
14/04	MUSSELBURGH	AS-IS
17/04	RIPON	OCCHI VERDI
25/04	SANDOWN	ETTERBY PARK
04/05	COLOGNE	POLAR FLIGHT
04/05	WOLVERHAMPTON (A.W)	ONE SINGER
05/05	NEWCASTLE	CAN CAN LADY
05/05	DONCASTER	RAMIKE
05/05	NEWCASTLE	STAKIS CASINOS BOY
11/05	BEVERLEY	THREE ARCH BRIDGE
12/05	REDCAR	ONE SINGER
17/05	HAMILTON	ONE FOR BAILEYS
18/05	RIPON	ALCONLEIGH
26/05	SANDOWN	PLAN FOR PROFIT
28/05	RIPON	THREE ARCH BRIDGE
28/05	RIPON	PRINCELY HEIR
29/05	CARLISLE	SHONTAINE
30/05	WOLVERHAMPTON (A.W)	OH NEVER AGAIN
30/05	WOLVERHAMPTON (A.W)	GLOBETROTTER
01/06	SAN SIRO	GOTHENBERG
02/06	HAMILTON	PEKAY
03/06	PONTEFRACT	LAND OF DREAMS
04/06	NEWCASTLE	ATLANTIC VIKING
13/06	SOUTHWELL (A.W)	CANADIAN FANTASY
14/06	LEICESTER	PERICLES
17/06	ASCOT	FLY TO THE STARS
20/06	AYR	CAN CAN LADY
20/06	AYR	AIX EN PROVENCE
25/06	CARLISLE	RAINBOW RAIN
26/06	CARLISLE	JUST GRAND
27/06	NEWCASTLE	ATLANTIC DESIRE
27/06	WOLVERHAMPTON (A.W)	PERICLES
30/06	SOUTHWELL (A.W)	MIRROR FOUR SPORT
01/07	HAMILTON	CANADIAN FANTASY
04/07	HAMILTON	INDIGO DAWN

04/07	BEVERLEY	PRINCELY HEIR
09/07	EPSOM	LEND A HAND
11/07	YORK	SHARP PLAY
12/07	WARWICK	INDIGO DAWN
13/07	HOPPEGARTEN	GOTHENBERG
15/07	BEVERLEY	CEE-N-K
16/07	CATTERICK	LEND A HAND
19/07	REDCAR	BALLY SOUZA
19/07	REDCAR	NIGHT MIRAGE
19/07	NEWMARKET (JULY)	TADEO
21/07	BEVERLEY	LEND A HAND
21/07	AYR	TILER
21/07	SOUTHWELL (A.W)	INDIGO DAWN
23/07	CATTERICK	TOP OF THE FORM
25/07	THIRSK	ALCONLEIGH
25/07	THIRSK	BALLY SOUZA
26/07	NEWCASTLE	DARWELL'S FOLLY
30/07	GOODWOOD	CLOUD INSPECTOR
31/07	GOODWOOD	FLY TO THE STARS
31/07	GOODWOOD	DOUBLE TRIGGER
02/08	LINGFIELD (A.W)	MISTER ASPECTO
02/08	HAMILTON	NIGHT MIRAGE
03/08	NEWCASTLE	FRUITS OF LOVE
04/08	RIPON	ATLANTIC DESIRE
08/08	SALISBURY	ATLANTIC DESIRE
09/08	LINGFIELD (A.W)	MISTER ASPECTO
10/08	LEOPARDSTOWN	PRINCELY HEIR
10/08	REDCAR	STAR RAGE
11/08	THIRSK	GAELIC STORM
11/08	THIRSK	SHONTAINE
14/08	BEVERLEY	FIZZED
16/08	RIPON	TADEO
16/08	RIPON	AIX EN PROVENCE
17/08	DIELSDORF	CELESTIAL KEY
18/08	HAMILTON	CHASKA
19/08	YORK	DOUBLE ECLIPSE
23/08	REDCAR	LOVE ME DO
23/08	BEVERLEY	ALBERICH
24/08	DIELSDORF	CLOUD INSPECTOR
25/08	RIPON	TYCOONESS
25/08	EPSOM	GAELIC STORM
29/08	CHESTER	VICKI ROMARA
01/09	HAMILTON	DOUBLE ALLEGED
11/09	DONCASTER	LEND A HAND
15/09	MUSSELBURGH	TAKE A RISK
16/09	DONCASTER	LAND OF DREAMS
20/09	AYR	EQUITY PRINCESS
25/09	PONTEFRACT	NASKHI
26/09	REDCAR	SINON
27/09	CATTERICK	GAELIC STORM
28/09	NOTTINGHAM	TADEO
28/09	DIELSDORF	CELESTIAL KEY
29/09	HAMILTON	SHONTAINE
29/09	BATH	ST HELENSFIELD
04/10	WOLVERHAMPTON (A.W)	PERICLES
13/10	AYR	PEKAY
19/10	SAN SIRO	LEND A HAND
20/10	PONTEFRACT	SHARP CRACKER
22/10	NEWCASTLE	LOVE ACADEMY
01/11	WOLVERHAMPTON (A.W)	DON SEBASTIAN
01/11	NEWMARKET	TRIGGER HAPPY
04/11	REDCAR	GYPSY PASSION
08/11	NEWCASTLE	STAR RAGE
10/11	LINGFIELD (A.W)	PLAN FOR PROFIT
10/11	LINGFIELD (A.W)	INDIGO DAWN
24/11	SOUTHWELL (A.W)	DOUBLE EDGED
25/11	LINGFIELD (A.W)	UNCONDITIONAL LOVE
29/11	NEWCASTLE	STAR RAGE
10/12	LINGFIELD (A.W)	INDIGO DAWN
10/12	LINGFIELD (A.W)	MAREEBA

1998

02/01	SOUTHWELL (A.W)	PLAN FOR PROFIT
09/01	SOUTHWELL (A.W)	SPIRIT OF LOVE
16/01	SOUTHWELL (A.W)	MISTER ASPECTO
19/01	SOUTHWELL (A.W)	SHONTAINE
24/01	WOLVERHAMPTON (A.W)	MISTER ASPECTO
04/02	WOLVERHAMPTON (A.W)	DARWELL'S FOLLY
07/02	LINGFIELD (A.W)	NETTA RUFINA
09/02	SOUTHWELL (A.W)	SHONTAINE
16/02	SOUTHWELL (A.W)	MADMAN'S MIRAGE
18/02	WOLVERHAMPTON (A.W)	MISTER ASPECTO
25/02	WOLVERHAMPTON (A.W)	NUIT D'OR
03/03	LINGFIELD (A.W)	SOME MIGHT SAY
21/03	WOLVERHAMPTON (A.W)	DARWELL'S FOLLY
31/03	NEWCASTLE	WHITE HEART
04/04	HAMILTON	TOUCHEZ DU BOIS
07/04	NOTTINGHAM	STINGRAY
08/04	RIPON	SHARP PLAY
23/04	BEVERLEY	FIZZED
25/04	WOLVERHAMPTON (A.W)	STAR RAGE
03/05	DIELSDORF	SHARP PLAY
04/05	DONCASTER	SPIRIT OF LOVE
12/05	YORK	SINON
14/05	YORK	ATLANTIC DESTINY
16/05	THIRSK	SHARP PLAY
16/05	THIRSK	RAFTING
22/05	PONTEFRACT	FUTURE PROSPECT
23/05	HAYDOCK	TADEO
25/05	SANDOWN	ASSET MANAGER
26/05	REDCAR	ROBIN LANE
29/05	AYR	YAVANA'S PACE
06/06	HAYDOCK	SHINING DESERT
10/06	HAMILTON	EQUITY PRINCESS
10/06	HAMILTON	SOCIETY SNOOP
12/06	YORK	GAELIC STORM
20/06	ASCOT	FIZZED
23/06	BEVERLEY	THREE GREEN LEAVES

26/06	NEWCASTLE	ASSET MANAGER
27/06	NEWCASTLE	NASKHI
27/06	NEWCASTLE	GAELIC STORM
30/06	HAMILTON	ROBIN LANE
30/06	HAMILTON	TAMPA LADY
01/07	REDCAR	KAMEEZ
02/07	CATTERICK	YOUNICO
03/07	SANDOWN	YAVANA'S PACE
04/07	NOTTINGHAM	ARABIAN DESERT
04/07	CARLISLE	OUR PEOPLE
07/07	NEWMARKET (JULY)	FRUITS OF LOVE
08/07	NEWMARKET (JULY)	TAMPA LADY
10/07	CHEPSTOW	WHITE HEART
10/07	HAMILTON	ROBIN LANE
11/07	LINGFIELD	FIZZED
16/07	DONCASTER	NASKHI
20/07	BEVERLEY	THREE GREEN LEAVES
20/07	BEVERLEY	NASKHI
22/07	CATTERICK	LAABED
24/07	WOLVERHAMPTON (A.W)	FUTURE PROSPECT
28/07	GOODWOOD	LAND OF DREAMS
30/07	GOODWOOD	DOUBLE TRIGGER
31/07	GOODWOOD	GYPSY PASSION
03/08	RIPON	NETTA RUFINA
08/08	ASCOT	SPIRIT OF LOVE
12/08	BEVERLEY	ZEITZ
12/08	BEVERLEY	PENNY MOOR
13/08	BEVERLEY	TOUS LES JOURS
22/08	FAIRYHOUSE	TADEO
22/08	CHESTER	TILER
23/08	DIELSDORF	CELESTIAL KEY
27/08	MUSSELBURGH	ICE
29/08	REDCAR	OUR PEOPLE
31/08	EPSOM	TISSIFER
02/09	YORK	PLAN FOR PROFIT
03/09	YORK	ICE
03/09	YORK	ALBERICH
07/09	HAMILTON	STOLEN TEAR
08/09	GALWAY	YAVANA'S PACE
08/09	NEWCASTLE	THREE GREEN LEAVES
09/09	DONCASTER	SPIRIT OF LOVE
09/09	KEMPTON	ATLANTIC DESTINY
09/09	KEMPTON	TISSIFER
10/09	DONCASTER	DOUBLE TRIGGER
10/09	CHEPSTOW	DOUBLE EDGED
17/09	YARMOUTH	ETTERBY PARK
19/09	WOLVERHAMPTON (A.W)	INVESTMENT HERO
26/09	ASCOT	WHITE HEART
27/09	MUSSELBURGH	ACICULA
08/10	YORK	ICE
08/10	YORK	GAELIC STORM
09/10	ASCOT	ROBIN LANE
10/10	CORK	THREE GREEN LEAVES
12/10	AYR	AMARICE

15/10	NEWMARKET	ACICULA
17/10	NEWMARKET	SPIRIT OF LOVE
19/10	PONTEFRACT	THREE GREEN LEAVES
19/10	SOUTHWELL (A.W)	LOVE ACADEMY
20/10	FOLKESTONE	SPITZBERGEN
22/10	BRIGHTON	SHARP CRACKER
23/10	NEWBURY	GAELIC STORM
24/10	DONCASTER	ROBIN LANE
30/10	NEWMARKET	ETTERBY PARK
05/11	BRIGHTON	SPITZBERGEN
07/11	DONCASTER	YAVANA'S PACE
13/11	SOUTHWELL (A.W)	LOVE ACADEMY
09/12	LINGFIELD (A.W)	LOVE DIAMONDS
21/12	LINGFIELD (A.W)	LADY CAROLINE
22/12	SOUTHWELL (A.W)	LOVE ACADEMY

1999

01/01	LINGFIELD (A.W)	JOHN BOWDLER MUSIC
01/01	LINGFIELD (A.W)	THEKRYAATI
12/01	LINGFIELD (A.W)	LOVE DIAMONDS
23/01	WOLVERHAMPTON (A.W)	THEKRYAATI
23/01	WOLVERHAMPTON (A.W)	LOVE BLUES
23/01	LINGFIELD (A.W)	THREE BAY TREES
26/01	LINGFIELD (A.W)	HORMUZ
30/01	LINGFIELD (A.W)	LOVE BLUES
03/02	WOLVERHAMPTON (A.W)	THEKRYAATI
12/02	SOUTHWELL (A.W)	KENTUCKY BULLET
04/03	LINGFIELD (A.W)	HORMUZ
25/03	DONCASTER	WHITE HEART
27/03	DONCASTER	KENTUCKY BULLET
28/03	NAD AL SHEBA	FRUITS OF LOVE
05/04	NEWCASTLE	DOONAREE
05/04	NEWCASTLE	ROYAL REBEL
05/04	NEWCASTLE	TILER
15/04	RIPON	TONIC
15/04	RIPON	HAMMER AND SICKLE
17/04	THIRSK	TISSIFER
21/04	CATTERICK	DOONAREE
25/04	DIELSDORF	ICE
30/04	MUSSELBURGH	RAFTING
06/05	CHESTER	HARRYANA
06/05	SOUTHWELL (A.W)	JOHN BOWDLER MUSIC
08/05	BEVERLEY	STAR RAGE
13/05	YORK	ICE
18/05	GOODWOOD	GAELIC STORM
25/05	PONTEFRACT	DRAMATIC QUEST
28/05	PONTEFRACT	AROUND THE WORLD
31/05	REDCAR	HAMMER AND SICKLE
02/06	BEVERLEY	ATLANTIC PRINCE
02/06	BEVERLEY	EASTWAYS
07/06	PONTEFRACT	TURTLE
12/06	LEICESTER	YAVANA'S PACE
12/06	LINGFIELD	CAROUSING
16/06	HAMILTON	WINDY GULCH

Date	Course	Horse
17/06	RIPON	HORMUZ
18/06	AYR	FORUM GIRL
18/06	ASCOT	FRUITS OF LOVE
18/06	AYR	SHONTAINE
18/06	REDCAR	FEZ
22/06	BEVERLEY	MARDANI
24/06	NEWCASTLE	ASTON MARA
26/06	DONCASTER	FEZ
28/06	MUSSELBURGH	NETTA RUFINA
01/07	CATTERICK	EVESHAM
01/07	CATTERICK	TOUS LES JOURS
03/07	BEVERLEY	HORMUZ
05/07	RIPON	BAILEYS BLACK TIE
06/07	PONTEFRACT	KASHRA
07/07	EPSOM	LINDEN GRACE
08/07	OVREVOLL	GAELIC STORM
08/07	LINGFIELD	ISLAND SONG
09/07	YORK	MARDANI
10/07	YORK	FEZ
10/07	ASCOT	DRAMATIC QUEST
16/07	HAMILTON	WINDY GULCH
16/07	CARLISLE	BAJAN BELLE
17/07	RIPON	YOUNG SUE
20/07	BATH	ISLAND SONG
21/07	THIRSK	RAFTING
24/07	REDCAR	STAR RAGE
24/07	NEWCASTLE	ST HELENSFIELD
24/07	NEWCASTLE	HIDDNAH
25/07	CHESTER	RAFTING
26/07	FOLKESTONE	ISLAND SONG
27/07	GOODWOOD	KASHRA
29/07	OVREVOLL	GAELIC STORM
29/07	GOODWOOD	THEKRYAATI
31/07	THIRSK	LADY MELBOURNE
31/07	GOODWOOD	CAROUSING
31/07	THIRSK	HAPPY DIAMOND
02/08	CARLISLE	LOVE BLUES
04/08	NEWCASTLE	WINDY GULCH
10/08	AYR	SPLASH OUT
11/08	HAMILTON	CAEROSA
11/08	BEVERLEY	STAR RAGE
12/08	BEVERLEY	LOVE LANE
13/08	WARWICK	ROBIN LANE
13/08	EPSOM	AWAKE
20/08	NEWCASTLE	PARADISE GARDEN
21/08	RIPON	BAILEYS BLACK TIE
22/08	LEOPARDSTOWN	ROYAL REBEL
24/08	HAMILTON	BREAK THE CODE
28/08	REDCAR	HARRYANA
28/08	NEWMARKET (JULY)	KASHRA
28/08	GOODWOOD	YAVANA'S PACE
30/08	EPSOM	HAPPY CHANGE
31/08	BADEN-BADEN	WHITE HEART
04/09	EPSOM	YAVANA'S PACE
06/09	HAMILTON	GOLDEN MIRACLE
07/09	LEICESTER	DARWELL'S FOLLY
11/09	GOODWOOD	STAR RAGE
13/09	MUSSELBURGH	COOL INVESTMENT
15/09	BEVERLEY	KIND REGARDS
18/09	NEWBURY	ALBERICH
26/09	MUSSELBURGH	ETTERBY PARK
27/09	HAMILTON	GOLDEN MIRACLE
29/09	NEWCASTLE	HIGH CHEVIOT
07/10	YORK	CAEROSA
13/10	WOLVERHAMPTON (A.W)	DARWELL'S FOLLY
13/10	LE CROISE-LAROCHE	HERE COMES RISKY
14/10	REDCAR	KAYO
15/10	NEWMARKET (JULY)	GAELIC STORM
16/10	NEWMARKET (JULY)	KAYO
20/10	NEWCASTLE	KAYO
23/10	NEWBURY	AWAKE
25/10	LINGFIELD (A.W)	VIRGIN SOLDIER
26/10	BATH	CAEROSA
26/10	REDCAR	FOOTPRINTS
30/10	NEWMARKET (JULY)	WINDY GULCH
03/11	MUSSELBURGH	LITTLEPACEPADDOCKS
03/11	MUSSELBURGH	VIRGIN SOLDIER
07/11	MULHEIM	SPIRIT OF LOVE
08/11	LINGFIELD (A.W)	VIRGIN SOLDIER
11/11	LINGFIELD (A.W)	ALBERICH
12/11	SOUTHWELL (A.W)	VIRGIN SOLDIER
17/11	WOLVERHAMPTON (A.W)	VIRGIN SOLDIER
22/11	SOUTHWELL (A.W)	VIRGIN SOLDIER
30/11	SAINT-CLOUD	SINON
18/12	LINGFIELD (A.W)	DOUBLE BANGER

2000

Date	Course	Horse
05/01	LINGFIELD (A.W)	SHAMSAN
08/01	LINGFIELD (A.W)	GLENWHARGEN
10/01	SOUTHWELL (A.W)	SHONTAINE
10/02	WOLVERHAMPTON (A.W)	WASEEM
15/02	WOLVERHAMPTON (A.W)	OUR PEOPLE
18/02	SOUTHWELL (A.W)	XELLANCE
25/02	SOUTHWELL (A.W)	AMBUSHED
20/03	SOUTHWELL (A.W)	ATLANTIC RHAPSODY
08/04	HAMILTON	HIDDEN BRAVE
12/04	WARWICK	FOOTPRINTS
22/04	HAYDOCK	YAVANA'S PACE
24/04	NEWCASTLE	ALMOST FREE
30/04	DIELSDORF	AKBAR
04/05	WOLVERHAMPTON (A.W)	XELLANCE
15/05	REDCAR	BAILEYS PRIZE
19/05	HAMILTON	INCA STAR
24/05	LEOPARDSTOWN	ROYAL REBEL
25/05	NEWCASTLE	VIRGIN SOLDIER
26/05	PONTEFRACT	SHARP PLAY
27/05	WARWICK	ELSIE BAMFORD
27/05	WARWICK	FLUMMOX

27/05	HAYDOCK	ATLANTIC RHAPSODY
31/05	RIPON	BOUNCING BOWDLER
02/06	AYR	CELTIC SILENCE
03/06	CATTERICK	ELSIE BAMFORD
03/06	NEWMARKET	THREE GREEN LEAVES
04/06	PONTEFRACT	CAROUSING
06/06	LINGFIELD	ICE
10/06	DONCASTER	DOWN TO THE WOODS
10/06	EPSOM	MURGHEM
11/06	RIPON	INCA STAR
12/06	WINDSOR	TONIC
12/06	PONTEFRACT	WASEEM
12/06	NOTTINGHAM	JULIUS
12/06	FRAUENFELD	CELESTIAL KEY
12/06	FRAUENFELD	AKBAR
15/06	NEWBURY	LITTLEPACEPADDOCKS
17/06	YORK	ICE
18/06	CARLISLE	SEA SQUIRT
19/08	NEWBURY	MURGHEM
20/08	DIELSDORF	AKBAR
22/08	HAMILTON	KIND REGARDS
22/08	YORK	ROYAL REBEL
23/08	YORK	BOUNCING BOWDLER
25/08	THIRSK	STAR RAGE
26/08	REDCAR	ATTACHE
26/08	WINDSOR	HAPPY CHANGE
27/08	YARMOUTH	BRANSTON FIZZ
28/08	WARWICK	XELLANCE
28/08	NEWCASTLE	LOTS OF LOVE
28/08	EPSOM	RIBERAC
28/08	NEWCASTLE	KIND REGARDS
03/09	LUCERNE	COOL INVESTMENT
04/09	HAMILTON	BRANSTON PICKLE
04/09	HAMILTON	DOUBLE HONOUR
05/09	LINGFIELD (A.W)	EXCLUSION ZONE
06/09	EPSOM	RIBERAC
09/09	DONCASTER	DOWN TO THE WOODS
13/09	SANDOWN	ATTACHE
13/09	BEVERLEY	LOVE EVERLASTING
15/09	AYR	CAROUSING
16/09	NEWBURY	BOUNCING BOWDLER
23/09	ASCOT	RIBERAC
23/09	HAYDOCK	TURKU
24/09	ASCOT	KIND REGARDS
24/09	DIELSDORF	AKBAR
26/09	NEWMARKET	JULIUS
30/09	REDCAR	GAELIC STORM
10/10	AYR	TAKAMAKA BAY
19/10	NEWCASTLE	TOMASINO
20/10	WOLVERHAMPTON (A.W)	LUNA FLIGHT
20/10	NEWBURY	GAELIC STORM
20/10	WOLVERHAMPTON (A.W)	FORUM FINALE
26/10	MUSSELBURGH	AURA OF GRACE
28/10	LEOPARDSTOWN	GAELIC STORM

01/11	MUSSELBURGH	CELTIC MISSION
01/11	MUSSELBURGH	ALBUHERA
09/11	LINGFIELD (A.W)	EXCLUSION ZONE
25/11	WOLVERHAMPTON (A.W)	SPIRIT OF LOVE

2001

08/01	SOUTHWELL (A.W)	ROBANDELA
30/01	WOLVERHAMPTON (A.W)	ROBANDELA
07/04	MUSSELBURGH	AND BEYOND
07/04	MUSSELBURGH	ROBANDELA
10/04	PONTEFRACT	SHAYADI
12/04	MUSSELBURGH	GOLDEN WELLS
17/04	NEWMARKET	PROCEED WITH CARE
19/04	RIPON	TOMASINO
21/04	NEWBURY	GOLDEN WELLS
23/04	WINDSOR	CELTIC MISSION
24/04	MUSSELBURGH	SOPHIELU
25/04	EPSOM	ROMAN KING
27/04	SOUTHWELL (A.W)	KAURI
05/05	NEWMARKET	ZINDABAD
06/05	NEWMARKET	ROBANDELA
12/05	HAMILTON	DESERT DEER
15/05	YORK	AND BEYOND
15/05	YORK	SARATOV
21/05	MUSSELBURGH	STANZA
22/05	BEVERLEY	RIBERAC
24/05	GOODWOOD	AKBAR
25/05	PONTEFRACT	DESERT DEER
26/05	DONCASTER	ATTACHE
26/05	KEMPTON	VIRGIN SOLDIER
30/05	NEWBURY	DRAMATIC QUEST
31/05	AYR	ALBUHERA
31/05	GOODWOOD	DOUBLE HONOUR
01/06	NOTTINGHAM	FRAGRANT STORM
07/06	HAYDOCK	TAKAMAKA BAY
09/06	HAYDOCK	DOUBLE HONOUR
13/06	HAMILTON	MISTER COSMI
17/06	LEICESTER	TAKAMAKA BAY
17/06	LEICESTER	ZINDABAD
19/06	ASCOT	AND BEYOND
19/06	ASCOT	TAKAMAKA BAY
21/06	RIPON	TURKU
21/06	ASCOT	ROYAL REBEL
23/06	REDCAR	EUROLINK ARTEMIS
23/06	AYR	LEO'S LUCKYMAN
27/06	THIRSK	SCOTTISH RIVER
02/07	PONTEFRACT	FALCON HILL
05/07	NEWBURY	KAYO
05/07	HAYDOCK	FORUM FINALE
05/07	SOUTHWELL	STAR RAGE
06/07	NEWCASTLE	EUROLINK ARTEMIS
08/07	SANDOWN	DESERT DEER
13/07	YORK	ICE
13/07	YORK	LOVE EVERLASTING

14/07	ASCOT	FALCON HILL
14/07	YORK	AKBAR
15/07	HAYDOCK	CELTIC MISSION
18/07	LINGFIELD	LOTS OF LOVE
23/07	WINDSOR	BAJAN BLUE
23/07	AYR	PARADISE GARDEN
24/07	AYR	RACING BAILEY'S
25/07	LEICESTER	SIR GEORGE TURNER
27/07	THIRSK	RYDERS STORM
28/07	ASCOT	FAR PAVILIONS
29/07	NEWMARKET (JULY)	ALBUHERA
30/07	YARMOUTH	TIGNE
31/07	GOODWOOD	MISTER COSMI
02/08	GOODWOOD	RIBERAC
03/08	AYR	SAPHIR INDIEN
05/08	NEWBURY	LOVE EVERLASTING
07/08	CATTERICK	PENNY PICTURES
08/08	NEWCASTLE	DANTON
08/08	NEWCASTLE	FIGHT YOUR CORNER
12/08	ASCOT	RIBERAC
12/08	REDCAR	EUROLINK ROOSTER
15/08	BEVERLEY	BANDARI
18/08	HAYDOCK	YAVANA'S PACE
21/08	HAMILTON	RACING BAILEY'S
24/08	NEWCASTLE	ELA D'ARGENT
25/08	NEWMARKET (JULY)	FALCON HILL
27/08	NEWCASTLE	FASHIONABLE MAN
28/08	RIPON	KAYO
31/08	EPSOM	BOUNCING BOWDLER
07/09	HAYDOCK	LOTS OF LOVE
08/09	THIRSK	RISKER
09/09	LONGCHAMP	YAVANA'S PACE
10/09	NEWCASTLE	LOVE REGARDLESS
11/09	LEICESTER	ROBANDELA
12/09	GOODWOOD	RAJAB
14/09	DONCASTER	DARASIM
15/09	EPSOM	STUNNING FORCE
17/09	LE CROISE-LAROCHE	HERE COMES RISKY
19/09	GOODWOOD	SIMEON
20/09	AYR	LEGAL APPROACH
21/09	NEWBURY	FIGHT YOUR CORNER
21/09	NOTTINGHAM	AFFRAY
22/09	NEWBURY	ALBUHERA
22/09	AYR	BANDARI
26/09	GOODWOOD	ROBANDELA
28/09	HAYDOCK	CELTIC MISSION
29/09	HAYDOCK	LOTS OF LOVE
30/09	MUSSELBURGH	DOUBLE GAMBLE
30/09	ASCOT	LEGAL APPROACH
02/10	NEWMARKET	SIR GEORGE TURNER
04/10	NEWMARKET	TISSIFER
11/10	YORK	KAYO
13/10	ASCOT	GOLDEN WELLS
13/10	ASCOT	FIGHT YOUR CORNER
16/10	AYR	LORD PIERCE
20/10	CATTERICK	BAILEYS PRIZE
21/10	NAAS	CELTIC MISSION
21/10	LONGCHAMP	YAVANA'S PACE
22/10	PONTEFRACT	BANDARI
23/10	WOLVERHAMPTON (A.W)	ASHKALANI STAR
27/10	DONCASTER	FALCON HILL
03/11	NEWMARKET	RIBERAC
06/11	DONCASTER	SIMEON
07/11	MUSSELBURGH	CELTIC STYLE
07/11	MUSSELBURGH	XELLANCE
08/11	WINDSOR	ROBANDELA
09/11	DONCASTER	DOUBLE HONOUR
19/11	SOUTHWELL (A.W)	CHEENEY BASIN
10/12	SOUTHWELL (A.W)	OLIVIA ROSE
11/12	WOLVERHAMPTON (A.W)	UNDER CONSTRUCTION
26/12	WOLVERHAMPTON (A.W)	ALBERICH

2002

03/01	LINGFIELD (A.W)	ATLANTIC QUEST
11/01	WOLVERHAMPTON (A.W)	THUNDER CANYON
29/01	SOUTHWELL (A.W)	CHEENEY BASIN
31/01	SOUTHWELL (A.W)	MAZURY
05/02	SOUTHWELL (A.W)	TAKES TUTU
16/02	LINGFIELD (A.W)	TAKES TUTU
18/02	WOLVERHAMPTON (A.W)	BENNY THE VICE
09/03	WOLVERHAMPTON (A.W)	TWO MARKS
15/03	WOLVERHAMPTON (A.W)	BEACON WOOD
21/03	DONCASTER	SYSTEMATIC
23/03	DONCASTER	FALCON HILL
23/03	DONCASTER	DOUBLE HONOUR
25/03	WOLVERHAMPTON (A.W)	HEARTHSTEAD PRIDE
25/03	WOLVERHAMPTON (A.W)	DOWN TO THE WOODS
27/03	LINGFIELD (A.W)	FORTUNATE DAVE
03/04	RIPON	SHANOOK
03/04	RIPON	SIMEON
04/04	LEICESTER	SYSTEMATIC
13/04	HAYDOCK	SIMEON
20/04	NEWBURY	ZINDABAD
24/04	CATTERICK	FASHIONABLE MAN
26/04	WOLVERHAMPTON (A.W)	COLLARD
26/04	SANDOWN	SIMEON
27/04	RIPON	DARASIM
01/05	PONTEFRACT	HEARTHSTEAD PRIDE
02/05	REDCAR	OUTEAST
03/05	NEWMARKET	TAKES TUTU
04/05	NEWMARKET	DESERT DEER
04/05	THIRSK	KETAN
05/05	NEWMARKET	ATLANTIC QUEST
07/05	CHESTER	FIGHT YOUR CORNER
11/05	THIRSK	OUNDLE SCOUNDREL
11/05	LINGFIELD	BANDARI
13/05	REDCAR	KETAN
14/05	YORK	SYSTEMATIC

Date	Course	Horse
15/05	YORK	ROYAL BEACON
16/05	YORK	ZINDABAD
18/05	HAMILTON	BEAMISH PRINCE
21/05	GOODWOOD	REVOLVING
25/05	NEWMARKET	MASTERPOINT
27/05	CARLISLE	EXCLUSION ZONE
29/05	RIPON	THE BONUS KING
30/05	AYR	HELM BANK
03/06	SANDOWN	AKBAR
04/06	REDCAR	DECOY
04/06	LEICESTER	OLIVIA ROSE
08/06	DONCASTER	DANCINGINTHESTREET
08/06	EPSOM	THE BONUS KING
08/06	DONCASTER	LEO'S LUCKYMAN
15/06	BATH	AFFRAY
18/06	THIRSK	PURRING
19/06	ASCOT	HELM BANK
20/06	ASCOT	SYSTEMATIC
20/06	ASCOT	ROYAL REBEL
21/06	AYR	ELA D'ARGENT
22/06	WARWICK	RAISED THE BAR
22/06	ASCOT	ZINDABAD
22/06	REDCAR	KATINA
24/06	WINDSOR	SCOTT'S VIEW
24/06	MUSSELBURGH	KNAVESMIRE OMEN
26/06	WARWICK	DECOY
26/06	WARWICK	DANCINGINTHESTREET
28/06	CHANTILLY	AND BEYOND
02/07	HAMBURG	DOUBLE HONOUR
02/07	YARMOUTH	GATEMAN
03/07	CATTERICK	SCOTT'S VIEW
05/07	HAYDOCK	BOUNCING BOWDLER
05/07	BEVERLEY	SCOTT'S VIEW
08/07	MUSSELBURGH	SHARP SECRET
11/07	DONCASTER	WILFUL
12/07	CHESTER	SCOTT'S VIEW
12/07	BEVERLEY	ALMOST TWILIGHT
12/07	BEVERLEY	ILOVETURTLE
12/07	YORK	BOURBONNAIS
13/07	ASCOT	MANA D'ARGENT
14/07	CURRAGH	GATEMAN
15/07	AYR	WESTERN DIPLOMAT
17/07	CATTERICK	TWO MARKS
19/07	CARLISLE	BORU BORU
20/07	HAYDOCK	LEGAL APPROACH
20/07	WARWICK	KNAVESMIRE OMEN
22/07	AYR	DOUBLE OBSESSION
23/07	AYR	PIE HIGH
23/07	AYR	NUIT SOMBRE
26/07	THIRSK	SHARP SECRET
26/07	ASCOT	GARROS
29/07	YARMOUTH	SHARP SECRET
30/07	GOODWOOD	SCOTT'S VIEW
30/07	GOODWOOD	BANDARI
01/08	GOODWOOD	TAKES TUTU
02/08	GOODWOOD	DARASIM
03/08	NEWMARKET (JULY)	KNAVESMIRE OMEN
03/08	GOODWOOD	SCOTT'S VIEW
03/08	NEWMARKET (JULY)	PIE HIGH
03/08	DONCASTER	KENTUCKY KING
04/08	COLOGNE	LOVE REGARDLESS
04/08	NEWBURY	LOVE EVERLASTING
07/08	PONTEFRACT	KNAVESMIRE OMEN
07/08	NEWCASTLE	NUIT SOMBRE
10/08	ASCOT	MANA D'ARGENT
10/08	ASCOT	BOUNCING BOWDLER
11/08	COLOGNE	YAVANA'S PACE
16/08	NEWBURY	SYSTEMATIC
20/08	YORK	BANDARI
20/08	YORK	BOURBONNAIS
23/08	NEWMARKET (JULY)	RHEINPARK
25/08	BADEN-BADEN	MISTER COSMI
28/08	CATTERICK	MISS HOLLY
02/09	HAMILTON	LOVE YOU ALWAYS
04/09	YORK	SCOTT'S VIEW
05/09	REDCAR	THUNDER CANYON
07/09	HAYDOCK	TAKES TUTU
13/09	DONCASTER	SYSTEMATIC
14/09	GOODWOOD	ITEMISE
19/09	YARMOUTH	KNAVESMIRE OMEN
21/09	NEWBURY	DESERT DEER
21/09	NEWBURY	LEGAL APPROACH
27/09	REDCAR	AMUNDSEN
27/09	HAYDOCK	MURGHEM
27/09	ASCOT	LOVE EVERLASTING
28/09	ASCOT	MANA D'ARGENT
29/09	ASCOT	SCOTT'S VIEW
29/09	ASCOT	SYSTEMATIC
30/09	HAMILTON	FRESH AS A ROSE
30/09	HAMILTON	ROBANDELA
30/09	HAMILTON	NIGHT MIST
03/10	NEWMARKET	KNAVESMIRE OMEN
03/10	NEWMARKET	DESERT DEER
06/10	DUSSELDORF	LOVE REGARDLESS
07/10	PONTEFRACT	SHANTY STAR
12/10	ASCOT	ROBANDELA
12/10	ASCOT	LOVE EVERLASTING
21/10	WOLVERHAMPTON (A.W)	THUNDER CANYON
22/10	SOUTHWELL (A.W)	NIGHT SHIFT BLUE'S
25/10	DONCASTER	KNAVESMIRE OMEN
09/11	DONCASTER	KNAVESMIRE OMEN
09/11	DONCASTER	MARINAS CHARM
09/11	DONCASTER	LOTS OF LOVE
25/11	SOUTHWELL (A.W)	RANSOM O'WAR
14/12	WOLVERHAMPTON (A.W)	BIG LUCIANO
20/12	WOLVERHAMPTON (A.W)	GRETA D'ARGENT

2003

Date	Course	Horse
04/01	SOUTHWELL (A.W)	MISS HOLLY
04/01	SOUTHWELL (A.W)	HERNE BAY
20/01	WOLVERHAMPTON (A.W)	COOLBYTHEPOOL
01/02	WOLVERHAMPTON (A.W)	COOLBYTHEPOOL
07/02	JEBEL ALI	TAKES TUTU
07/02	WOLVERHAMPTON (A.W)	EASTERN DAGGER
17/02	WOLVERHAMPTON (A.W)	DUBAI TOWER
26/03	CATTERICK	SHANOOK
10/04	MUSSELBURGH	JEBAL SURAAJ
16/04	BEVERLEY	HANS CHRISTIAN
23/04	EPSOM	THEORIST
23/04	CATTERICK	SHANTY STAR
23/04	CATTERICK	STUNNING FORCE
26/04	LEICESTER	DELSARTE
26/04	SANDOWN	DESERT DEER
28/04	HAMILTON	FANTASTIC LOVE
29/04	NOTTINGHAM	ATTRACTION
30/04	PONTEFRACT	MORSON BOY
30/04	PONTEFRACT	GRETA D'ARGENT
30/04	PONTEFRACT	RUSSIAN VALOUR
02/05	NEWMARKET	DELSARTE
03/05	BRIGHTON	STUNNING FORCE
05/05	DONCASTER	MORSON BOY
09/05	HAMILTON	PARKVIEW LOVE
09/05	NOTTINGHAM	THE PERSUADER
12/05	REDCAR	DUBAI TOWER
15/05	YORK	THE PERSUADER
17/05	THIRSK	ATTRACTION
19/05	BATH	JACK DURRANCE
20/05	BEVERLEY	THE PERSUADER
23/05	HAYDOCK	CAKE IT EASY
23/05	HAYDOCK	FISIO THERAPY
23/05	HAYDOCK	GREAT SCOTT
24/05	NEWMARKET	PANTONE
24/05	DONCASTER	PEARL OF LOVE
26/05	CHEPSTOW	RAPHOOLA
27/05	SANDOWN	RUSSIAN VALOUR
27/05	SANDOWN	JEBAL SURAAJ
27/05	LEICESTER	EASTERN DAGGER
28/05	RIPON	WATERSTONE
28/05	LINGFIELD (A.W)	RAPHOOLA
30/05	AYR	INVESTMENT AFFAIR
30/05	CATTERICK	RAHAF
30/05	AYR	THINK TANK
31/05	MUSSELBURGH	ATLANTIC QUEST
02/06	CARLISLE	KAHYASI PRINCESS
02/06	LEICESTER	LEICESTER SQUARE
04/06	BEVERLEY	PENNY CROSS
04/06	BEVERLEY	GREAT SCOTT
04/06	BEVERLEY	ATTRACTION
04/06	BEVERLEY	COOLBYTHEPOOL
06/06	HAYDOCK	FINANCIAL FUTURE
07/06	EPSOM	GATEMAN
07/06	EPSOM	PARKVIEW LOVE
10/06	REDCAR	STAGECOACH RUBY
11/06	HAMILTON	VENETIAN PRIDE
13/06	SANDOWN	PANTONE
14/06	YORK	WESSEX
15/06	CARLISLE	PENNY CROSS
15/06	FRAUENFELD	FINANCIAL FUTURE
15/06	CARLISLE	CHANTRESS
18/06	ASCOT	PEARL OF LOVE
18/06	ASCOT	ATTRACTION
19/06	RIPON	COOLBYTHEPOOL
19/06	ASCOT	FANTASTIC LOVE
19/06	RIPON	NUIT SOMBRE
19/06	ASCOT	RUSSIAN VALOUR
20/06	ASCOT	SHANTY STAR
20/06	AYR	LUCKY STORY
21/06	AYR	ATLANTIC QUEST
21/06	AYR	CHESTER LE STREET
23/06	MUSSELBURGH	INVESTMENT AFFAIR
24/06	BRIGHTON	STAGECOACH RUBY
29/06	DONCASTER	LEO'S LUCKYMAN
30/06	PONTEFRACT	LUCKY STORY
01/07	HAMBURG	KNAVESMIRE OMEN
01/07	HAMILTON	ANNABEL LEE
02/07	CATTERICK	WHISPERED PROMISES
04/07	BEVERLEY	MY DAISYCHAIN
04/07	SANDOWN	MISTER MONET
04/07	SANDOWN	NUIT SOMBRE
05/07	BEVERLEY	KAHYASI PRINCESS
07/07	RIPON	BLACKWATER FEVER
08/07	NEWMARKET (JULY)	ATTRACTION
11/07	HAMILTON	COOLBYTHEPOOL
11/07	ASCOT	DOUBLE OBSESSION
11/07	YORK	MORSON BOY
12/07	ASCOT	MANA D'ARGENT
16/07	CATTERICK	THINK TANK
18/07	PONTEFRACT	INVESTMENT FORCE
18/07	HAMILTON	COOLBYTHEPOOL
19/07	HAYDOCK	KAHYASI PRINCESS
21/07	AYR	CARTE SAUVAGE
22/07	AYR	SHAYADI
22/07	AYR	MUNAAWASHAT
23/07	LEICESTER	TEDESKA
23/07	LEICESTER	PANTONE
24/07	DONCASTER	GRETA D'ARGENT
25/07	THIRSK	SUZUKA
25/07	ASCOT	KAHYASI PRINCESS
26/07	ASCOT	DOUBLE OBSESSION
29/07	GOODWOOD	DARASIM
30/07	GOODWOOD	LUCKY STORY
30/07	GOODWOOD	KNAVESMIRE OMEN
01/08	AYR	BESSEMER
13/08	HAMILTON	SPECTROMETER

Date	Course	Horse
13/08	HAMILTON	BAILEYS DANCER
13/08	HAMILTON	MARINAS CHARM
13/08	BEVERLEY	CARACARA
14/08	BEVERLEY	WHISPERED PROMISES
14/08	BEVERLEY	HERNE BAY
15/08	CATTERICK	VICTORY VENTURE
16/08	NEWMARKET (JULY)	ROYAL BEACON
18/08	WINDSOR	MARINAS CHARM
19/08	HAMILTON	MY DAISYCHAIN
23/08	CURRAGH	PEARL OF LOVE
23/08	BEVERLEY	PENNY CROSS
24/08	DEAUVILLE	DARASIM
24/08	BEVERLEY	MASTERPOINT
25/08	EPSOM	FORT
29/08	CHESTER	CHANTRESS
01/09	HAMILTON	WOODY VALENTINE
06/09	HAYDOCK	GATEMAN
06/09	THIRSK	MBOSI
06/09	HAYDOCK	THE PERSUADER
06/09	HAYDOCK	BAILEYS DANCER
09/09	LEICESTER	GOLD HISTORY
10/09	DONCASTER	MARINAS CHARM
12/09	DONCASTER	LUCKY STORY
13/09	DONCASTER	GRETA D'ARGENT
14/09	LONGCHAMP	DARASIM
15/09	REDCAR	YOSHKA
17/09	SANDOWN	DUKE OF VENICE
19/09	AYR	GOLD HISTORY
19/09	AYR	TAFAAHUM
20/09	CATTERICK	BLOEMFONTAIN
10/10	YORK	NERO'S RETURN
14/10	LEICESTER	PENRITH
14/10	AYR	MEKURIA
18/10	CATTERICK	CHASE THE RAINBOW
19/10	SAN SIRO	PEARL OF LOVE
20/10	PONTEFRACT	DENISE BEST
25/10	DONCASTER	NERO'S RETURN
28/10	NOTTINGHAM	ASIATIC
03/11	REDCAR	GO PADERO
08/11	DONCASTER	SCOTT'S VIEW

2004

Date	Course	Horse
19/02	WOLVERHAMPTON (A.W)	ALWAYS FLYING
21/02	NAD AL SHEBA	SCOTT'S VIEW
23/02	WOLVERHAMPTON (A.W)	JOMACOMI
05/03	WOLVERHAMPTON (A.W)	GOLDEN QUEST
11/03	NAD AL SHEBA	SCOTT'S VIEW
24/03	LINGFIELD (A.W)	GOLDEN QUEST
26/03	DONCASTER	KING OF DREAMS
29/03	NEWCASTLE	ETMAAM
06/04	PONTEFRACT	AKASH
06/04	PONTEFRACT	WINGED D'ARGENT
08/04	MUSSELBURGH	MASTER MARVEL
11/04	MUSSELBURGH	GRAN DANA

Date	Course	Horse
11/04	MUSSELBURGH	JOSEPH HENRY
12/04	KEMPTON	SCOTT'S VIEW
14/04	NEWMARKET	GATEMAN
15/04	NEWMARKET	GOLD HISTORY
28/04	PONTEFRACT	WOODY VALENTINE
30/04	MUSSELBURGH	LOVE IN SEATTLE
30/04	NOTTINGHAM	JOSEPH HENRY
01/05	NEWMARKET	BANDARI
02/05	NEWMARKET	MASTER MARVEL
02/05	NEWMARKET	ATTRACTION
04/05	MUSSELBURGH	MAN OF LETTERS
04/05	WARWICK	PREMIER DREAM
06/05	CHESTER	BANDARI
07/05	CHESTER	SYSTEMATIC
08/05	THIRSK	SNAP
08/05	BEVERLEY	ROYAL ISLAND
14/05	HAMILTON	NEVER WILL
14/05	NOTTINGHAM	TWOFAN
15/05	THIRSK	MYSTICAL GIRL
16/05	RIPON	HEARTHSTEAD WINGS
17/05	BATH	ETMAAM
20/05	NEWCASTLE	WHAT'S UP DOC
20/05	NEWCASTLE	ROYAL ISLAND
22/05	BADEN-BADEN	DARASIM
23/05	CURRAGH	ATTRACTION
24/05	LEICESTER	NUFOOS
24/05	CARLISLE	CARTE ROYALE
27/05	AYR	LEO'S LUCKY STAR
28/05	PONTEFRACT	PENRITH
31/05	CHEPSTOW	ALWAYS WAINING
01/06	SANDOWN	GOLDEN QUEST
01/06	SANDOWN	BANDARI
01/06	SANDOWN	MYSTICAL GIRL
12/06	YORK	ETMAAM
13/06	DONCASTER	FIEFDOM
15/06	ASCOT	DOUBLE OBSESSION
16/06	RIPON	ACT OF THE PACE
16/06	HAMILTON	MUNAAWASHAT
17/06	RIPON	YOSHKA
17/06	RIPON	SPIRIT OF FRANCE
18/06	ASCOT	ATTRACTION
18/06	REDCAR	CARTE DIAMOND
23/06	CARLISLE	KING OF LOVE
24/06	THIRSK	SNAP
26/06	WINDSOR	GATEMAN
28/06	PONTEFRACT	LEO'S LUCKY STAR
29/06	HAMILTON	DUNLEA DANCER
01/07	EPSOM	WOODY VALENTINE
02/07	SANDOWN	MELROSE AVENUE
06/07	PONTEFRACT	BENDARSHAAN
07/07	CATTERICK	YOSHKA
07/07	NEWMARKET (JULY)	BANDARI
08/07	WARWICK	I'M SO LUCKY
09/07	YORK	ELLIOTS WORLD

09/07	YORK	CARTE DIAMOND
10/07	NOTTINGHAM	GENEROUS OPTION
15/07	HAMILTON	MISTER MONET
17/07	NEWMARKET (JULY)	BENDARSHAAN
21/07	CATTERICK	JANE JUBILEE
21/07	AYR	SHAMARDAL
23/07	ASCOT	MANA D'ARGENT
24/07	ASCOT	ALWAYS WAINING
24/07	ASCOT	MISTER MONET
25/07	NEWMARKET (JULY)	KING OF DREAMS
28/07	GOODWOOD	SHAMARDAL
29/07	MUSSELBURGH	JANE JUBILEE
29/07	GOODWOOD	DARASIM
29/07	CARLISLE	TOBY'S DREAM
02/08	CARLISLE	BAILEYS DANCER
04/08	PONTEFRACT	REQQA
04/08	NEWCASTLE	SPY KING
07/08	HAYDOCK	MISTER MONET
11/08	HAMILTON	SPY KING
11/08	BEVERLEY	CAN CAN FLYER
17/08	YORK	ELLIOTS WORLD
20/08	SANDOWN	BRAHMINY KITE
21/08	DEAUVILLE	MISTER MONET
27/08	THIRSK	SECRET HISTORY
29/08	BEVERLEY	NUFOOS
30/08	CHEPSTOW	TORRENS
04/09	KEMPTON	MYSTICAL GIRL
11/09	MUSSELBURGH	JUST A FLUKE
11/09	GOODWOOD	GOLD HISTORY
11/09	GOODWOOD	HEARTHSTEAD WINGS
11/09	CARLISLE	SECRET PACT
14/09	THIRSK	HADRIAN
15/09	BEVERLEY	KING'S ACCOUNT
17/09	AYR	MARKET TREND
18/09	CATTERICK	SECRET PACT
19/09	HAMILTON	LOVE PALACE
23/09	PONTEFRACT	WISE OWL
26/09	ASCOT	FORT
29/09	NEWCASTLE	CROSSPEACE
02/10	NEWMARKET	ATTRACTION
04/10	WINDSOR	HANSEATIC LEAGUE
08/10	YORK	MAFAHEEM
12/10	AYR	WINGED D'ARGENT
12/10	AYR	KING'S ACCOUNT
15/10	NEWMARKET	ALWAYS WAINING
15/10	REDCAR	EXIT SMILING
16/10	NEWMARKET	SHAMARDAL
16/10	NEWMARKET	CONTACT DANCER
17/10	MUSSELBURGH	SWIFT SAILOR
17/10	MUSSELBURGH	GO PADERO
17/10	MUSSELBURGH	KINDLING
22/10	DONCASTER	WINGED D'ARGENT
23/10	DONCASTER	CROSSPEACE
02/11	CATTERICK	GO PADERO
02/11	CATTERICK	LADY KARR
02/11	CATTERICK	MCELDOWNEY
04/11	NOTTINGHAM	STARCHY
05/11	YARMOUTH	QUIZZENE

2005

14/01	SAKHIR	LOVE REGARDLESS
28/01	WOLVERHAMPTON (A.W)	HEYBROOK BOY
27/03	MUSSELBURGH	ALRAFIDAIN
27/03	MUSSELBURGH	SWIFT SAILOR
29/03	PONTEFRACT	NERO'S RETURN
29/03	PONTEFRACT	TAKHMIN
31/03	DONCASTER	TARRAMAN
02/04	KEMPTON	MARKET TREND
06/04	NOTTINGHAM	WINGED D'ARGENT
12/04	MUSSELBURGH	BARCARDERO
13/04	BEVERLEY	MR ROONEY
14/04	RIPON	SECRET HISTORY
18/04	PONTEFRACT	ADORATION
20/04	CATTERICK	STAGE SCHOOL
20/04	CATTERICK	MELROSE AVENUE
21/04	BEVERLEY	SECRET HISTORY
22/04	SANDOWN	QUIZZENE
23/04	HAYDOCK	BAY STORY
23/04	LEICESTER	HIDDENSEE
24/04	DIELSDORF	ROYAL ISLAND
29/04	MUSSELBURGH	GENEROUS OPTION
01/05	NEWMARKET	CROSSPEACE
02/05	DONCASTER	HIDDENSEE
03/05	CATTERICK	AUVERGNE
03/05	LEICESTER	MICHAELS PRIDE
04/05	CHESTER	QUIZZENE
11/05	YORK	SECRET HISTORY
12/05	CARLISLE	ROYAL ENGINEER
13/05	NOTTINGHAM	YOU TOO
14/05	NEWBURY	I'M SO LUCKY
15/05	RIPON	IN FULL CRY
21/05	CARLISLE	MARIAS MAGIC
21/05	CARLISLE	WINDHOVER
21/05	CARLISLE	ALWAYS BAILEYS
28/05	MUSSELBURGH	TRIVANDRUN
01/06	BEVERLEY	ADORATION
03/06	HAYDOCK	EMERALD BAY
04/06	HAYDOCK	GOLDEN QUEST
07/06	REDCAR	MICHAELS PRIDE
09/06	RIPON	BARCARDERO
12/06	DONCASTER	STAGE SCHOOL
12/06	DONCASTER	BLACK CHARMER
16/06	BEVERLEY	LOVE IN SEATTLE
16/06	BEVERLEY	REAL COOL CAT
17/06	YORK	MELROSE AVENUE
18/06	WARWICK	NUFOOS
18/06	YORK	BANDARI
20/06	NOTTINGHAM	EMERALD BAY

22/06	EPSOM	HADRIAN
22/06	CARLISLE	DESERT REALM
23/06	LEICESTER	REAL COOL CAT
23/06	SALISBURY	MICHAELS PRIDE
25/06	NEWCASTLE	CRIME SCENE
27/06	MUSSELBURGH	LUBERON
27/06	PONTEFRACT	EMERALD STORM
01/07	HAYDOCK	MARY GRAY
01/07	BEVERLEY	RICE MOTHER
01/07	SANDOWN	I'M SO LUCKY
02/07	BEVERLEY	MICHAELS PRIDE
04/07	RIPON	SOUND BREEZE
09/07	HAMILTON	ARNPRIOR
13/07	HAYDOCK	HADRIAN
14/07	HAMILTON	MCELDOWNEY
15/07	HAMILTON	SPIRIT OF FRANCE
15/07	PONTEFRACT	MAGGIES FARM
15/07	CARLISLE	MUZDAHER
18/07	BEVERLEY	BAAN
18/07	BEVERLEY	CARIBBEAN DANCER
18/07	AYR	SOUND BREEZE
18/07	AYR	NIHAL
20/07	SANDOWN	MARIAS MAGIC
20/07	LEICESTER	UNIQUE MOMENT
21/07	BATH	MICHAELS PRIDE
23/07	NEWBURY	BAY STORY
24/07	PONTEFRACT	SOUND BREEZE
25/07	YARMOUTH	CARIBBEAN DANCER
26/07	GOODWOOD	PRINCE OF LIGHT
26/07	GOODWOOD	GOLDEN QUEST
26/07	BEVERLEY	RIVER LENA
27/07	MUSSELBURGH	SUPREME CHARTER
29/07	GOODWOOD	ALWAYS BAILEYS
06/08	AYR	DIABLERETTE
06/08	HAYDOCK	ROYAL ISLAND
07/08	LEICESTER	ATLANTIC WAVES
07/08	REDCAR	SUNDAY SMILE
10/08	HAMILTON	DOCTOR SCOTT
11/08	SANDOWN	WINGED CUPID
16/08	HAMILTON	MCELDOWNEY
16/08	YORK	PRINCE OF LIGHT
16/08	HAMILTON	WEEKEND FEVER
17/08	EPSOM	MELAAYA
17/08	CARLISLE	MARY GRAY
18/08	YORK	NIHAL
22/08	HAMILTON	MCELDOWNEY
24/08	CATTERICK	LOVE PALACE
24/08	BRIGHTON	MCELDOWNEY
25/08	MUSSELBURGH	RULE FOR EVER
26/08	THIRSK	MUZDAHER
26/08	THIRSK	HEARTHSTEAD DANCER
28/08	BEVERLEY	ROAD TO LOVE
29/08	NEWCASTLE	MARIAS MAGIC
29/08	NEWCASTLE	LIGHTNING AFFAIR

03/09	NEWMARKET (JULY)	PRINCE OF LIGHT
04/09	YORK	LOVE ANGEL
05/09	NEWCASTLE	STEPPING UP
07/09	EPSOM	LINAS SELECTION
08/09	BATH	LOVE ANGEL
09/09	DONCASTER	ELLIOTS WORLD
10/09	GOODWOOD	NERO'S RETURN
10/09	MUSSELBURGH	SPIRIT OF FRANCE
10/09	LEOPARDSTOWN	ATTRACTION
10/09	DONCASTER	LEO'S LUCKYMAN
12/09	MUSSELBURGH	BENDARSHAAN
15/09	PONTEFRACT	SWIFT SAILOR
15/09	AYR	LUBERON
16/09	AYR	RULE FOR EVER
16/09	NEWBURY	WINGED CUPID
17/09	CATTERICK	DESERT D'ARGENT
18/09	HAMILTON	NAKHEEL
19/09	CARLISLE	JAAD
23/09	HAYDOCK	KINDLING
24/09	RIPON	LONDON EXPRESS
26/09	HAMILTON	HEARTHSTEAD WINGS
26/09	HAMILTON	REGAL CONNECTION
28/09	NEWCASTLE	RAZED
28/09	NEWCASTLE	DREAM MOUNTAIN
01/10	EPSOM	ADORATION
01/10	EPSOM	KINDLING
01/10	EPSOM	BAAN
01/10	REDCAR	COALPARK
08/10	YORK	AUSTRIAN
09/10	NEWCASTLE	FRUIT SALAD
10/10	WINDSOR	KILBARRI
14/10	REDCAR	FENNERS
15/10	CATTERICK	KINGS HEIR
16/10	MUSSELBURGH	THREE THIEVES
17/10	PONTEFRACT	NAKHEEL
19/10	NOTTINGHAM	SOUND BREEZE
22/10	DONCASTER	DESERT D'ARGENT
03/11	MUSSELBURGH	KINDLING
03/11	MUSSELBURGH	COTE D'ARGENT
05/11	WOLVERHAMPTON (A.W)	SPITTING IMAGE
05/11	DONCASTER	CROSSPEACE
20/12	SOUTHWELL (A.W)	SPITTING IMAGE

2006

01/01	SOUTHWELL (A.W)	SPITTING IMAGE
08/02	LINGFIELD (A.W)	SOHO SQUARE
13/02	WOLVERHAMPTON (A.W)	MAGIC MOTH
15/02	LINGFIELD (A.W)	ORVIETAN
18/02	WOLVERHAMPTON (A.W)	RANSOM STRIP
20/02	LINGFIELD (A.W)	REBELLION
27/02	WOLVERHAMPTON (A.W)	SOAPY DANGER
03/03	WOLVERHAMPTON (A.W)	CITY WELL
03/03	WOLVERHAMPTON (A.W)	MARMOTA
11/03	WOLVERHAMPTON (A.W)	LUCKY LARK

23/03	LINGFIELD (A.W)	REBELLION
04/04	PONTEFRACT	LONDON EXPRESS
12/04	CATTERICK	UNIQUE MOMENT
19/04	BEVERLEY	SOAPY DANGER
20/04	NEWMARKET	ATLANTIC WAVES
20/04	RIPON	PEPPERTREE LANE
21/04	THIRSK	LOVELACE
28/04	SANDOWN	LINAS SELECTION
29/04	RIPON	HEARTHSTEAD WINGS
02/05	SOUTHWELL (A.W)	MCELDOWNEY
03/05	PONTEFRACT	STEADY AS A ROCK
04/05	MUSSELBURGH	CRIME SCENE
05/05	MUSSELBURGH	JIDAAR
06/05	THIRSK	ASPASIAS TIZZY
10/05	RIPON	ALWAYS FRUITFUL
12/05	HAMILTON	WINDS OF CHANGE
18/05	CARLISLE	MIDDLEHAM
19/05	YORK	PEPPERTREE LANE
21/05	RIPON	SIR ARTHUR
27/05	CATTERICK	MCELDOWNEY
28/05	NEWMARKET	AGAINST THE GRAIN
29/05	REDCAR	CALL ME GEORGE
31/05	SOUTHWELL (A.W)	MAKAI
01/06	AYR	MARMOOQ
02/06	CATTERICK	MCELDOWNEY
10/06	HAYDOCK	SOAPY DANGER
14/06	HAMILTON	UNIQUE MOMENT
16/06	NOTTINGHAM	WHIFFLE
21/06	HAMILTON	GIGS MAGIC
21/06	HAMILTON	HINTON ADMIRAL
22/06	BEVERLEY	DRUMFIRE
22/06	RIPON	DUBAI'S TOUCH
22/06	BEVERLEY	SIR ARTHUR
22/06	RIPON	SCOTLAND YARD
23/06	ASCOT	SOAPY DANGER
23/06	ASCOT	LINAS SELECTION
23/06	ASCOT	I'M SO LUCKY
24/06	AYR	SILENT WAVES
27/06	BEVERLEY	UNIQUE MOMENT
29/06	HAMILTON	ADAPTATION
01/07	NEWCASTLE	CHAMPERY
01/07	WINDSOR	LUBERON
02/07	WARWICK	RASLAN
03/07	PONTEFRACT	DUBAI'S TOUCH
04/07	BRIGHTON	LUCKY LARK
04/07	HAMILTON	BALTIC PRINCESS
05/07	CATTERICK	KIRKLEES
06/07	YARMOUTH	MAJOUNES SONG
07/07	WARWICK	RASLAN
08/07	BEVERLEY	CHAMPERY
08/07	CARLISLE	ARGENTINE
08/07	SANDOWN	ROAD TO LOVE
09/07	AYR	FROSTY NIGHT
09/07	BRIGHTON	TENCENDUR
10/07	RIPON	SCOTLAND YARD
13/07	NEWMARKET (JULY)	SOAPY DANGER
14/07	YORK	LUBERON
14/07	HAMILTON	ADAPTATION
15/07	YORK	LINAS SELECTION
15/07	CHESTER	PRINCE OF LIGHT
15/07	YORK	CODEWORD
17/07	AYR	OTRANTO
19/07	CATTERICK	DOLLAR CHICK
20/07	EPSOM	FIVE A SIDE
20/07	HAMILTON	MOVETHEGOALPOSTS
21/07	NEWMARKET (JULY)	PRINCESS TAISE
22/07	LINGFIELD	DARFOUR
24/07	AYR	VOODOO MOON
24/07	BEVERLEY	SILENT WAVES
25/07	AYR	JOSEPH HENRY
26/07	SANDOWN	OLD ROMNEY
26/07	LEICESTER	ALWAYS BEST
27/07	SANDOWN	DOCTOR SCOTT
27/07	YORK	NIHAL
28/07	THIRSK	CARWELL
28/07	THIRSK	AZURINE
30/07	ASCOT	ROAD TO LOVE
01/08	GOODWOOD	CROSSPEACE
01/08	BEVERLEY	WELD IL BALAD
03/08	EPSOM	WHITE DEER
03/08	GOODWOOD	ROAD TO LOVE
04/08	GOODWOOD	CROSSPEACE
05/08	THIRSK	PALO VERDE
05/08	GOODWOOD	PRINCE OF LIGHT
07/08	CARLISLE	AYAM JANTAN
07/08	CARLISLE	REGAL CONNECTION
10/08	YARMOUTH	WINGED FLIGHT
12/08	AYR	FIRST MATE
13/08	REDCAR	BAILEYS ENCORE
15/08	CARLISLE	COALPARK
16/08	HAMILTON	OLD ROMNEY
17/08	SANDOWN	MARIOTTO
18/08	NEWCASTLE	MAYOR OF LONDON
18/08	NEWBURY	DUBAI'S TOUCH
19/08	RIPON	PEPPERTREE LANE
22/08	YORK	LONDON EXPRESS
26/08	SANDOWN	DRUMFIRE
28/08	EPSOM	NERO'S RETURN
09/10	CATTERICK	CHEENEY BASIN

310

INDEX

Abell, David 88
Aberdeen 29
Aberfoyle 31, 32, 37, 38, 44, 49
  James Bond Club 42
  Park School 42
Accordion geldings 184-185
Achray, Loch 49
Adam, William 218
Adaptation 200
Aerials and Electronics 31
Aga Khan 23, 131
Against The Grain 189
Aintree, Grand National 18, 45, 46-47, 48
aircraft, Piper Cherokee 16
Alba Televisions 31
Albion, Debbie 17-18, 103-104, 133, 138-139, 151, 160-163, 234, 259
Alderson, Gail 181
Alexander Goldrun 221, 224
all-weather racing 105-108
Alonso, Fernando 268
Always Flying 114
Always Fruitful 229
Always Trying partnership 114
Andrew, HRH Prince 218
Animal Farm 85
animal welfare 134-138
Annandale 194
Anne, Queen 200
Arena Leisure 130, 263
Argyle Cavalier 201
Arlington Million 83, 160
Armigerent 289
Arnold, Rupert 146
Ascot 76, 179, 200, 206, 245
  Britannia Stakes 215
  Chesham race 115, 201
  Coronation Stakes 222
  Gold Cup 188, 212, 214, 265
  1995 100, 194, 201, 207, 208, 211
  Hardwicke Stakes 120, 182, 183-184
    run at York 23
  King Edward VII Stakes 215
  King George V Handicap/Stakes 182, 201, 202, 215
  King George VI and Queen Elizabeth Diamond Stakes 182, 242-243, 244-245
  Krug race 206
  Norfolk Stakes 114
  Princess Alexandra Stakes 214
  Princess Margaret Stakes 87
  Queen Mary race 226
  Queen's Vase 128, 201, 202, 215
  Royal Lodge Stakes 91, 92, 205, 206
  Royal week 28, 95, 100, 194-195, 199, 201, 220
    2006 200-201, 214-216, 229
  Sagaro Stakes 207, 208
  St James's Palace Stakes 96, 99, 125, 126, 130, 179
  White Rose Stakes 113
  Wolverton Handicap 215
Ascot Sales 45
Ashforth, David 255-256, 257
Association of Veterinary Surgeons 41
At the Races 146, 245, 263, 264
Atlantic Waves 12, 121, 126, 142, 143, 149, 165, 166, 170, 176, 177-178, 189, 288
Attraction 19, 121, 156, 160, 169, 176-177, 188, 192, 201, 214, 217-227, 228, 235
Austen Brothers' Circus 47
Australians 187, 197
Austrian 22, 125, 170
Awaasif 176
Ayr 63, 115

Baan 143, 215
Bailey, Alan 45
Bailey's Encore 234
Baileys Horse Feeds 56, 73, 230
Balding, Clare 73, 163, 183, 267
Balding, Ian 75
Balkan Knight 243
Ballydoyle 214, 265
Bandari 23, 120, 174, 280, 289
Barclays Bank 79, 80, 102
Barr, Sam and Mrs 203
Barrons, David 106
Bartholomew, Hermione 44
Batt, Peter 28
Bawtry 55
BBC 46, 60, 163
Bearsden Gas 42
Bedale hunt 284
Beecroft, Mark 59, 60, 61
Bell, Kate 52
Bennett, Brian 'Jock' 106, 112, 117, 160, 171-172, 174, 251, 278
Berkhamsted, Greenland Park Stud 75, 87
Berlin, Kit Kat Klub 37
Berry, Jack 76, 140
Best Mate 18, 132-133, 158
Bestbuybaileys 64
Bethell, James and Sally 287
Better Be Bold 203-204

betting in horseracing 274-275, 277-278
Beverley 59, 61, 63, 141
  Hilary Needler Trophy 219
Beware Of Agents 142
Biddlecombe, Terry 158
Bijou D'Inde 96, 100, 115, 121, 126, 178-179, 238, 277
Billy Two Rivers 159
Birmingham 30
Black Charmer 12, 120-121, 143, 288
Blue Square 244
Blum, Gerry 96
Blythe Knight 131
Bollin Eric 280, 289
Boquilobo 177
Bosra Sham 121, 222
Bosworth Field, Battle of 15
Bottomley, Andrew 125, 154-155, 168
Boyd, George 44
Boyfriend, The 37
Braintree 45, 48, 53, 54, 82
Branston Abby 88
Brave Inca 129
Brig o'Turk 49
Brigadier Gerard 33, 59
British European Airways 30
British Horseracing Board 146, 212, 257-258, 264, 271
British Overseas Airways Corporation 30
British Racing School, Newmarket 156
Brocatello 269
Brown, John 67, 277, 278
Buckley, Chris and Mark 248
Burns, Maurice 183
business, future of 249-252
Bustino 243

Cabaret 37
Cadeaux Genereux 115, 179
Call Me George 164
Calver, Peter 75
Campsie Hills 41
Cape, Isaac 15
Cape Cross 217, 227
Carlisle 61-62
Carroll, John 92, 184
Carson, Willie 51, 60, 61, 97, 238, 253, 267
Caskieben 194
Catterick 63, 93, 174, 199, 284
Cauthen, Steve 155
Cecil, Henry 59, 82, 92, 113, 152, 272
Celtic Silence 114-115, 127, 128
Celtic Steps 284
Celtic Swing 235, 254
Champery 289

Champfis 272-273
Channel 4 243
Channel 4 Racing 67, 73, 105, 232
Channon, Mick 13, 28, 108, 129, 152, 178, 222, 279
Chantilly, Prix Du Jockey Club 125
Charlton, Roger 219
cheating 265, 268-270, 271, 272-274
Chelmsford 54
Cheltenham 239
Cheltenham Festival 131
Cheltenham Gold
  Cup 18
Cherry Mix 244
Chesmore, Paddy 33, 34
Chesmore, Sue 34
Chester Vase 88
Chin, Stanley 234
Chippenham Lodge Stud, Cambridgeshire 88
Chorist 158
Cistercian monks 15
Clark, Jim 268
Classic Cliché 208
Classic victor, first 89, 94-95 see also Mister Baileys
Cleethorpes 54
Cleveland and South Durham Animal Rights
  Group 47
Clydesdale Bank 42
Coatbridge 33
Cochrane, Ray 63
Coffey, Gary 106, 244
Cointreau 42
Cole, Paul 152, 208
Cologne 185
Colonel Collins 97
Condell, Declan 66, 153, 162, 247-248
Coneghan, Jack 29, 30
Connolly, Billy 38
Contact Dancer 180
Coolmore 189, 190, 191
Coral 123-124
Corbiere 46
Cosgrove, Anthony 249
Coverham 69
Craft Express 63
Craig, Tommy 34, 44, 45, 56-57, 59, 67
Crediton, East Burrow Farm 212, 213
Crime Scene 215, 235
Crisford, Simon 83, 145
Crosspeace 21, 215, 266, 267, 280, 290
Crow 46
Crump, Captain Neville 14
Cumani, Luca 59, 71, 93, 152
Cummins, Bart 187
Cunningham, Michael 46, 184

Curragh, The 131, 179, 186, 187-188
  International Stakes 188
  Irish 1,000 Guineas 96, 179, 221
  Irish Derby 23
  Phoenix Stakes 267
  Shelbourne Hotel Goffs Million 289

Dad's Army 144
Daily Telegraph 97
Dalgleish, Keith 185
Dalgleish, Kevin 131
Dancing Brave 243, 268
Dante 176
Darley, Kevin 114, 163-164, 215, 221, 233,
  234-235, 236, 242
Darley Flying Start scheme 247
David (cousin) 32-33, 38
David Copperfield 79
Davies, Stephen 269
Daws, George 69
Dawson, Cliff 57
Daylami 182
De Rothschild family 47
Deauville 23, 179, 222, 226
  Prix Morny 87-88
declarations, 48-hour 146-147, 253, 263-264
Denbera Dancer 126-127, 178
Derby, Lord 83
Desert D'Argent 121
Desert Orchid 157-158, 203
Desert Realm 215
Dettori, Frankie 92, 93, 100, 125, 190, 208,
  238, 288
Deuters, Chris 262
Diaghilef 201
Dickens, Charles 79
Dickinson, Michael 18, 122, 152
Directory of the Turf 44, 55, 59, 74, 287
Distance View 99
dogs 151
Doncaster 63, 73
  CIU Serlby Stakes 21
  Doncaster Cup 207, 208, 237
  Flying Childers race 100-101
  Lincoln meeting/handicap (run at Redcar) 110,
    130, 131
  Racing Post Trophy 22
  St Leger 46, 70, 266, 279, 280, 288, 289
  Tote Portland Handicap 63
Doncaster Sales 23, 34, 48
Donna (sister-in-law) 54, 55
Donoughue, Lord 257
Double Blue 94, 95, 204
Double Eclipse 201, 207, 210, 211
Double Honour 21

Double Trigger 19, 24, 91, 93, 95, 100, 103, 117,
  122, 125, 126, 178, 186, 188, 194, 201, 203, 204,
  205-213, 214, 217, 237, 265, 280, 290
Douglas, Michael 84
Down, Alastair 211-212, 254
Doyle, Mick 128, 180, 182
Druids 194
Drumfire 289
Drymen 33
Dubai 45, 82, 191, 197, 287
  Burj Al Arab Hotel 191
Dubai, Nad Al Sheba 191
  UAE Derby 125
Dubai Millennium 88
Dubai Turf Classic 103, 180, 182, 274
Dubai World Cup 107, 176, 179, 191-192
Dubai's Touch 289
Dunbar 34
  Westbarns, Tilton House Stables 44
Dunfermline College of Physical Education 43
Dunlop, Ed 65, 280
Dunlop, Harry 65
Dunlop, John 59, 65, 82, 152, 252
Dwyer, Kevin 55-56

East Kilbride 30, 32
Easterby, Peter 65
Easterby, Tim 65
Eddery, Pat 65, 159, 238
Edinburgh 33, 43, 44, 46
Edredon Bleu 158
Edward IV, King 15
Efisio 218, 220
Ekland, Britt 109
Ela-Mana-Mou 204, 205
Eldorado 132
Electrocutionist 242, 244
Elizabeth II, HRH Queen 199
Elliott, R. P. 'Bobby' 59, 61, 62, 63, 71, 76, 92,
  204, 273
Elsey, Bill 203
Emerson, Ralph Waldo 91
Emirates Racing Association 192
Empire Day 288-289
Enforcer 244
English Ballet 235
Epsom 71, 177, 233
  Amateurs' Derby 269, 280
  Derby 33, 86, 88, 90, 177, 239
  1994 96, 97-98, 177
  2006 150, 175, 189
  Woodcote Stakes 188
Eradicate 116
Erhaab 97
European Breeders' Fund 190

Even Top 238
Evening Standard, London 253, 265
Eventing 259
Evry 88
Exeter 18, 132-133
Fabre, Andre 242
Fahd Salman 48
Fahey, Richard 264
Fair, Tony 63
Fairhurst, Chris 79, 80
Fairley, Greg 189, 234, 236
Fallon, Kieren 92, 180, 235, 238, 273-274
Fanning, Joe 93, 142, 164, 177, 189, 215, 233, 234, 235-236, 237, 289
Favourite Racing 267
Feerick, Valentine 234
Ferguson, Sir Alex 17, 25, 104, 189, 200, 276
Ferguson, John 106, 110, 192
Ferguson, Sarah 218
Ferguson, Mr (Deirdre's father) 37, 38, 39, 53, 80, 81
Ferguson, Mrs (Deirdre's mother) 37, 38
Ffrench, Royston 164, 233, 234, 266
Fibresand 107
Fight Your Corner 88, 128
Filho, Dr Rogerio F. De Sousa 18
Fleetwood Mac 278
Flintoff, Freddie 19
Flip (whippet) 36
Flirtation 218, 220
Floors Castle 218, 227
Floors Castle Stud 218
Florimund 268-269
Fly To The Stars 100
Forest Wind 88
Form Book 61, 66, 141, 145-146, 267
fox-hunting 136-137
Francis, Dick 274
Francome, John 73, 156, 183, 232, 243
Freeman, Sarah 181, 183
Freud, Clement 105
Friars Haugh 158
Friel, Joe 101
Fruits Of Love 103, 116, 176, 180, 181-183, 184, 245, 254-255, 274

Gaelic Storm 237
Gallagher, Dean 88-89
Gartmore Bridge 31
General Billy 58
George Washington 123, 149, 176
Germany 82, 190
Gilbert and Sullivan 37
Given, James 20, 153, 248
Glasgow 17, 29, 38, 43, 85, 179

Bridgetown 28
Cardonald College of Further Education 39-40
Knightswood 29
Langside College 39
Shawfield 35
Springburn 28
Union Street 31
White City 35
Glasgow Celtic FC 198
Glasgow Herald 46, 47
Glasgow Rangers FC 197, 198
Glasgow University Veterinary School 35, 39, 40-41, 42, 43, 45
Gloucester, Richard, Duke of 15
GNER 211
Godolphin 13, 21, 22-23, 76, 83, 88, 105, 106, 125, 126, 128, 144-145, 153, 168, 188, 189-190, 191, 202, 213, 215, 251, 284
Goff's sales 23, 180, 204
Gold, Angus 123, 141
Golden Quest 23, 265
Goodwood 16, 28, 179, 188, 202, 236, 290
  BCG (formerly the Gordon) Stakes 266
  Champagne Vintage Stakes 91
  Coutts Glorious Stakes 266, 267
  Goodwood Cup 23, 207, 208, 209, 210-211, 265, 266
    1998 212, 237
  Goodwood Festival 194, 265-267
  Gordon Stakes 113, 120
  Sussex Stakes 98, 99
  Vintage Stakes 91, 121, 266
Gosden, John 71
Gothenburg 188, 201
Graff, Markus 23, 109, 131, 145
Graham, Billy 95
Grand Lodge 92, 93, 94, 99, 116
Great Leighs 107
Greek Well 149
Green, Lucinda 157
Green Shield stamps 30
greyhound racing 34-35, 66-67, 68
grouping of horses 112-113
Grundy 243
Guest, Rae 60, 61
Guillambert, Jean-Pierre 234

Hadrian's Wall 42
Haggas, William 287
Haigh, Paul 84, 254
Hall, Sally 90
Hall, Sam 90
Hambleton 71
Hamdan Al Maktoum, Sheikh 120, 122, 123, 157, 234, 289 *see also* Maktoum family

Hamilton 16-17, 21, 74, 128, 200
handicapping 270-272
Hannon, Richard 13, 21, 59, 178, 251, 266
Hansel 180
Happy Love 143
Harland, Ian 111-112, 249, 250
Harper, Chris 98
Hartington, Lord 153
Haslam, Patrick 102
Hawick 46
Haya of Jordan, Princess 192
Haydock Park 59-60, 61, 179, 264, 280
  Cock of the North Stakes 76
Haydon, John 213
head lads 247-248 *see also entries for individuals*
'Heart of the Country' 137
Heart's Cry 242
Hedley, Jane 157-159
Hern, Major Dick 82
Herries, Lady 254
Highest Accolade 176
Hills, Barry 13, 59, 65, 82
Hills, John 65, 218-219, 287
Hills, Michael 184
Hills, Richard 122, 123,234, 288
Hinari 56, 59, 70, 73
Hinari Disk Deck 63, 186
Hinari Hi Fi 59, 60, 61
Hinari Televideo 63, 76, 186
Hinari Video 59, 60, 61-62
Hogg, Wayne 269, 280
Holland, Brendan 154, 248, 250
Holland, Darryll 101, 183, 184, 188, 208, 237,
  272, 273
Hollinshead, Reg 235
Holy Roman Emperor 267
Home, Alec Douglas 196
Hong Kong, Sha Tin 88
  Champions Mile 222, 226
Hong Kong Jockey Club 185
Hood, David 58
Hoppegarten, Berlin-Brandenburg Trophy 188
Horatio Nelson 189
Horgan, Con 161
Horse & Hound 14, 50, 132, 166-167, 259, 270
horse deaths 131-134
'Horse Whisperer' 240
Horseracing Regulatory Authority 268, 271, 273
Howard de Walden, Lord
  86-87, 92
Huckerby, Richard 24, 206
Huggins, Ron 24, 203-204, 205, 206-207, 210-211,
  212-213, 290
Hughes, Richard 186, 269
Huntingdon 58

Huntingdon, William, secretary to 54
Hurley, Liz 109
Hurricane Run 131, 242, 244

I'm So Lucky 215, 216, 229
In Full Cry 12, 121
In The Wings 168
Independent 239
Inland Revenue 79-80
interviewers 73-74
Investors in People 175

Jaber Abdullah 142, 189, 190
Jacobites 195
Jacobs, Klaus 141-142, 216, 243
Jacobs, Renata 141, 243, 244
Japan Cup 182
Jarnet, Thierry 208
Jarvis, William 92, 94
Jenkins, John 56
Jervaulx Abbey 15
Jill (cousin) 47
Jockey Club 55, 56, 57-58, 66, 70, 78, 146, 148, 174,
  232, 257, 270, 272, 275
  Portman Square HQ 57-58
jockeys 233-239 *see also entries for individuals*
Johnston, Angus (son) 18, 27, 32, 137, 151, 198,
  285
Johnston, Charlie (son) 18, 26, 27, 65, 66, 72, 136,
  151-152, 195, 197, 198, 221, 231, 242, 243-244,
  245-247, 249, 250, 274, 285, 286
Johnston, Clan 194
Johnston, Deirdre (wife) 18, 25, 28, 49, 69, 78, 79,
  80, 87, 91, 95, 106, 115, 116, 125, 133, 136, 153,
  161, 162, 164, 167, 169, 176, 179, 182, 184, 195,
  196, 197, 198, 199, 200, 201, 216, 217, 219, 221,
  225, 226-227, 233, 249, 250, 272, 283, 284-287,
  290-291
  as Deirdre Ferguson 37-39, 40, 42, 43, 48-49
  at Bank End Stables 51, 52-53, 54, 55, 58, 61-62,
    64, 66, 68
  sister 37, 38
Johnston, Jimmy (uncle) 29, 30, 31
Johnston, Lynn (sister) 28, 30, 31, 33
Johnston, Mary (mother) 28-29, 30, 31, 33, 133,
  197, 198
Johnston, Ronald (father) 28, 29-31, 32, 33, 34, 35,
  36, 38, 44, 45, 46, 72, 85, 133, 135, 195, 196, 198
  father 29
  mother 30
Johnston, Sharon (sister) 28, 30, 31, 33, 36, 38, 43,
  44, 49, 198-199, 290
Joseph Henry 233, 236
Jumeirah Racing 105
Junius filly 96

Just Precious 63, 73
Justine (stable lass) 174

Katrine, Loch 31, 38
Kayf Tara 208
Keaney, John 176, 184
Keaney, Terence 184, 185
Keegan, Kevin 20
Keeneland yearling sales 22, 23, 280
Kempton Park 106, 107, 147
  King George VI steeplechase 107
Kennedy, Robert 75, 87, 88
Kennet Valley Thoroughbreds 289
Kentucky, Vinery Stud 98
Key Point 87
Khalid Abdullah 268, 269
Kimberley Clark 24, 203
Kimbo 45
King Of Kings 188
King's Theatre 92, 94, 97
Kingmambo 126-127
  colt 280
Kingsley, Charles 71
Kingsley Klarion 154, 264
Kirklees 266, 289
Knight, Henrietta 157, 158
Knowles, George 56
Kris 86
Kris Kin 99

Lady of the Lake, The 31
Lai, W. M. 'Eddie' 185
Lake District 42
Lammtarra 243
Land Of Dreams 100-101, 104, 183
Lara, Brian 217
Larnach, Andy 155-156, 163
Laurie, John 144
Lebretton, Mikaelle 285
Lee, Alan 109
Legal Fiction 90
Leicester 155
Lend A Hand 104, 121, 183, 188, 237
Leopardstown 188
  Matron Stakes 223
Les Arcs 158
Lester, Geoff 124
Leyburn 79, 80
Lifewatch Vision 76, 87, 186
Linas Selection 141, 215, 216, 229, 243, 244, 253, 266, 279, 288
Lindsay, Flora 35, 39
Lingfield 95, 107, 108
  Derby Trial Stakes 120
Liverpool, I. M. Marsh College of Physical

  Education 43
Lloyd Webber, Andrew 144
Local Suitor 87-88
London 30, 41, 86
  Portman Square 57
London, Tower of, princes in 15
London Express 245
Longbridge 69
Longchamps 211
  Poule D'Essai Des Poulains 125
  Prix de L'Arc de Triomphe 139
  Prix Du Cadran 188, 208
Longfellow, Henry Wadsworth 243
Lonsdale, Gordon 41-42
Louth 53
Love You Always 128
Lovelace 289
Luberon 253
Lucky Story 179, 180
Lungo, Len 152

Macken, Eddie 157
MacLeod, David 159
Madaares 170
Magic Moth 138-139
Magnier, John 190, 280
Majestic Desert 222
Maktoum Al Maktoum, Sheikh 104, 121
Maktoum family 13, 17, 22-23, 81, 82, 83-84, 88, 104, 110, 114, 190-191, 192, 193, 250, 260, 288 see also Hamdan Al Maktoum, Sheikh; Mohammed Al Maktoum, Sheikh Maktoum bin
Man and Boy 85
Mana D'Argent 269
Manchester United 17, 174
Mangle, John 70
Mann, Charlie 256
Maraahel 244
Marina Park 75, 87, 88, 201, 205, 206
Mark Johnston Book of Training Whippets 26, 35
Mark Of Esteem 88, 179, 238
Matiya 121
McCartney, Paul 137, 138
McCluskey, Arthur 46
McCririck, John 73-74, 86, 239, 242, 244, 271, 275
McEldowney 199, 214
McGrath, Jim 97, 105, 210-211, 244
McKeown, Dean 87, 90, 92, 238
McKeown, Mrs 90-91
McManus, J. P. 277
medication 255
Melbourne Cup 186, 187, 208
Melrose Avenue 194, 202
Mercer, Joe 59, 104
Mercer, Manny 114

Merryman II 14

Middlebrook, Gary 162

Middleham 12, 13, 14, 15, 16, 56, 66, 69, 70, 71, 72-73, 90, 95, 102, 110, 144, 192, 203, 213, 242, 253, 277, 287 *see also* Wensleydale

Black Lion 204

Brecongill Stables 90

Kingsley House 13, 14, 16, 23, 37, 70-71, 72, 74, 75, 76, 79, 83, 84, 87, 88, 101, 103, 151, 176, 178, 180, 193, 227, 228, 229, 250, 251, 279-280

RaceRiders café 152, 163

Park Farm 12-13, 14, 16, 17-18, 24, 261, 284

Spigot Lodge 101

'Swine Cross' 15

Warwick House Stables 14-15, 102

Middleham Castle 15

Middlesbrough 47

Midland Bank 53, 80

Miesque 126-127

Milbank, Charlie 45, 67

Mill Reef 33

Milligan, Kate 79

Milngavie 205

Minnelli, Liza 37

Mister 45-46

Mister Baileys 20, 89, 90-92, 94-95, 96, 97-100, 103, 121, 122, 124, 125, 126, 176-177, 178, 203, 205, 206, 208, 217, 222

Mister Monet 179

Mohammed Al Maktoum, Sheikh Maktoum bin 17, 22-23, 48, 82-83, 105, 106, 113, 114, 115, 116, 125, 126, 128, 178, 191, 192, 215, 247, 259, 276, 280, 288-289 *see also* Maktoum family

Moore, George 69

Moore, Mason and Bell 50, 52

Morning Line, The 243-244

Morrison, Stuart 115, 179, 277

Motherwell 33

Motivator 126, 177

Mujadil 183

Mullins, Willie 72

Munich 88

Murphy, Andrew 248

Musselburgh 93

Nakheel 12, 119, 120, 121-125, 126, 141, 142, 148-150, 288

Nashwan 243

National Trainers' Federation (NTF) 14, 56, 146, 147, 196, 255, 263, 264

Nero's Return 269, 280

Neville, Anne 15

Newbury 91, 107, 226

Hungerford Stakes 222-223

Lockinge race 222

Mill Reef Stakes 88

Newbury, Gainsborough Stud 104, 105, 110, 237

Newcastle, Gosforth Park 90, 91, 179, 263, 272-273

Fighting Fifth Hurdle 17, 58, 88-89

Newcastle greyhound stadium 66-67

Newmarket (racecourse) 107, 131, 144, 155

1,000 Guineas 19, 83, 127, 193

2004 121, 157, 220-222, 224

2,000 Guineas 20, 44, 98, 176, 179, 188, 237, 238

1994 92, 93-95, 96, 98-99, 103, 122

2004 121, 124

2006 120-121, 123, 141, 142, 149

Cesarewitch 180

Cherry Hinton race 220, 222

Craven meeting 122, 131, 141

Dewhurst Stakes 22

Feilden Stakes 123, 142, 177

Group 2 Princess of Wales's Stakes 242

Nell Gwyn Stakes 127

Sun Chariot Stakes 222

Sweet Solera Stakes 235

Zetland Stakes 207

Newmarket (town) 14, 23, 54, 67, 78, 82

Animal Health Trust 149

British Racing School 156

Collin Stud 44

Darley Stud 105, 106, 110, 282

Exeter Road 76

Hamilton Road 70, 71, 110

October Sales 48

Shadwell Estate 105, 157

Stetchworth 44

Newtonstewart 45

Nijinsky 33, 90, 96

Nonesuch 29

North Somercotes, Bank End Stables 50, 51-52, 53-54, 55, 63-64, 68, 70, 72, 77

Northallerton 197

Noseda, Jeremy 288

Nottingham 219

Oborne, Peter 265

O'Brien, Aidan 21, 118, 123, 149, 187, 215, 232, 248, 266, 268, 287

O'Brien, Vincent 136

O'Byrne, Demi 136

O'Connor, Warren 100

O'Donohoe, Daragh 288-289

O'Gorman, Bill 117

Oh So Sharp 222

Oliver, Andy 248-249

Oliver, Ken 46

Olympian Odyssey 176, 177

Orvietan 105

Ouija Board 224, 280, 281
  sire 217
owners, racehorse 276-277 *see also entries for individuals*
Oxx, John 23, 131

P&O 22
Palace Episode 22, 168
Palestine 28, 29
Palmer, Brian 56, 59-60, 63, 70, 75, 76, 79, 80, 101, 111, 248, 276
Palmer, Val 51, 60
Palo Verde 278
Papal Bull 177
Paris 42
Parsons, Tony 85
Pauline (secretary) 248
Payne, Ken 69
Peacock, Matt 176
Pearl Kite 83
Pearl Of Love 201
Peppertree Lane 21, 189, 215, 280
Perratt, Linda 189
Persian Punch 133, 188, 212
Peslier, Olivier 184
Peter (brother-in-law) 54
Piggott, Lester 66, 97, 98, 238
Pipe, Martin 48, 59
Pitman, Jenny 46
placing horses 282-283
Platts, Paul 90
Polytrack 107
Pontefract 119, 120, 174
Pope, Major Michael 56-57
Prescott, Mark 71, 173
Press Association 215-216
Price, Captain Ryan 160-161
Prince Of Light 12, 121, 170, 266
Princely Heir 104, 132, 183, 188
Princess Taise 235, 289
prize money 19, 21, 120, 178, 188, 232

Queen Elizabeth Forest Park 31
Question of Sport, A 60
Quick Ransom 87, 115, 161, 178, 179, 186, 205, 206, 238, 277
Quinn, Richard 92

Rabjohn, Stephen 162
Raceform 58
Racehorse Owners' Association 262
Racing Channel 236

Racing Post 14, 26, 40, 67, 74, 84-85, 98-99, 101, 118, 121-122, 131, 141, 145, 147, 148-149, 151, 152, 164, 166, 172, 174, 177-178, 182-183, 185-186, 199-200, 211-212, 215, 216, 223, 244, 253-255, 264, 269, 272-273, 277-278, 279, 283
  100 Greatest Racehorses 208
  100 Greatest Races 99
  A Fair Deal for Stable Staff campaign 255-259, 261, 262
  Flat Horses of 2005 227
  Today's Trainer section 21
Racing UK 263, 264
Randall, John 185
Rapscallion (Scallywag colt) 45, 46, 48, 50, 56
Raymond, Bruce 104, 237
Rebellion 105
Redcar 93, 130, 131, 234, 236
  EBF Reg Boyle Bookmakers Maiden Stakes 205-206, 207, 210
  Brocklesbury race 116, 139
Richard III, King 15
Richards, Gordon 59
Richmond, Hurgill Lodge Stables 83, 160
Right Angle Club 104, 189
Road To Love 245, 253, 266, 290
Rob Roy 31
Robellino 90, 96
  colt *see* Royal Rebel
Roberts, Michael 83, 92, 208
Roberts, Monty 240
Robin (Grimsby Council clerk of works) 64
Robinson, P. 131
Robinson, Stephen I. 15
Rockavon 44
Rooster Booster 158
Rosie Oh 58
Rothschild, Mrs James de 47
Rowe, Richard 58
Rowland, Val 61, 63
Roxburghe, Duke of 17, 19, 115, 153, 217, 218-220, 222, 223-224, 225, 226, 276
Royal Academy 238
Royal Island 109, 131
Royal Rebel 151, 188-189, 212
Royal Veterinary College, Potters Bar 181-182, 183
Royston, Newsells Park Stud 106, 141, 243
RSPCA 240-241
Rumplestiltskin 126
Rumpold 98, 99
Russell, John 45, 67
Russian Valour 114

Ryan, Kevin 71

S&H Stamps 30-31
Sadler's Wells 121, 123, 149, 269
Saeed bin Suroor 125, 208, 242, 251, 287
Saeed Manana 83
St Andrew's University 43
Saint Clements 284
St Moritz 109
Salman, Fahd 48
Saluter 158
San Siro 188
Sanderson, Carrie 156-157
Sandown Park 186
  Henry II Stakes 151, 164, 207, 208
  Hong Kong Jockey Club Trophy 185
Save with Safety scheme 24
Savill, Peter 17, 21, 114, 115, 127, 151, 188, 189, 212, 235, 254, 271
Scallywag 46, 47, 48
  colt see Rapscallion
Scargill, John 203
Schermuly 116
Schilling, Mrs 195
Schumacher, Michael 268
Scott, Brough 73
Scott, Charlotte 31
Scott, Sofia 31
Scott, Sir Walter 31
Scottish National Party 33
Scottish nationalism 195-199
Scottish sectarianism 197-198
Sea Bird 99
Seagram 46-47
Secretariat mare see Fruits Of Love
Shakespeare, William 15
Shalapour 23, 131, 132, 145, 146
Shamardal 22, 104, 125, 127, 128, 179-180, 214, 227-228, 259
Sharpo filly 96
Sheila's Cottage 14
Shepherd, Nicky 162, 171-172, 259, 260
Silent Waves 266, 289
Silent Witness 222
Silver Kris 284
Singh, Chandrapal 156
Sir Ivor 33
Sir Percy 22, 121, 149, 177, 189, 193
Sixties Icon 288
Skilton, Penny 13, 157, 163
Slip Anchor 86
Sly, Pam 22, 91, 127, 193

Smith, Harvey 135, 136
Smith, Robert 135
Soapy Danger 109, 141, 215, 216, 229, 242, 243, 244-245, 259, 279, 281, 288
socialist friend 86
Soho Square 105
Song 59
Sousa Filho, Dr Rogerio F. De 18
Southwell 18, 105, 107, 145, 146
Soviet Song 222, 224, 226
Speciosa 22, 91, 127, 193
Spencer, Jamie 281
Spirit Of Love 178
Spitting Image 105, 106
Sporting Life 28, 48, 67, 83, 176, 194, 254
Sportsman 124, 263
Star Rage 88-89, 201
Starkey, Greville 63
Starstreak 113-114
starting stalls, Steriline 147-148
Steady As A Rock 289
Stenton, Edward 48, 50, 52, 53
Stephenson, Arthur 59, 155, 156
Stepping Up 22, 125, 170, 284
Stevens, Dave 123-124
Stewart, Alec 219
Stone, Keith 155
Storm Cat 22
Stoute, Coral 287
Stoute, Sir Michael 13, 21, 71, 95, 118, 177, 178, 183, 232, 266, 268, 269-270, 287, 289, 290
Strategic Choice 208
Stronachlachar 38
Stroud, Anthony 82-83, 115, 282
Sun 45
Sunday Times Rich List 218
Sunderland greyhound stadium 66-67, 171
Sundrop 221
Sure Jumper 34
Surrey 15
Sweden, Jagersro 237
Sweet Robin 201
Swinburn, Walter 65, 185

Tabor, Michael 277
Tacolino 286
Taggart 103
Tartan Tie 116
Tate, James 18, 152, 246, 280
Tate, Lucinda 152
Tate, Thomas 18, 152
Teal 14

Teleprompter 83, 160
Teslin 289
Teuchters 38
Thatcher, Margaret 85
The Grey Bomber 46
The Minstrel 239
Thetford, Shadwell stud 105, 157
Thirsk 200, 219, 278
Thompson, Derek 73
Thomson Jones, Harry 82
Thornhill 38
Thornton, Chris 101
Thoroughbred Times 223
Thumblerigger 96
Thurso 42
Timeform 105, 282
  Racehorses annual 91-92
Times, The 14, 109, 194
Tomkins, Mark 139
Torso 33
Towcester 58, 118
Tregoning, Marcus 22, 177, 189
Triple Crowns 90, 96
Tripoli 29
Trossachs, Gateway to the 31
Turkey, Veliefendi, Group 2 Bosphorus Cup 100
Turner, Ian 47
Tyne Tees TV 166

UK Racing 146
Unconditional Love 201

Venner, Paul 56, 63, 73, 90, 91, 96, 97, 98
Viner, Brian 239
Vinnie Roe 212

wages, stable staff 255-262
Walk In The Park 177
Wall Street 84
Walton, Kate 13
Walton, Peter and Tony 13
Walwyn, Peter 82
War of Attrition 129
Warren, John 153, 231
Warwick, Earl of 15
Water Babies, The 71
Waterloo 83
Watt, Gordon 287
Watton, Robynne 181-182
Watts, Bill 83, 112, 160
Weatherbys 78

Weaver, Jason 60, 92, 93, 94, 95-96, 97, 98, 100, 101, 179, 206, 208, 238
Webbon, Peter 271
Wensleydale 14, 15 *see also* Middleham
  High Moor 15-16, 70, 71, 183, 192, 205
  Low Moor 113, 165, 205
Wesley, John 14
Wessex, Earl and Countess of 109
Wetherby 48
What's The Verdict 94
whip use 238-241
Whippet Club of Scotland 35
whippets 26, 35-36, 39, 66, 67-68
Whitaker, Richard 48
White Heart 104
Whitsbury Manor Stud, Hampshire 98
Wilde, Kevin 66-67
William Hill 67, 274, 277
Williams, Tyrone 92
Willoughby, James 216
Wilson, Julian 268-269
Windsor 268, 269
Windsor Castle 199
Winged Cupid 22, 125, 126, 145, 168, 170, 289
Winged D'Argent 151, 164, 214, 265
Winning Post, The 243
Winter, John 44, 67
Woking 30
Wolverhampton 18, 107, 108-109, 138, 242
Woolf, Cliff 93-94
Wright, Howard 253-254

yard managers 152-163, 169-170, 171-172 *see also*
  entries for individuals
Yarm 45, 47, 48
Yavana's Pace 156, 183, 184-186
Yeats 214, 265
Yes Indeed 34
York, Knavesmire 21, 23, 71, 97, 108, 189, 200, 288
  Acomb Stakes 179
  Dante Stakes 96-97
  Ebor 87, 272
  Ebor meeting 108, 161, 238, 244
  Gimcrack 91, 92
  Great Voltigeur Stakes 120, 208, 244, 279
  John Smith's Day 243, 244
  Wachenfeld German Wines Maiden Stakes 83
Youmzain 279

Zafonic 87

10